The Embattled University

The
Embattled University

Edited by
STEPHEN R. GRAUBARD
&
GENO A. BALLOTTI

GEORGE BRAZILLER
NEW YORK

For information address the publisher:
George Braziller, Inc.
One Park Avenue, New York 10016

Standard Book Number:
0-8076-0581-6, cloth edition
0-8076-0580-8, paper edition
Library of Congress Catalog Card Number: 71-128778

With the exception of *"Quo Warranto?*—Notes on the Governance of Universities in the 1970's," by Daniel Bell, which appeared in the Spring 1970 issue of *The Public Interest,* the essays in Part I of this book, "The Embattled University," appeared in the Winter 1970 issue of *Dædalus,* the Journal of the American Academy of Arts and Sciences. The essays in Part II, "Dialogues on the University," appeared in the Fall 1969 issue of *Dædalus.*

First Printing
Printed in the United States of America

CONTENTS

Part I: *The Embattled University*

Part II: *Dialogues on the University*

PART 1
The Embattled University

STEPHEN R. GRAUBARD

Preface

IN THE 1960's many of the assumptions on which American society rested were called into question. The older generations were sometimes skeptical of established institutions; the young were often actively hostile. Schools, colleges, and universities seemed particularly vulnerable. They, perhaps more than other institutions, were obliged to cope with the effects of a cultural revolution that had its greatest initial impact on (and impetus from) youth, a growing segment of the total population now in a position to make its influence felt. Attempts to explain the character of the new generation have often foundered on a too great preoccupation with externals in dress and behavior. Behind both lay a more fundamental dissent; many adolescents and young adults, in rejecting established patterns, saw options for themselves and acted on those possibilities in a way their parents had never done. Their strength lay in their numbers, but also in their cohesion and willingness to challenge authority. By raising questions about the legitimacy of rules and procedures previously taken for granted, they were able to exert a force that had important consequences for educational institutions.

To live in the university today is to be aware of subtle changes that have taken place—the erosion of authority once unquestioned and the setting aside of precedents once thought to be inviolable. Although the president or dean may seem to be doing all the things his predecessors did, and professors may appear to have rights and responsibilities scarcely different from those traditional to their positions, all authority operates in an institutional environment that is altered. Initiatives for reform come from new quarters; the possibilities for independent action are considerably more circumscribed. If professors retain the right to choose their colleagues and trustees the obligation to determine how monies shall be used, both accept limits of a kind that would have seemed unthinkable a decade ago.

STEPHEN R. GRAUBARD

The question for the 1970's is whether the political institutions of the country will soon begin to reflect tendencies already clearly observable in those institutions where an explicit questioning of established norms has by now become conventional. Were this to happen, we would be justified in saying that the student agitation of the 1960's prefigured more general attitudinal changes that soon affected the whole society, influencing the ways in which problems were perceived and the manner in which officials proceeded to cope with them. If, however, as is entirely possible, the larger society, particularly in its political institutions, shows reserve and even dubiety about the changes that have taken place, preferring arrangements that are more traditional, tensions already existing will be exacerbated. Between a political authority, unsympathetic to many of the tendencies of these last years, and a higher educational system, increasingly pressed to respond to the demands of the young, relations are apt to be difficult.

As long as colleges and universities depended primarily on the generosity of alumni or the willingness of state legislatures to make provision for educational purposes, the possibilities for institutional independence, although limited, were substantial. There was no incentive for the small liberal-arts college in New England to express values or pursue policies similar to those of the large mid-Western state university. The well-being of one was not thought to be intimately related to the well-being of the other. Each had its own purposes, each its own sources of support, distinct from those of the Catholic, urban, or woman's college. When, however, as now, it is becoming obvious that large new funding for higher education will increasingly come from federal sources, the issue of institutional independence takes on a very new character. The relation between what takes place on an individual college or university campus, the attention given the event, and its influence on public opinion, particularly as that finds expression in Congress, all become crucially important. Congress is not simply more sensitive to the smallest disturbance; Senators and Representatives take for granted their obligation to speak on educational matters. Financial support gives the right of criticism to the taxpayer whose disillusion or unhappiness the elected official is expected to register, and this creates a new and powerful constituency with which the colleges and universities are obliged to contend.

Reliance on the good opinion (and good will) of the nation, as expressed in Congress, may pose very great difficulties for academic institutions. This is particularly true if there are indeed "two nations" in the United States today, as Disraeli insisted there were in the England of the nineteenth century; these, however, are not the rich and the poor so much as the young and the old. If this view is admitted, the colleges and universities of the country emerge as "enclaves of the young" whose "turf" will never be very congenial to adults holding certain opinions or pursuing certain kinds of activities. This is not to suggest that all colleges and universities now reveal a common physical and moral aspect, or that all challenge in the same way practices and values that still dominate in the market place or in legislative halls. Rather, the question arises whether we may not be assisting in a confrontation of a kind that did not occur when the generational differences were less acute and when institutions of higher learning were more privileged and isolated preserves, less dependent on the good opinion of an undifferentiated general public.

Such questions were not being asked a decade ago. It is an evidence of what has happened to American colleges and universities in recent years that a book written about higher education in the early 1960's could not be reprinted today without major alterations. In the fall of 1964, just before the events of Berkeley, *Dædalus* published an issue entitled "The Contemporary University: U. S. A." Even a cursory glance at the Editor's *Preface* to the issue will suggest that the work was not intended to be a celebration of the American university, which at the time enjoyed considerable prestige both at home and abroad. The *Preface* reflected any number of ambiguities that existed about the directions in which the university appeared to be moving. Thus, for example, questions were raised about the "price" paid by the university for its opportunities to engage in research and service of a kind that it had never aspired to do in the pre-World War II era. In the post-Sputnik and pre-escalated-Vietnam moment, when universities were showered with tangible and intangible gifts—vastly increased private and public spending and unparalleled public confidence and esteem for higher education—the Editor wrote:

It is difficult enough to know what a proper professional education ought to be in fields which are rapidly changing; it is even more difficult to determine how the undergraduate ought to be educated. . . . This is not simply a matter of raising questions about the adequacy of a particular curriculum. It extends to more basic matters such as how a college community ought to be organized, what services it must provide, and what demands it may legitimately make of young people. When the content

STEPHEN R. GRAUBARD

of specific courses is at issue, that is a matter easily resolved. When, however, the utility of courses generally is brought into question, more fundamental issues are touched. The problem today is not simply to know how mechanical inventions may be used to bring popular lectures to audiences of a thousand, or even how to introduce new methods for language instruction, but what the significant educational experiences of young and intelligent men and women ought to be.

Are these references to statements in the 1964 *Dædalus* issue (along with others that might be produced) intended to suggest that by that date, in any case, today's educational difficulties were prefigured, and that demands were being made for their early resolution? It would be pleasing to be able to report such prescience and resolve. Actually, neither is claimed. To refer to the earlier issue of *Dædalus* is only to emphasize how much has actually changed. There is an urgency about the university situation today that did not exist in September, 1964; it is not an accident that the 1964 issue carried the neutral title "The Contemporary University: U. S. A.," and that the present volume is entitled *The Embattled University*. The earlier issue was conceived and written in time of peace; the second was conceived and written in time of war, not war as the nation knew it in 1917-18 or in 1941-45, but war as it came to know it after 1965.

Colleges and universities, while significantly affected by the earlier global conflicts of the century, particularly by World War II, were slow to anticipate the likely consequences for themselves of the growing American involvement in Vietnam. It is well to remember that the Berkeley rebellion antedated by several months the larger commitment of American forces to the Asian war, and that, in any case, it seemed to reflect a California situation not thought to be common elsewhere. The idea that colleges and universities might soon be more generally involved—that peaceful sit-in movements to promote the integration of the races would provide the models for action in quite different spheres—seemed scarcely possible.

That disorder has been the condition of university life throughout the non-Communist industrial world these last years and that this has been true even when Vietnam scarcely figured as a prime matter of political dispute are facts emphasized in Stanley Hoffmann's essay in this volume. Clearly, the issues he raises with respect to bureaucracy, meritocracy, and technocracy need to be examined in their American context. Substantial numbers of students, men and women, in a great variety of colleges and universities, have involved themselves actively (or sympathetically) in movements whose objectives have been political and social. However effective (or ineffective) these efforts have been, they have engaged many hundreds of thousands in actions that were in one way or another tied to Vietnam, race, and poverty. American student protest and university reform have therefore been at one and the same time responses to the universal conditions of modern industrial society and to the more particular conditions that prevail in this country.

While the mass media, painting with broad brush strokes, have sought to depict the youth of America in ways that would suggest total transformations in their life styles—from a preoccupation with careers and suburban comfort to a preoccupation with politics, drugs, and sex—the facts are less spectacular than the headlines suggest. There are still significant numbers of young people for whom a successful professional career is the single most important objective in life, as there must be hundreds of thousands who are no less excited by the victory of their college football team on a Saturday afternoon than their fathers or grandfathers ever were. Politics have not intruded everywhere in the culture of the young, nor has social conscience become the principal goad to action. Yet, a change has taken place. Minorities, not as small as some would suggest, have appeared, asking insistent questions about the university and the society, questions that were not commonly put even as recently as half a decade ago. While one may argue that radical critics are not many in number and that the motivations for their criticisms are various, this does not alter the fact that they have generally elicited favorable responses to their points of view from many of their peers and not infrequently from significant numbers of their elders. Students, particularly those who are both vocal and articulate, have led recent movements to change American politics and American higher education.

Erik Erikson, in his "Reflections on Dissident Youth," speaks about the universal qualities of adolescence but dwells more particularly on what he defines as an "intensified adolescence." There is reason to believe that the particularly aggravated condition of young people in the United States and elsewhere in the 1960's was in no small measure the result of a whole series of major societal changes. If this view is accepted, youthful behavior that might otherwise be regarded as aberrant can be viewed in a quite different perspective. It is not important that this behavior be approved of; it may in fact be exceedingly dangerous both for the individual and the society, but if its genesis is seen in a new way, it serves to underscore conditions in modern industrial society that call for closer scrutiny.

This is not to suggest that the particular kinds of confrontation of these last years in colleges and universities will continue into the 1970's or that new generations of students (student generations are, by all accounts, notoriously brief) will show the same political and intellectual proclivities that have recently been commonplace. Rather, such a view would indicate that the largely favorable student response to the opinions of their contemporaries was not entirely fortuitous. Many student leaders, whose names are already receding from memory, were able to mobilize for change in the universities precisely because they were responding to a set of generalized conditions which invoked common responses among the young. Students considered themselves members of a class. They separated themselves from their parents and teachers, acknowledging only those who were prepared to show tolerance for their point of view. Some—the more dogmatic and passionate— insisted on the necessity of total adherence to their opinion; others —perhaps the majority—were interested in some kind of dialogue. However, it had to be on issues that they deemed important. Everything else was said to be irrelevant.

Many students hold views with respect to war, race, poverty, drugs, and sex that are not shared by the overwhelming number of adults in American society. While it is possible to argue that the adult views are changing—that their sympathy for the opinion of the young is growing—there are evidences to suggest precisely the opposite trend. It is much too early to predict how this tension will resolve itself.

Statements of university purpose that would have raised no controversy in 1960 are heatedly discussed today. The whole climate of opinion about the university is altered, and if some students are unhappy with what they have wrought, feeling that they have not even begun to accomplish their objectives, there are many outside who wonder how the university can tolerate such insupportable conduct. Alumni magazines and newspaper columns are filled with nostalgia for other days when authority was less uncertain about its rights and when the legitimacy of every action was not the subject of daily dispute.

How have faculty members—once the guardians of academic

tradition—responded to these demands for rapid change? It would be impossible to render in short compass the varieties of faculty opinion and sentiment that now exist. Just as it is foolhardy to suggest unanimity among students, so any suggestion of faculty consensus must be ruled out. There is, in fact, the possibility that faculty opinion is more divided than that of almost any other group for whom the university matters, ranging from those who share the views of the students most active in the various protest movements to those increasingly wary of the confrontations that are taking place. Faculties of law, engineering, education, business, and medicine are often scarcely less divided on specific issues than are the liberal arts faculties. The greatest enthusiasm and the deepest depression co-exist in the same faculties. The differences about purposes and strategies are considerable, and whatever unity may once have existed is now for all practical purposes destroyed.

If the student bodies of the country have become more political, so also have the faculties. Issues that would not have been thought appropriate subjects for faculty debate a few years ago are now regularly raised. There is a new uncertainty about faculty prerogatives, and with it a new questioning of traditional modes of appointment, course and curricular development, testing, and the like.

While it would be unjust to suggest that faculty members have been content to follow where students have chosen to lead, there is no advantage in denying the importance of the student initiatives. Even on matters where one would have expected the debate to originate with professors, there is evidence to suggest that the principal energy behind proposals for reform has come from students, graduate and undergraduate. If faculty ranks have been divided as a consequence, it is not simply because some are more amenable to change than others. The student pressure within universities has brought into the open the conflicting interests of individual faculty members. What are, in fact, the professor's teaching obligations? How can he be said to discharge these? How is he to manage his responsibilities as a scholar (if he claims these), give adequate service to the profession, advise local, state, or federal bodies and independent groups, and still serve the college or university that provides him with his academic place?

Although these questions seem to be simple variants of the old problem of how to be both an effective teacher and a productive scholar, the dilemma actually has a new dimension. The turmoil of recent years has raised a new specter for many who teach. As adults with many obligations, their roles are necessarily more complex than those of the students who confront them. Their adequacy as parents is constantly called into question by the criticism, implicit and explicit, of their action (or inaction). Their professional obligations are endangered by young men and women who will disappear from their lives, leaving them to work out difficulties with colleagues they must see in departmental and faculty meetings for years after the issue that originally divided them has long been obscured. Finally, many feel acutely their inadequacy as citizens, an inadequacy never previously recognized. It is as if they too want to protest—not only against war, racism, and poverty, but also against all the smaller injustices that they have tolerated in silence. Some join the students; others resist them. Still others, embarrassed by the situation, think back with nostalgia to a time when it was possible to get on with one's work and when men had a keener sense of their own limitations.

Presidents and deans are hard put to respond to these conflicting pressures. The problems of governance are admirably stated in several essays in this volume, perhaps most explictly, though with very different emphases, by Clark Kerr, Morris Abram, and Ralph Dungan. Each in his own way is seeking to explain the new chemistry of internal politics in the university, while giving attention also to the influences that are impinging on the university from outside.

Questions of university governance, however, cannot be raised without reference to university purposes. This point, made several times throughout the book, is given a particular urgency in the essay "The Role of the University: Ivory Tower, Service Station, or Frontier Post?" by Salvador and Zella Luria. For them, it is not a question of whether colleges and universities are in fact presently carrying out their responsibilities adequately, but whether there is not a need for these institutions to assume new responsibilities and to develop attitudes different from those that have prevailed until now. To put the question in this form is to ask what others in the volume also insist on—that we see ourselves as citizens of a new time, for which the institutions of yesterday must be adapted. Whether the problem is to accept the fact of universal higher education, with all that implies, as Martin Trow insists, or to marry two intellectual styles, now present in the university but separate and hostile to each other, as Jill Conway suggests, or simply to aim for securing a curriculum that is interesting and a form of university government that is fair, as Peter Caws argues, there is no way to avoid the complex clash of interests that has, in recent years, expressed itself on so many college and university campuses.

Edgar Friedenberg suggests that the university is in trouble not because it has failed, but because it has succeeded, having only too happily proceeded to do society's bidding. The vaunted autonomy of the university, he implies, was always more a fiction than a fact. He is not at all sanguine about the possibility of the society "providing a home and a place of their own for young men and women in which they can develop a sense of personal commitment and a basis for moral judgment." This, he thinks, is the purpose that a college or university ought to have.

For those who hold such a view there is nothing surprising in the fact that there has been a massive loss of public confidence in America's higher educational system. They would argue that such a result was to be expected just as soon as colleges and universities began to experiment and to liberalize themselves in the ways that they have done.

The problem may indeed be political. Were alumni and state legislatures prepared to support and sustain colleges and universities only as long as they did certain things and studiously avoided doing others? Is the time now at hand when institutions of higher learning will be penalized for becoming too political, for harboring in their midst significant numbers of students and faculty who do not share with the majority of the American people the political views and the moral preferences that are expressed in the choices of representatives to Congress and to state legislatures? Is there, in short, some significance in the fact that an educational reform (one hesitates to call it revolution) has taken place without a comparable political reform having occurred? Are we seeing in the educational change an evidence of the overwhelming preferences of the young, preferences that must one day soon express themselves also in comparable strength in Washington? These questions are of no small importance. Does the university turmoil of these last years constitute the first evidence of a new disposition to experiment largely with established institutions? Or, may we see in a few years that the United States remains—indeed has always been—a profoundly conservative country, not at all disposed to accept either a new politics, a new world view, or a new education?

At this moment, these are all open questions. If colleges and universities are not simply to bide their time, waiting for the larger public to appreciate them, there must be a new formulation of the purposes for which they exist. Are they to be judged by their capacity to train professional men and women or ought their objective to be the moral improvement of their students? What kinds of political involvement ought they to encourage? Is the university to be a department of state whose professors and students have special privileges and obligations, or ought it to serve as an independent critical body within the state? There was a time when the university imagined it could be all these things; today, there is some ambiguity whether it can begin to fulfill any of these functions adequately.

The old college and university catalogue statements of purpose will no longer suffice. State legislatures and the U. S. Congress wait to be instructed, but that instruction must avoid the shibboleths of the past that no longer carry conviction. The students have put the university on trial; the university must respond by redefining its role as traditionally conceived; first, in its relationship to its several constituencies—faculty, administration, trustees, students, and alumni; second, in a reformulation of the rights and responsibilities of each of these to the other.

The question, of course, is whether the colleges and universities have a sufficient understanding of what they are becoming to persuade those within the society on whose financial support they depend of the legitimacy (indeed necessity) of accepting the innovations already introduced and of considering others that may soon be advanced. If they succeed in this, the political change that did not occur in the 1960's may well occur in the 1970's; if they fail, the educational change of the last decade may only serve to create new political and educational tensions.

The propensity to imagine that the future will be like the present, only more so, is as dangerous as the illusion that the past can be recaptured. Academic institutions, responding to opportunities provided by government and industry in an expanding economy, assumed responsibilities in the 1950's and 1960's that contributed to a significant change in their character. Now, questions are raised about many of the activities that universities have chosen to pursue. If students reject the university's involvement in certain kinds of defense-related research, and if some are prepared to use pressure to prevent such research, there is analogous questioning going on in other places. Given the tensions within the university, political leaders look with new eyes at academic institutions, asking whether they are in fact suitable sites for certain kinds of research. One hears new talk of the necessity of establishing separate research institutes, only loosely (if at all) tied to universities. An organizational pattern that made American institutions of higher education

unique in the world, involved in ways that universities abroad
would not have thought to be possible, is suddenly brought into
question.

Out of the turmoil will almost certainly develop new institutional arrangements. Colleges and universities will be pressed to
assume new obligations, to respond to demands from individuals
and groups previously not heard from. It is too early to say whether
the result will be an expanded effort in certain areas, a reduced
effort in others, but a general disposition to remain faithful to the
American formula of "teaching, research, and service." These terms,
so vague, admit of almost any activity; they favored certain kinds
during the decades since the end of World War II; they may favor
others in the coming years.

American colleges and universities have known financial ad-
versity many times in their histories; it might be truthfully said
that it has been their normal condition. For a brief moment, events
conspired to change that situation. Now it would appear that
"normalcy" has returned; private institutions are financially embarrassed; public institutions are financially pressed. The political
climate is altered; universities figure on the front pages of daily
newspapers less for their football exploits than for their disciplinary
problems. If American higher education was ever offered an opportunity to explain itself, that opportunity is presented now. To do so,
however, when divisions within academic institutions and in the
society are so deep, is not going to be easy. It may be the greatest
obligation that falls on colleges and universities at this time.

A prime necessity, clearly, is a more accurate understanding of
the ecology of higher education in this country today. Until the
dependence of the stronger institutions on the weaker is understood
(and the obverse as well), until the relations between institutions
within a state or region are reconceptualized, until there is a greater
awareness of what democratization of higher education implies for
the professions and for society generally, there will be a continued
tendency to believe that each institution must look to its own well-
being, seeking its own support in places where such support traditionally was to be found. The need, clearly, is for new thought on
why the nineteenth-century educational models, even where they
survive, no longer serve as they once did. More than at any time in
the past, colleges and universities must consider the injunction of
James Bryce, who suggested that "a university should reflect the
spirit of the times without yielding to it." To discover the spirit is

arduous enough; to know where and how to resist (and why) may be even more difficult.

The American Academy of Arts and Sciences is much beholden to the Danforth Foundation for providing the support that made this volume (and another that is to be published later) possible. Not the least of the benefits of the grant given the Academy by the Danforth Foundation is that it has led so many people inside academic institutions (and also outside) to reserve time for reflecting on the present condition of colleges and universities. The grant both permitted a study of academic goals and governance and encouraged an exchange of views that would not otherwise have taken place.

This Preface is written by one of the Editors; it would be inappropriate for it to carry the name of both. However, those who know how this volume came into being will recognize that it is the work of many hands. That fact is recorded on the title page.

MARTIN TROW

Reflections on the Transition from Mass to Universal Higher Education

Autonomous and Popular Functions of American Higher Education

IF WE consider American higher education today with any degree of detachment, we are struck by a paradox. On the one hand, the system seems to be in serious trouble and perhaps even in crisis. Almost all major universities and many others as well have been the scene of student disturbances and even insurrections. Events at Berkeley and Columbia, at Harvard and San Francisco State, have become national news; on many other campuses militant blacks and whites and dissident faculty confront their university's authority with bold demands, threats, strikes, and sit-ins. On the other hand, if looked at from another perspective, and especially from a European perspective, American higher education is successful and thriving, and, indeed, provides the model for educational reformers in almost every European country. American research and scholarship make contributions to every field of learning and dominate many. In applied science and technology we are the envy of the world: As Servan-Schreiber has observed, the Americans have worked out "a close association between business, universities, and the government which has never been perfected nor successful in any European country." Our universities are deeply involved in the life of the society and contribute much to the efforts to solve its problems—from social medicine to the inner city. And finally, this sprawling system of some 2,500 colleges and universities enrolls over 40 per cent of the age grade, over 50 per cent of all high school graduates, and those proportions are steadily rising.[1] In some large states like California, where roughly 80 per cent of high school graduates go on to some form of higher education,

1

our system of mass higher education begins to be very nearly universal. Whatever one's assessment of those figures and their implications, they must be counted a considerable achievement.

But there must be too much irony in a celebration of the triumphs of American higher education just at present, when scarcely a day goes by without another report of a confrontation or disruption on a campus. There is perhaps more profit in considering its difficulties. I believe these, of which student unrest is only the most visible, can be better understood in light of the heightened tension between the autonomous and the popular functions of American colleges and universities, arising out of the movement from mass toward universal higher education.

American colleges and universities, almost from their beginnings, have performed these two sets of functions. The distinction is between those activities and purposes that the university defines for itself and those that it takes on in response to external needs and demands. The autonomous functions are intrinsic to the conception of the university and the academic role as these have evolved in Europe and America over the past 150 years, and are now shared with universities all over the world. The popular functions, most broadly developed in the United States, are best seen as services to other institutions of the society. The line between them is not hard and fast; ultimately, it can be argued, all university activities are in some sense responsive to societal interests. But the distinction is a useful one, perhaps most clearly to Europeans whose universities until recently have largely confined themselves to their traditional and autonomous functions and have resisted accepting tasks set for them by other parts of the society or the population at large.

At the heart of the traditional university is its commitment to the transmission of the high culture, the possession of which has been thought to make men truly civilized. This was really the only function that Cardinal Newman and more recently Robert Hutchins have thought appropriate to the university. Closely related to this, and certainly central to our conception of liberal education, is the shaping of mind and character: the cultivation of aesthetic sensibilities, broad human sympathies, and the capacity for critical and independent judgment. The second autonomous function of the American university is the creation of new knowledge through "pure" scholarship and basic scientific research. Third is the selection, formation, and certification of elite groups: the learned professions, the higher civil service, the politicians, and (though less in Britain than in the United States and on the Continent) the commercial and industrial leadership.[2] These functions involve values and standards that are institutionalized in the universities and elite private colleges, and are maintained by them autonomously and even in resistance to popular demands and sentiments.

The popular functions fall into two general categories. First, there is a commitment on the part of the American system as a whole to provide places somewhere for as many students as can be encouraged to continue their education beyond high school. For a very long time it has been believed in this country that talented youth of humble origins should go to college. But the extension of these expectations to all young men and women—that is, the transformation of a privilege into a right for all—dates no further back than World War II. In part, this notion is a reflection of the erosion of the legitimacy of class cultures and of the growing feeling in every industrial society, but most markedly in the United States, that it is right and proper for all men to claim the possession of the high culture of their own societies.[3] In school and through the mass media, ordinary people are encouraged to send their children to college to share in the high culture, for its own sake as well as for its instrumental value in gaining entrance to the old and emerging elite occupations. Higher education is assuming an increasingly important role in placing people in the occupational structure and, thus, in determining their adult class positions and life chances. Social mobility across generations now commonly takes the form of providing children with more education than their parents had, and the achievement of near-universal secondary education in America by World War II has provided the platform for the development of mass higher education since then. The tremendous growth of occupations demanding some form of higher education both reflects and further stimulates the increase in college and university enrollments. All this shows itself in yet another way, as a marked rise in the educational standard of living of the whole population. Throughout the class structure, already fully accomplished in the upper-middle but increasingly so in the lower-middle and working classes, "going to college" comes to be seen as not just appropriate for people of wealth or extraordinary talent or ambition, but as possible and desirable for youngsters of quite ordinary talent and ambition, and increasingly for people with little of either.[4] We are now seeing what was a privilege that became a right

3

transformed into something very near to an obligation for growing numbers of young men and women.

If one popular function is the provision of mass higher education to nearly everybody who applies for it, the second is the provision of useful knowledge and service to nearly every group and institution that want it. The service orientation of American higher education is too well known to need discussion. But the demands on the universities for such service are increasing all the time. In part, they reflect the growth of the knowledge base created by the scientific explosion of the past few decades. Not only is much of this new knowledge of potential applied value to industry, agriculture, the military, the health professions, and so on, but also new areas of national life are coming to be seen as users of knowledge created in the university. We may know more about how to increase corn production than how to educate black children in our urban slums, but it is likely that the universities will shortly be as deeply involved in efforts to solve our urban and racial problems as ever they were in agriculture.

The Academic Division of Labor

How has American higher education been able to fulfill both its autonomous and its popular functions? Put differently, what have been the institutional mechanisms through which the colleges and universities have been able to contribute to the transmission and creation of knowledge, and also serve the variety of other demands the society has made on them?

The chief such mechanism has been the division of labor between and within institutions. A very large number of American colleges are essentially single-function institutions, either autonomous or popular. Swarthmore College, Haverford, and Reed are essentially preparatory colleges for graduate and professional schools. Their faculties for the most part are men who have taken a Ph.D. in distinguished universities, but who prefer a career in a teaching college rather than in a big university. In addition, there are the elite private universities which are highly selective in admissions and which subordinate service to basic research and the transmission of the high culture.

By contrast, a very large number of American colleges are essentially service institutions. The roughly two hundred teachers colleges, the many small, weak denominational colleges, the less

4

ambitious engineering schools, the over eight hundred junior colleges—these are serving primarily vocational ends, preparing youngsters from relatively modest backgrounds for technical, semiprofessional, and other white-collar jobs.

There is another group of institutions—most notably the big state universities—which performs the autonomous and popular functions within the same institution. On the one hand, these institutions, along with the state colleges and junior colleges, have taken the brunt of the enormous expansion in enrollments in recent decades. They are centers for community service of every kind; they train the teachers, the social workers, the probation officers, and market researchers, and the myriad other new and semiprofessionals required by this service-oriented post-industrial society. On the other hand, they are also centers of scholarship and basic research, and contribute to the advancement of knowledge in every academic subject. Moreover, they offer, in their undergraduate colleges of letters and sciences, the full range of academic subjects, some of which center on the transmission of the high culture and are concerned less with public service than with the cultivation of sensibility and independence of judgment, a sense of the past, of the uniqueness of the individual, of the varied forms of human experience and expression—in brief, all the desired outcomes of liberal education.

Within such universities, the popular and autonomous functions are insulated from one another in various ways that serve to protect the highly vulnerable autonomous functions of liberal education and basic research and scholarship from the direct impact of the larger society whose demands for vocational training, certification, service, and the like are reflected and met in the popular functions of universities. These insulations take various forms of a division of labor within the university. There is a division of labor between departments, as for example between a department of English or history and a department of education. There is a division of labor in the relatively unselective universities between the undergraduate and graduate schools, the former given over largely to mass higher education in the service of social mobility and occupational placement, entertainment, and custodial care, while the graduate departments in the same institutions are often able to maintain a climate in which scholarship and scientific research can be done to the highest standards. There is a familiar division of labor, though far from clear cut, between graduate departments and professional schools. Among the faculty there is a division of labor, within many departments, between scientists and consultants, scholars and journalists, teachers and entertainers. More danger-ously, there is a division of labor between regular faculty and a variety of fringe or marginal teachers—teaching assistants, visitors, and lecturers—who in some schools carry a disproportionate load of the mass teaching. Within the administration there is a division of labor between the dean of faculty and graduate dean, and the dean of students. And among the students there is a marked separation between the "collegiate" and "vocational" subcultures, on one hand, and academically or intellectually oriented subcultures, on the other.

Despite the strains that have developed around these divisions of function between and within American colleges and universities, they have worked surprisingly well, surprising especially to ob-servers in European universities who have opposed the encroach-ment of popular functions on the universities as incompatible with their traditional commitments to increasing knowledge, transmitting the high culture, and shaping the character of the elite strata. Ameri-can higher education, as a system, has been able to do those things and *also* to give a post-secondary education, often within the very same institutions, to millions of students, while serving every in-stitution of society, every agency of government.

The enormous expansion of American higher education, both in its numbers and its range of activities, is putting great strains on these insulating mechanisms and thus is threatening the autono-mous functions of the university.[5] The expansion of the university is involving it more directly in controversial issues and is there-fore increasing the number and range of significant publics in the larger society that are attentive to what goes on in the university. This in turn is causing severe problems for boards of trustees and regents and for the over-all governance of universities and the pro-tection of their autonomy. These problems are reflected on campus, in the growing politicization both of the faculty and the student body (which also has other sources). The intrusion of politics onto the campus has many consequences, among them the threat to the procedures by which these institutions govern themselves. At the same time, the growth in enrollments brings to campus large numbers of students who do not accept the authority of the institu-tion's traditional leadership to define the form and content of higher education: Some of these are disaffected middle-class whites, while increasing numbers are militant blacks. The progressive politicization of the campus threatens most the intellectual activities that require the suspension of commitment and an attitude of skepticism toward all received truth and conventional wisdoms. The central question for the American university is whether its indefinitely expanding popular functions are compatible with the survival of its autonomous functions of disinterested inquiry, whether in the classroom or through research and scholarship.

Governing Boards and Their Changing Publics

The role of trustees in American higher education is a peculiar one. They are, by law, the ultimate authority over these corporate bodies: They own the physical resources of the institution; they select its chief administrative officers; they possess the formal authority that is exercised by delegation by the administrative officers and faculty alike. And yet two parallel tendencies have been at work to reduce the actual importance of the trustees in recent decades. On the one hand, more and more power has been drained away from the trustees with the growth of major alternative sources of funds for academic programs over which the trustees have, in fact, had little or no control; and on the other, administrators and faculty have come increasingly to assert that powers that have over time been delegated to them are theirs by right. The growth of the contract grant system has enormously increased the power of the faculty in relation to administration as well as to trustees; and the tight competitive market for academic men, together with institutional ambitions for prestige in the academic league standings, have insured that trustees rarely exercise control over the funds granted to research professors. Trustees have been relatively ineffective in controlling even capital expansion, one remaining bastion of their power, when funds for new buildings come to support new research programs for which professors and administrators have jointly applied. Moreover, administrators are increasingly turning to outside funding agencies, especially to foundations, to support new academic programs, to set up experimental colleges, or to bring more minority-group students on campus. And again, trustees are really not consulted about these. External sources of funds mark a major diminution of the trustees' power to shape the character or guide the direction of "their" institution.

Secondly, the broad encompassing concept of "academic freedom" has meant that both administrators and faculty members come to feel that the powers they exercise over instruction, admissions, appointments, the internal allocation of resources, and even, increasingly, the physical design of the campus are all theirs by right. Some of the forces that have led to the extension and deepening of the concept of academic freedom have had to do with the enormous influence of the most distinguished American universities as models for all the others. Characteristically, it is in the most distinguished universities that the academic community has gained the widest autonomy, the broadest control over its own conditions of life and work. Many lesser institutions have come to see faculty power and institutional autonomy as a mark of institutional distinction, to be pursued as part of the strategy of institutional mobility to which so much of the energies and thought of academic men is devoted. The power of the faculties in the most distinguished universities flows precisely from their academic distinction, through the familiar academic transmutation of prestige into power. The faculties of weaker institutions see the relation, but endeavor to turn the causal connection on its head: They mean to gain the power and transmute it into prestige, for their institutions directly and themselves indirectly. Whatever its justification, the growth of faculty power has meant a diminution of the power of trustees and regents.

Boards of trustees traditionally have looked in two directions: inwardly to the government and direction of their universities; outwardly, to the groups and interests which provide the support for, and make claims for services on, the university. On the one hand, as I have suggested, trustees have been losing power over their own institutions: Many things are done and funded behind their backs, so to speak. At the same time (and this applies more to public than to private universities), their constituencies and their relation to their constituencies have been changing. Boards have traditionally dealt with very specific "relevant publics": legislative committees, wealthy donors, alumni organizations. In the leading universities, their job has been to get support from these publics while resisting inappropriate interference. And in this task trustees of public universities have not been so different from those of private universities: In most of their relationships, they have been dealing with people very much like themselves—in many cases graduates of the same state university, men of similar sentiments and values and prejudices. These relations could be, for the most part, cozy and private. Under these circumstances some of the leading state universities, such as the University of California, could until recently imagine themselves to be private universities operating largely on public funds, in a relationship to public authorities not unlike that of the British universities.

Today, the constituencies, the relevant publics, of state universities are much wider, more heterogeneous, and less familiar. In part, the growth of relevant publics has accompanied the simultaneous expansion of the universities and of their functions. For example, eleven years ago the University of California consisted of two major campuses, three small undergraduate colleges, and a medical school, with a total enrollment of about forty thousand, operating on a state budget of a little over one hundred million dollars. Today the university consists of nine campuses with over a hundred thousand students and a state budget of over three hundred million dollars, with nearly as much again from outside sources. The student body and faculty are not only bigger, but more heterogeneous, reflecting a variety of interests, many of which touch directly on sensitive and controversial issues. The schools of agriculture still do research on more fruitful crops and more effective pest control, but other students and faculty are active in support of the movement to organize migratory farm workers; the schools of education still produce schoolteachers and administrators, but also provide expert advice to school boards embarked on programs of total integration, while other faculty testify in defense of black militants and invite Black Panthers to give lectures on campus; administrative officers still define and defend academic criteria for admissions, while their colleagues press for the admission of larger numbers of minority-group students outside the ordinary procedures. And California, like many other universities, is now embarking on a major commitment to the solution of urban problems that inevitably will involve it in the most intense and passionate political controversies.

As a result of the expansion of the public universities, both in numbers and in the range of their activities, more and more people have come to take an interest in them and to feel that they have views on them that ought to be heard. In some uncertain sense, the constituency of the University of California, for example, has become the population of the state. But it is out of just this uncertainty about the nature and composition of the university's relevant publics that the Regents' anxieties arise. As the constituency of the trustees has grown, it has become less distinct. It is unclear just

9

who the relevant publics are to which the Regents should attend. Moreover, with the disruption of the old cozy relations between the Regents and specific limited publics, they can no longer know their constituents' minds by consulting with them or by reading their own. And as the Regents lose touch with their constituents, so also they come to be less well known and trusted by their new constituents. To this new mass public, they are not people one can telephone or one has talked to; they are merely a remote part of the apparatus of government—the powerful people who need to be pressured. And some unrepresentative part of the anonymous public begins to write letters complaining about the university, and the Regents, for want of a genuine relation to these new publics, begin to read them and become anxious and worried. One important difference between the older specific and differentiated publics and the emerging mass undifferentiated public is that the former reflect specific interests that can be met, or compromised, or educated, or resisted. A mass public, by contrast, does not have interests so much as fears and angers—what it communicates to the trustees is "why can't you clean up that mess at the university—all those demonstrating students and unpatriotic faculty."

These two tendencies—the trustees' sense of a loss of control over "their" university and the emergence of a mass public of uncertain size and composition and temper with whom the trustees have no clear representative or communicating relationship—can undermine a board's conceptions of who they are and what their role is, and generate in them anger and anxiety. And out of that fear and anger, trustees appear to be more inclined to intervene directly in the academic life of the university: its curriculum, faculty appointments, and student discipline. In California where these developments are far advanced, these interventions are creating a serious crisis of authority within the university—what might be called a constitutional crisis—centering on who actually controls the curriculum and appointments of staff, which is not yet resolved. If it is not resolved, or if it leads to bitter struggles between the faculty and administrators and the Regents, or between the university and the state government, then the university's capacity to sustain a climate of intellectual excellence will be gravely threatened, and its ability to perform all its functions, but most especially its functions as an international center of learning, will be seriously weakened.

California is in many ways a populist democracy. The governor and legislature discuss and revise the university's annual operating budget in an atmosphere increasingly directly political and responsive to popular sentiments and indignation; and the whole electorate votes directly on proposed bond issues that are required for capital expansion. The Board of Regents, the majority of whose members are appointed to sixteen-year terms, was conceived precisely as a buffer between the university and popular or political pressures, to protect the necessary freedom of the university to explore issues and engage in educational innovations that might not have popular support at any given moment. But the board appears increasingly unable to perform that function. Instead of defending the university to its external publics, it begins to function as a conduit of popular sentiment and pressure on the university. And this, as I have suggested, places all the functions of the university in grave jeopardy.

But the problems I have been discussing are not confined to public state universities and populist societies. The emergence of a mass undifferentiated and angry public indeed poses a special threat to public universities. But the more general pattern in which university expansion creates new and easily neglected bodies of constituencies can be illustrated in the events that took place at Columbia University in the spring of 1968. The physical expansion of Columbia, situated right at the edge of Harlem, made of that community a highly relevant and attentive public. Over many years Columbia has been expanding its operations into areas and buildings from which minority-group people have "necessarily" been evicted. But its board of trustees, and unfortunately also its administration, had not begun to see that Harlem was at least as relevant to Columbia's fate as were its alumni, its wealthy donors, and the great foundations. And it was the representatives of the black community, within the university as students, who precipitated the crisis that then was exploited by white radicals and greatly exacerbated by undisciplined police action.

Many of the popular functions of the universities in the past—mass education and public service—have indeed been popular in the other sense of the word and have gained the support or indifference of the general public. But it seems inescapable that the university in the future will be involved much more frequently in highly controversial issues and actions for which mass support cannot always be gained. The expansion of the universities, both

11

in size and function, means that we will be living in an environment increasingly sensitive to what the university does, and especially to what it does that has direct effects outside the university. It is not generally recognized how much the university's freedom and autonomy were a function of popular indifference and of the management of special interest groups outside the arena of popular politics. But for various reasons the society is less and less indifferent, at the same time as trustees and regents are less able to perform their traditional function of defending the university through the forms of elite politics. And this is especially clear in the university's relations to the racial revolution.

Black Studies and Black Students

Almost every major college or university in the country is trying, in one way or another, to contribute to the enormous social movement that goes by the name of the "racial revolution." The first and most common response of universities is to increase the proportion of black students in their student bodies; the second is to develop programs or departments or colleges of black or ethnic studies; the third is to increase their commitment to the solution of urban problems.

The way a university responds to each of these challenges conditions the way it will or can respond to the others. How it goes about recruiting minority-group students heavily affects the character of a program or department of black or ethnic studies, and that in turn affects the ways in which an institution can try to approach a wider variety of urban problems. Moreover, how a university deals with all three of those programs will greatly influence how well its autonomous functions—of liberal education and basic research and scholarship—survive the current waves of populist sentiment and pressure.

But much of the discussion surrounding the need to increase the numbers of black students and faculty in our colleges and universities has focused on the mechanisms of black recruitment and the organization of a black curriculum. There has been little discussion of the characteristics and attitudes of black students and of differences among them. But the success of all these efforts may depend greatly on what black students in universities want from the institutions and the extent to which their hopes and desires are compatible with its basic values and processes.

We can usefully distinguish four positions among black students in colleges and universities today:

1. The revolutionaries, represented by but not confined to the Black Panthers, whose attention and energies are focused primarily on the black ghettos and the larger society, and who see the university chiefly as a base of operations and a pool of resources for revolutionary organization.

2. The radicals, who focus more on the university, but see it in its present form as a racist institution and in need of fundamental reorganization as a part of the radical transformation of society. They reject existing forms of university organization and governance: the way it selects its faculty, admits students, defines its curriculum, and awards credits and degrees. They demand "open enrollment," the abolition of "white" standards for appointments, admissions, and performance, and the full commitment of the institution, or a major part of it, to the racial revolution. They are likely to be separatists, demanding autonomous departments of black studies and special provisions for the recruitment and housing of black students. They differ from the revolutionaries chiefly in being less ideological, less interested in a world revolution along Maoist lines, and more in transforming the university. They are prepared to disrupt the university, to damage its buildings and close its classes, and indeed to destroy it, if necessary, to reconstruct it as an institution devoted to "the welfare of the people." Their hostility to the "racist" university as it exists is so great that they doubt that there is anything useful they can learn from it.

3. The militants, who also focus their attention on the university, but who accept, with some reservations, its basic character as a center for the creation and transmission of knowledge and values through free and objective inquiry. They push hard, however, in an active and organized way for a larger role for blacks in the university, both in numbers of students and faculty and in resources devoted to their special interests and problems. They may support departments or programs of black studies, but are prepared to see these integrated into the structure of the university, conforming (again with some reservations) to its academic norms and standards. They are

13

prepared to demonstrate forcefully, but not (deliberately) in ways that threaten to destroy a university that they wish to reform. Most importantly, they differ from the radicals in having a greater interest in gaining an education for themselves in the university.

4. The moderates, who are largely committed to gaining skills and knowledge and training for careers in a multi-racial society. These people often support the demands of the militants, but draw back from confrontations and disruptions, and are little interested in, and indeed may oppose, separatist forms of education represented by departments of black studies. These students are often strongly committed to taking their skills back into the larger black community, where they may in fact be highly militant in relation to the white society and its institutions.

Individual students often straddle or combine two of these positions, shifting tone and emphasis on different issues and in different circumstances. Moreover, individuals will often use the rhetoric and arguments of one position while acting more consistently with another. In the general inflation of rhetoric, black militants often sound like radicals, making sweeping condemnations and demands when in fact their intention is to increase the numbers of black students and to gain somewhat larger resources for them in their institutions. Similarly, often under pressure and out of fear, moderates may sound like militants, expressing support for demonstrations when in fact they want nothing so much as to be allowed to get on with their studies. But this inflation of rhetoric is not merely a personal or group tactic; it has consequences for individuals and institutions. Students are captured by their own rhetoric, committed to positions and actions they may not have intended; the institution and the larger community often respond to the words and not the intentions, adopting either more submissive or more intransigent positions than are appropriate.

The inflation of black rhetoric, coupled with certain illusions and misconceptions among white faculty members and administrators, serves to obscure the actual character of black students on any given campus and the real distribution of sentiments and interests among them. The distortion is usually toward an exaggeration of the importance and influence of the radical and revolutionary blacks, as compared with the moderate and militant reformers.

14

The Transition from Mass to Universal Higher Education

A case in point is provided by the events surrounding the strike called by the Third World Liberation Front at Berkeley during the winter of 1968-69 in support of demands for an autonomous department of ethnic studies. The leadership of this organization and of its black component, the Afro-American Student Union, was predominantly radical. It had the support of black and white revolutionaries and also of many militants, though some of those opposed the more violent and destructive forms the strike took. It may be useful to sketch the background and context of this damaging strike.

At Berkeley, as at numbers of other major universities, the decision was made several years ago to increase the number of minority students in the student body. This was to be done both by encouraging black and Mexican-American students who qualified for admission in the ordinary way to apply to Berkeley and also by recruiting others whose high school records did not make them admissible through the ordinary procedures, but who might be admitted under a special rule which allows 2 (later 4) per cent of the student body to be admitted outside the ordinary admissions criteria of the university. At Berkeley an Educational Opportunity Program was set up in 1966 to encourage youngsters from ethnic minorities to attend the university and specifically to admit some of them under this special 2, later 4, per cent rule. The first director of this program, acting under the Chancellor's authority, was a man of great energy and commitment who developed relations with many of the black communities in the Bay Area and began to increase the numbers of students coming to Berkeley from those communities. In fall, 1966, the Berkeley EOP recruited and enrolled 130 students; in 1967, the number doubled to about 260, and in 1968 it doubled again. By January, 1969, there were over 800 EOP students at Berkeley, with the number still growing. His successor has continued this policy with similar energy and devotion. As a result of the efforts of this program and of other programs, and of the ordinary processes of admissions, there were in 1968-69 some 1,200 black students at Berkeley.

I do not believe that anyone ever made a decision about the nature or characteristics of the black students to be recruited to Berkeley. The assumption was that the numbers were small and ought to be larger for many reasons, and that the way to do this was to go into the black neighborhoods and recruit students from substantially all-black high schools. Indeed, the Chancellor himself

15

held the view that the university had a special responsibility to the most deprived black students. Increasing numbers of these youngsters have been going on to junior colleges, but, in his view, the university was richer and more powerful than these, and thus carried a larger responsibility to just those youngsters from the most handicapped and deprived backgrounds.

The resulting relationship between Berkeley and its growing numbers of minority students is conditioned by three factors: first, the characteristics of the minority students themselves, especially the values and attitudes that they bring with them to the university; second, the attitudes toward and perceptions of the minority students held by the faculty and especially by the administrators; and third, certain characteristics of the campus itself.

First, the black students recruited to Berkeley by and large have been militant and radical, clearly much more so than the black community as a whole. It may be that they reflect the attitudes of the average minority-group students of college age. It seems equally likely that there is a self-recruitment of more militant and radical blacks to the university, and a special interest in them on the part of the administrative officers who have headed the special program. There is, I think, a widely held belief that radicalism and militancy among young blacks is itself a sign of special energy and intelligence and, indeed, of potential leadership qualities. The youngsters with these characteristics recruited to the campus have brought their values with them and are indeed shaping the continued recruitment of black students to Berkeley.

Second, the romantic view of black militancy by white faculty and administrators is itself a factor of great importance in the present situation. It arises in part out of a generalized sense of guilt among liberal white men about the situation of Negroes in America—a sense that indeed blacks ought to be very angry, and that to be very angry and to express that anger in militant and radical forms are evidence of a certain freedom from older cultural constraints and a mark of being among the leaders of the emerging black community in America.

There is also the sheer ignorance of most white people regarding the distribution of attitudes and values among the black population, as a result of which young militant blacks are taken to be far more representative of their race than they in fact are. It was a source of great surprise and some embarrassment to members of the university community to discover that over 90 per cent of black voters across the country voted for Hubert Humphrey in 1968, and that in California the Peace and Freedom Party, which carried the most radical and revolutionary racial slogans on its banners, gained very little support, even in the black ghettos.

The attitudes I am describing have affected the recruitment of black students to Berkeley and have exaggerated the significance of the black militants among the black students on the campus. For example, it was widely assumed that the Afro-American Student Union did, in fact, represent the black students on the Berkeley campus and express their views. It was also widely assumed that all black and other minority-group students supported the strike of the Third World Liberation Front during the winter quarter of 1969, and in their relations with the minority students on the campus the administration carefully dealt with the Third World Liberation Front as their legitimate leadership. But no one really knew how representative that body was, nor indeed how many black and minority-group students did not support the strike and even continued to attend class in the face of considerable fear and intimidation all during the strike. There has been, in general, a marked indifference in the university to the moderate or moderate-militant black and minority-group students, an indifference that in some cases has bordered on contempt.

There are two elements in this that are worth pointing to. The first is the invisibility of the Negro, which Ralph Ellison wrote about in his penetrating novel some years ago. In the university, both faculty and administrators are still inclined to deal with black students as group members, imputing to them a variety of characteristics and attitudes that reflect the guilt and wishes and assumptions of the whites themselves. The black students themselves, as individuals with unique characteristics, are largely invisible. It is in many ways more convenient to assimilate them to an Afro-American Student Union or Third World Liberation Front, where they comprise another political force which has to be accommodated in the university and with which one can negotiate and deal. Whatever the difficulties of that, it is still less difficult than to confront black students as people in all their uniqueness and individuality, differing sharply among themselves in their attitudes and orientation to the university.

In addition, there is the powerful ideological weapon of "Uncle Tomism." Uncle Tom, as an epithet, is assigned by radical and revolutionary blacks to any blacks less militant than they. It is a way of dismissing and discrediting the views of those who are still committed to an interracial and integrated society, and who do not in all cases support violent or other militant tactics. The term is reserved especially for moderate black students who want to use the university in traditional ways—to gain an education and increase their skills and opportunities in their future careers. Ironically, the university has accepted the black militants' definition of the non-militant Negro as an Uncle Tom, and has paid little attention to the interests of the very considerable number of black and other minority-group students who have not supported the Third World Liberation Front. This is, I think, in part because of the romantic apotheosis of black militancy among white liberal academics that I spoke of earlier, and in part because the militants can cause more trouble and are more powerful than the non-militants, who by the very fact of their not being organized can be safely ignored. And indeed they are ignored.

The black students recruited recently to the campus have brought their own values and culture with them. Many of them have had painful experiences throughout their school careers and have found schools and teachers unrewarding and punishing. They arrive at Berkeley and often begin to have the same kinds of unhappy and unsuccessful experiences in class that they have had before. Some very quickly cease going to class altogether, and for many the university, which so far as they can see is just another punishing kind of school which offers them little personal reward or psychological support, becomes the object of enormous anger and resentment. Berkeley, unlike some private and residential institutions, has never paid a great deal of attention to the emotional lives of its students, nor has it made any special effort to socialize them to the campus community. Nor has it been greatly concerned with the extent to which students hold the values which are essential to teaching and learning in the university. The university has traditionally concerned itself with the purely cognitive aspects of the student's life, and allowed his social and emotional life and moral development to take care of itself, or to find a home in the extra-curricular forms of collegiate life. This was never very satisfactory, but it was not disastrous so long as the university recruited largely middle- and upper-middle-class students who already shared many of the views of themselves and the university that their teachers did, and whose attitudes, if not strictly academic, were at least not hostile to the university as it existed. These assumptions cannot be made about young militant blacks from the urban ghettos of the Bay Area,[6] but still nothing much has been done to socialize minority-group students to the university world after they are admitted. Indeed, even to suggest such an attempt is often seen as encouraging them to betray their identifications with their own ethnic communities.

Currently almost the whole of the attention of the university in this area is directed to problems of the curriculum and the organization of black studies. The issues have been autonomy, the recruitment of the faculty, the role of students in decision-making, and so forth. Those who have seen the report of the Harvard committee on black studies (the Rosovsky Report) will remember that the question of black studies there was embedded in a matrix of concern for the individual student and his sense of belonging, concerns that grew out of an awareness of his loneliness and anxieties on the campus. As much was said about the necessity for a black student union and for the integration of black students into the residential houses as about the curriculum of the black studies program.[7] In the Rosovsky Report, we see a sensitivity to the black student as an individual with special difficulties in adjusting to a university community. At Berkeley, as at many large public universities, there is no tradition for this kind of concern; instead, it deals with black students as an organized political force and bargains with them about the forms of a college of ethnic studies. The absence of a concern for the individual and his adjustment to the campus will have the most profound consequences for the relation between the university and minority-group students.

The decision at Berkeley to proceed with a College of Ethnic Studies will have consequences for the university, I suspect, as a source of continuing conflict and turmoil. It will also have consequences for the university's new broad commitment to urban problems. The proposed College of Ethnic Studies, at Berkeley as elsewhere, has in my view less to do with education than with politics. Some of the leaders of the Third World Liberation Front who are centrally involved in the creation of the new college see it primarily as a base for political action in the black ghettos and for the training of revolutionary cadres for the future. The real target, for them, is not the university, which is only incidental or instrumental, but rather the black community itself, which gave the bulk of its votes in the last election to Hubert Humphrey. For the radical and revolutionary Third World leaders, that is the real

19

challenge—it is their brothers in the community who must be reached and shown the true nature of a racist society and the true nature of their own interests. And the disputes over the college, not all of which are yet resolved, have not centered on its academic character or curriculum, but on its degree of autonomy, its freedom from the ordinary constraints of the university which might inhibit its primary mission in the black community.

Chancellor Roger Heyns was aware of the problem. In a statement to the Academic Senate at Berkeley, in which he reaffirmed the necessity for the continued application of ordinary university procedures to the new college, he observed:

I have a protective view about the proposition that the unit should engage in community service. I assume this does not mean service which is useful in the teaching and learning process as in field work or internships—to which there can be no objections. But I am very wary of any unit of the university becoming an instrument of community action.

If the academic community chooses to use the University or any part of it as a base of political action, if it tries to identify the University with its causes, and mobilize the prestige and the resources of the University to goals which it chooses, then it has made the University an important piece of political real estate. And it will follow, inevitably, that others, outside the University, will then regard its control and management as important goals which *they select*.[8]

These are good and strong words. But I think they are illusory. I do not believe the Chancellor will be able to control events after the college has been established. The new college emerges out of a strike marked by many acts of violence and vandalism which the Chancellor himself has enumerated; it will grow and develop under the threat of renewed strikes and violence. The campus is desperate for peace; its faculty committees and its administration will be very reluctant to disrupt fragile agreements and ambiguous understandings by denying the college what it wants, especially if the college is prepared to get what it wants through regular university procedures. I believe the procedures will be defended (though they, too, have been attacked by faculty groups); but they can be operated with enough flexibility to demonstrate that they need not be "obstructive." My doubts on this score apply to staffing, curriculum, and admissions, but also, in the present context, to the college's role in the community. An active role in the ethnic communities is absolutely central to the concerns of many Third World faculty and students. The notion that their college will not be allowed to be "an instrument of community action," in the Chancellor's words, is, I believe, quite unrealistic. The further assumption—that such activity will not involve organizing and educating people and groups in that community for political action, but will be merely field work in connection with some course of study—is equally illusory. And, indeed, many of the Third World leaders and their supporters affirm in the strongest terms that the university should change its relation to the community, and precisely be an instrument for change in it. They point to the fact that the public land grant universities have long accepted their role as agents of social change, and merely demand that they broaden their conception of that role and of the forms of change it can effect in the community. The power of this strong tradition in American higher education, coupled with the moral and political power of the militant black movement itself, will make it extremely difficult for the Chancellor, or university presidents elsewhere, to try to prevent directly political activities in the community based in the new colleges of black or ethnic studies.

If my concerns are in fact realized, what are the consequences for the universities' new broad entry into the field of urban problems? The question is almost rhetorical. American universities have had some experience of service in public areas which involve political controversy. But surely the problems in this regard are likely to be greater in the area of urban affairs than in agriculture or medicine. The heart of the matter is whether the university can find a way to approach urban problems without being transformed into a political weapon or arena. I believe it can if the university can remember and respect its own unique qualities as a center for basic inquiry and rational discussion of issues, as a source of new ideas and critical examination of existing policy and practice, and as a training ground for the variety of professions and semi-professions whose skills are in such short supply in the areas of urban problems. At best the university cannot avoid being drawn into areas of controversy, and its autonomy will be further strained by the appearance, if not the reality, of partisanship. Facts are, or quickly become, political weapons, and reports and recommendations, however firmly based on facts, have a tendency to support one position in a debate and not others. But if there is a continued concern for the quality of the knowledge base, a dedication to the effort to illuminate issues and to increase the number and variety of policy options, a scrupulous attention to negative evidence, and a sensitive avoidance of the technocratic contempt for the ordinary political processes, then the university may indeed survive its most ambitious program of service to the community.

But these are just the qualities that one can hope for, but not assume, in a college of ethnic studies. Some of its founders *know* what the problems are and know what must be done. "Enough of this endless study and discussion," they say. "After a hundred or two hundred or three hundred years of it, let us now do what needs to be done." However justified this may be for a radical political program, it cannot but complicate the university's broad involvement in the problems of the city, with which it inevitably will be associated in the public mind. As a result, it seems likely to me that the university will come to be seen as the source of direct and radical intervention in the politics of the minority communities themselves. The reaction to political action based in the university, as Chancellor Heyns observed, will be political reaction from the community and the state.

I have suggested that some of the problems at Berkeley have had their roots in the casual and almost unnoticed decision to increase the numbers of minority-group students by recruiting youngsters through special admission directly from the ghetto high schools. This decision has shaped succeeding events at Berkeley, including the strike and the ensuing proposals for a college of ethnic studies. But given a commitment to increase the numbers of minority students on campus, a commitment almost unanimously supported throughout the university, is there any alternative to the way Berkeley went about it? Was all this not inevitable, an inevitability embodying, as I have heard said, a kind of cosmic justice which visits on the university an appropriate suffering for its decades of neglect of the minority groups in the population? I do not believe it was inevitable, nor do I see a divine spirit at work in our current travail. I think there is another way to increase our service to minority groups in the state and nation—and that is by helping to strengthen and expand the strata of black and other minority-group professionals and semi-professionals: teachers, lawyers, engineers, social workers, probation officers, professors, scientists, researchers, students of urban problems. Education in the freshman and sophomore years, after all, is not our strength at Berkeley, nor at many other big state universities; on the whole, we do it badly, and what success we have is with students who come to us already motivated and well-educated, who can use the resources of the university in the service of their own self-education. Youngsters from local black high schools need much more than that. But we are ill-equipped to give them the kinds of counseling and personal attention and patient concern that they need and deserve. Ironically we are much closer to being able to provide this kind of education to our juniors and seniors and graduate and professional students. And there, I think, is our special opportunity. The university can recognize and accept its unique qualities as a center for advanced undergraduate, graduate, and professional training, and for scholarship and research, and not use a program of special admissions to compete unreflectively with junior colleges and state colleges for youngsters just out of high school. We might, instead, come to be seen as a place where the minority-group draftsman and technician could return to school to become an engineer; the school aide, a teacher; the teacher, a trained administrator or educational specialist; the advanced undergraduate or graduate, a scientist or academic man. This would mean not a smaller, but a different commitment. It is true that many graduate departments and schools are also making special efforts at recruiting minority-group students. But what is required is a much fuller commitment by the university in this direction. For example, it may mean that we have to find ways of being more hospitable to older undergraduates with broken academic careers, and to use our special admissions programs for the man of thirty-five who left college ten or fifteen years ago, who does not meet the ordinary criteria for admission to the university, but who needs additional training to go beyond his dead-end white-collar job. And we might have to search out such people—in industry and politics, the civil service and community poverty programs and schools—with as much energy and initiative as we now use in looking for youngsters to come as freshmen. It may well be that one way to organize the education of many of them would be in a school of urban studies.

All this implies an effort to broaden and strengthen the black middle class. But somehow middle-class Negroes have a bad name among white academics—indeed, the name is Uncle Tom—and we have come to identify leadership in the minority community with radical militancy. That is not, I think, a service either to the minority communities or to the university.

The question, of course, is not whether public universities should or should not enroll more minority-group students, or develop programs of studies centering on their history and culture and experience and problems, or commit more of their resources and energies

23

to such programs. There are many good reasons, moral and intellectual and pragmatic, for making those commitments. The question is the form such programs of special recruitment, ethnic studies, and the like should take; or, more precisely, what criteria we should use in making those decisions—decisions we are in danger of making either unreflectively, as with recruitment, or in direct response to confrontation as a way of gaining peace, as with ethnic studies. The answers lie in a clearer sense of the kinds of programs that are compatible with one's conception of the university. And here, of course, we come to what may be irreducible value preferences. Insofar as one sees the university as merely a political instrument, functioning at present chiefly to arm and legitimate a racist and utterly corrupt society, then indeed one need not worry overmuch about its survival; one may want to use it, or seize it, or, failing that, to unmask and then smash it. But if one sees the university as a vulnerable institution that in some respects can stand apart from politics and society and provide an arena for the critical examination of all views of man and society, then the survival of this function in the university is a matter of some consequence for the way in which the university performs its other, more directly service functions.

"Compulsory" Higher Education

The growth of American higher education and the powerful wave of popular sentiment that accompanies that growth are affecting its relations to its environment, with trustees and regents, at the point of greatest strain. But the same forces, both within and outside the universities, are affecting the internal fabric of the universities: the character of their undergraduates and graduate students and faculty members, and their processes of governance. It begins to appear as if the expansion of American higher education, in numbers and functions, is transforming it from a system of mass higher education into one that will bear responsibility for nearly all of the college-age population—that is, into a system of universal higher education. That development, clear in trends and projections, is obscured by the fact that currently only about half of all high school graduates across the country go directly from high school to some form of higher education. But in the upper-middle classes and in states like California the proportion of youngsters going on to some form of post-secondary education is already over 80 per cent. For youngsters in those places and strata, universal higher education is here: Nearly everybody they know goes on to college. And those strata and areas are growing inexorably. Many of the difficulties now being experienced by American colleges and universities reflect the strains of this transformation from mass to universal higher education.

In the recent past, attendance in our system of mass higher education was voluntary—a privilege that had in some places become a right, but not yet for many an obligation. Whether seen as a privilege, as in certain selective, mostly private, institutions, or as a right, in unselective, mostly public, institutions, voluntary attendance carried with it an implicit acceptance of the character and purposes of the institution as defined by "the authorities." The authority of trustees or administrators or faculty to define the nature of the education and its requirements could be evaded, but was rarely challenged by students. With few exceptions students played little or no role in the government of the institution.

The growth of enrollments and the movement toward universal higher education has made enrollment in college increasingly obligatory for many students, and their presence there increasingly "involuntary." In this respect, in some strata and places, colleges begin to resemble elementary and secondary schools, where it has long been recognized that compulsory attendance increases problems of student motivation, boredom, and the maintenance of order. The coercions on college students take several forms. The most visible in recent years has been the draft, which has locked many young men into college who might otherwise be doing something else. But other pressures will outlive the reform or abolition of the draft: the unquestioned expectations of family and friends and the consequent sense of shame in not meeting those expectations; the scarcity of attractive alternatives for youngsters of eighteen and nineteen without college experience[9]; the strong and largely realistic anticipation that without some college credits they will be disqualified from most of the attractive and rewarding jobs in the society as adults. As more and more college-age youngsters go on to college, not to be or to have been a college student becomes increasingly a lasting stigma, a mark of some special failing of mind or character and a grave handicap in all the activities and pursuits of adult life.

The net effect of these forces and conditions is to make college attendance for many students nearly involuntary, a result of external pressures and constraints some of which do not even have the legitimacy of parental authority behind them. The result is that we are

MARTIN TROW

finding in our classrooms large numbers of students who really do
not want to be in college, have not entered into willing contract with
it, and do not accept the values or legitimacy of the institution.

In the past, the relative accessibility of higher education
brought large numbers of students to American colleges and universities who had little interest in learning for its own sake, but who
had strong ambitions to rise in the world and wanted the degree and
sometimes the skills that would help them better their status. We
are now seeing large numbers from more affluent homes who similarly enter college without much interest in bookish study, but who
also are less interested in vocational preparation or social mobility—
who either have little ambition for a middle-class career, or else take
it completely for granted, or, as in many cases, both. These students
also differ from the members of the old "collegiate culture" who took
refuge from the higher learning in the "gentleman's C" and the distractions of college sport and social life. But these students, already
securely lodged in the middle and upper-middle classes, were not
inclined to challenge any authority, especially when the institution
made its own relaxed compromises with their styles and evasions.
For the members of the old collegiate culture, as for the vocationally
oriented and the serious students with an interest in academic work,
a willing contract with the college of their choice was implicit and,
for the most part, honored.[10]

The entry of large numbers of "involuntary" students introduces
into the university considerable resentment and hostility directed,
among other things, to its conceptions of achievement and ambition.
There have always been large numbers of people, in this as in other
societies, whose ambitions were modest or who felt that the human
price of striving and ambition was not worth the problematic gain.
But these views are represented more strongly in the university today, where they assert their legitimacy in ways the institution seems
peculiarly unable to counter. Part of the attack is on the *ends* of ambition and takes the form of the rejection of academic institutions
and programs that threaten to fit people for jobs and careers in a
"sick society." Part of the complaint is that academic or intellectual
work is *intrinsically* dehumanizing, separating people from one another, destroying their human qualities, authenticity, and so forth.
This sentiment sometimes takes the form: "Look, stop trying to put
us on your treadmill; your own lives are spent running around doing
pointless things. We just want to look at the flowers and love one
another." This point of view, in its pure form, is clearly incompati-

26

ble with any kind of consistent goal-directed effort. But many students, under the constraints to be enrolled in college, hold views close to this while continuing to attend classes and earn credits. Such students pose a special problem for the university. They are not only bored and resentful at having to be in college, but they are also quite vulnerable to the anti-rational or politically radical doctrines currently available in the university—and especially to those that explain and justify their distaste for formal academic work and their reluctance to get caught up in the patterns of striving and achievement.

There is no doubt that many student complaints have real objects—bad teaching, faculty indifference, and the impersonal people-processing of the big universities.[11] But it is sobering to learn that much the same anger is expressed by students in the most varied kinds of colleges and universities—in small liberal arts colleges as in multiversities, in innovative and permissive colleges as in conservative and traditional ones. Where does all the anger come from? Surely some of it comes from forcing youngsters into college who have no interest in bookish study, at least at this point in their lives. There may be other things for them to do now, and perhaps better times for them to be exposed to the disciplines and pleasures of formal study.

Problems of Graduate Education: A New Breed

There are interesting parallels between developments in undergraduate and in graduate schools. The rapid expansion of higher education, along with other developments in the larger society, has also brought into faculties and into departments young men whose commitments to academic values are weak or ambivalent. In part, this is because increasing numbers of students are entering graduate school who have little interest in the discipline and for whom graduate school is a chance to continue their liberal education, sometimes under more favorable conditions. There are visible among an increasing number of graduate students (and some of the ablest) a sharp recoil from professional training and, indeed, a rejection of that ambition to achieve distinction in one's field that we have always assumed to be a chief motive of our best graduate students, as of their teachers. For these students any ambition or striving, even for a successful academic or scientific career, involves the loss of per-

27

sonal authenticity and human qualities, and in social terms is a sell-out to a basically corrupt and sick society. In these respects, it resembles the rejection of ambition and fear of success that are even more widespread among undergraduates. These new graduate students also reflect the enormous growth of higher education and of affluence that allows undergraduate interests to be pursued in graduate and professional schools. They cannot be said to be involuntary students, even in the metaphorical sense in which I have referred to a class of undergraduates. But insofar as their interests and motives are at odds with the purposes of graduate training and the values and expectations of the faculty, tensions and resentments develop among them that are not unlike those we find among the reluctant undergraduates.[12] For these students, graduate study has certain attractions that are quite independent of the department's central function of providing professional training for scholars and college teachers. The university is a pleasant, stimulating, and protected environment that affords the students the leisure to read in areas that interest them and, in a sense, to pursue the liberal education that many feel they did not really gain as undergraduates. It also provides the necessary conditions for the political activities in which some are involved.

Some of these students do in fact drop out of graduate work, especially from departments in vertebrate disciplines that have rigorous professional standards and do not allow themselves to be used as extensions of undergraduate liberal arts colleges. In many other departments, especially in the humanities and social sciences, professional training has always been tempered by the encouragement of the continued general intellectual growth of the graduate students. And, in some, the discipline and the faculty itself are divided on the relative importance of technical training, on one hand, and a broad general education and familiarity with the literature of other fields of study, on the other. This reflects an older struggle within universities between gentlemanly, aristocratic attitudes toward learning and the conception of the discipline as a body of knowledge that grows by patient systematic inquiry employing the technical apparatus of scholarly and scientific research. The disdain for "narrow technical studies" or professional training, as well as for the kinds of research that lead to a successful academic career, is common both to the gentlemanly conception of the university as well as to these graduate students, who would be horrified to be accused of behaving like gentlemen or aristocrats. (And indeed in other respects they do not resemble those older models.) Many professors of sociology and English, of history and anthropology, would argue that it is precisely the combination of professional skills and broad learning that is the best preparation for a life of scholarship and future work of high distinction. So the students of whom I am speaking often find encouragement from their teachers for studies that in their teachers' eyes are an appropriate part of their professional training, but to the student represent more accurately a rejection of the discipline and of the scholarly or scientific career.

The irony, of course, is that some of these students do in fact "succeed" in their graduate studies, sometimes with the help and sponsorship of faculty members who are themselves least in sympathy with the dominant professional and research orientations of their fields and departments. These students are rarely the most brilliant in their class (that usually requires a serious professional orientation as well as a general interest in ideas), but they are often very able and can meet the sometimes modest professional requirements of their department without too great an effort. These students often also hold teaching assistantships (though rarely research assistantships). And in some departments a very large part of undergraduate education is carried by TA's, many of whom are deeply hostile to their own departments and to the subject as it is taught there. In the sections of large undergraduate lecture courses that they teach, such TA's can effectively sabotage the design of the course, developing alliances with undergraduates who are similarly hostile to the institution in which they are studying. Increasingly these TA's, led or protected by sympathetic (often junior) faculty members, in fact create their own courses, which are explicitly designed to counteract the "conservative establishment" courses offered by the rest of the university. These courses, which as they multiply develop into a kind of shadow university, provide an academic base for dissident and politically active undergraduates.

Some of these students eventually pass their qualifying exams and, for want of an alternative, proceed on to college or university teaching, with or without a dissertation in hand. And some join our own ever-expanding departments as junior colleagues, in many cases with their own values—their sharp and painful ambivalence toward success and an academic career, their hostility to the discipline as a cumulative body of learning, to research, and to the organization of the academic departments, curriculum, and university—unchanged.

From another perspective these students and junior colleagues reflect a failure of graduate departments to socialize their students effectively or to gain from them a commitment to their purposes and values and conceptions of the discipline and the university. This is in part due to the values these students hold on entry to graduate school, values which are reinforced by currently fashionable cultural and political ideologies and sentiments, and by their peers. It also reflects the loss of confidence of the faculty in its own values and its inability or reluctance to communicate them with conviction. Perhaps most important, these departments are no longer (if they ever were) normative communities. And that, in turn, reflects the growth of the departments, the increasing specialization of knowledge, and the privatizing centrifugal pulls of research (as compared with the centripetal force of teaching and of curriculum design). The core values of a department may still be assumed, but they are not continuously reasserted, redefined, and reinforced by men coming together and acting around them. The breakdown of a department as a moral community reflects these centrifugal forces, and then in turn reacts back on and contributes to them. Academic men are even less likely to interact around the shared work of a department when they discover deep divisions among them about the central purposes and conceptions of the subject and department. All this has marked consequences for each discipline, but it also contributes to the general weakening of academic authority and of the ability of graduate departments to socialize their graduate students to a common conception of the academic and scholarly role.

In short, we are steadily recruiting people to college and university faculties who are deeply hostile to the central values and functions of the department and institution they join. We see them increasingly at scholarly conventions and as supporters or leaders of student demonstrations. We are beginning to see them in growing numbers on departmental and university committees, where the old assumptions regarding the shared unspoken values of academic men, cutting across disciplinary lines, can no longer be sustained. And where these shared values are no longer shared, whether because of political students or dissident faculty, the old forms of university government by discussion and consensus begin to break down. The consequence is the steady politicization of government at every level and in every arena, attended by the withdrawal of men whose sense of obligation to university service does not extend to polemical politics.

The Transition from Mass to Universal Higher Education

The Management of Internal Conflict

This leads me to the impact of external pressures and student activism on the internal government and climate of universities. A number of forces work to limit the extent and intensity of disputes within the university; these forces tend to mute disputes and press toward compromise and accommodation between differing points of view. One of these is the broad acceptance of the legitimacy of the multiple functions of the university. The practical effect of this conception of the university as multiversity is to remove from dispute the sharpest and fundamentally irreconcilable issues; disputes then can take the form of arguments about the relative emphasis to be given to different views or the relative support to be allocated to different programs. And even those disputes are further diluted in situations in which there is secular growth or expansion throughout the university, and where disputes then become merely questions of priority and time.

Disputes are also softened by a general agreement to conduct them within the regular academic and administrative machinery— the system of committees and meetings through which major universities govern themselves. They are still further softened by the institutional (and often also the geographical) insulation of conflicting views. For example, the humanistic scholars are typically centered in a university's college of letters and sciences, or its equivalent; the service orientations in the professional schools and some of the graduate departments. Historians and engineers may have different conceptions of the primary functions of the university, but they rarely have occasion to confront each other in argument.

Conflict between different conceptions of the university is also minimized by making the department, rather than a college or the university, the unit of effective educational decision. The departments, or most of them, are more homogeneous than the faculty as a whole, and they have their own strong mechanisms for compromise and accommodation, not least of which is to minimize the number and importance of issues involving collective decisions, allowing the privatization of intellectual life, a withdrawal to one's own classroom and research. On the graduate level, the university *is* for all practical purposes the aggregation of departments and professional schools, their satellite research centers and institutes, and the supporting infrastructure of libraries, labs, buildings, and administrative help. The departments effectively govern their own appointments and promotion of staff (subject to certain review procedures by extra-departmental committees), admit their own graduate students, and organize their instruction. On the undergraduate level (I am speaking here of the central liberal arts college), there is, of course, the necessity to organize some structure of education that is not confined to a single department. The form this takes at many institutions is a set of distribution requirements—so many units required in fields outside one's major, so many in a major field, the remainder in electives. This system, whatever its failings as education, has the substantial virtue of reducing the amount of academic decision-making that is necessary. This reduces the occasions for conflict involving educational values and philosophies, thus letting men get on with their own work. What we see there is a spirit of *laissez-faire*, within broad administrative constraints set by limitations of space, time, staff, and other resources, that mirrors the broader philosophy of the multiversity as a whole.[13]

This pattern may be seen as an institutional response to the problem of combining post-secondary education for large numbers of students of the most diverse character with the highest standards of scholarly and scientific work. But the events of the past few years have revealed basic weaknesses in the system which are in a sense the defects of its virtues. One of these is the lack of a central, widely shared sense of the nature of the institution and a weakness in its capacity to gain the loyalties and devotion of its participants. This means that the institution operates on a relatively thin margin of error. Closely related to this is its tendency to generate both among students and faculty somewhat diffuse resentments, feelings of frustration and alienation from an institution which provides services and facilities, but which seems singularly remote from the concerns of individuals, responsive only to pressures and problems that are organized and communicated through the regular channels, and not always even to those. It is this kind of institution marked by weak faculty loyalties, vague resentments, and complex administrative arrangements that is showing itself to be highly vulnerable to political attacks from without and within.

These attacks have other consequences than the disruptive demonstrations and sit-ins that are most widely publicized. The attacks, whether from a governor or a radical student group, work to politicize a campus, to polarize a faculty, and to force its members to make choices in an atmosphere of passion and partisanship. The differences that crystallize around the issues I have been describing differ from the ordinary issues of academic politics: For one thing, they involve the students more directly; for another, they are more stable, more closely linked to deep-rooted values and conceptions of the nature of the institution. Moreover, at many of the leading universities they are being institutionalized in the form of faculty caucuses and parties, which will persist as permanent elements in the governmental process, further contributing to the polarization of faculty out of which they arise. Perhaps most importantly, these tendencies threaten to disrupt the informal processes of consultation, negotiation, and compromise, among and between faculty and administrators, by which universities are ordinarily governed. And they threaten to break through all the devices for softening conflict that I was describing.

In their place are put forward two powerful democratic models for the government of institutions. One is the model of representative democracy, complete with the party system and judicial review. The other is the model of direct democracy in the self-governing small community. Both models, as well as a combination of the two involving the formalization of the governmental process in addition to the provision of a high degree of participatory democracy, have been advocated for the university. Such systems would require a relatively high and continuous level of faculty involvement in the issues and instruments of university government, as well as a basic decision regarding the extent of citizenship—that is, the role of the students in the decision-making machinery. And, indeed, both of these issues have been raised in a recent student-faculty report on university governance at Berkeley, which calls for a high level of participation by both faculty and students in units of government at every level, from the campus as a whole down to the individual departments.[14]

Many arguments can be made against such a proposal—its cumbersomeness; the impermanence of the students (they do not have to live very long with the consequences of their decisions on a campus); their incompetence to decide certain matters; and so forth. But, in my own view, more important than any of these is the absolute level of political activity and involvement required of teachers and students under these arrangements. The casual and rather informal methods by which faculty members and administrators govern a campus may have many failings, most clearly visible to those who are not part of such a government. But their chief virtue is that they have allowed students and teachers to get on with their work of teaching and learning. Some students and faculty who want to radically transform the universities are at least consistent in wanting to change the form of governance by making the process of government itself a central part and focus of a university education. But liberal education, scholarship, and research are not inherently political activities, even when they take politics as their subject. And they are threatened by a highly politicized environment, both by its partisanship and demand for loyalties and commitments, and also by its distractions, its encroachments on one's time and energies. The reactions of academic men who are not much interested in university governance is usually to withdraw their attention and let others govern. But this works only if those others, who *are* interested in politics, share the faculty's basic values and are concerned to create and protect an environment in which the old functions of teaching and research can go on without distraction or intimidation. That is an unlikely outcome of any arrangement that makes its own government a central activity of the university, insures that all disputes pass through its formal machinery, and brings students and faculty with a passion for politics to the center of the governing process. But that is the direction of much student and faculty sentiment at the moment, and of "reforms" on many campuses.

The demand for participatory democracy by those who see it as an instrument for radical change in the university involves a paradox that makes it suspect. Genuine participatory democracy, as those who have seen it at work in university departments or New England town meetings know, is an inherently conservative form of political organization. In these bodies there is a strong pressure for consensual decisions, arising largely out of the potential divisiveness of disputes unmediated by any representative machinery. The anticipation that one is going to have to continue to live and associate with one's colleagues or neighbors outside the political arena is a powerful inhibitor of actions or changes which some of them object to strongly.

But the forms of participatory democracy can be a vehicle for radical action when they involve large aggregates of people who do not comprise a genuine community, and whose relations with one another are not diffuse and continuous, but segmental and fleeting. Under those circumstances, participatory democracy becomes plebiscitary democracy, manipulated by small groups of activists who speak in the name of the passive masses. (And the demand for constant participation insures the passivity of most students and faculty, who have other things to do than govern themselves.) For a university government based on the forms of participatory democracy to be used for radical change, it must be captured and manipulated by political activists. The conditions making for this kind of manipulation grow as activist groups among faculty and students gain in strength, tactical experience, and ideological fervor. Those conditions are also strengthened by persistent and, in some universities, highly successful attacks on the legitimacy of existing forms of university governance.

The Quest for Legitimacy

It is widely recognized that events over the past decade, perhaps coinciding with other more fundamental and long-range developments in the society, have greatly weakened the legitimacy of institutional authority. The loss of authority and of confidence in that authority is nowhere more evident than in our colleges and universities. The constant attacks on the universities for their "irrelevance," their neglect of students, their "institutional racism," their implication in the war in Vietnam and in the "military-industrial complex" have deeply shaken the belief of many academic men in their own moral and intellectual authority. Many academic men no longer really believe they have a right to define a curriculum for their students or to set standards of performance, much less to prescribe the modes of thought and feeling appropriate to "an educated man." Indeed, the very notion that there are qualities of mind and sensibility to be gained from experience in a college or university is often treated with amusement or contempt, as merely a reactionary expression of middle-class prejudices.

This crisis of confidence is at the heart of the crisis of university governance. One common response in universities is to try to reestablish the legitimacy of institutional authority not on the older grounds of wisdom, technical competence, or certification, but on newer grounds of responsiveness to democratic political processes. And this coincides with demands from the student left for "more responsive machinery of government which will reflect the interests and sentiments of all the members of the university community," including, most particularly, the student body. And everywhere reforms and changes are under way to increase the role of students in university government—not merely in areas of traditional "student affairs," but directly within the faculty and departmental committees that deal with such matters as the curriculum, faculty recruitment, and student admissions. But this has not been done only to gain the perspectives and advice of students on academic issues. That could be done by co-opting students who are especially highly qualified or interested in a given area, and who would be likely to make the most thoughtful and helpful contribution to discussions. Changes currently proposed or being made reflect a greater interest in strengthening the legitimacy of academic decisions than in improving their quality. And that has meant borrowing the legitimacy of student government—its legitimacy as a democratically elected body—by assigning to it the authority for selecting the student representatives on academic committees. This effort to borrow legitimacy by university authorities helps account for the exaggerated importance that they attach to all organized groups and for their relative indifference to the majority of unorganized students, black and white.

One consequence, of course, is to increase greatly the political component in academic decisions; for the student governments in our major universities are primarily political, not academic, bodies. Their leading officers are now often nominated by political groups and parties, representing more or less elaborately articulated positions on general academic-political issues, and they are elected after heated and well-organized campaigns. To be nominated and elected, these students must themselves be highly political men who give to student politics a large part of their time and energy. They are consequently not likely to be students who are most deeply involved in their studies—in nineteenth-century history or solid state physics, for example—and in this important respect they are less likely to share the values and perspectives of the academic men whose committees they join. Moreover, on those committees they see themselves as representing constituencies with attitudes and interests, and this, coupled with the continuing fear of every student politician of being outflanked on the left, makes their position highly resistant, if not impervious, to change through reasoned argument in the ordinary give-and-take of committee discussion. By contrast, faculty members on committees have been more likely to represent no one but themselves and therefore can change their minds or views without concern for a constituency or for charges of "selling out." This may change with the institutionalization of parties and caucuses among the faculty, and that would similarly increase the purely political component of academic decisions.

In most discussions about student representation in university government two assumptions are made: first, that the student representatives do, in fact, reflect "student" views and perspectives; and, second, that while these may differ in certain respects from those of faculty and administrators (properly reflecting the special experience and age of students), they will arise out of fundamentally common values and conceptions of the university. Students are seen, in these discussions, as junior colleagues or apprentices in a common enterprise of teaching and learning. There is no doubt that many students do, in fact, have the character of junior colleagues, equally concerned from their own special perspectives with an environment in which teaching and learning can most fruitfully be carried on. And faculty members who have served on committees with able and serious students know just how valuable their perspectives can be on many issues, and how important they can be as a corrective to the administrative considerations and research orientations most strongly represented on those committees. But not all students are, in fact, junior colleagues: Some are indifferent timesavers, and still others are hostile antagonists. The nature of the political process surrounding student government in large universities these days makes it likely that student leaders will be far more political and almost certainly more radical than the average student. Moreover, they are likely to be more dogmatic and doctrinaire in rhetoric and action in their official positions than they might be in private. Nor can we safely assume that the leaders of student governments will share basic commitments to learning, scholarship, and academic freedom with the faculty members.[15]

Universities are fragile and vulnerable to disruption; in the face of bitter attacks, academic men and administrators lack confidence in their own authority and want to borrow that of elected student representatives. Both these facts help explain why academic men so rarely criticize student representatives and so commonly make them the objective of fulsome flattery. But by making student government the source of student representatives on faculty and administrative committees, universities may be shredding the very delicate procedures by which they govern themselves, procedures which depend on mutual trust, shared values, rational discussion, civility, and discretion. Insofar as important academic committees become arenas for ideological confrontation, short-run political maneuvers, and immediate exposure to publicity, they cannot function. Under those circumstances, serious scholars and students would refuse to serve on these committees,[16] and university government will be carried by political students, the minority of academic men who enjoy polemical politics, and the hapless administrators who have no choice.[17]

Where Next?

The growth of numbers, functions, and political pressures within universities takes many forms and has many consequences. I have touched on only a few of those which I believe are especially serious threats to the university's core functions of liberal education, scholarship, and basic research. I have not spoken of the crisis in undergraduate education arising out of the complete collapse of any generally shared conception of what students ought to learn; nor of the role of teaching assistants in the big state universities, who carry a great part of the undergraduate teaching, begin to see themselves as exploited employees, and organize in trade unions. Nor have I done more than touch on the changing character of our undergraduates, on the boredom of some and the apparently unquenchable anger of others, and on the meaning of their demands for "a relevant curriculum." Merely to point to these issues is to affirm that I do not judge the state of our universities by the conventional measures of success that I mentioned in my opening sentences. But I cannot close without at least acknowledging the most pressing question of all: Given the inexorable movement toward universal higher education in this country, what is likely to happen? How will American colleges and universities respond to the enormous strains and dislocations already visible within them?

I can see a number of possibilities, some of which have already begun to emerge:

Progressively more repressive sanctions by public and private authorities may be enacted against disruptions in the universities and colleges and against people and activities perceived as "radical" or "subversive." These sanctions, if carried very far, are likely to bring teachers and students into direct confrontation with the state or the governing bodies, and result in further disturbances and loss of autonomy, morale, and a measure of academic freedom.[18]

There may be an acceleration of the movement of academic men, especially research scholars in the natural and physical and social sciences, out of the universities and into various public and private research centers which are (or seem to be) better protected against attacks from left or right. Certainly there are models for the separation of teaching and research in the continental and Soviet systems of higher education. Although this shift would run sharply against strongly held conceptions of the academic career in the United States, it is likely to be present as one alternative for many academic men in the event of a deepening crisis in the university.

The system may develop an even sharper and more effectively insulated differentiation of character and function within and among institutions. Some universities may self-consciously commit themselves to the primacy of disinterested inquiry in research and teaching, and select students, staff, and service missions with that primary criterion in mind. Parts of other institutions—departments, schools, research centers—may attempt to do the same. It is problematic, and will surely be variable, how effectively universities or parts of universities will be able to insulate themselves against the powerful populist forces afoot in higher education.[19]

There may evolve alternative forms of undergraduate education, breaking radically with the bookish and academic traditions that still link even the more "innovative" efforts at "relevance" with the high literary and scientific cultures. Much of the demand for "relevance" on the part of undergraduates is a revolt against formal learning and a wish to be involved immediately and directly in the society and its problems and opportunities. It is no use telling such students they should not be in college, but in the world and at work; the meaning of universal higher education is that these students have little choice but to be in some college, and that our system of higher education "owns" the years from eighteen to perhaps twenty or twenty-two of most of our youth. What may, perhaps must, emerge are various forms of nonacademic learning and service, organized by colleges and universities, allowing youngsters to define themselves as college students, earning credits for "degrees" and certificates, but off the campuses and free from classrooms, library, and laboratory disciplines. I believe we must reduce the involuntariness of college attendance for many who do not want to study if the college and universities are to survive in recognizable form for those who do. The creation of nonacademic forms of "higher education" off campus may be the most important innovation on the agenda for our colleges and universities.[20]

Finally, a word on the great state university. It is a matter of continual amazement that an institution so deeply involved in public service in so many ways has been able to preserve its autonomy and its critical and scholarly and research functions. The question is whether its new commitments to public service, on campus and off, will seriously endanger that autonomy and the disinterested and critical intellectual life that it allows. One answer, very tentatively is: that depends on *how* it performs these new services. The issue is very much in doubt. But if the autonomous functions of the great state universities are threatened and then crippled by the political pressures arising out of their commitments to service, then those functions, at their highest levels of performance, will be confined to the private universities or forced outside the university altogether. And if that happens, something very precious—the presence within institutions of popular democracy of the highest standards of intellectual life—will have been lost in America.

REFERENCES

1. *A Fact Book on Higher Education* (American Council on Education: Washington, D. C., 1969), p. 9048.

2. And in Europe the preparation of teachers for the selective secondary schools where the children of those elites are educated and prepared for their own accession to elite status.

3. This is now as much a scientific as a literary culture.

4. For discussion of the forces associated with the growth of mass higher education in the United States, see Martin Trow, "The Democratization of Higher Education in America," *European Journal of Sociology,* Vol. 3, No. 2 (1962).

5. This essay will focus on the problems of the great American "multiversities," public and private.

6. Nor can it be made about many white undergraduates today. On this, see below, on "compulsory" higher education.

7. *Report of the Faculty Committee on African and Afro-American Studies,* Faculty of Arts and Sciences, Harvard University (January 1969). The program of black studies recommended by the Rosovsky Committee and accepted by the Harvard faculty has been greatly modified under pressure, and is no longer a model for Berkeley or the country.

8. *Campus Report* (University of California, Berkeley), Vol. 3, No. 10 (March 6, 1969). Italics his.

9. And, of course, the "attractiveness of alternatives" is also defined by social norms held by family and friends.

10. The contracts and mutual understandings, of course, differed enormously for the great variety of students and the almost equally great variety of institutions.

11. Indeed, one function of political action on campus for many students is to introduce them to other students with similar values and attitudes, and to the pleasures of belonging to a community of like-minded people working together in a common task with common ideals and purposes. The euphoria in evidence in some demonstrations and sit-ins (for example, the occupation of Stanford's Applied Electronics Laboratory in the spring of 1969) is some indication of the deep intrinsic rewards for participants in political activism around issues whose moral content seems to be absolutely clear and simple. It is important that this kind of communal life and action does not seem to be possible within the framework of the university itself; it is difficult and dangerous *outside* the university (for example, in communes or community action programs); it is relatively easy and highly rewarding *inside* but *against* the university.

12. Of course, for undergraduates and graduate students alike who are locked into school by the draft, the term "involuntary" is not at all metaphorical.

13. For a fuller discussion of the triumph of *laissez-faire* over general education in American universities, see Martin Trow, "Bell, Book and Berkeley," *The American Behavioral Scientist* (May-June, 1968).

14. *The Culture of the University: Governance and Education,* Report of the Study Commission on University Governance (University of California: Berkeley, January 15, 1968). See also my "Conceptions of the University," *American Behavioral Scientist* (May-June, 1969).

15. An example of academic discussion (cant is perhaps too strong a word) on this issue is the following from the pen of the Chancellor of the Minnesota State College System: "Let us admit that, despite differences in age, experience, maturity, and background, our students should be viewed as colleagues-in-learning who must be actively and meaningfully involved in shaping all of the institutions of the campus—its curriculum, faculty, social life, administration, learning resources—its total image." G. Theodore Mitau, "Needed: Peacemakers and Social Engineers," *AAUP Bulletin* (Summer, 1969), p. 157.

    This statement shares with many others on this theme these characteristics: a) it imputes to all students the qualities of "a colleague in learning" possessed by only some; b) it recommends a larger role for students in college and university government without either specifying the forms, mechanisms, or possible limits of their participation, or anticipating the probable consequences for the institution; c) it encourages students to make unlimited demands on the faculty which, if (when) not met in full, will surely increase student feelings of frustration and anger.

16. There is already a noticeable withdrawal of participation by academic men from those areas of the university government which are most exposed to student attack. The withdrawal thus far is largely due to changes in the style of "debate," and to a distaste for threats and personal abuse

in the gutter language sometimes employed by radical students to whom ordinary civility and rational discourse are contemptible middle-class evasions.

17. I am speaking here chiefly of undergraduates and campus-wide government. In the graduate departments and professional schools, a strong case can be made for participation of graduate students in at least some departmental decisions. But what kind of participation, in what kinds of decisions, will properly vary from department to department (depending on its size, the character of its students, and other factors), and should not be governed by any institution-wide formula or policy.

18. Continued campus disturbances may have even more serious consequences for the political climate of the larger society.

19. I suspect that, in the foreseeable future, institution-wide policies and standards in most multiversities will work more to dilute than to defend scholarship and academic freedom. Under great pressures, university administrators will be tempted to take popular positions on academic issues. For example, one of the few issues on which the New Left and the far right agree is that an overemphasis on research embodied in the doctrine of "publish or perish" is the prime enemy of good teaching in our big universities. University presidents can come out squarely on the side of virtue by instructing academic committees to give greater weight to "teaching effectiveness" in the appointment and promotion of faculty. Some will go a step further and instruct these committees that this is the appropriate place for student evaluations to enter the appointment and promotion procedures.

"Effective teaching" is notoriously hard to assess or even to define. In the present political climate, to stress it further in the assessment of faculty is to put even more pressure on teachers to seek the approval of their students, with subtle but serious implications for academic freedom and the fate of certain controversial subjects. A serious move toward the improvement of undergraduate teaching in the big public universities might start with an improvement in the ratio of teachers to students, which in turn would allow the institution to reduce the very large role of graduate teaching assistants in the undergraduate courses. But that would be expensive, and not nearly so popular.

20. We should also be able to increase the amount and legitimacy *within* the university of "expressive" activities—painting, music, the dance, the performing arts generally—for students prepared to submit themselves to these demanding, though less bookish, disciplines.

For another approach, the Swedes are just beginning to discuss the idea of an "education bank," under which all citizens would have a commitment from the state for one or two years of further (higher) education which they can take at any time during their lives if they choose to leave school during or on completion of their secondary schooling. The Swedes will very shortly also be bringing nearly all their youth to the point of university entrance; they anticipate mass but not universal higher education. An "education bank" would increase the voluntariness of university entrance and deserves consideration in the American context.

JILL CONWAY

Styles of Academic Culture

A STUDY of the aims and purposes of the university cannot be separated from an inquiry into its social functions. The question of governance is secondary. It flows from the function of the university; it does not define it. I shall discuss first the general functions of the educational community within American society and then consider those which are specifically discharged by the university in undergraduate and graduate education. This discussion will be developed in historical terms because I do not think that we have adequate theoretical models for analyzing the relationship between the university and society. It is certainly not helpful to analyze the social evolution of the university through analogies to biological organisms or economic structures. Potential for growth or for productivity does not necessarily indicate that an academic institution is serving intellectual ends, nor indeed does it show that human needs are being met within the university community or within the larger society in which the university is lodged. Much of the discussion of contemporary university problems proceeds on the assumption that we do possess satisfactory models of societal change upon which we can base our theories concerning desirable directions for institutional development. Yet the length and repetitiveness of the contemporary debate on the university illustrates that we are incapable of utopian thinking on this subject and that we cannot move beyond pragmatism in trying to imagine forms and goals of the university of the future. In such a situation, we had better have recourse to Clio or to poetry and metaphor because the tools of the social sciences may only dull our perceptions.

Historically, educational institutions have performed functions in American society which have not always been perceived and which are only related to intellectual goals by a combination of peculiarly American factors. One thinks of Benjamin Franklin's account of the importance of self-education as a way to wealth and of Thomas Jefferson's belief in popular education as the rock on which to build a stable republic. Although the Founding Fathers clearly understood the economic and political significance of education for American society, not until the nineteenth century was the educational community invested with the function of controlling class conflict and stimulating nationalism in an immigrant population. Horace Mann was the first educational theorist to state clearly that the common schools were as important as agents of social stability as they were for political equilibrium. For him, the advent of industrialization in Massachusetts was not an indication that the social conflicts of European industrial society might also trouble the republic. Instead he wrote in 1848 that "education . . . beyond all other devices of human origin, is the great equaliser of the conditions of men—the balance-wheel of the social machinery."[1] By making Franklin's way to wealth available to all in the common schools, Mann believed, the economic and social inequities of Europe would not be duplicated in America. Thus the key to the preservation of social democracy was the development of universal education. The school could also be harnessed to a national goal by teaching its pupils to value the great political heritage of the United States. No matter how diverse the social and ethnic background of students in the common schools, they would all learn "those articles in the creed of republicanism, which are accepted by all, believed in by all, and which form the common basis of our political faith. . . ."[2] The school, therefore, was to be the one institution in America that held the social machinery in balance, preventing grinding class or ethnic conflict and preserving republican beliefs in the face of all competing ideologies.

Mann's expectation that the school could carry out this function while teaching the conventional Victorian literary curriculum rested upon an unexamined assumption that literary culture was the key to economic success. A generation later, John Dewey—recognizing that the system of public education had not functioned as a social equalizer, as Horace Mann had so confidently predicted—was forced to clarify the connection between democracy and education. Dewey's diagnosis of the problem seems curiously inverted to European minds. He felt that the school had not functioned as an agent of democracy in America because it had taught the literary and aesthetic values of a European aristocracy. A redesigning of the curriculum was needed to forge a truly democratic educational system purged of aristocratic values and sterile aestheticism. European aristocratic culture had been one of leisure whereas American democratic culture would be one of work. The organizing principle that would define the new function for the school in society would be the development of students' minds in relation to the predominant system of production. In equating consciousness with the system of production, Dewey was adopting a Marxist view of culture and asserting that class conflict could be avoided in American industrial society if the school were used so that all its pupils saw themselves in the same relationship to the means of production.[3]

In this way, the connection between the school and social equality was maintained, but at a cultural loss that has rarely been considered. Because of the mythic dimensions of the school as custodian of the democratic future, the educational community is automatically perceived in America as the community that can resolve all social problems. In fact, the instinctive American response to the perception of a social problem is to devise another educational program to deal with it. Such a response harmonizes the democratic urge with the future-orientation of capitalism. Today, however, this response stands revealed as politically naïve because the mediation of conflict is essentially a political task and cannot always be reconciled with intellectual goals. Indeed, due to the development of serious social and ideological conflict within American society, the institution that normally mediates conflict is subject to extreme stress, but lacks the flexibility for decision-making characteristic of most political organizations. Although it is a truism to say today that the university is being politicized, the historical forces that have led to this development are not often understood.

Another function that educational institutions perform in American society is the recruitment and certification of an elite. American social thought has never come to terms with the problem of elites because the myth of a universally accessible educational community has made it possible to dodge the question. Yet American educational institutions have reached a *de facto* solution to the problem of elites through recruitment by the most vigorous competition. It is the recognition of this function by students today which tempts them to reject the whole idea of competition within the academic community. Similarly, as the ruling professional group within American society becomes suspect, the institutions which have recruited and certified that professional elite also become suspect. The route to power, once thought to be subject to a democratic process, is seen to lie through cleverness and intellect—qualities which, as Richard Hofstadter has pointed out, are deeply distrusted in American popular culture.[4]

The political function of mediating conflict and the social function of recruiting and legitimating an elite must be distinguished from the third function of the educational community in America. This is the intellectual function of creating and disseminating knowledge, the task which we usually associate with universities. There are historical reasons why the intellectual function of the educational community is a complicated and ambiguous one in American culture. The university as a Western European institution grew out of an established church which could claim to define and disseminate the truth. Yet in colonial America because there was no clear religious establishment, there was real uncertainty about which religious groups should be authorized by society to transmit their orthodoxies. This ambiguity was resolved by permissiveness so that any religious group which could support a college came to receive a charter from the state. Thus the traditional pluralism of American intellectual life developed from the acceptance of the idea that there was no single body of religious truth which must be conveyed. Once these denominational institutions became secularized, their intellectual functions became even more equivocal within the broader context of American culture.

Two historical forces combined to produce secularization of learning in the late-nineteenth century. These were the foundation of state universities, creations of the secular state, and the adoption of the ideal of pure science from the contemporary German university. By becoming secular institutions, however, American universities became exposed not only to scientific values, but to the commercial values of the dominant business community in the gilded age. The social group which possessed authority and wielded it unquestioningly in post-Civil War America was the business community, and hence lay governance of universities became government by businessmen. This fact is perfectly exemplified in the history of the foundation of the first secular institution dedicated to pure research, Johns Hopkins University. Of the twelve lay trustees of Johns Hopkins, seven were businessmen, none were professional educators, and five were not college graduates.[5] They recognized that their task was to discover a new idea of the meaning and purpose of the university, and that this discovery could come about only through finding and supporting some great educational statesman as president of the new university. But neither the search nor the subsequent support was thought of as merely enabling the new university to develop. The trustees were determined to "place the Concern in the top rank, if money, experience and hard work on their part will do it."[6] The entrepreneurial attitude could not be more vividly demonstrated, nor could the confidence of businessmen that they had contributions to make to academic life of more than a purely financial nature.

The attitudes of the Johns Hopkins trustees are symbolic of the extent to which lay governance had distinctive and unique consequences for the American university. Because of the entrepreneurial attitude to learning, the great industrial fortunes of the nineteenth century were turned over to the endowment of education. This endowment, however, was not a passive one; it was accompanied by the assumption that industrial capitalism had much to contribute to the way in which knowledge was produced and disseminated in America. A natural consequence of this easy liaison between the university and the business community was that the intellectual function of the university came to be progressively defined as the creation and diffusion of knowledge valued in relation to its technological utility. Renaissance humanism and classical culture played no part in an industrial scheme of values, and they came to occupy a smaller and smaller part of the curriculum in all but the most patrician centers of learning on the East Coast.

As a result, American culture became technological more or less by default. The classical and humanistic traditions were not so much attacked as assumed to be irrelevant. This departure from Western European traditions of learning allowed American universities to lead the world in coming to terms with the machine, but at the cost of becoming efficient machine-like systems for producing a standard product. The expressive, intuitive, emotional aspects of human experience scrutinized in Greek drama and reflected upon by the great humanists did not find an important place in the American college curriculum—in part because, as Marx pointed out, self-expression has no necessary place in an industrial system; and in part because by the logic of American

47

cultural development the expressive, intuitive, and emotional sides of the human personality were seen as "soft" aspects of feminine irrationality rather than as masculine intellectual qualities. The definition of separate masculine and feminine spheres of cultural activity has historically been part of the patterning of American society and serves to explain why there was so little resistance to the definition of knowledge as abstract and scientific in the nineteenth century. Part of the rebellion of youth today consists of affirming that intellectual excellence can be demonstrated by intuitive and expressive achievement in a way that has equal validity with the rational problem-solving of the older curriculum. William James adopted the terminology of the frontier to characterize the tough- and the tender-minded. In doing so, he unwittingly demonstrated the extent to which the stereotypes of a frontier society dictated styles of intellectual life. The tough-minded have made the social sciences in America "hard data" sciences that occupy the cultural middle ground between humanistic knowledge and knowledge that is of technological value. The dominant intellectual style dictates that the social scientist may think about man as a social being, but only with a degree of mathematical precision which approximates that of the machine.

Thus special social and cultural factors have given a characteristic American twist to the intellectual function of the American university even though that function was borrowed from Western European culture. All the functions of the university—social, political, and intellectual—can be understood only in the larger context of American society and culture. Today the young radicals recognize what the political and intellectual functions of the American university are. They insist that the political function be made overt, and that the intellectual function be radically changed to develop a more expressive culture. The social function of the university is more in question in society at large than it is among students, faculty, or university administrators. It is difficult, however, to see the ways in which student expectations concerning the university as a political institution can be met since the university can only continue to mediate conflict in society through a process of infinite expansion. Furthermore, it is questionable whether a future orientation should always prevail in resolving social conflict. Time, money, and energy should be directed toward the solution of social problems *now,* rather than continuing the Horace Mann-John Dewey approach to educational reform for the next generation. It is also possible to argue that some limitation of university growth might lead to a beneficial redirection of resources and energy on political action. A genuine ideological flowering in the United States might be a welcome departure from the pragmatic tradition in politics. In this way, the breakdown of political consensus is probably essential for the preservation of universities that can perform their essential intellectual services.

The present crisis in universities should not be regarded as the result of a breakdown of authority which brings in its train the politicization of a community which was formerly a-political. It should be viewed instead as a crisis in which the university is no longer able to carry on the political task which it has hitherto managed with some success. If the problem of politics and the university could be considered in this manner, we might be able to move toward some original thought on the problem of elites in American society. Although American thought preserves the fiction that the educational system operates in the direction of abolishing elites, they do exist and the universities create them. What troubles American society today is the irresponsibility of the professional elite which it has created and which claims the classical liberal freedoms to dispose of its skills to the maximum of personal profit. It is one of the ironies of American history that the development of the graduate school and the ideal of pure research meant that scholars could escape to some extent from the dominant commercial culture, but could also avoid social responsibility generally. Certainly some recognition that a university-trained elite exists must be a precondition for defining the responsibilities of its members. Some of these responsibilities are obvious today. Faculty members must refuse to engage in research which might pollute or destroy the human environment. They must also recognize the responsibility to teach and to use their skills with reference to values other than their commercial worth in the market. The assumption of this kind of responsibility seems the only path which exists today toward acceptance and support of the university by the rest of society. A wider social responsibility might, in fact, strengthen the intellectual caliber of the university because it might end the isolation from the rest of society which has been the normal lot of American intellectuals since the rise of the graduate school.

This laboratory-like isolation of academic culture lies at the heart of the discontent concerning the way in which the university discharges its intellectual tasks. The curriculum is irrelevant to the young because it does not automatically provide the means for coming to grips with the immediate, pressing problems of human experience. A student who works away at the history of industrialization and intellectual responses to it for two or three years will eventually be able to develop some intellectual stance toward the media and mass culture. But if the quality of mass culture is a deeply felt personal experience every day of his life, he will need some outlet for that emotion before the three years are up. A student who feels daily that industrial technology has endangered the balance of the human environment will reject being made a unit in a rationally designed learning process no matter how efficiently it is administered—not because it is intellectually unsatisfactory, but because it is deeply disturbing emotionally.

This attempt to eliminate emotion from intellectual effort creates the deepest gap between the generations. The young seek to bring the rational and irrational aspects of human experience into significant relationship. Their style of intellectual life is religious. Their elders cling to the identity of the objective scientist and wonder at the storms of emotion raging through the laboratory. One route toward a satisfactory new curriculum would be to redesign it so that man would be at the center once again. Man can be viewed scientifically and religiously at one and the same time since he is both an evolving part of nature and an irrational being for whom reason alone cannot explain experience. Certainly in the humanities and social sciences, we must abandon the rigid programming of knowledge. No discipline in the social sciences today possesses sufficient methodological unity that students need to pass through a three- or four-year program to master some coherent world-view at the end. Any synthesis which our curriculum in the humanities and social sciences conveys should be one built up by the individual student.

In this respect, as in so many areas of thought today, we can benefit from examining the medieval world. We could achieve freedom for the student to synthesize by returning to a medieval notion of study. A faculty member should teach what he is master of to any group of students who are admitted to the university and who want to work with him. A single final examination on a pass/fail basis should elicit the student's synthesis when he feels that he is ready to be examined. Much of the boredom of undergraduate life would disappear if we really required students to be self-motivating and obliged them to develop their own intellectual positions rather than training their critical talents. Since the lines of our conventional academic disciplines are blurring, we have less and less justification for requiring students to observe them. Since in the present state of the social sciences and humanities we have no *summa* to offer students, we must encourage them to arrive at one on their own. These remarks refer, of course, to the undergraduate curriculum and the teaching of the humanities and the social sciences. I cannot speak to the problem of the curriculum in science and the proper manner of teaching it. I would only insist that science find its place in the undergraduate curriculum as it relates to man in his human predicament. It must not be taught in an entirely pre-professional manner, as it is in most undergraduate programs today. This intrusion of professional discipline into the undergraduate curriculum requires students to develop one set of intellectual talents at the expense of others which might personally be equally valuable. Professional commitment should remain an adult choice rather than something externally imposed.

Some such rearrangement of the undergraduate curriculum and the examination process should dispose of many of the problems of university governance in undergraduate studies. Student needs would become self-defining. In the realm of undergraduate teaching, salaries could be made commensurate with the capacity and interest of faculty in teaching students. This capacity might or might not have much to do with their eminence as scholars. Departments would be less important if their control of the curriculum were removed and their examining functions much restricted. So far as the curriculum is concerned, students could seek out their own relevance. This would be creative chaos as opposed to the deadening routine which makes the predominant state of mind for the undergraduate one of boredom. Much of our present stress in rigorous training in abstract thought might disappear from the undergraduate curriculum, but students might find themselves engaged in a learning process involving moral and emotional growth as well as training in critical thought.

Such an undergraduate program would, of course, need to be carefully separated from graduate training, and criteria other than undergraduate records would have to be developed for entry into graduate school. The whole transition between college and graduate school needs to be much more carefully scrutinized than it is at present. At the moment, the graduate school is simply being given, by extension, all the social, political, and intellectual functions attributed to the educational community by theorists like Jefferson and Horace Mann. In addition, because the graduate school is the last stage of formal education, it is the place at which another uniquely American expectation concerning education comes most strikingly into play. This is the expectation that one's education will be the automatic path to some meaningful social role.

No other society has produced quite the literature of complaint about education that America has. Henry Adams is only the most striking example of the American belief that the mere process of acquiring intellectual skills should place one in a situation where significant social action and power are immediately to hand. This expectation cannot be fulfilled unless there is some underlying harmony between the goals of education and the vocational structure of society at large. During the nineteenth and the first half of the twentieth centuries, professional training was a direct path to a desired social role for men. There was a smooth passage between earning a graduate degree and a place as an entrepreneur of knowledge or skill in the existing hierarchy of professions or in the upper echelons of business management. The situation of women with access to higher education, however, was very different during this period. Indeed, the expectation that higher education would lead women to meaningful social action, when frustrated, led women to become radical critics of American society and culture.[7] Somewhat the same thing is happening today among a significant proportion of men and women in graduate school, because the economy has moved to a stage at which the service industries are of major importance. The role which seems both meaningful and useful to the young has, therefore, become that of service. Consequently many graduate students seek to alter the institution of the graduate school so that there will once again be some underlying harmony between the kinds of training they receive and the kinds of vocational roles which they value. It is questionable, however, whether the graduate school—the institution where knowledge must be generated—is the appropriate place in the educational community for this ideal of social service to be expressed. The concept of service advanced by the young is purely pragmatic and relates only to forms of service that can be perceived at the moment. While an ideal of social service is consistent with the generation of knowledge, it need not necessarily further that process. We might find that representatives of the service sector of the economy would perform no better as lay directors of universities than the businessmen who first took on the tasks of lay governance. They might be just as likely to influence the university toward intellectual efforts that were focused completely on the present. Certainly the process of generating knowledge cannot be directed solely with reference to the needs of any particular social or economic group without serious loss of intellectual vitality.

The solution to this problem could be found for the present by devising some form of institutionalized service between college and graduate school. The channeling of candidates from undergraduate to graduate school is now an arbitrary process since choice of intellectual vocation can have little reference to life as lived outside an academic institution. There should probably be a two- to three-year period between college and admission to graduate school in which potential graduate students can have actual experience of some form of social service. Those whose temperamental bent was purely intellectual would not suffer from such service. Those who went on to professional schools like law or medicine would quickly bring their service experience to bear on legal and medical problems. Indeed, some of the more harmful trends in recruitment into the medical and legal professions might be reversed by such an expedient. Better still, those talented enough to make real contributions in their field without graduate education would have the opportunity to become effective in society without spending four or five years within a learning process of little benefit to them. By this device, we might counteract the obsession of American society with technical expertise and postgraduate education.

Since the financing of graduate education must become more and more a federal matter, the implementation of such a plan calls for a simple piece of legislation requiring all candidates for financial aid to demonstrate some such period of social service. Graduate schools might then impose the same qualification on applicants who did not receive government grants. This enforced involvement with the outside world is easily defensible. It is no more than a peaceful equivalent of military service, long thought acceptable in Western democracies. At the same time, it would

JILL CONWAY

insure that vocations to intellectual life were tested in terms of some experience outside the university. At present, students enter graduate school as clerics entered the unreformed religious orders—not because of true vocations, but because they are comfortable places, considering the options in the external world. The monastic orders ceased to be important cultural forces in Western Europe when clerics were chosen that way. This may be the fate of the graduate schools unless we can define what constitutes a real intellectual vocation.

When the trustees of Johns Hopkins began their search for a new idea of the university and for an American Newman to give it form, they were forced to ask what constituted an intellectual vocation. They understood it to be a "search for truth aside from any consideration of practicality or usefulness."[8] The definition sounds naïve a hundred years later because we have lost the happy Victorian confidence that what is defined as knowledge can be pursued aside from some liberal consensus about what is practical and useful. Now that the liberal consensus has gone, who has the right to say what truths shall be pursued in graduate schools? The answer must be that in order to escape a state-imposed syllabus of errors, faculty and students must come to some agreement about curriculum in a manner that gives equal weight to the intellectual concerns of both. The counter-course must be taken into the curriculum no matter how noisy the process may be. To make the definition of truth in our confused times a generational prerogative is to invite the kind of academic turmoil in which we all live. It is also to insist that the scientific and religious styles of intellectual life must inevitably be opposing ones. Yet if the contemporary disillusionment with the promise of science is not to degenerate into an exaltation of the irrational, the two intellectual styles must be harmonized.

REFERENCES

1. See Lawrence A. Cremin (ed.), *The Republic and the School: Horace Mann on the Education of Free Men* (Teachers College, Columbia University: New York, 1957), p. 87.
2. *Ibid.*, p. 97. Both quotations are from Mann's *Twelfth Annual Report* (1848) to the Massachusetts Board of Education.

54

3. See John Dewey, *Democracy and Education* (Macmillan: New York, 1916). See especially the essay entitled "The Nature of Subject Matter."

4. Richard Hofstadter, *Anti-Intellectualism in American Life* (Knopf: New York, 1963).

5. See Hugh Hawkins, *Pioneer: A History of Johns Hopkins University* (Cornell University Press: Ithaca, 1960), pp. 4-7.

6. See James Cary Coale to William Gilman, Nov. 20, 1874, cited in Hawkins, *Pioneer,* p. 7.

7. See, for example, the writing of Jane Addams on women's education and its effect on her generation. Her ideas are most readily available in Jane Addams, *Twenty Years at Hull-House* (Macmillan: New York, 1909).

8. Hawkins, *Pioneer,* p. 292.

EDGAR Z. FRIEDENBERG

The University Community in an Open Society

AT THIS stage in our history, the rapidly growing heterogeneity of the university both in function and clientele would certainly have led to trouble and confusion even if there were no inherent conflict among its functions. But there are fundamental conflicts that, though they stem from the heterogeneity of the university community, reflect far more than the ugliness of the kind of academic urban sprawl that has developed. As the size and jumble of the university community have increased, the university's functions have acquired conflicting meanings and value to its various constituencies. The question of governance, I believe, resolves itself into that of whether a morally defensible ordering among those functions can be achieved and made viable under the actual conditions of our society. If it cannot—and this is quite possible—then the passage of the university system should not be greatly mourned, nor unduly delayed by a series of organ-transplants and excisions designed to relieve immediate crises at further cost to the university's integrity.

The central function of higher education in America has always been vocational. Harvard was founded to train clergymen; and as the society has become more a mass, open society, its dependence on the university system for vocational training and placement has, of course, become far greater and more complex. It is well understood that the university serves society by selecting and training a wide range and enormous number of technicians who, granting its present mode of organization, are essential. The university is the instrument of the continuous talent search by which an industrial democracy assures itself that it is not systematically ignoring lower-status social groups as a potential talent-

56

source, thereby denying them access to opportunity and itself the value of their contribution.

In a mass, industrial democracy, no function could be more legitimate. Nor could any function be more heavily burdened by ideology. The furious controversy that has recently been aroused by Arthur Jensen's conclusion that there are significant innate differences of cognitive style between blacks and whites that, in this culture, operate to the disadvantage of blacks and especially hamper them in school is, for example, totally ideological.[1] *Any* difference between individuals or between social groups may be either an advantage or a disadvantage, depending on circumstances. Stupidity is often a virtue which must be feigned by those unfortunate enough to lack it; while if the Esquimaux had feet a yard long and a foot wide, they wouldn't need snowshoes. Jensen's findings, if valid, certainly establish that blacks are less well adapted than whites to respond successfully to the demands of the dominant institutions of industrial democracy, especially its schools. They leave entirely open the question of whether this is a sign of inferiority, superiority, or neither. But they are nevertheless threatening because the conflict to which they point may be impossible to resolve for a society ideologically committed both to equality of opportunity and to popular sovereignty. Even if Jensen is right, there are two ways in which this resolution could be achieved, but both appear to be politically impossible for a mass democracy. One is to provide equal respect and rewards to people with the kinds of cognitive styles blacks—or poets, or hippies, or mystics, or police, or sexual deviants—possess. There are such people; and they are indeed different from one another and from the norm. This requires, in short, genuine pluralism: a great many small events, some competitive, in which different kinds of excellence could be demonstrated and rewarded.

The second way is for society to respond openly and generously to need, without requiring that the needy—which at different times and in different ways includes all of us—prove anything or win any race at all. Except, perhaps, in its Malthusian aspects, this is now technologically possible through the instrumentality of an enormously high technical level of productivity distributed through a high guaranteed annual income or a universal credit card—instead of a university degree. But our society lacks the political means to make any such commitment. The anxiety and *ressentiment* such proposals arouse among the bitter coalition of the self-made, the self-condemned, and the vast number of poor whose sole satisfaction seems to come from the prospect of others more impoverished still; of industrial leaders fearful that too few people would work unless compelled to by threat of humiliation and want, and union officials who fear that a general rise in the standard of living unrelated to membership in the labor force would deprive them of a *raison d'être* make it impossible. Taken together for these and other reasons, the majority of the American people seem incapable of regarding misery as anything but failure; and loathe the most miserable of their number. The major premise of our ideology of opportunity is that each should have an equal chance to succeed; but the minor premise is that only those who do succeed may be rewarded, and that refusal to compete should be punished or subjected to therapy as "dropping out."

The educational system has played a complex and delicate role in mediating among these competitive hostilities and ideological problems. It has, in effect, become a steeplechase in which comparatively few people fail utterly; but the hazards are so cunningly designed that many more fall somewhat behind and are cooled out. The more successful students have been precisely those whose cognitive skills and ideological positions have been most suited to the demands of middle and upper managerial positions in existing institutions; so that the school has served to reify these qualities as characteristics of the worthiest members of society. But, in so doing, it has also established the educational system as the supervisor of legitimate people-racing in our society. It provides the anthrodrome; its staff are the judges and referees; it determines which events shall be accepted as part of the decathlon, which styles of competition are legitimate and which are cheating and hence grounds for disqualification and exclusion from subsequent competition.

All this is familiar enough; but its converse side is less frequently stressed and is more useful in understanding contemporary academic stress. Victories won in and certified by the educational system may be honored by the society with increments of status without arousing much resentment among the underclass, so long as the educational system is thought to operate on universalistic principles. If, in fact, you are admitted to fair competition, you are expected, in our society, to be a good loser. But the educational system, consequently, must become as nearly as possible the sole route to success and recognition; no contender is to be seeded out of the earlier events. It is this, I believe, which accounts for the absurd profusion of curricula in American schools and colleges, and the universal insistence on diplomas of various kinds as qualifications for posts and professions not even remotely related to the skills those diplomas reputedly certify. They are not intended to mean anything in themselves, but they have two useful social functions. They do attest that the bearer has been thoroughly socialized in the educational system and knows the score and the name of the game, which insures that life in bourgeois America will not end like a performance of *Turandot:* The name is not "love," though the score may be. And they get society off the hook by ratifying its universalist pretensions: Nobody got anything free, there has been no favoritism or nepotism, the plastic little girl who won the national championship at baton-twirling is really the best. Her mother made her practice four hours a day, and the school taught her how to relate to strangers.

When a social group—ethnic or otherwise—whose characteristics have kept it at a competitive disadvantage becomes strong enough politically to demand a better life in America, it cannot simply demand a bigger reward as an elementary human right. Having previously accepted universalism in principle, it must complain not of *inhuman* treatment, but of *unjust* treatment—that is, of discrimination. The response of the liberal segment of society is not to redress its grievances directly, which would be politically disastrous, but to scurry around trying to think up ways of being sure it wins more events without actually cheating or showing favoritism. My own formal doctoral training happens to have been in that aspect of education called "evaluation"—that is, the design and construction of tests. For the past six or seven years, since whites have become more aware of the American racial crisis, I have, like most others trained in this area, often been called upon to participate in conferences at which funding agencies sought technical help in searching out the academic proficiency which they insisted must lie undiscovered among blacks so that this might be recognized and rewarded. They had already, of course, attempted to provide support for those whose superior promise could be identified by existing academic records or testing techniques.

Urgent as the need for a massive increase in support for black and other "disadvantaged" students was and is, it seems grotesque for these agencies to conceive their problem as a matter of test-bias. Indeed, the urgency of the problem makes this preoccupation with tests and contests grotesque. What is needed to respond more adequately to the needs of "disadvantaged" groups is not a more thorough and ingenious canvass among them for the qualities society rewards, but a broader and more adventurous—and more gracious—conception of what constitutes a socially valuable attribute. It is certainly desirable that a much larger proportion of blacks receive National Merit Scholarships than have done so in the past. It is even more fundamentally desirable that awards committees broaden their definition of what constitutes National Merit, to permit them to recognize a variety of individuals, and sometimes without demanding victory in any competition. But this might yet be fruitless if the only consequence of such recognition is to channel the recipient into the educational system, albeit under much more favorable circumstances than he would otherwise have had. A student admitted to the university by such pluralistic devices might still find himself cooled out rather quickly because the university itself was unable to recognize diversity of cognitive style and continued to define any effort to do so as "lowering standards."

Yet there remain only three possibilities, no matter what may be demanded. Unless the university *does* learn to respect a less rationalistic definition of cognition as an acceptable means toward academic achievement, or the society learns to respect personal, idiosyncratic ways of growing up and learning outside degree-granting institutions—those who, whether for ethnogenetic or purely personal reasons, are less adept at competitive striving and linear rationality will lose out in this society, as they have been doing so far. Because the second of these alternatives seems even less likely than the first, the present intense demand for black studies programs, controlled by black personnel, has arisen. The opposition to these as academically unsound reflects, I believe, the recognition of the more conservative faculty that they are indeed intended to provide protected enclaves in which black students with poorer conventional academic skills can survive. In view of the history of the university system, this recognition cannot be accepted as an adequate reason for resisting these programs. Virginity cannot be defended unsuccessfully more than once; and if defended successfully for too long, future development is arrested. The university system has, quite properly, recognized social demand in accepting faculties of engineering, of educational studies, and other studies that quite clearly lack the cultural breadth of the humanities. This is the device by which we achieve an increasingly open society. Those trained in these disciplines, too, have a different cognitive style—both because of differences in training and differences in background that are associated with these vocational choices. In any case, the "new men" are different. New black men are no more likely to do violence to the academic tradition than white and may be a little more human.

Once one accepts in principle, then, that the university system is to be maintained as virtually the sole channel of mobility, the university must respond to demands for variation in the definition of achievement needed to recognize the way in which different social groups develop different styles and different merits; and if, in fact, they develop none, illusory merits will doubtless have to be ascribed to them. Society must recognize the claims to dignity and opportunity of all its constituent groups. If the university is to continue to stand astride the only legitimate highway to advancement, it must quit demanding tolls in coins that only some travelers can acquire and calling this "maintaining standards." But the acceptance of more diverse modes of response nevertheless leads to conflict precisely with those groups which have forced themselves most recently and with greatest discontinuity to their earlier experience to make it on the more conventional terms already prevalent in the university system. No datum has more consistently recurred in current conflict within the university than the observation that the students who are least responsive to and most intolerant of the growing demands are whites whose parents never attended college; while those most sympathetic to and often so over-identified with the blacks as to court repudiation by them are higher-status white students who take college for granted, but are unable to tolerate its moral failures. To accede to the demands of blacks is not only to violate prejudices that many first-generation working-class students hold; it is also to change the rules of the game they have learned so laboriously and to discredit as irrelevant and morally fatuous or worse the instrument they have sought, at great sacrifice, for their deliverance. Those who have just been seated at the Round Table after a long and arduous journey are likely to get rather upset when informed that Camelot is no more authentic than Disneyland, and that Excalibur, according to the small print, was made in Hong Kong.

This, I believe, is the major source of friction between the "jocks" and commuters, who still try to take the university system seriously on its own terms, and the higher-status white activists and blacks who denounce it. The Vietnam war has, of course, infinitely exacerbated this conflict, both because it has discredited the university system morally and, more directly, because the immediate vocational opportunities to which university education leads are so likely to be war-connected. These opportunities are, moreover, *more* likely to be war-connected for lower-status students than for higher; because these, differentially, tend to locate themselves in the technological rather than the humanistic curricula. Concretely, to bar recruiters from war-industry and ROTC programs from campus is to destroy insolently, before their eyes and without their consent, the staircase that conservative students had come to college to climb. On the basis of this social model, I cannot but be convinced that black students, once they find themselves more at ease in what was never Zion, will join the jocks and repudiate their activist supporters, whose style they already seem to find grandiose and rather hysterical. Besieged college and university presidents on recent media presentations have seemed correspondingly less hostile to the blacks whose attacks on the university system, though often more aggressive than those of white activists, are also far more superficial. These men are trying, I believe, to convince black student leaders that the university system is still relevant to them, however strongly their more privileged white dissident colleagues may condemn it.

For these reasons, then, current academic conflict is complexly rooted in the university's function in the transmission of vocational opportunity to members of a society in which personal advancement, or making it, is the major basis for self-esteem. The university, moreover, serves as differential as well as transmitter; it keeps society from being overturned by permitting individuals to move at very different rates and still think they're wheels—which they are at least in the sense that it is they who bear the vehicle's burden. But conflict about the function of the university in contributing to economic and social opportunity, central as it is, is still, I believe, less fundamental a social problem than those which have now arisen *between* its vocational function and other functions less ideologically acceptable in our society and hence less frequently explicitly discussed.

The University Community in an Open Society

A major function of the university has been to serve as a community in which many of its members have found intense and protracted satisfaction and have married or formed permanent friendships or taken lovers. This is why college and university life has become a pastoral legend in American folklore, and why alumni continue to attend class reunions in a nostalgic and futile effort to recapture briefly their student experience. Both the nostalgia and the futility have become clichés as aspects of such events. But nostalgia—grief for your own place, the guilt and loss of having uprooted yourself—is an emotion that a great many Americans would be better and more sensitive for having allowed themselves to feel, though it is more agonizing than any other experience that still leaves its victim with a future. Nostalgia is not recognized in America as the kind of suffering that teaches people anything of value, because a culture that sets its highest premium on mobility as a way of getting its business done discounts it in advance as romantic immaturity. But people who have learned to respect this agony are less likely than others to set fire to peasant huts with their cigarette lighters, and this is a desirable form of self-restraint.

The futility, moreover, is ironical, because the university is still, for some of its students, the source of the kind of intense community alumni recall nostalgically; but alumni cannot recognize this because it is these students whose styles they find most repellent and who seem to them to be trying to destroy the university. So some may be; those who love their home would sooner burn it than see it defiled. But it is nevertheless precisely the militants who have found within the university fellows with a common vision of its purpose who care enough about it to risk beatings and imprisonment in the service of that vision and who are currently having the experience the alumni think they remember—not the jocks, at a time when the football hero has become anachronistic, and certainly not the commuters who would just as soon be in correspondence school if you could really make it there and the mail service were better. The more conservative alumni are more likely to be nostalgic than the liberals who, being dedicated to progress, will have gone on through several further stages of their life-cycle without much thought about their college days. But as conservatives they cannot recognize their deeper kinship with the radicals and hippies who make the university their home and not just a stopover on their career-line.

It must be granted that the fact that college life—as we used to think of it—should have become a basis for community is largely an unintended, and in some ways a paradoxical, development of American life. The educational system is designed to make schooling both a transient and a highly competitive experience, which is highly inimical to the development of a sense of community. At most stages, no such sense develops. A high-school homecoming is, in Kurt Vonnegut Jr.'s word, a real *granfalloon;* though some working-class youth, having been less hung-up than their middle-class peers in academic competition and less oriented onward to college, *do* find the high school a home-from-home and may continue to return to it as a social center for a year or two after they have graduated or dropped out, until their friends have left. But schools, generally speaking, are ill-designed to foster intimacy and a sense of identity among their members. The devices that are intentionally employed to foster school spirit destroy spontaneity and intimacy in the interests of an automatic *esprit de corps* which is anything but homelike.

But the unintended consequences outweigh the intended. College life, though growing continuously more competitive through the years as the educational system grows more universalistic, is still much less competitive than life outside the sanctuary. There is not the constant press for conspicuous consumption. The definition of the student role as impecunious and economically dependent is neither desirable nor just, and fosters the exploitation of students as sweated labor in undergraduate instruction. But it also provides the only enclave in American life in which poverty is not dishonorable and makes it far easier for people to accept one another for what they are, to establish cooperative living arrangements and open expression of feeling. There is a certain *Schadenfreude* to be got from the fact that the custom of exploiting students by making them the university's serfs has backfired into what appears to be a permanent rejection of the middle-class community's more vulgar and driven patterns both of consumption and of uptight family life. The systematic age-grading is harmful in its broad social consequences; the universities are now perceived by the general public as ghettos that are becoming useless because they no longer manage to protect the community from the dangerous young aliens they contain. But this view, too, fosters a sense of identity and empathy among students as such—not strong enough to prevent them from being divided into warring factions by conflicting interests and values, but strong enough to leave them with a viable subgroup even when this happens. And, finally, the fact that our society withholds adult status till after the human sexual prime so that the peak of erotic intensity occurs during college years enhances students' impact on one another and the probability that something human and personal, if not necessarily agreeable, will develop. Sexuality in the young, though intensely competitive, resists the control of a competitive society, for the attributes that lead to erotic and economic success are different. The difference tends steadily to lessen, for in every society higher status characteristics come to be defined as erotically desirable: witness the vicissitudes of obesity. The conventional institutions of student life, as John Finley Scott has shown in his studies of the college sorority as a national marriage-brokerage system for conventional girls, function so as to rationalize students' erotic relationships and bring them into the university's total network of transactions.[2] But the fraternity and sorority system is declining and has largely been replaced by informal though enduring relationships; there are more liaisons and fewer conquests. This, too, adds to the confusion and hostility of the alumni who would never have claimed that a sexual relationship could be moral in itself, though marriage might make it legitimate and even obligatory.

For these sound, if accidental reasons, the campus has come to serve the middle-class young as a community and sometimes as the locus of their best real experience of personal relationships. That, despite its growing impersonality and dedication to a competitive *ethos,* our society has not only permitted this, but enshrined it in sentimental myths of college life is explicable, I suggest, largely because the process—as long as colleges were largely highly class-selective in the clientele they served—served the class interests of those who supported the colleges without their having to admit that such a thing existed. Simple and quite genuine patterns of affiliation could be counted on to provide American society not only with the ivy equivalent of an old-boy network at the top, but with lower networks that served both to support and ensnare potential aspirants from lower levels. Catholic universities help educated Catholics to go on feeling Catholic, which helps make subsequent discrimination unnecessary. Similarly, during the period of more than a decade that I taught at Brooklyn College, I came to feel that the college's sustaining vision of itself as the channel of opportunity for poor but bright and often radical students from excluded social groups had become a myth that was exploited rather cynically. In all that time, there were only four or five members of genuinely excluded ethnic groups—blacks or Puerto Ricans—among my students. They were not poor; they came, for the most part, from the homes of tax accountants, furniture dealers, or other petty-bourgeois; and their brightness was often nullified by extreme provinciality. My colleagues continued to refer with satisfaction to the college's high academic rating nationally. But Norman Podhoretz's comment in *Making It*[3] suggests that the most alert Brooklyn youth of the kind the college was supposed to serve had already perceived what I came to see more slowly: that the true *national* function of the City College system was not merely to educate academically competent New York City youth and provide them with increased opportunity, but also to provide a reliable drainage system to keep them from flooding out the Ivy League and the western and midwestern state universities, which might have provided access to greater economic opportunity, but which would certainly have responded with ambivalence to the opportunity to provide this service.

There are clearly certain serious conflicts between the university's functions in providing economic opportunity in an egalitarian society and serving simultaneously as a base for community among the young. Competition itself poisons community; and young people for whom intimacy and communion are primary values deeply resent being forced to adopt standardized, competitive patterns of behavior by an impersonal grading system and examinations that are as objective and, hence, as unresponsive to their individualized qualities and feelings as they can be made. But this is what their peers who are using the university as an anthrodrome, and who are more concerned about the rewards to which academic success leads than with the quality of their college experience, need for their purposes. This, surely, is why the demand for ungraded curricula, experimental colleges, and the abolition of many forms of examination so neatly divides the activists and hippies from the more conventional and usually lower-status students who resist it.

But there are less direct but equally important reasons why the function of the university as a base of community interferes with its function as anthrodrome. As I have discussed more fully elsewhere, it is the community function of the university which most antagonizes the larger community outside.[4] Their hostility has several sources: a sense, more flattering than realistic, that student life is "privileged" and libertine compared to their own; the way in which the student-role is defined so that students—about the most sweated labor in America outside agriculture—are perceived as not working and as being supported by their parents or the welfare state. But most infuriating of all is merely the fact that a community exists. Below the level at which the corporate network can provide a sense of identity and of membership in a colleague group, most Americans today are bereft of intimacy and belong to very little that has meaning for them. Divided as it is, the university is one of the few institutions that still shelters enclaves of people with common values who can talk to one another; and there is a fine irony in the frequency and bitterness with which its critics complain that it has become irrelevant to human life. They are right; but of what other institution in our society would it even occur to anyone to make this complaint? The Congress, the American Medical Association, the Chase Manhattan Bank? Except for their undoubted capacity to do irreparable mischief, nobody seriously *expects* them to be relevant any longer. Fly Jefferson Airplane, and hope for the best.

This sense of being part of a meaningful coalition and bound by realities of feeling and genuine goals to its other members is, I believe, more coveted, and the source of more bitter conflict—inner and outer—in our society than any other treasure it might, but seldom does, afford. It is this, rather than sexual gratification, that remains the illicit satisfaction; though attacks on satisfying communities are usually directed against their putative licentiousness, which is often the only language in which their detractors can identify what they think they're missing. But the jealousy and sense of deprivation, and correspondingly the hostility, engendered are intense. So far as I know, no hippy commune has been allowed to survive in America; it is either busted by outraged neighbors or destroyed by ogling tourists who move in on it looking for thrills, or both. On campus, such communities enjoy some, though declining, protection. In any case, the presence of a viable community on campus is embarrassing to the students in the anthrodrome. It generates norms of conduct by which they find themselves put down, reminds them that there are satisfactions their commitments to the future forbid them to share, and, more directly, reduces the value of their credential in the community they hope will honor it. It antagonizes and drives away the officials with whom they hoped to negotiate for preferment. The conflict between the university as community and as anthrodrome is an absolutely real one, a conflict of interests as well as tastes; and it seems either fatuous or disingenuous, therefore, to deny that what advances the interests of one is likely to be costly to those of the other.

Meanwhile, constituencies of the university other than students are, of course, involved in the conflict. Generally speaking, the interests of the faculty and administration coincide with those of the anthrodrome and are opposed to those who would find community in the university. The university is indeed fundamentally involved in the industrial and governmental activities that its critics find most reprehensible and that even its supporters no longer defend. But these activities are not merely the stuff of which academic careers are made and the source of needed financial support. They also provide the upper stages of the anthrodrome itself. The more conventionally ambitious students need them as the next step in *their* careers. And an even more fundamental commitment to the anthrodrome has been made on what may be irreversible epistemological grounds. The very conception of what constitutes knowledge in every discipline; the prevailing empiricism that reduces research even in the humanities to objective and often quantitative terms; the official dominance of "value-free" social science that willingly sells itself to the highest bidder, though now with the hope that the arrangement may be handled with discretion—all these serve the needs of the anthrodrome and have a chilling effect on the community. The self-definition of the college administrator as the broker among the various interests that affect the university, whose professional responsibility actually *precludes* his attempting to exert any moral leadership among the university's various *liaisons dangereuses,* also serves the anthrodrome; as does the university's peculiar orientation to public relations, which leads it to court public support and hence public approval even under circumstances that would clearly favor instead a policy of coolly reminding the public that it, too, is dependent on the university as a major source of revenue and employment and that it might be well advised to avoid excessive harassment even of those it does not particularly like.

So far, I have made no reference to the official functions of the university on which it bases its formal claims to esteem and support: the creation and propagation of knowledge, or, as we now more frequently say, research and teaching. This omission is the more striking since these functions might be expected to support the community within the university and require its support in turn, rather than the anthrodrome. Both teaching and research are in essence, at their best, particularistic activities. No commitment to equality of opportunity can make a teacher as useful to the students he does not turn on as he is to those he does; no amount of ambition can help a student learn much of value from a teacher who has no interest in either students or what he is teaching. But the university has evolved a highly effective device to protect universalism under these conditions: rigid control of instruction through scheduling, credits, and the definition of the process as one involving abstract, symbolic communication rather than feeling, touch, or spontaneity. The effect of this is to keep instruction almost entirely in what the great psychoanalytic theorist Harry Stack Sullivan called "the syntactic mode" and so remote from the reality of sense-data and personal experience as to seem quite unreal. This makes academic freedom, defined as the freedom to teach whatever content one wishes provided the content remains turned-off, quite innocuous, especially in a mass democracy on which concepts, as such, have no influence until they have been legitimated by the mass media as what beautiful, or powerful, people believe. It also makes teaching both puerile and detached. An effective college teacher must be more interesting, provocative, and profound than daytime TV, or lose the attention of his students. Many do.

It is true that college faculty neglect teaching in favor of research as leading to more rapid professional advancement. But it is also true that teaching in the mass university of today has become a rather degrading experience; like trying to put on an authentic display of Berber folk-dances in a Casablanca dive into which a group of sailors have been lured on the pretext that other more urgent interests would be satisfied. Neither party to this shady transaction is innocent, and the more authentic the folkloric spectacle is, the more hostile the clientele becomes, since the quality of the performance is in itself a rebuke to its genuine, if base, desires.

The Selective Service Act, with the 2-S deferment, is of itself enough to make a whore of any professor. But for this the anthrodrome might in any case suffice. If freedom of opportunity requires that instruction take place in mixed groups in which those to whom what is being considered can only be an instrument of no intrinsic interest outnumber and swamp those with whose culture it already connects, teaching must remain an unrewarding and inauthentic activity. Liberalism's answer to this is familiar and compelling: Make it connect, find new ways to reach the disadvantaged and the merely uninterested and stimulate their interests. But education can only be planned and organized experience and must build on experience already had; it cannot be grafted onto a lifeless trunk or one which rejects it as incompatible with its development. Techniques for "reaching" or "motivating" students to learn something they do not care about initially seem to me most often devices for inducing them to abandon their own past for the sake of a deal with society that will pay off in the future. The anthrodrome is willing enough to do that—that is why it came to the university—but the process of helping it does not feel much like teaching. Nor would curriculum revision intended to adapt to its interests help very much, for students who come to higher education primarily to advance their careers quite often have no interests in either ideas or experience as such—and, indeed, sense that such interests would hamper their advancement in this society. What they want is a degree and the tricks of their trade.[5]

Under these conditions, then, both the significance of teaching as a university function and its potential contribution to the university community diminish, and too massive a claim for support should not be based on it. In the case of research, a quite different set of difficulties arises. There can be no question that our society, unless revolutionized, will continue to support and conduct the kind of research now done in our universities. Whether this is useful or leads to fundamental knowledge is irrelevant. Complex, literate societies usually maintain some costly and prestigious institution in which the kind of knowledge useful to their elites is codified, recorded, and interpreted. Such institutions take on a sacred character, and a threat to them is interpreted by the elite as a threat to the integrity of the society (which, from their point of view, it is). The Alexandrian priesthood must have been at least as outraged and dismayed by the burning of their library as the leading citizens of Canada were by the destruction of the computer at Sir George Williams University last year. When barbarians burn centers of learning, the end of an era may indeed be at hand; and the following era will possibly define knowledge differently and rebuild the library as a tourist attraction, if it recognizes such a social role as "tourist."

Since history is written by and from the point of view of ruling elites, especially before there is mass literacy, the destruction, physical or functional, of centers of learning is automatically recorded as a tragedy—though whether the quality of life in Alexandria was on the whole improved and liberated or impoverished by the burning of the library I do not know; it certainly delayed the birth of Lawrence Durell by nearly two millennia and marked, if it did not cause, the end of Alexandria as a major power.

If the United States is to continue its present course as a major power, it will continue to maintain knowledge factories whose product resembles that of the current multiversity. Such an institution will do what we call research, because in an open, technically advanced society empirical knowledge, which is the only kind useful for manipulating persons and objects in the environment, is the kind that becomes sacred. When an American speaks of "the advancement of knowledge" or "expanding the frontiers of learning," he almost always means the kind of learning that will enable him or his kind of people to control something or do something effective to somebody else: that is, science.

Scientific knowledge, in our society, is usually defined as morally neutral in itself; moral judgments may be made only about the uses to which knowledge is put, not about knowledge itself. This seems to me absurd. A moral judgment, though not a simple one, may be made about the *kind* of knowledge that makes it possible for me to think of a child as an object to be napalmed or of the manufacture of napalm as productive. It is not just our values nor our place in history that makes us not even wince at the idea that the *value* of our most gruesome armaments is included as part—and a very large part—of our gross national *product*. It is our epistemology as well—the character of what we regard as knowledge and respect as such—that has become an expression of our national character. This conception of knowledge also makes it possible for us to insist that people die later and in a somewhat different way than they would have otherwise, though so far no less frequently; and this, which we call modern medical science, is usually considered good. A complex moral judgment, then; but a moral judgment on the nature of science all the same.

It is clear that Western and especially American culture is locked into this empirical conception of knowledge, and equally clear that this favors the anthrodrome—those who enjoy doing and pushing more than feeling and being and reflecting on the process. The research function, then, is one more function of the university that favors them over the community-seekers. It is less clear, however, that the research function must be carried out within the same institution as the other functions of the university. This function, and this function alone, can dispense with the presence of young persons assigned the transitory and subordinate status of students. In many societies this separation is usual: The research institute has no teaching functions; the teaching institutions do not expect their staffs to make what we call contributions to knowledge —that is, to do research and publish it.

This separation, if it were real, would have a great deal to recommend it. Much research done in American universities is done there simply because this is cheaper and keeps it decentralized and out of sight. It is harder for a snoopy reporter to put the pieces together if the answer to what happened to all those sheep lies concealed under the scanty ivy of the University of Utah rather than in the Dugway laboratory itself. Now that such functions have become an awkward source of controversy for the universities, a reverse process has set in, one in which universities divest themselves of formal institutional connection with the research institutes and laboratories to which they now assign their more macabre military contracts—a device which seems hardly sufficient to protect them from complicity and will probably not even save them embarrassment. For this separation is quite unreal and within the context of American life and values probably cannot be made real.

The problem is again epistemological; empirical research is the only knowledge-function that has enough prestige, or is considered useful enough, to command genuine support in America. It is assumed, for example, that in a college devoted to teaching rather than research course-loads should be two or three times greater than in a university where the staff is expected to do research. But this assumption misses the whole point, which is that university teaching has come to be accepted as the kind of half-assed process it is because of the primacy of research; and to do it better means to do it entirely differently and probably in a much more leisurely, intimate, and unstructured way. The gain to be sought is in the quality of the relationship rather than in the number of units to be serviced. But no support for collegiate education on this scale is likely. Even if it were, the results would not be likely to be very promising for reasons Christopher Jencks and David Riesman make clear in *The Academic Revolution*: The highest prestige *colleges* in the country ought to be free to do the best teaching, being relatively less impoverished and having better trained faculty than the more marginal institutions.[6] But, in fact, they function as what Jencks and Riesman call university colleges: that is, they orient their teaching, their grading, and their curricula to the demands of graduate schools and pride themselves on the number of people they send on successfully to the doctorate, which ties them securely to present departmental organization and precludes serious curricular experimentation which, again, would jeopardize the career interests of their faculty, the ambitions of their more striving students, and the college's prestige.

All the major functions of the university which the society endorses and supports are opposed to its function of providing a home and a place of their own for young men and women in which they can develop a sense of personal commitment and a basis for moral judgment. These, indeed, infuriate our society, which prefers decorum to morality and success to either. They distress and frighten the universities' officials because they threaten the universities' sources of support. These officials avoid the moral issue when they can; those few who have attempted to respond to it with a measure of understanding and respect for their students have often been driven from their posts by outraged and punitive governing boards —sometimes, as in the cases of the excellent Kerr-Meyerson administration at Berkeley and that of John Summerskill at San Francisco State under which the first real experimental college program of the decade was developed, at the point at which these administrations seemed clearly on the verge of a triumphant reconciliation among discordant factions, though on terms more generous than the governing board could stomach. Leadership of this quality is too rare, however, to have been much of a challenge to regents and trustees. Much more often, university officials have redefined attacks on the ethical position of their institutions as empirical problems of governance. This, I suppose, is why the present volume of essays has been commissioned.

Most efforts to solve this problem have taken the form of structural alterations: changes in the composition of policy-making bodies within the university and sometimes token representation of students on the governing board. These measures are desirable as ways of providing more status and dignity for students and more respect for them; indeed, there are few campuses beyond the most parochial in which student sentiment and values are ignored today as they were even at schools like Columbia or Swarthmore until a few years ago. But such measures do not touch the heart of the difficulty, because the difficulty is not structural but moral.

The American university system, like Dr. Frankenstein and Dr. Faustus, is in trouble not because it has failed, but because it has succeeded; and succeeded in undertakings to which it would not have committed itself had it not relinquished moral responsibility in favor of empirical mastery in the first place. If this is too harsh an indictment, it is so for one reason only: that it attributes too much autonomy to the university. University faculty, especially, are inclined to be taken in by their own traditional, but increasingly deceptive pretense that they run the place. In fact, universities are run as America is run: indirectly, by a power structure that depends on the ambitions of the faculty and the lust of its individual members to be close to sources of power to induce it to organize itself so as to do what is expected of it. Power within the university aligns itself to power outside it.

REFERENCES

1. Arthur R. Jensen, "How Much Can We Boost IQ and Educational Achievement?" *Harvard Educational Review*, Vol. 39, No. 1 (Winter, 1969), pp. 1-123.

2. John Finley Scott, "The American College Sorority: Its Role in Class and Ethnic Endogamy," *American Sociological Review*, Vol. 30, No. 3 (June, 1965), pp. 514-27.

3. In the view Norman Podhoretz attributes retrospectively to his high school English teacher, he soliloquizes: "*Slum Child, filthy little slum child*. I was beyond saving; I deserved no better than to wind up with all the other horrible little Jewboys in the gutter (by which she meant Brooklyn College). If only I would listen to her, the whole world could be mine; I could win a scholarship to Harvard, I could get to know the best people, I could grow up into a life of elegance and refinement and taste. Why was I so stupid as not to understand?" *Making It* (Random House: New York, 1967), p. 10.

4. Edgar Z. Friedenberg, "The Campus Community and the Community," *New American Review #6* (New American Library: New York, 1969), pp. 146-62.

5. By far the most vivid and insightful treatment of what such purveying to an aspiring urban proletariat does to the joy of teaching is to be found in Herbert Gold's sadly neglected essay on a crisis in his career as an instructor at Wayne State University a few years ago—a crisis whose illustrative significance has been greatly enhanced by subsequent events in Detroit: "A Dog in Brooklyn, A Girl in Detroit: A Life Among the Humanities," *The Age of Happy Problems* (Dial Press: New York, 1962).

6. Christopher Jencks and David Riesman, *The Academic Revolution* (Doubleday: Garden City, New York, 1968), pp. 20-27.

S. E. AND ZELLA LURIA

The Role of the University:
Ivory Tower, Service Station, or Frontier Post?

THE TERM governance recalls the word *gouvernail* or rudder: that which steers a vessel toward its goal. One can describe the rudder and its operation without any assumptions as to the destination of the ship. But is that the interesting problem? In dealing with the governance of the university, are we not asking at least as much where it goes as how it gets there?

A more significant, although still imperfect, analogy is that of biological evolution. Biochemistry and physiology tell us how organisms function, whereas evolutionary biology tells us how the organisms that exist came to be, and why they appear to be so well adapted to the existing conditions as to give to evolution its seemingly purposive and to some extent predictable character. The purposiveness of evolution is only an apparent one: It stems from the passive adaptiveness of living organisms to their environment. In social phenomena, including the conduct of the university, a dimension other than structure and history enters the picture: the dimension of conscious purpose. Man sets goals and tries to fit the means to those goals. Thus, the goals of the university at any given stage of society must dictate its structure, even though vestiges of obsolete structures may remain as tokens of the past—such as the pageantry of commencements and of football games.

If the goals of a university must dictate its structure, what determines the goals themselves? Inevitably these goals and the set of values that underlies them reflect the values and goals of the society around the university. The critical question is the nature of the reflection. Is it to be an undistorted, uncritical reflection, like that of a plane mirror whose function is simply to reproduce what is presented to it? Or a protective reflection, like that of an insulating surface that excludes external influences from the interior of an object? Or a critical reflection that analyzes the input of external signals and filters it through a discriminating system of evaluative devices?

In less fanciful terms, the key question for any institution, and for the university in particular, is its ethical interaction with the society in which it operates. This interaction may result in acceptance of the predominant values, which become identified as the university's own; or it may lead to a rejection of society's values and a withdrawal into the traditional ivory tower; or it may generate a critical, creative relation between society and university. It is the thesis of this article that the latter kind of interaction both befits the university and ultimately benefits society the most. It is an interaction that requires, on the part of the university, a complex mixture of commitments: commitment, on the one hand, to being a creative force in the historical process, deeply and passionately involved in the affairs of society, and, on the other hand, to providing society with the intellectual stewardship that can come only from rigorous, dispassionate analysis of reality.

Traditionally, our universities have had three functions—education, scholarship, and service. In earlier times, the educative and scholarly functions were closely allied, and the service function was only a minor one. In the complex technological society of today, the service functions have grown enormously, and the educational and scholarly functions (at least in the natural and social sciences) have come increasingly close to the service functions. The university provides society with experts and expertise. The reasons for these changes are to be found not only in the demands of society to which the university responds, but also in the fact that the organization of the university and its sources of livelihood reflect the structural organization of our society itself. This has generated the entrepreneurial system of the American university, in which the policy-initiating bodies—both administrations and faculties—acting in the manner of capitalist entrepreneurs have become actively and competitively involved in seeking out what kinds of intellectual pursuits society could use (and therefore be willing to support) and in developing the corresponding programs of research, education, and service. Unquestionably, this entrepreneurial system has contributed to make the American university the flourishing and effective institution that it is today. In fact, this aspect of the American university provides a model for many of the reforms now attempted in Europe and elsewhere to make universities in those countries more efficient and more responsive to social realities.

But the entrepreneurial system, for all its productive activism, has an inherently passive quality. Drawing its inspiration from the surrounding society, it asks itself only what it can do for society as it is, rather than what role it can play in the evolution of society. Yet, many people believe that the university has a critical responsibility to interact with society in an active rather than a passive role. One may even go further and state that, in a society that is losing its traditional religious-metaphysical sources of values, the university, as the institution charged with the intellectual and educational formation of the youth, has the responsibility of stepping into the resulting vacuum and providing the seat of the search for new functional sets of values. In brief, the university must be prepared to be the intellectual and ethical forum of the lay society.

The great religions of humanity—Judaism, Christianity, Islam, Marxism-Leninism—even though they embodied realistic reactions to social situations existing at a given time, inevitably became immobilized in dogmatic, authoritarian codes of intellectual beliefs and moral behaviors because of their metaphysical assumptions. The challenge of technological society, with its rapidly changing objective situations, poses the problem of generating an evolutionary system of values suitable to such an unprecedented social environment. A biological analogy can provide some useful hints.

Biological evolution is an essentially opportunistic process. It selects what is fit (that is, reproductively successful) in *the immediate present*. Yet what is finally selected are those lines of descent that remain fit (in the same reproductive sense) over longer times, even in changing situations. Thus, evolution selects populations for adaptability (the capacity to tolerate a range of situations) and for plasticity (the ability to respond to changing situations with a change in genetic structure). Both of these properties are functions of the range of genetic endowments present in a population. Any biological analogy to social phenomena is bound to be somewhat distorted because social and cultural evolution does not duplicate biological evolution. Cultural evolution is Lamarckian—treasuring its acquired characters—and is deeply influenced by conscious purpose, whereas biological evolution is Darwinian and knows only causes, not purposes. Yet both processes have one feature in common: the role of adaptability and plasticity in determining long-run fitness. If a culture and a society are to flourish, their conceptual and ethical frameworks must fit the real and changing environment. Hence, these frameworks must be adaptable, plastic, intrinsically self-critical, and persistently self-revising. No agency in society is better suited to carry out the function of criticism and revision than the university, permeated as it is (or should be) with the spirit of free inquiry and the commitment to factual truth.

There is a danger that the plasticity of social attitudes and ethical values may be interpreted in a purely automatic way. Plasticity can mean several different things: a creative sensitivity and responsiveness to changing environmental conditions, or a passive submission to external pressures, or an aimless swaying with the winds of change. The third interpretation leads to acquiescence with and encouragement of all sorts of faddism; the second, to the very identification with the societal establishment that the entrepreneurial activities of universities tend to foster. Passive acceptance of the goals and values of society deprives the university of the claim to intellectual leadership and encourages its involvement in ventures of dubious ethical and intellectual value.

It is interesting to note here that adoption by the university of a passive attitude toward society as a source of values differs little in its consequences from the opposite choice—to ignore such values and to live in a self-centered illusion of spiritual purity. Withdrawal into the ivory tower amounts in practice to an endorsement of the *status quo*. In fact, by removing a large segment of intellectually alert individuals from the field of actual involvement in the affairs of society, the attitude of the ivory tower encourages the use of rational knowledge for irrational purposes. The scholar who scorns involvement in the life of the commonwealth assumes a burden of responsibility for the misuses to which the products of his scholarship may be put by the society from which he has supposedly kept himself aloof.

The remaining alternative is for the universities to accept openly an active role in social experimentation. Even though to do so represents a departure from some cherished illusions of neutrality and detachment, it amounts only to acknowledging the real situation and making the university's role in society less ambiguous. The university today is a major business enterprise, preempting facilities of increasing magnitude and competing with other sectors of the community for funds and *Lebensraum*. Moreover, through its service functions, whether carried out institutionally or by individuals, the university plays a much greater role in the affairs of society than many of its members are willing to admit. But this role has too often been a passive rather than a creative one—that of a service station rather than a frontier post. The university will be on sounder ground if it makes its role in social affairs explicit and creative by exploring the problems of society in the spirit of free, critical experimentation that has characterized its involvement in the natural sciences. In fact, such an approach to society's problems is clearly appropriate to the university's mission of intellectual stewardship.

The tasks that face the investigator in the social sciences are, of course, different from those encountered in the natural sciences. The natural scientist searches for the laws that rule events in the world of material objects, inanimate or living. Understanding of these laws allows prediction of future events under defined conditions and permits the evolution of a technology directed to the solution of specific practical tasks. Engineering and medicine are typical technological outgrowths of natural science. In their technical content (not in their applications!), these outgrowths are as value-free and socially neutral as their parent sciences. They are part of the intellectual enterprise of man, which aims both at understanding the world we are part of and at developing means to control and alter it. How these means are then used is where the problem of responsibility comes into play.

The social sciences attempt, in principle, to follow the same patterns, searching for laws that rule human events and deriving predicting schemes, on the basis of which a social technology may evolve. But here the distinctions are more easily blurred. The perception of social events and their interpretation are deeply influenced by the fact that the social scientist is part of the society that he studies. Furthermore, experimentation in the affairs of society can seldom be done under the relatively neutral conditions available to the natural scientist since all experimentation involves active involvement in the process of social change. The question of responsibility cannot be separated from the testing of hypothesis: Studying society in a scientific, experimental way means interfering with the course of events. There can hardly be value-free social inquiry and experimentation. The university has attempted to preserve an apparent neutrality and detachment by segregating its own activities in the social sciences into scholarly and service functions. It has carried out supposedly value-free research in its academic departments and has done its practical interaction with society by lending its talents and know-how to outside agencies—government, industry, foundations, or other institutions.

Such segregation of functions provides only the appearance of a value-free, "scientific" atmosphere in the social sciences. Most social science theory and research rests on unstated ethical assumptions. In a stable society, the prevailing unanimity of social values makes it easier to ignore the implicit assumptions. But when the supposed unanimity breaks down and deep divisions become apparent within society, the range of value choices is wider and the implications of these choices are clearer. The illusion of a value-free position becomes untenable.

At such times, many of the service activities of social scientists stand revealed as *de facto* participation in the practices of the social Establishment. Likewise, the academic critics of the *status quo*, hesitant to involve the supposedly neutral university in controversial social experiments, can exercise their role as experts only within agencies or groups committed to social reform. Thus, the insistence that the university preserve a value-free intellectual environment leads to a displacement of the active, creative market place of ideas away from the university.

The consequences of this displacement affect the content and the course of social experimentation. When carried out by agencies committed to specific social theories, it tends to avoid self-criticism and to generate self-fulfilling predictions. If this experimentation were done by diverse scholars from within the university, as an integral part of professional research, it could more easily be carried out in a spirit of intellectual integrity and mutual criticism, with awareness of the underlying assumptions, willingness to accept results that contradict the assumptions, and commitment to full disclosure of findings and conclusions. The findings of experimentation in social affairs done under such conditions would be more easily interpretable to the public at large, who in the last instance must make the relevant choices.

Restraints on the university from open independent participation in social experiment are numerous: faculty tradition of scholarly detachment, administrative concern over financial support, and trustees' conservative interpretation of their responsibility. Encouragement of greater participation, on the other hand, comes from many sources: pressures of the local communities reacting to the impact of the universities on their economic and social life; demands of socially deprived groups claiming their share of education and services; and prodding by concerned groups of students and faculty committed to the search for effective solutions to social ills.

Inevitably, students' misgivings against society translate themselves into criticism of the academic community. Interestingly enough, student critics object not only to the university's pretended detachment from pressing social problems and to its actual participation in the activities of society's Establishment, but also to the "neutral," scholarly approach in much of their social science education. These criticisms ought to be heeded because they have much to offer in a constructive direction. At its best, student criticism is not a nihilist reaction to an affluent society, but a demand for integrity of purpose and for more unity between theory and practice, both in the university and in society. In the United States, student unrest is not so much a revolt against traditional values as a revulsion against a society that at times seems to betray its own proclaimed values.

Is it possible for the university to find a response that recognizes the legitimacy of the new challenges and yet preserves both the structure of the university as a viable institution and the integrity of its intellectual and educational mission?

The concept of a critical and constructive experimentation in the area of social inquiry may offer a positive answer by providing a kind of "engagement" (in the sense of the French word *engagement*) different from that of partisan action groups or political parties. The university may use critical experimentation in social situations in order to find out what approaches are effective in altering such situations and what results are to be expected from such actions. Such experimentation may take place within the university itself—for instance, in creating educational and employment opportunities. The recent beginnings toward developing and promoting experimental programs for black and other minority students are obvious examples; much more can be done in this and similar areas. External experimentation may involve, for example, organizing economic or political structures directed at the solution of specific community problems.

Once the university accepts a responsibility to experiment in

81

the process of social change, its educational role also takes on new dimensions. In a return to the true humanistic and Socratic traditions, the university can train its students to explore and evaluate, in a meaningful societal setting, the consequences of specific choices and decisions. The insulating partitions between learning, teaching, and acting in the real world become less rigid, and the intellectual enterprise acquires a new, more integrated character.

Factual knowledge obtained in active experimentation and providing a rational basis for decision-making can even contribute a source of personal values. In the same way that being part of the process of biological evolution confers biological meaning to the life of individual organisms, being part of the intellectual enterprise as a rational source of social decision as well as of transmissible knowledge confers meaning to the life of the individual man. By fostering participation of its students in the human enterprise as intellectually trained and socially involved individuals, the university can contribute more effectively to their personal development.

The involvement of the university in social experimentation within the framework of rigorous intellectual inquiry is important in another respect. In the complaints recently raised against the universities, one hears much talk of the need for relevance. This is too often interpreted as a demand that scholars, scientists, and students relinquish the pursuits of "purely intellectual content" and engage in other, more immediately applied tasks. Coupled with this demand is a rising criticism of the natural sciences (as sources of a technology whose anarchistic applications threaten human society) as well as of the humanities (as some sort of bead-game played by parasitic inhabitants of the ivory tower). Criticism of natural science is particularly disturbing when it takes the form of anti-rationalism, rejecting the most valuable content of the intellectual tradition because it has failed to solve the social problems that arise from the technological revolution. Yet it may well be that only a rational application of a scientific social technology tested by experiment can solve the problems that arise from industrial technology.

The university can make a meaningful response to the criticism of its scholarly activities neither by kowtowing apologetically to all faddistic pressures nor by assuming an attitude of supercilious indifference. It must be responsibly involved in the affairs of society, in the dual role of scientific experimenter and custodian of the integrity of the intellectual enterprise. Thus the university responds to the challenge by becoming purposefully and actively engaged in the adventure of the social process.

How can the governance of the university foster a lively, critical, constructive "engagement" in the activities of an evolving society? There is a role to be played by every group in the university community. Student involvement in the decision-making process as well as in the actual day-to-day machinery of university operation is already becoming widespread and is needed to make the university responsive to the problems of present and future generations. Faculty initiative is more necessary than ever to preserve in such a university the rigorous process of intellectual integrity and to assure that all university activities retain the educational and evaluative content too often lost sight of in the passive kinds of service activities. The trustees, if their role is to endure and to be a useful one, must see as their trust the preservation of community support to the university even when the latter makes itself a gadfly of society and even an active participant in social experimentation.

We are all too familiar with the concern that radical students may destroy the university in the process of trying to change society, the university being the societal structure most readily available to their criticisms and vulnerable to inside disruption. But, in fact, the university is worth preserving for the very purposes proclaimed by the radical reformers. In our society, the university may be the most effective structure through which intellectual forces can be put to use in influencing the course of social evolution in a rational way. In order to be effective in this role and to prove its critics wrong, however, the university may have to assume responsibilities and attitudes different from its traditional ones.

PETER J. CAWS

Design for a University

PROBABLY MORE worthless nonsense is written about education than about any other subject except religion. Because of this proliferation of verbiage, it is one of the hardest subjects to write about effectively. Almost anything that can be said is drowned by a hundred other pronouncements on the same point. The best thing to do under the circumstances is to keep quiet until the hubbub subsides; but since there is no prospect that it will ever do so, it is easy to succumb to the temptation to add to it, even though it is more than doubtful that the expenditure of paper or the claim on the reader's attention can really be justified. This is the more true in a publication such as this; the sense of futility is increased because one is probably preaching to the converted, most of one's readers have probably thought the same or better thoughts on their own, and few of them are the people in whose hands the fundamental decisions of public policy lie which must eventually be taken if the situation in American schools and colleges is to improve.

Here we all are, nevertheless, united between the covers of a book, constrained by events to think broadly once more about higher education. To have posed the problem of the governance of the university betrays the conviction—which by now nearly all of us share—that something is badly wrong with the governance of the university. The same goes for the curriculum, which can hardly be separated from governance when it comes to institutional design. And the attempt to describe an ideal university, which will occupy the latter part of this essay, presupposes that real ones fall short in some fundamental way. Unfortunately we do not always share our perceptions of these shortcomings, and this leads to a paradox in the treatment of such subjects that needs to be confronted if not resolved.

Academic people are trained to follow their own lines of thought, and most of them have fundamental convictions about what is wrong, which they are prepared to expound to their colleagues and anyone else who will listen, perhaps in an essay like this one. While each thus satisfies his private whims, the real problems get increasingly out of hand. This kind of individualism, when openly acknowledged, is one of the virtues of the academic mind; the key to the educational process remains the committed teacher and researcher who, in spite of group investigations, team teaching, and a new suspicion of the magisterial attitude, is still most effective when operating singly out of a personal unity of knowledge and outlook. But the problems that face us now are collective, and to make a significant difference in the face of them will take a *common* purpose and an *agreed* strategy. The opportunity of arriving at these must not be allowed to slip away while each of us is coming to terms privately with the scope and implications of the problem.

In spite of the relative pessimism of these opening remarks, there can be no doubt that the conditions for a solution to the current difficulties do exist. There are enough talent, enough money, enough intellectual energy in the United States to provide a first-class education up to the capacity of every individual. That is the *sine qua non* of a truly democratic society, and the intuition of the Founding Fathers was correct about its possibility, indeed on a scale more generous than they envisaged. The trouble is, in fact, that there are too many possible solutions. Almost any curriculum, almost any form of governance, adhered to with sufficient intellectual and moral passion, will do. What gets transmitted under ideal conditions from one generation to another, when the details have been forgotten, is a certain standard of scholarship or social behavior—not even a *particular* standard (there can, after all, be honest disagreements about these things), but a conception of what it means to *have* a standard. One may try to justify the content of a curriculum, the form of a system of government, in terms of a psychological or philosophical or political theory, but this activity has very little connection with its acceptance or rejection, which will rest on reactions at a far less sophisticated level. It is probably a mistake, in fact, to attempt the justification in terms of abstract theory of methods which, if they are to be effective at all, will have to be widespread throughout the system. (I would include in this prohibition theories about what is happening now—the generation gap, the black experience, the student radicals, the new or old New Left.)

What is problematic, then, is not the resources, but their distribution; not finding *the* right solution, but agreeing on *a* right solution; not getting the complex details right, but getting the simple outline right. The point is that the solution, whatever it is, will have to be understood and accepted by faculty, students, trustees, legislators, voters, and so on. So it had better be simple, or at least it had better incorporate a few salient and simple essentials. At another stage in the history of the system it might (if the intuition of the Founding Fathers to which I referred above really was correct) be possible to justify a more complex set of principles, since there might exist the general ability to understand them. Now, alas, it is doubtful whether any general ability to understand even the most simple principles is really widespread in the society; and if all these people are to be convinced, complex justifications are at all costs to be avoided.

I take my point of departure from two principles of an almost frightening banality—which nevertheless, if generally adhered to, might improve things considerably. They are, first, that the curriculum of the university ought to be interesting, and, second, that the government of the university ought to be fair. It will at once be pointed out that there may be disagreement about what is fair or interesting. I therefore add two qualifications designed to resolve such disagreement: The curriculum must be interesting, *as judged by the students who are compelled to follow it;* and the government must be fair, *as judged by the faculty and students who are ruled by it.* If a president makes an arbitrary ruling against a faculty member, and the faculty thinks it is unfair, then it *is* unfair. And if a teacher gives a lecture that students think is boring, then it *is* boring.

There is at first sight nothing striking about these principles, except indeed their banality. But the great thing with principles, as is well known in logic but hardly understood in most other areas, is that from the simplest beginnings, by a sufficient insistence on the drawing out of consequences, unexpected complexities can emerge. And if to the logical development we add an insistence on practical application—which again, in most areas, is hardly ever referred to a starting point of principle—the situation may become truly revolutionary. Imagine for a moment that every class actually became interesting or every decision fair! Of course it cannot be expected actually to *happen;* we can be counted on to keep *theoria* and *praxis* at the usual prudent distance from each other. It is just this comfortable separation—an inexhaustible tolerance of discussion, an immovable resistance to genuine change—that has been driving our young revolutionaries into hysteria.

I stress interest, not relevance; the term is of wider scope and lets in many things that the sterner criterion of relevance might exclude. It is not logically impossible, of course, that some irrelevant things might also be uninteresting, and that is most often what is meant when elements of the curriculum are attacked as irrelevant. All would be forgiven if they were interesting. But note that it is impossible for something to be relevant and uninteresting. Interest, again, is the governing category, not (for example) utility. The useful will be interesting to those who care about it.

Also I stress fairness, not participation. The formula does not *entail* student involvement in curriculum planning or faculty participation in government. There are practical reasons why these things are desirable, but they do not follow from the principles. Here as elsewhere one is driven to democracy not because participation is in itself a desideratum, but because there is no evidence that anything else can be trusted. Representative government is not necessary to insure that everybody's interests are served, since they might happen to be served by a benevolent despotism; it is necessary because the benevolence of the despot cannot be guaranteed.

The concept of government implicit in all this is very wide; it runs from the hiring of the president to the grading of a freshman theme. The concept of fairness is very narrow; it involves only that the governed shall not be put at a positive disadvantage by the action of government. And the concepts of interest and of fairness overlap and reinforce each other. The grossest case of unfairness known in the university world—but one which, unfortunately, is all too frequent—arises when a teacher bores a student and then gives him a low mark. Not, of course, that a teacher can be expected to interest everybody; everything is boring to somebody. But if a student is bored, the least that can be done for him is to release him without prejudice, from the course or perhaps from the university. Releasing people from the university without prejudice (and without a degree) is something we have not yet learned to do gracefully, and I will have more to say about it later. If *everybody* is bored and unless strong reasons to the contrary present themselves, the teacher should be released from the university without prejudice. This too is difficult.

Despite its narrowness, the concept of fairness does have one extension that is of some importance. The government of the university must be fair not only to those within it, but also to those outside it. If by a restrictive admissions policy it excludes from participation in its advantages a class of people who might profit from them, then its fairness in the external sense can well be challenged. The thorny question thus raised is in one sense beyond the scope of our present concern, but the university is implicated in society and cannot escape the charge of unfairness if it helps to perpetuate an inequality in that society. In one way it is too great a burden on the admissions apparatus of individual colleges and universities to expect them to solve this problem. The right to an education up to the limit of one's talent, as long as the society has the resources to provide it, is a right the satisfaction of which ought to be more explicitly incorporated in the Constitution than it is. The main point to be made in this context is that there needs to be not just a university here and another there, but a university *system* serving not the values of society, but the aspirations of each member of it without exception.

This preliminary discussion of principles may take on more meaning as we move into the problems of designing an institution to embody them. And that will raise sooner or later the question of what a university really is. One difficulty is that only about a hundred years ago there were no universities in the United States. The institutions which now bear that title, but claim a longer pedigree, started out under other names—colleges, seminaries, and the like. They grew into universities by adopting some functions and abandoning others, and this happened piecemeal, so that in most cases the question of the integral character of the institution was never raised explicitly. Within the last hundred years, large numbers of new institutions calling themselves universities have come into being, but with rare exceptions they have taken their form from established universities either in this country or elsewhere and have not set out to confront the question of what one would create if one could really start from scratch and redesign the educational system as a whole.

Two alternative strategies offer themselves: to take some existing institution and see what would have to be done to it to bring its operation into line with the basic principles enunciated above; or to imagine a new institution expressly created for the purpose of putting these principles into action. It will be objected that both of these lines have in fact been followed. People are always trying to correct the flaws in existing institutions, and a number of new ones have been created—are even now being created—with the express intention of avoiding the errors and follies of the past. My criticism of most of these activities rests on two grounds: namely, that these enterprises are usually carried on by committees; and that if theoretical justification is claimed for them, it is nearly always much more pretentious than what I have suggested—new approaches to liberal education and that kind of thing. The trouble with committees is that it is almost impossible for them to arrive at an *integral* view of anything. I have already pointed out one difficulty with complex justifications; another is that if expressions like "liberal education" are used at all, the difficulty multiplies itself since not only the people who are to be convinced, but almost certainly the proponents of the scheme themselves will be unclear about what is meant. The expression "liberal education" should really be stricken from the vocabulary, as (for reasons which I shall suggest below) the liberal arts college ought to be removed from the university.

Let me revert for a moment to the committee problem. Most plans for educational reform fall short not so much because they are not comprehensive as because they are not coherent; they have not been thought through as a whole by a single mind and are likely to show the signs of their joint composition. One of the most bewildering features of the present agitation in the academy is the proliferation of committees, all manfully struggling over essentially the same problems, all producing virtuous documents which shift the emphases somewhat, usually (under the pressure of circumstances) roughly in the right direction, but which fail to signal the radical changes that are genuinely needed. A much better approach would be for institutions to pool their resources—not, heaven forbid, by creating even larger and more synoptic committees, but by offering some kind of prize for the best solution to the problem, whatever it happens to be. One or more out of a large number of submissions in a competition of this sort might come close to being satisfactory; and, starting from the best, a process of modification (perhaps, this time, even by a committee) might really lead to a new and a more hopeful beginning. I offer this suggestion in all seriousness. Given the nature of our present difficulties, it is foolish to insist that problems either of curriculum or government at university X must be solved by a consideration of the matter *ab initio* by the students and faculty of university X. Granted that they have to rule on the acceptability of the proposed structure, still the resources of intellect and ingenuity in the country at large are almost bound to be greater than their own resources, and there is nothing shameful in admitting this fact. American education at all levels is bedeviled by this multiplicity of effort. Prodigious quantities of useful time are wasted in the duplication from state to state, from school district to school district, from college to college, of the *constructive* activity of curricular design and the drafting of schemes of government, when local energy should largely be devoted to the *critical* consideration of these matters, starting from the *best* models that can be found anywhere at all.

The design that I shall sketch in the following paragraphs is not intended as a candidate in my ideal competition. To describe a potential university in any detail would require a document comparable to those which describe actual universities—that is, something like a bulletin or catalogue. Also, in spite of the distinction drawn above between constructive and critical activities, the ideal will not have sprung full blown from the imagination, but will take its main lines from the shape of the educational enterprise as it has defined itself in a democratic setting and from the constraints imposed by current problems. Its function, in common with all utopian speculation, is at least in part a negative one, directed against what is actually the case—against certain notable failures of our present system which, as I see it, spring from flaws in its design. Further, there is to be recognized, as always, a whole set of implicit assumptions imposing its own modality on the scheme. Some of these are unconscious; some can be quickly identified. Among the latter, in particular, is the assumption that what we want is an egalitarian and democratic society. If we really wanted a system based on the concept of an elite, instead of just having one by accident (and that is what some people do want), some rather radical changes in design would be needed.

One further assumption needs explicit treatment, since it has to do with the definition of what a university is. This requires a short excursus. Whatever else may be said of them, universities clearly are part of a complex system whose primary function is educational. If the educational system really *is* a system, no part of it can be discussed adequately without reference to the other parts, and any project for reform in one area must take account of its probable impact on the others. This poses a dilemma for the critic of the university who wishes to restrict his attention to the university alone. A first-rate university can only be the apex of a first-rate educational system, whereas the rest of the system in America, taken collectively, is at present about fourth-rate. Nobody wants a fourth-rate university, but anything better will overload the system and will be swamped with remedial cases. Our universities, taken collectively, are about third-rate, and the problem is already evident. (I do not deny the existence of Exeter and Groton, of Harvard and Yale, but address myself to the general case.) The critic can only assume that the rest of the system could in principle be reformed, and I shall—in harmony with the optimistic notes struck earlier—assume this, although there will not be space to go into the mechanism for it. The central conception of the university will therefore ignore the defects in the rest of the system. (In order to preserve a semblance of relevance to contemporary society, it will be necessary to have some components of a remedial sort, which might be thought of as dispensable once there was no longer any need for them. It was in this spirit, as I understand it, that the Pentagon was originally constructed.) Assuming, then, a working system of elementary and secondary schools, technical institutes, and the like, I define the university in a negative way: It is the place where people go when they have exhausted the resources of all the other available institutions, but have not exhausted their own capacity for full-time intellectual work in an institutional setting. I mean this definition to be taken quite seriously and to apply to students and faculty alike. Its force will become clearer as we proceed.

I mention in this definition students and faculty, but make no reference to administrators. This reveals another assumption. The role of administrators will be taken up in its place, but I assume as axiomatic that the definition of this role *follows* the design of the university and not the other way around, whereas faculty and student roles are recognizable independently of and prior to their institutional embodiments. To put the same point in another way: There might be a university without administrators, but there could be no administrators without a university; there might, on the other hand, be professors and students without a university, but there could be no university without professors and students—without, that is, persons playing these respective roles.

If a university is to consist of faculty and students, the first question to be raised in designing it is how they get there. This broaches the subjects of admissions and hiring, and appears to require administrators at once. And of course it does—people to ac-

PETER J. CAWS

knowledge applications, sort dossiers, check credentials, make out income tax forms, write checks, and so on. Our main concern, however, is with the criteria according to which some students are admitted and others rejected, some scholars invited to join the faculty and others not invited to do so. The students are comparatively easy to deal with: Those students will be admitted, up to the capacity of the institution (which will be unspecified, but finite), who meet the definitional criterion proposed above; they have been through the elementary and secondary schools and learned what was taught there, they may or may not have spent a year or two doing something else, but they now want to learn more, to devote most of their time to it, and to do it under institutional supervision. They have looked at the other institutions (technical, professional, and so forth) open to students of their age—and they must *really* have looked and be able to show that they have—in the light of their career interests, if any, and decided that none of them are suitable. They bring with them from the last institution they attended a certificate which testifies that they can profitably undertake further full-time education, that they themselves have untapped resources. All students satisfying these criteria must be found a place in a university if the society is to live up to its Constitutional obligations.

Some features of the present system which have to do with the desire of students to enter the university require comment at this point. Students are often driven into college (the obvious point of entry to the university for somebody just leaving school) because an alternative institution does not exist or is not yet ready for them. Or they may be driven into it for social or economic reasons, without any particular desire to profit from it intellectually. An example of the first case is the man who knows he wants to become a doctor, but has to go to college before he can be admitted to medical school; an example of the second is someone who needs a B.A. as a mark of general culture, or as a union card for white-collar work, or as a talisman against underprivileged or minority status. These cases arise because of the belief of outsiders (counting the medical school and its admissions committee as outside for the time being) that something that can be acquired only in the college is indispensable to the training of certain kinds of persons—candidates for medical school, or for a particular job, or even for recognition as educated members of society. This desideratum cannot be of a merely technical nature, which could clearly (at least in the first case) be taken care of by a special course or two or by on-the-job training; on the

92

contrary, it is openly admitted to be *general education*. Millions of
pages are devoted to it in the literature. But there are several puzzling things about it.

First of all, there is the assumption that the education the student
has received outside the university—in the schools and from other
people in a less formal setting—is not in fact the required general
education; and that, this being the case, it is up to the university
through its liberal arts college to remedy the lack. The puzzling
thing about this is that by the time the student gets into the college,
the schools have had at him for twelve years or so and society at
large for seventeen or eighteen. What can they have been up to all
that time? Whatever one may say about the slow rate of development of the human animal, there seems to be little reason to doubt
that by the age of eighteen it is possible to acquire the chief manual
and intellectual skills and to internalize as much of the culture as
will ever be held in common. We do not manage it, but it could be
done. After eighteen the processes of learning and acquisition continue indefinitely, but again there is little reason to suppose that the
years between eighteen and twenty-two constitute, for the general
population, a particularly auspicious period for *generalized* intellectual development. They may indeed be almost totally wasted
intellectually, since it is in just this period, plus or minus a few
years, that all kinds of quite specialized and non-intellectual interests begin to develop.

It may be, of course, that professional schools, employers, and so
forth just do not want to take in people who are too *young*. And in
this they may be quite right. But young people grow older whether
they are in a college or not, and recent events suggest that they
often grow more mature in spite of what happens to them in college
rather than because of it. There is of course a determinable statistical proportion of the age group, usually with specialized interests formed earlier, for whom these years are ideal from the point
of view of intellectual development, and they always constituted
one component of the undergraduate population in the older universities. The other component was traditionally made up of students whose primary reason for attendance was *explicitly* social,
and that might seem to provide a justification for the liberal arts
college, as indeed for some small private colleges it still does. But
things are now taken so seriously that it is hardly possible, particularly in large public universities, to admit this: Colleges are always regarded by their presidents, deans, and commencement

speakers as *educational* institutions, and thousands of students who would much rather be elsewhere continue to flounder through their required courses. The enterprise, which might have been honestly frivolous and sometimes used to be, has become in many cases ponderously fraudulent.

The trouble can be summed up by saying that in the liberal arts colleges too many people are being taught the rudiments of their culture too late. *The entire curriculum of the liberal arts college is remedial*, at least until it becomes specialized. The liberal arts college, as an instrument of general education, ought to be abolished. Of course at present it cannot be just because of the weaknesses of the school system, which almost guarantee a profound ignorance of the major features of their world and their culture on the part of entering college freshmen. The general education component of the liberal arts college, therefore, stands as one of those Pentagon-like features referred to above—invented out of what should have been a temporary necessity, pending the adjustment of what it might have been hoped were temporary troubles, perpetuated because abnormal conditions persisted, until indeed, both in the military and in the educational cases, they have come to seem normal. But the principles of university admission as formulated above can remain constant; the university begins where the rest of the educational system leaves off and can get rid of general education just as soon as the schools take up an honest responsibility for it.

Having raised the question of admissions, it may be as well to go on at once to the related questions of retention ("good standing") and eventual separation, to use the most neutral term possible. The problem of governance arises more acutely here than in the case of admissions; for while admissions are in principle at least covered by a general rule, retention and the decision as to what credentials (degrees and the like) are to be given to the student on separation involve judgments that will have to be made by somebody for each individual case. I will suggest general rules for these also, but their application will be more difficult. The general rule for retention is that, apart from "criminal" cases, the student should be retained as long as he continues to meet the requirements for admission—that is, as long as the teachers with whom he studies are prepared at the end of their association with him to testify that he can profit from further work. (I assume that they will not so testify if, while he has the necessary mental equipment, he has shown no disposition whatever to use it.) And the general rule for separation is that the student should be given a certificate stating that he has completed a certain number of years' study at the institution, with such annotations as to special ability as may be appropriate (as discussed below).

The implicit recommendation in this last general rule is that degrees as we now know them should be abolished. One of the most striking features of the American educational system, which has been sharply thrown into relief by recent events, is the extraordinarily narrow range of conditions under which it is possible to leave an educational institution with honor. There are in fact only three major points in the full-time educational career of the average student at which an honorable separation is possible: graduation from high school, marked by a high school diploma; graduation from college, marked by the award of a bachelor's degree; and graduation with some higher degree. The first two of these normally come at the ages of seventeen or eighteen and twenty-one or twenty-two respectively, the last some indeterminate number of years later. Any other mode of termination of the process of formal education marks the student as in some sense a failure. The high school dropout who, six months before graduation, escapes from what is often an incredibly inappropriate mode of life for a person of his age, has by comparison with his less adventurous colleague who completes the year and gets the diploma an academic score of zero, at least in the eyes of many of the people in whose hands his future career will lie.

Diplomas and degrees were originally invented to mark stages in a carefully planned educational sequence and were awarded not only for having reached the appropriate chronological point without academic mishap, but for having met some definite and definitely situated challenge, such as a series of examinations. In America such formal points of transition have long since been done away with, and diplomas and degrees (with the exception of some higher degrees) are gained by a process of accretion of credits, without any of the drama or stress of the old system. Furthermore, only the most simple and sanguine of observers could pretend that the courses leading up to these degrees are integral or even coherent in the sense that every component is indispensable and interdependent with every other. This being the case, there seems to be no real point to diplomas and degrees except, again, a social one, as providing an excuse for a certain amount of pageantry and self-congratulation.

PETER J. CAWS

I would seriously advocate a standard form of credential, uniform in its concept across the entire nation, which would state simply the institution attended and the number of years of attendance, together with qualifications (if any) earned in special fields and attested to by professionals in those fields. This credential would be given to every student leaving the institution, whenever he happened to do so. The number of years might well be cumulative as between different institutions, so that, assuming eight years of elementary and junior high school, a beginning high school senior who dropped out would receive his eleven-year certificate automatically, with no questions asked. The special qualifications would ideally be inscribed not according to the judgment of the local expert in the subject, but according to some system of judgment (perhaps, although not necessarily, by examination) administered on a national scale by professionals in that area. In some fields, of course, this would be much too formal a mechanism; a fourteen-year certificate, awarded to a student getting married at the end of her sophomore year and attesting to some skill in home economics, ought not to require something like a bar examination before it could be awarded. On the other hand, a sixteen-year certificate in mathematics, equivalent to a B.A. with a major in the subject, might well have its specialist notation certified by the American Mathematical Association. Prospective employers, examining such a certificate, would naturally look to see what institution the student had last attended and make a judgment, just as is now done, in the light of its known quality. But a bright student attending a poor college would have a chance of improving his professional standing considerably with such a national certification. Of course, in one sense something like this happens now with the Graduate Record Examination, but under such a scheme it is to be hoped that the professional organizations themselves, rather than a purely administrative testing service, might undertake the burden of judgment.

I would at this point apologize to the reader for these constant diversions from the subject of government, were it not for the conviction that a great many of our present problems in government spring from a failure to understand fully the nature of the enterprise in which we are engaged, and that, this point once clarified, many of them would solve themselves. Government strictly speaking does come into play, as remarked earlier, in cases where the general rule cannot easily be applied—when it is not certain whether a

96

student who clearly can profit from further work really will do so, or whether somebody leaving an institution deserves a special local mark of distinction or censure on his certificate. Who should decide these questions? This raises once again the issue of definition.

If the university is a place where people with certain kinds of talent and ambition go, it is also the community of these people, and according to sound democratic principles should be governed by them or—to the extent that they themselves are the governed—by persons exercising power derived from their consent. (They might, in fact, be legally constituted *as* the community; the existence of boards of trustees, which at the moment most often serve as the legal embodiment of the institution, is not really necessary for that purpose, and elected bodies—perhaps with representation from the community—might well take their place.) The community consists of students and faculty; it is surely unnecessary here to repeat that these two classes find themselves in a symbiotic relationship, that each requires the other, and that, except in anomalous cases such as endowed institutes for research, no university exists more for one than for the other. Invoking the elementary principle of fairness, then, it would seem to follow almost with deductive force that decisions about membership in the community or the collective endorsement by the community of the credentials of some departing member should be made by representative bodies of faculty and students. And again, in a discussion which is already becoming too lengthy, it is surely unnecessary to rehearse the steps by which institutions whose origins in Europe were genuinely communal arrived by metamorphosis at the hierarchical structure with which we are all only too familiar, whose model has become the corporation rather than the community.

One might, in fact, pose the question raised at the beginning of this part of the discussion—Where do the faculty and students come from?—as a question about the criteria for membership in the community of faculty and students. In its simplest form, the criterion would simply be acceptance by the other members of the community; the remarks above about admissions, retention, and so forth serve to indicate conditions under which this acceptance ought normally to be forthcoming, at least in the case of students. For the faculty, some other form of departmental or divisional organization is no doubt essential, whether or not along traditional lines, if only because the competence of any one faculty member to judge the professional standing of his colleagues extends only over a contiguous proper subset of the faculty as a whole. Thus, admission to the faculty—the initial appointment—will not look very different in the ideal university from the way it looks now.

Retention, however, does need some examination. I do not wish to go into the arguments for and against tenure, but the question seems to me to involve two totally distinct issues: the security of the individual as far as earning his livelihood is concerned; and the nature of the services in exchange for which this security is offered. Tenure, as it affects the first of these issues, has been a necessary and desirable institution. On the second point, however, it has led to abuses. Given that membership on the faculty is assured, a periodical re-examination of an individual's status within it, with a consequent adjustment if necessary, would be extremely salutary. The nature of the adjustment might be more or less severe depending on the outcome of the evaluation, and, given the mores of the academic profession, it would only in extreme cases lead to loss of status. But occasionally it might; and the very possibility that it might would go far to correct a situation in which a minority of privileged faculty members on tenure continues to enjoy high salaries and light teaching loads long after intellectual energy and sense of professional responsibility have been allowed to dwindle away.

Still I have said nothing about administrators. There is indeed a whole segment of the university population as now defined, ranging from trustees to janitors, which is left out by this analysis. And it is deliberately left out. Trustees, presidents, deans, registrars, secretaries, janitors, and the like are not, strictly speaking, part of the university at all—not, at least, as these positions are now interpreted and filled in most American institutions of higher education. They are ancillary to the real business of the university, and only the supplanting of the community model by the corporation model has put them in their present dominant position. I do not wish to be misunderstood as casting any doubt at all on the integrity of persons in such positions or on the way in which they have filled them, once appointed (and given that the duties and powers involved had the warrant of historical precedent). But in the ideal university administrative personnel would be appointed only as needed for the day-to-day running of the institution and would be under the *control* of the community of faculty and students. As in the case of the Pentagon, the military analogy may be helpful; the principle involved is that of civilian control, which in the academic case has been lost sight of more completely, if that is possible, than in the case of the Joint Chiefs of Staff and their respective Secretaries. In that case, at least, the position of Secretary of the Army exists and is occupied by a civilian, however little real control civil government may exercise over the military establishment.

Again, this does not mean that most of the higher administrative positions now common in the university would be abolished, nor that—as at present—most of them would not be filled from the ranks of the faculty. But it does mean that on taking up such positions a more explicit change in status might have to be insisted upon. The life of the university is intellectual, and justification for membership in it should rest on intellectual qualifications and no others. I am aware that the theory of the multiversity makes this sound like a throwback to ivory-tower detachment, a failure to understand the new responsibility of the university to society, and so forth; but the error in such a conclusion is patent. The university, in fact, can only fulfill its obligation to society by remaining rigorously intellectual. That is its *métier*, and although under the umbrella of the multiversity many other activities are sanctioned, they might just as well be carried on by other institutions, and in a properly designed educational system they would be. The point may seem, and indeed to some extent may be, merely semantic: The needs of society are to be served, and if—as now so often happens—the people who have the training and talents to serve it are also university teachers, what is more natural than that the agencies of service should be located where they find themselves? But it is only too clear what difficulties the concept of the multiversity leads to, once it is allowed to lose its center of historical continuity, which resides solely in the coming together of committed persons for intellectual ends. The commitment of its members to the community of learning has been steadily eroded by nonintellectual commitments, not only external but also internal.

Part of this erosion has come about because of historical developments in the society at large that have had an impact on the university unanticipated by those whose official task was, among other things, precisely to anticipate them. The recent necessity—felt first, to their honor, by students and now increasingly by faculty also—of taking the government of the university, to some degree at least, back into the hands of the academic community as I have defined it constitutes an incredibly damaging indictment of American university administration. Under ideal circumstances administrative officers would indeed make the decisions at which these committees are struggling to arrive, subject to the approval of the community; there would be (as there has not been) a clearly defined mechanism of accountability, regularly exercised, and the students and faculty would get on with what they ought to be doing—namely, intellectual work—in the confidence that, to repeat a formula already invoked (and one that ought to be familiar enough to Americans), the powers exercised over them were justly exercised and derived from their consent, and that any abuse of these powers could immediately be corrected by their withdrawal of that consent. A certain amount of active participation in government, provided it does not take too much time, will probably always be desirable, if only to prevent a repetition of the scandalous failure of administration to be sensitive and responsive to changing conditions. But if the proportion of this involvement rises too much, as it is bound to do when a faculty member accepts a full-time administrative position, then the status in the academic community of the faculty member concerned must come into question.

In many public institutions there are regulations about the amount of outside work (consulting, additional teaching, and so on) a faculty member is allowed to undertake; these restrictions have always seemed to me rather bureaucratic, but they do suggest a possible criterion of continued membership in the faculty. I would propose that, instead of reporting outside activities, every member of the faculty should report the proportion of time spent in nonintellectual as opposed to intellectual activities. I use the term "intellectual" in its straightforward sense to mean "requiring the exercise of intellect." The key term is *exercise;* it is possible to know many things and even, to some extent, to reason and to understand without *exercising* any faculty at all. Administrative work under pressure (and what administrative work, these days, is not under pressure?) leads often to a kind of habitual or mechanical conduct, to a preoccupation with time and with the *fact* that problems are resolved, rather than to a preoccupation with substance and the *manner* in which they are resolved. I speak from experience, and again do not wish to be misunderstood as criticizing the beleaguered administrator in his person. But it simply cannot be argued—and hardly any administrators do argue—that the work of running the average administrative office in an American university requires the exercise of intellect for more than a small fraction of the day. Most committee work, for example, is non-intellectual and could perfectly well be done by a reasonably intelligent robot if sufficient information could be put at its disposal.

If he devoted more than a certain proportion of his time—say 50 per cent—to non-intellectual work, the faculty member would be put on adjunct status with reduced participation in academic affairs; if more than some other proportion—say 75 per cent—he would cease to be a member of the *academic* community altogether. Not that his voice would cease to be heard—indeed, just as happens now, people in administrative positions would be expected to have great influence with the faculty because of the conspectus of university affairs provided by their vantage point at the intersection of many different academic circles. But if their active intellectual life had in fact shrunk to the degree indicated by my suggested percentages, it is likely that the criteria of judgment according to which they habitually operated would to that extent begin to diverge from those intuitively adhered to by people still in the thick of the intellectual enterprise. Not that administration *need* involve such a shrinkage: In a well-run institution with adequate clerical help, deans and even presidents might very well occupy themselves with intellectual concerns more than half the time. As it is, they always promise themselves they will, but they hardly ever do. There can, in fact, be detected a kind of crisis of authenticity on the part of university administrators, attested to by the indignation with which they privately greet (and not always privately) arguments like this one. The crisis could, of course, be simply resolved by crossing the line back from administration to teaching and research; but just as it is difficult for students to leave the university with honor at any other point than their proper commencement, so it has been made difficult for administrators to sustain their own conception of their prestige or, for that matter, to sustain their salaries through the process of re-entry to the academic community. The only honorable exits for an administrator, at least in the eyes of many of them, are death, retirement, or apotheosis to an even more exalted administrative position. Some manage to sidestep into government or politics, but rarely—although there have been some notable exceptions —is a total rehabilitation successful.

In the ideal university, most high administrative offices would be held by faculty members for short and definitely terminating periods—say, three-year terms with a limit of two such terms consecutively. During their terms of office, they would throw themselves almost completely into administrative affairs, which is virtu-

PETER J. CAWS

ally essential if the full range of possibility is to be realized, but they would cease to be voting members of the academic community. At the end of their term of office, they would be received back into the academic community with honor and gratitude. In the anomalous situation where somebody actually preferred administrative to intellectual pursuits—a circumstance which would cast some doubt on the nature of his original commitment to the intellectual— he might with the consent of the faculty and subject to the mechanism of accountability referred to above continue to exercise his functions, and once in a great while this might turn out to be the best possible thing for the university. Great university presidents have not been absent from the scene, although they have been extremely rare. But the idea that there might be more than two thousand people in the country able and, what is more important, willing to occupy such positions with any dignity at all is grotesque. It is easy to see how the notion of the college or university presidency as a lifetime position came into being, but the proliferation of institutions of higher education should long since have suggested that a different solution would eventually be necessary. With several hundred advertised vacancies in the ranks of presidents, it may at last be realized that the eventuality has overtaken us.

Having got the faculty and students, along with whatever administrative personnel is needed, together into a university community, we have still to discuss how they sustain themselves there, what they do, and what kind of *place* it is. To start with the last of these: Ideally the university is a place not just to work (as though it were an office), but to live and work. Its physical design should reflect the nature of the living and working, and the ancillary services provided should be so arranged as to facilitate a certain quality of life and work. The university should be a community, and it should be an intellectual community; it may also be incidentally, but only incidentally, a community of another sort—social, domestic, and so on. Its members ought to live as close to it and participate as much in it as their own conception of the relation between their intellectual and private lives will allow. In the case of students, this will most frequently mean actually living on the premises; intellectual and private lives seldom coincide totally, but particularly in the case of students the closer the better. It cannot be too much stressed that being a member of a university cannot be much less than a full-time occupation. The separation between intellectual and private life is likely to be greater on the

102

part of the faculty than on the part of students, but even they will spend a high proportion of their waking time on the campus, and the phenomenon of the multiversity professor who comes three times a week and disappears will be unknown.

This state of affairs, of course, can only be realized if the physical conditions are right; there must be adequate library resources and study space, adequate laboratories and studios. The general rule should be that material things are as unobtrusive as possible and completely taken care of. Housing, meals, laundry, child-care, and other such mundane details should be in the hands of people professionally equipped to deal with them, and members of the university, whether faculty or students, should simply not have to worry about them. The point of this is not to offer them a life of luxury, but to submerge the practical to the level of habit, so as to make possible a genuine continuity of the intellectual. This condition has hardly ever been achieved in America, although it used to be standard, for example, in the older universities in England. Even there it is giving way. The harassed married graduate student, struggling to make ends meet, is familiar all over the world. His life is the antithesis of what it ought to be. (I am not suggesting that students ought not to be married, just that they ought not to be harassed or have to struggle to make ends meet.)

But how, it will be asked, can the financial conditions for all this possibly be achieved? That brings us to the question of sustaining people once they get into the university. Here it seems to me quite clear that every student ought to be on full scholarship, and that these scholarships should run for reasonable amounts of time—four full years for an undergraduate, three to five for a graduate student. The conditions for retention of a scholarship would be essentially the same as conditions for remaining as a member of the university community. The means of achieving this on a sound financial basis seems to me comparatively simple. A university, in order to be recognized as such, would have the responsibility of laying down the minimal conditions for facilitation of the intellectual life on the part of its members, and a national scheme of financial support would be put in operation. But it would be at least partly self-sustaining if something like the following could be done: For every year of full scholarship support (and everybody, regardless of means, would automatically have such support) a student would be assessed, in perpetuity, and starting immediately after the end of his last year on scholarship, an annual tax of some definite proportion of his income—say, .5 per cent. (The figure might have to be higher, or it might be lower; I do not have the actuarial skill to make the computation exactly.) This tax would be collected by the federal government as an integral part of income tax and would be identified on income tax returns. But it would be credited to the college that had originally given the scholarship, on a pro-rata basis if more than one was involved. Colleges whose alumni became prosperous would thereby automatically become prosperous; but no college would be allowed to fall below a certain minimum level of support, according to an agreed formula—a provision which would be extremely important for new institutions having as yet no alumni. The money now given by the foundations, the states, and the government might well continue to be given and would constitute a reserve for cases in which the formula led to inequalities.

The principal drawback to this scheme is that it puts a premium on training students to make large amounts of money. In this, however, it merely accepts a regrettable, but apparently inescapable feature of society as presently organized (and assumes no social revolution of a radical kind). Although it might certainly be hoped that the university would produce some alumni who were comparatively indifferent to such things, most of them would try to make as much money as possible anyway. Since there is, as various studies have attested, a rough correlation between financial success and level of educational achievement, institutions that were better from an intellectual point of view might be expected to reap a corresponding financial reward. The scheme is, in a way, only a formalization of what already happens informally through alumni associations and so on, but it would remove the strong element of charity and patronage characteristic of alumni giving and also the striking differential now to be observed between institutions with a strong alumni spirit and institutions with none. Alumni spirit is characteristic of the kinds of institution mentioned earlier as having a primarily social function, and the wealth of their alumni often has little to do with the educational benefits they received during their college years. A percentage assessment would of course, incidentally, tap private fortunes as well as earned salaries; it would not at once erase the social differential between old private and new public institutions. But it would go a long way toward removing at least part of the problem of educational financing, past the age of compulsory school attendance, from the political arena.

There remains the question of curriculum, the nature of the central activity of the university. "The curriculum" is, at least, a familiar phrase. But on examination it reveals an assumption about higher education which we have all tacitly accepted, but which is in flat contradiction with the theoretical foundations of our form of government and with what is known about the process of intellectual development beyond the elementary stages. (Not much *is* known, as a matter of fact, since learning theory has taken most of its data from animals and children.) Democratic principles require that adults should be self-determining agents; normal eighteen-year-old humans are adults; therefore, normal eighteen-year-old humans should be self-determining agents. We do not bring them up to be in any but peripheral senses, under the mistaken impression that the education of the young is best understood by the old. But education is the central and most serious part of their lives and by then they ought to be in charge of it. To what extent, then, should we lay down the course it should take?

Obviously education cannot be entirely unstructured, and in certain areas—notably mathematics and the sciences—it may be genuinely necessary to tackle the material in a certain order. At the very early stages, in the schools, there may even be some point in arranging the areas themselves in a certain order. Even in "soft" disciplines, there may be better and worse ways of mastering content, and professors of those disciplines are likely to know these ways better than students do. So the notion of *a* curriculum, leading to some well-defined academic end, is still a useful one; it is *the* curriculum to which I am objecting. Borrowing Kantian language, the point could be made by saying that there is no categorical curriculum, although there may be many hypothetical curricula. But to enter upon one of these, the student must know what end he wishes to pursue, and this is what democratic principles forbid us to decide for him.

But how is the student to choose his academic ends? In order to do so intelligently, he must know what the alternatives are, and this throws us back to the question of general education raised and lamented above. One component of general education does, perhaps, properly belong in the college, although it is hardly ever included. This is what might be called the scope of intellectual inquiry, the interrelation of the disciplines, the "map of knowledge." It consists of what George Sarton used to call "knowledge of the second kind"—not knowing all subjects, but knowing what all subjects are *about;* not having the facts and theories on the tip of one's tongue, but knowing where to go to find out about them. The first course in the ideal university would in fact be a kind of prospectus of what was available there, taught jointly by the most talented and most lucid minds the university possessed. After that, there would be no required courses. But there would be plenty of opportunity for students to find out, from professors in each discipline, how best to proceed in gaining a mastery of that discipline, supposing that to be what they wished to do.

Something like this, it is true, is beginning to emerge in various universities now. There is great reluctance to turn students loose with their own destinies at such a tender age, but the conviction is beginning to spread that this must be done. In the emancipation of the student, however, we are in danger of overlooking the other half of the academic community. The professor, it is true, is in a slightly different position: The student pays, directly or indirectly, for what he learns; the professor is paid for what he teaches. It is therefore reasonable to assign teachers to courses. But the ideal relationship between students and professors would be a dialectical one, setting what the former want to learn over against what the latter want to teach, and arriving at a synthesis acceptable to both. A teacher would, as now, be hired by his department or by some equivalent (and autonomous) subdivision of the faculty. But there would be no list of courses made up by some third person before he ever came to teach or any student signed up to learn; in consultation with his colleagues (both faculty and student), it would be determined from semester to semester—but as far in advance as prudence required—what the content of his teaching would be.

All this sounds like chaos, like anarchy, like the widespread institutionalization of self-indulgence for students and faculty alike. But is there really any evidence that the population at large would be worse educated under this system than it is now? And would not the responsibility for failures, if any, in the academic system be more readily and more justly attributed than it is now? We can no longer argue—if we ever legitimately could—that young people do not know what is good for them; that we submitted to intellectual discipline, while they want to be entertained. Whatever we submitted to, the conditions of our society were such that we had an interest in doing so, and all my principle requires is that the same conditions be guaranteed to the present generation. That, too, may be a greater challenge than the universities can meet by themselves; whether or not it is will be seen in the event. But what will almost certainly follow—and if the notion of the university as a community is realized, it will follow with much less difficulty than might be feared—is a radical change in the internal organization of the curriculum. None of the habitual features of that organization—courses, hours, grades, semesters, examinations, and so on—should be exempt from scrutiny, and the feeblest imagination that still has life in it can think of alternatives for all of them.

Imagination is, of course, what is needed, and imagination leading to more systematic and coherent projects than the fragment I have presented here. At an earlier point I made in passing a suggestion for tapping the imagination with which the academic community taken as a whole is, I am convinced, more richly endowed than we often give it credit for. There may be other ways of doing it, but it must be done. And it must, I repeat, be done integrally; we need a model for the whole system, not just the university; even one for the whole society, not just the educational part of it. The work involved really has three components: a factual component to tell us exactly where we are; an imaginative component to tell us where we might ideally be; and a political component to indicate how, given the constraints of the actual situation, we might make practical moves toward the ideal. Incredible numbers of factual studies, some of them completely trivial, have been carried out, as have a few political studies, generally of restricted scope; but there have been hardly any imaginative ones. The order should be reversed. As I said at the beginning, there are many possible solutions; we cannot expect to arrive, in the teeth of social and political turmoil, at a unique ideal, ready to be implemented at once. But we might, if we had enough alternative models at our disposal, be able to choose the one most readily implemented and win ourselves some time in which we might see how to move to an even better one. "Imagination seizes power," as the French students, inspired by the Surrealists, cried last May. That is indeed as it should be, but imagination has work to do if it is to prepare itself for this responsibility.

CLARK KERR

Governance and Functions

THE GOVERNANCE of the American college and university is a residue of traditions and arrangements that are more the gift of history than of conscious thought. This system of governance is now in crisis as never before, and history alone will not dictate the future. The way out of this crisis, if there is a way out, will be extraordinarily difficult because of the peculiarities and complexities of the academic institution. The campus is inherently difficult to govern—even in theory.

One way of looking for solutions is from the perspective of the several functions of higher education which, in their many and changing combinations, affect both the general character of individual institutions and the degree of their internal variety. This functional approach suggests one general strategy for working out the manifold proposed adjustments now in controversy.

The Residue of History

Academic governance in the United States has at least four features that distinguish it from patterns elsewhere. The first is the heavy reliance on a board of trustees, regents, or managers composed of people drawn primarily from outside academic life and from outside governmental authority. There are boards or councils in Britain, Canada, and Australia, among other countries, as well as at some of the private universities of Japan, but they are nearly always much weaker than American boards in their exercised authority and are usually of a more mixed representation, including faculty and sometimes student representatives.

The second special feature is the comparatively strong role of the president, who is appointed without a specific term of office as a

108

full-time executive with a relatively large administrative staff. He has considerably more authority and opportunity for initiative, narrow as these limits may be, than his counterpart vice-chancellor or rector.

A third characteristic is the monolithic nature of the campus. To begin with, there is a campus as compared with the scattered endeavors, for example, in Paris or Buenos Aires. And on the campus, the central administrative organization is a single college of letters and sciences or arts and sciences. It includes most of the instruction and much of the research. Residence halls are simply residence halls, and not also academic units. Departments within the college are clearly subsidiary administrative units, as compared with the organization of a series of more or less autonomous faculties in many universities abroad—faculties of science and philosophy and law and medicine. Some of these monolithic colleges of letters and science in the United States are quite huge and have a single curricular policy and a single grading system.

The fourth identifying trait is the importance of external, but nongovernmental forces in the conduct of the affairs of the campus. In the United States, the alumni have an influence found almost nowhere else. Industry, agriculture, and professional associations have their points of contact, their advisory committees, their influence over funds. Private foundations advise about and finance endeavors according to their own systems of priorities.

This system of governance contrasts with others around the world. In Britain, the organized faculty has predominant influence, with the power of the University Grants Committee growing steadily. Universities are generally smaller in size and more divided internally into colleges and institutes (as in London, the largest, which still has under 25,000 students). In France, authority has resided until recently with the separate faculties and their deans and with the Ministry of Education; in Germany, it has rested with the individual full professor directing his area of scholarship and with the State government; in Russia, with the government formally and the Party informally and with the Academy that stands outside the universities with a degree of independence; in Japan, with the organized faculty; and in Latin America officially with the faculties, under their deans, and unofficially and intermittently also with students and heads of states. In Latin America, as elsewhere, Catholic universities give more power to the rector and more influence to the church than do others. As a general rule, faculties and governments are the dominating forces outside the United States.

The American system bears the marks of its origins in the Protestant sects of the early colonies. These Protestant sects emphasized the supremacy of the parishioners over the ministers; it was natural that they should also provide control by leaders of the community over the new colleges. If there was a model outside the colonies, it was probably Edinburgh which had a council largely composed of town councilmen and clergy. Similar arrangements existed at Leyden and Geneva. The earliest local councils were established in Italy when faculty members took refuge in the protection of the city fathers from the harsh rule of the students. Thus the rise of the city under control of its burghers was also a precedent for the board of the American college. It would have seemed natural, at a time when the church and the city were being placed under citizen control, to apply the same principle to the college. The populism of the nineteenth century in America added strength to this tradition—the college served the people and the board represented the people.

The president of the early college was like the minister of a Protestant church—in fact, most presidents were ministers drawn from the church. When the corporation became a more dominant institution, the president became more like the head of a corporation.

The single college of letters and science grew out of the unified classical college with its single curriculum and single faculty. Only at the University of Virginia, apparently following the French system, were the professors originally organized into eight separate schools. As the campus grew and departments were established, particularly after the Civil War and after the rise of science as against the classical curriculum, the college of letters and science became the administrative unit for the departments and the central unit for the budget, faculty appointments, approval of courses, and curricular requirements.

The involvement of private groups from outside the campus grew out of the dedication to service by the campus, particularly since the Civil War, the positions of power in society held by industrial and agricultural groups, and also the reliance on the private philanthropy of alumni and, later, of foundations as well.

Changes have taken place. Board members are no longer primarily from the ministry, but from business—as Veblen pointed out and did not like fifty years ago, but then he had not liked the

110

ministers either. The president is no longer a minister, but an executive. The college of letters and science is no longer so dominant,
with the growth of professional schools, research institutes, and
graduate divisions. The outside private forces have shifted in importance from the churches to agriculture, to industry, to the professions, to the contiguous population. Faculty members have organized into senates and increasingly attained dominant power in
academic areas, particularly since World War I. Students have gradually gained more freedom through the reduction of *in loco parentis,*
the rise of the elective system for choosing courses, and the establishment of extracurricular activities under their own control, mostly
in the period since the Civil War.

Changes have taken place, but the basic structural characteristics of a strong board, a relatively strong president, a largely monolithic internal structure, and a large role for private organizations
from outside academic life remain about as they were in 1900 and
in some respects in 1636.

The Pressures for Change

Substantive issues may or may not be settled easily and peace-
fully; but redistribution of power is always fought out with difficulty. The campus is currently passing from a concentration on
individual issues growing out of interests to a confrontation over
power growing, in part, out of principle.

There are more claimants for power than ever before, and there
is no more power to be divided. Someone must lose if others gain—
a zero-sum game. One gainer is the government, state and federal.
The major shift in influence since World War II has been to public
agencies. The reasons are clear. More of the institutions of higher
education are under public control, and more of the money in both
public and private institutions is public money. Public interest in
higher education has also risen. More young people attend from
more strata of society, and the actions of higher education, in research and service and dissent, increasingly affect more of the population. Higher education has become everybody's business. The
campus is no longer on the hill with the aristocracy, but in the valley
with the people.

State governments are exercising more fiscal control and more
influence over direction of growth, usually through coordinating
councils, than was the general situation historically. And, cur-

111

rently at least, there is a renewed state interest in the appropriateness of the relationships of students and faculties to political issues and to political action.

But the great new force since World War II has been the federal government. It now supplies one fourth of all funds spent by institutions of higher education. It has contributed more than one fourth of the new initiatives: toward science, toward residence halls, toward more equality of opportunity to attend college, and in many other ways. And it, too, has an interest in the conduct of the campus within the political arena. Federal interest as yet is fractionized among many federal agencies and several congressional committees, contrary to the situation in most other nations and contrary also to that in the fifty states where control is more unified; but this interest is increasingly concentrated in the Department of Health, Education and Welfare.

Less power and less influence on the direction of change now reside on campus; on campus, the big losers, particularly in domination of the budget, have been the board and the president. Their best instrument of control is now shared with others, and the American pattern is approaching the world pattern.

The public campus in disarray internally is particularly open to further intrusions from the state and the federal government. Internal harmony is the price of autonomy, and this price is not now being paid.

Less power on campus is met by new claimants for that power. The great new force is the students. There are more of them; they are more activist; they have more grievances against the campus and against society; and they are already making gains, and they may make more. For the first time, they are challenging the inner sanctum of the campus where the faculty and the administration have ruled supreme, challenging control over the curriculum and the use of the budget. Earlier they had asked for more freedom for themselves; now they wish to reduce the established authority of others. This is a harder challenge. The initial loser before this new force is the dean of students and then the president; before long, it may be the faculty. The sharpest challenges may come to be between the faculty which once supported the students against the administration and the students who, having disposed of the administration as an intervening power, directly confront the faculty. On campus, the students are the new men of power.

The faculty is in a less clear position. It is gaining power from

112

the administration in those segments of higher education where it has had little—the state colleges, the community colleges, and the lesser of the liberal arts colleges. About half of all faculty members are at such institutions. Gains take the form of stronger academic senates and faculty councils, but also, and potentially more significantly, of union organization. For the first time, unionization is penetrating higher education on an important scale, sometimes aided by state laws that favor unions and look upon academic senates as company-dominated organizations. When this happens, not only is some power shifted to the faculty, but it also comes to be expressed in the new form of employee-employer relations rather than the older collegial sharing of certain authority. There is a change in locus of power and in the philosophy of its expression.

In some places the faculty will gain power from the administration, often in major ways; but it may also lose to the students, sometimes in major ways. The net effect could possibly be a negative one for the faculty in terms of total power. It should be noted that not only are nearly all faculty members happy to take power from the administration, but also that some of them are happy to turn power over to the students. This is particularly true of younger faculty members who see the power of the older faculty members being taken away, and not their own—for they have little. Thus, while the faculty may lose power on a net basis, this does not mean that it will necessarily be unanimously unhappy about this shift.

The least clear trend in governance is what will happen to faculty power vis-à-vis the students. Students are historically changeable in their interests, and it is not certain how long the drive for influence in traditional faculty areas of dominance will continue. Also, faculties are historically conservative, and their capacity for resistance to change is quite substantial. Additionally, the public backlash against student activism can potentially strengthen the hands of the faculties as it did in Bologna centuries ago (and strengthen the hands of the public authorities at the same time). A crucial question will be the degree of unity within faculty ranks. Student seizure of faculty authority is likely only when it draws substantial support from within the faculty itself. Faculties recently have been on the run in the face of the sudden student attacks. If and when they consolidate their new positions, they may be virtually unmovable.

The two net losers are clearly the board and the president. The board is in an increasingly difficult position. Federal and state agencies make decisions it once made. The campus, particularly in the case of the universities and larger state colleges, is now too complex and too dynamic to be subject to detailed decision-making; yet many boards historically have been managerial boards. It is difficult to become a performance review board since nobody knows exactly what kind of performance is being reviewed: There is no quarterly test of profit or loss. The campus concentrates on inputs, not outputs, and performance is concerned with outputs, with value added to inputs. As a consequence, many boards respond to the special interests of their members and the current headlines.

The president loses to everybody, partly because he has had the most to lose originally, but also because he has no firm base of support in the power struggle, no natural constituency of his own. He long ago ceased to have much of what Veblen called "erudition"; he now ceases to be much of a "captain."

New outside groups also seek influence, chiefly the cities and the minorities, and they are not so discreet in their approaches as agriculture and the alumni have learned to become.

Several special situations exist. The Catholic colleges are moving from religious to secular control and from domination by the president to a sharing of authority with the faculty. Negro colleges are seeing the once masterful presence of the president—indispensable ambassador to the white power structure—reduced in stature as both faculty and students are less impressed than they once were. State colleges and community colleges, where the president historically has personally done all the hiring and firing, are witnessing faculty insurgence, and at some places even the commuter students have now become activist. Administrative authority is being reduced particularly in these three segments.

The forces that have the operative influence are those that can get the changes they want. Since World War II, these have been particularly the federal government and now the students. It is their changes which have prevailed and are prevailing. Nor is this surprising. The public interest in higher education has grown, and the methods of influence have always existed. The influence of youth has arrived on the "tidal wave" of numbers and the new tactics of confrontation. So much of the recent history of higher education has been written by federally sponsored science and by rising numbers of students that governance could not well escape these forces.

The nature of the power struggle has changed. Formerly it was the faculty demanding freedom from the authority of the president and the board in the name of academic freedom with the American Association of University Professors determining the basic lines that divided freedom from unwarranted control. Now it is the campus asking for autonomy from the government and, as yet, the lines have not been clearly drawn nor the protective agency devised that will differentiate autonomy from undue domination. The battle has moved to another part of the terrain, and there are new contestants.

Another change has been that part of the conflict has been internalized. The administration has always been looked upon as being partially foreign and thus subject to attack. The internal academic community has been viewed as composed of teachers and students. And now there is conflict within that community. Some of the students are against some of the faculty, and the faculty itself is divided. The academic community historically has faced its enemies outside and to the right. Now it finds attacks coming also from inside and mainly from the left. The "community of scholars" is now fighting within itself. The battle is not over a hated fascism without, but rather over a partially cherished syndicalism within.

A Confusion of Forms

The campus is a Tower of Babel in many ways, including governance. And Hell hath few terrors like confusion sharply challenged—which is where higher education finds itself today.

A. J. Muste once wrote that a trade union had a divided soul. It was an "army," but also a "town meeting" and a "business enterprise." It could not be all of these things at once and yet it had to be. So also the university: It is many things to many people and many things to itself. It is a guild where masters train apprentices, where expertise is supreme, a guild run by the masters, by the faculty. It is also a market place where students choose one campus instead of another and move from one campus to another, where they choose one course of study and one professor rather than another. Campuses and professors offer their wares, and students individually express their preferences. The customers pick and choose. The rules of the market place apply, even though the curriculum does provide a good many "tie-in" sales.

The university is also, to some degree, a democracy. Decisions are made that require the consent of the governed; rules are issued; and discipline is exercised. In a democracy, one man has one vote

115

and is entitled to a jury of his peers; and the students are in the majority.

It is a corporation with property, endowments, a reputation, a permanent life to preserve as against the difficulties of the moment. A board of directors should have the competence to manage the institution and look out for its long-run welfare. No group that comes and goes has the knowledge or the interest to do so. The directors represent the integrity of the institution.

It is a bureaucracy with rules to be applied impartially, accounts to be kept, and books to be stored as efficiently as possible. The executive runs the administration. It is a series of semi-autonomous service bureaus. Each bureau provides information to interested persons in industry, government, and agriculture. It needs an executive secretary working under a committee of the people being served. It is an agent of the state that spends state money and provides society with the research, skills, and consultation that are so essential to the progress of an industrial economy.

It is a church with a religion. It believes in the unfettered search for truth, in free expression of opinion without fear, in preservation of the past, including all books however offensive they may be currently, and in access on merit and the granting of grace on merit. Its principles are more important than service, or rules, or votes, or consumer preference. It is the keeper of the good, the true, and the beautiful; of culture. It perpetuates a spirit of inquiry and integrity. Its religion is not subject to compromise.

It is also a community, and the essence of community is that it is voluntarily held together by the common standards and interests of its members. Community follows the "will of the meeting" which requires more than a majority vote, and it is based upon a consensus about purpose and process. Traditionally, the academic community has been marked by tolerance among its members in their daily relations and by mutual persuasion as the basis of change; the application of power has been muted in the conduct of its internal affairs.

The university is all of these things, but it is also none of them in total. Perhaps most of all it has been a community with an implicit consensus that the guild of the faculty ran the curriculum and the research; the market choices of the students helped determine which campuses and which areas of study grew and declined; the democracy of the undergraduates governed extracurricular activities; the board watched out for the capital investment and the brand name; the president ran the day-to-day administrative affairs; the deans kept the students and the parents and the farmers and the doctors reasonably happy; the society was served in fact, but attacked on principle and expected to keep its distance; and everybody respected the academic faith and showed tolerance toward his fellow believer. Each element had its own domain. All elements had a common concern for the purposes of the community and the welfare of their fellow participants.

Much of this is now being challenged. The consensus is fading, and in some places, at some times, it no longer exists. The new crisis of governance is located in the dissolution of the old consensus. Without consensus, the campus can perish.

If Governance Followed Function

The functions of higher education are diverse, more so than the unholy trinity of teaching and research and service implies. And these functions are not inherently best subject to the same form of governance.

The main groups of functions are these. First are those associated with production: the talent hunt before and during college, the provision of professional and technical training, the conduct of research, and the extension of service. Second are those associated with consumption: the creation of opportunities for a general education, the invention and maintenance of interesting communities for daily living on campus, the provision of custodial services like medical care and counseling and guidance, and the provision of a holding operation where students can drop in and out as they change career and life plans. Third are those associated with citizenship: the provision of remedial work for people deprived at earlier levels of education, the conduct of basic "acculturation" to democratic principles and cultural patterns, and the development of commentary upon, criticism about, and dissent toward the surrounding society.

The faculty would seem to be in a particularly good position to govern professional and technical training, research, and dissent— these are the areas where expertise is or should be supreme—and to consider general policy for "acculturation" (if anyone can). The students are in an advantageous position to share in the governance of general education (with the interested faculty) and of community life (with sympathetic administrators); the administration is most suited to govern the talent hunt (with faculty advice), the service activities (with advice from the groups specifically to be served), the custodial functions (with student advice), the holding operations (with faculty advice), and the remedial activities (with faculty advice).

Important qualifications are necessary. As two examples, the balance of research effort and its conduct without secrecy are of concern to the entire community, and community life must be conducted within the limits of the general law applicable to all citizens.

This particular functional distribution of governance would mean major changes from common practice: The faculty would assume authority over the rules governing dissent (such campus rules will only be effective anyway with faculty approval); and students would share substantial authority over the pre-professional curriculum and over community life on campus—authority that now resides with the faculty for the former and the administration for the latter.

Two of these shifts of authority would run counter to current public opinion: that to the faculty on dissent when the public has its suspicions, and that to the students on community life when the public has its fears. But the only viable rules on dissent will be faculty rules and public law, and the only viable community life will be responsive to the students and acceptable to them. One of the problems of governance today is that changes which the campus requires are changes which much of the public abhors; and that the changes affecting political action and styles of life which find broad public support are anathema to the campus.

A missing link in governance in the United States is an over-all council of the total campus community—students, faculty, administrators, trustees, alumni—charged with discussing common concerns, such as academic freedom, institutional autonomy, continuity and integrity of operations, over-all functions, and governance. Such a council would seek to evolve and preserve a consensus about the community as a whole and to protect the academic faith. The Australian universities have done and are doing particularly well in providing such councils.

The board, composed largely of lay members, should, I believe, be kept, with some changes in some situations. The board, when properly constituted, can serve as a buffer against improper external pressures. It can be, and often has been, a dynamic force in assuring progressive change as against the conservatism of the fa-

culty. Additionally, it brings competence in handling many business
and financial matters, and serves as the guardian of the long-run
interests of the institution. Its role often needs clarification—particularly as to how it may best review performance; and its membership needs scrutiny—particularly as to how members may best
be chosen to assure an understanding of and devotion to the institution in its myriad aspects.

Clarification is also necessary of both the legitimate interests
and the limits of interference of state and federal governments.

All the points raised have certain implications for different types
of institutions. The faculty would have even more authority over
the university; the students would assume more influence over the
liberal arts college or the "cluster" college on a university campus;
and the administration would maintain much of its predominance
in the community college. Nevertheless, the central suggestion is
that governance should be related to a careful consideration of
functions.

The crisis over governance is due, in part, to the rise in importance of certain functions—the rise of the consumption functions as
pressed by the students and the rise of the dissent function as
pressed by students and some faculty. The existing system of governance has not been well adapted to these new emphases.

A Pragmatic Pluralistic Strategy

The problems of governance in higher education are so complex that no single solution is possible—situations vary from campus
to campus and within a campus from one major function to another.
Nor are perfect solutions likely—perfection from one point of view
is imperfection from another. Nor are permanent solutions likely—
institutions change and the interests and roles of their several constituencies change, and, also, experience accumulates.

Attempted solutions on the basis of ideology—all power to the
faculty or all power to the students or all power to the regents who
represent the people—are fraught with danger. There can be no
clear preference for one solution versus another solution on principle, given the nature of the academic institution; and ideological
solutions tend to be absolutist, authoritarian, and across-the-board
in a situation that calls for tolerance, a large measure of individual
freedom, and the precise fitting of governance to special situations.
Attempted solutions on the basis of power alone—on who has the

money or the votes or mob pressure—can tear a campus apart, and once torn apart it is hard to put together again.

A practical, pragmatic approach seems more sensible. An effort should be made to sort out the general issue of governance into its component parts, and then to approach each part in the light of the total problem. Area by area, the central questions should be who has an interest in the problem and who has competence to deal with it. The test should be performance. If performance is good, the argument for change is reduced. If performance is bad, the argument for change is enhanced. As an example, the undergraduate curriculum for non-majors is a disaster area on many campuses. The faculty as a whole has little or no interest in it, and many students are dissatisfied with it. Here is an area where the faculty cannot be proud of its record, and where the students have a great interest and some competence. Where the faculty has done well, as in some liberal arts colleges, the case for student participation is less persuasive.

This practical, pragmatic approach can lead to a whole series of agreements, area by area, at any moment of time. In fact, this approach is being followed, hesitantly and too slowly, in the United States, but particularly in Britain, Canada, and Australia. France and Germany, by contrast, are searching for across-the-board solutions of one-half power to the students or one-third power to the students in all areas. A more pragmatic series of solutions might lead to the conclusion that power should be total in some areas and zero in others.

Governance problems are best handled function by function. Also, academic governance is best conducted on a face-to-face basis within small communities. This suggests that separate institutions should be created to handle separate functions (particularly when the functions are not compatible—as, for example, specialized research versus general education for the non-majors). Where several functions are combined in single institutions, there should be considerable decentralization of governance. It also suggests that institutions, both in total and in their component parts, should be of modest size. Structure and governance are interrelated.

Massive size is an enemy of effective governance in the academic world with its great variety of activities, interests, and personalities. A campus of large size might best be viewed as a series of communities within a common environment, rather than as a single monolithic community; this is how Harvard is organized.

Higher education in the United States is now re-examining the system of governance given to it by history. A new series of consensuses is needed—not one over-all "best" solution, not one single preferred form. Variety in solutions should match the variety of situations, and this is almost infinite. Many small agreements will come closer to providing effective governance in totality than will any global approach. An examination of functions is essential to the success of the endeavor. The task is to match the form of governance with the function—to use the guild where the guild works best, democracy where democracy works best, and so forth. We are fortunate in having a variety of forms available to match against the variety of functions. The test of the matching will be found in the performance—let the governance fit the functions. Clarity about functions is becoming essential to sanity in governance now that the consensus which embraced the confusions of the past has disintegrated into conflict.

MORRIS B. ABRAM

Reflections on the University in the New Revolution

WE ARE currently in the midst of a revolution. The real nature of the profound social movement taking place today has been somewhat obscured because thus far it has been relatively bloodless, but we must acknowledge that it is indeed a genuine revolution. Much of its thrust concerns the distribution of power within the society. Part of its substance we should accept and absorb, but its proclivity toward violence and intolerance must be rejected if the liberal society is to survive.

There is little prospect that the over-all political aims of the revolution will be achieved, for there is no evidence that the society at large is in either a revolutionary or a pre-revolutionary stage politically.[1] But much of the revolution that deals with the arts, life styles, and various matters of personal taste has already been widely accepted. Portions of it—in the area of obscenity law, for example—have even been ratified by the United States Supreme Court.

The university has been the site of a good deal of the ferment and turbulence of the new revolution because it is the present habitation of its most articulate and dedicated leaders—and their followers. The university has come under severe pressure and attack because it is near, tolerant and vulnerable—and because, as an authoritative institution (which it must be), it can be made to appear authoritarian (which a good university certainly is not). I would not go so far as one foreign scholar who recently told me: "The American university has no educational problems—only the intrusion of political problems into educational affairs."

The campus phase of the new revolution has forced a re-examination of the nature of the university, its governance, and its role in society. Important questions have been raised, and many opinions shifted. I want to explore, here, some of the major issues I con-

122

sidered during my first year in office as President of Brandeis University. Many of these issues were raised by the students; some indicate the perception, sensitivity, and intellectual grasp of our young people, while others evince inexperience and confusion. Harris Wofford, President of the State University College at Old Westbury, Long Island, has said: "Maybe the students' role is as a giant Socrates, beard and all, asking very hard questions. They have stung us very hard, but we need to sting them out of their muddled thinking."

The "Neutrality" Issue

"Neutrality" is a critical campus issue and one on which my views have changed. There is a popular dialogue today that relates to the university's obligation to play a neutral role in our society. In my judgment, this dialogue is largely frustrating and unrewarding. Partisans in one camp describe a university that never was, while those in the other describe a university that never should be.

Of all the institutions in Western society, the independent judiciary has been the one traditionally acclaimed as the most neutral. Yet the Supreme Court is, after all, a court of men and can only aspire to neutrality, at different times rendering different decisions based on essentially the same facts and the same Constitution. But the Justices are not neutral about their commitment to neutrality. They have pledged themselves to use all of their skills and intellectual resources in the attempt to be neutral. One need read only a paragraph or two from a Holmes or Brandeis opinion to be struck by the passion with which these men aspired to dispassionate analysis.

Similarly, a university cannot be a totally neutral institution. As every other corporation, the university, an artificial being created by the law, acts through men. Its mission—education and research—and its commitment to the liberal belief that man is improvable in an ameliorative, evolutionary process comprise a rudimentary sort of constitution to which it is bound. Within these limits and by every effort, the university must—like the independent judiciary—strive to be objective and neutral.

The university plays a central role in transmitting present knowledge and extending the frontiers of truth, preserving what Whitehead termed "the connection between knowledge and the zest of life by uniting the young and the old in the imaginative consideration of learning."[2] It must remain a focal point from which new knowledge emanates and be a wellspring of criticism of the institutions of society. And it should encourage innovation in the realm of ideas. Whether the area is the natural sciences, the social sciences, the humanities, or the arts, one essential product of the university is originality. All of these functions constitute the mission of the university.

Since the university can never be neutral about its mission and its commitment, it must always determine whether a possible course of action fits the educational mission of the university and whether the consequences are defensible on educational grounds. The method the university employs to decide such questions must be fair and objective. For example, the draft is obviously not a purely educational issue; in its complexity, it impinges upon all the major concerns of our day. But insofar as the draft affects the educational mission of the university, it is of great concern to the campus community. If the university admits as students young people who perhaps would not ordinarily have been admitted, it is not being neutral; but this course of action surely is consistent with one view of its educational mission. Furthermore, while it is unlikely that we will ever be able to change things so that death no longer is the final resolution of life, our medical schools cannot be neutral in this area, for their responsibility remains to extend life to the limit.

Since the university is not and cannot be totally neutral, should it—as students of the New Left suggest—not only encourage a deep examination of the problems of society, but also become an instrument of social change? Should the university, determined advocate of innovation, be a revolutionary force? A university politicized, compelled to take stands and support political factions, radical or conservative, is a university doomed. The university should be crammed with people who take stands, who think, vote, and participate in every level of life, including politics. Revolutionary concepts in the realm of ideas may well be developed within its gates. But a politically programmed university can destroy the very procedures—freedom of expression and the free exchange of ideas— that make innovation possible; certainly it becomes an inhospitable place for men of wide and divergent views. The consequences of a decision to politicize the university are simply not defensible on educational grounds.

Changes in the Nature of the Student Body

In the past, university neutrality did not seem such a pressing issue because many of the students who exerted an influence over the quality and direction of active campus life belonged to a group that might have been called the "trade-off" group. These students, attending the university primarily in exchange for certain social or material rewards that were not related to the acquisition of knowledge, gathered their gentlemen C's. It would rarely have occurred to them to challenge the fundamental mission or position of the university; they wanted to indulge in hedonism under the sheltering arms of alma mater. In England before World War II, many of the "pass" degree students were trade-offs; they went to Oxford or Cambridge primarily for social reasons where, as Wordsworth acknowledged, they "sauntered, played or rioted" day and night. (Of course, there has always been a substantial group of students who recognize the multi-perspective goal of the university and enroll primarily to master the subject matter and to be subjected to the widest possible range of ideas. Many students were motivated by *both* traditional scholarship and trade-off drives so that few students belonged completely to either group. Nevertheless, these groups could be distinguished in a rough way by the *degree* of motivation toward learning or non-learning rewards, including the narrow benefits of a college degree.)

Today, trade-off students have all but vanished in most of the good universities.[3] Even where they do exist, contemporary trade-offs do not seem to have the yeast to cause any trouble or turmoil. They are not engaged with society, even in a general way, as are other students. Counterpoised against the societal concerns of today's turbulent young, the fraternal frolics of the trade-offs of the past look silly. Other groups have now pre-empted the stage with something more appealing to the age.

Replacing the trade-offs as the group most responsible for the prevailing climate among students is a group I would call the "find-out" group. Because the find-out student is an earnest, searching student, the traditional frolics that attracted the trade-offs do not appeal to him. But although his intentions are serious, his attention has not yet been absorbed nor his imagination riveted upon a specific academic discipline.[4] The find-out student does not see the university as a corporate body involving itself, even in its curriculum formation, in those matters that appeal to him.

Find-out students are now demanding several new types of university responses and focusing upon areas of the university never touched in the past. In addition to stating that the university should involve itself in the problems of society and become "relevant" to the broader community, they seek more control over the curriculum. Perhaps part of their frustration stems from the fact that, as Norman Birnbaum states: "We no longer have an effective conception of the general core of curriculum."[5] In the past, there was general agreement on what the educated man should know; from the quadrivium and the trivium on, there was a common language spoken in many tongues. Thomas Jefferson could be a man of law and letters, a diplomat, an architect, and an expert on both music and agriculture; today knowledge is so immense and disparate that the find-out feels he is going nowhere—and in the direction of everywhere. He therefore wants courses more "relevant" to his interests, with subjects running the gamut from drugs to sex to witchcraft.[6] His desire for control of the curriculum seems to spring from the wish to make the university more conducive to his quest for meaning in the academic world. (The complaint frequently heard that "a course or curriculum is not relevant" is an incomplete sentence. Something must be relevant to something else. The university, as a whole, is relevant only when it is relevant to society as a university—that is, as an educational institution. The liberal arts college has traditionally been a place where the student is taught not how to do a certain job, but how to attack and think about certain problems. The student is the one who makes what he learns relevant to his life.)

Can the University Meet the Needs of the Find-Out Students?

Universities are delicately balanced institutions designed to deal with delicate problems. Their life styles and independence have developed gradually from the Middle Ages until universities have become complex communities with many interests. Membership in these communities carries reciprocal rights and responsibilities (and those who accept the former cannot morally eschew the latter). No voice or viewpoint should be excluded, and a cardinal principle of the entire community must be acceptance of the rights of others. Given the nature of this community, I see three possible courses of action that universities can take in response to the find-outs.

First, the university can attempt to eliminate or change the find-out group. This course is undesirable and impractical because it would exclude many serious students, create a potentially explosive situation at the university, and no doubt quench a vital spark that could produce a better society beyond the campus.

Second, the university can be completely responsive to the new demands of the find-out group, ignoring the needs of other students and eliminating its traditional societal functions. This course is absurd. It would mean defeat for the traditional and classic learning process. Those who wished to learn in the classic sense or wanted to be involved in this process would attempt to go to new institutions in society for this purpose, but it is unlikely that these new institutions would be able to perform the traditional role so well. Society would thus lose those vital functions of innovation and the development of knowledge that are now performed by the university community.

Third, the university can attempt to satisfy both the find-out and structured learning expectations of students at the same time. This would mean integrating within the university innovative methods and curriculum options for one group of students, while maintaining a more or less traditional learning process under the control of an authoritative faculty for others. It is difficult and undoubtedly will produce tension, but I find it our only logical course. Those in the university may have to live with more options than presently exist; some excellent universities, including Oxford, have already done so for more than a century.[7]

This alternative does not mean the end of the conventional learning process, but it will require much additional effort on the part of the faculty, administrators, and students than has heretofore been exerted. Faculty will have to develop far more synthesis among the disciplines. (Generally, good faculties are politically and socially liberal, but they tend to be very conservative with respect to the defense of their own turf.[8]) Norman Birnbaum notes:

Originally instruments of mastery, the disciplines have become—despite our volition—means of perpetuating the irrationalities inherent in contemporary society's use of knowledge.[9]

Who knows but that the rigorously trained generalist in the wide overlaps of his primary field of interest may not be a better scholar and a better teacher than the intense specialist within a constricted field? This is not to deny the necessity of the latter, but only to suggest that in a great university the former may also have a value and an honored place.

If some of the best students in our society are simply not turned on by traditional isolated disciplines, perhaps a more engaging curriculum could be developed that is academically just as valid. For example, suppose we offered a course on "sovereignty" ‚in which students explored such questions as: How did the concept of sovereignty develop? To what extent does it unify or separate people? Why is it preserved? What are its virtues and its effects? What are the conditions for real independence? What are the relationships of sovereignty to economic growth? Does it play a role in the poverty or wealth of nations? Such a course could require a deep study of politics and economics, history and international relations. In addition, it would call for intensive work in anthropology and related disciplines. In fact, a course on "sovereignty" could require a study of war.

Obstacles to Revitalization of the Undergraduate College

A course on "sovereignty" would undoubtedly grip the interests of many contemporary students. The necessary interdisciplinary approach cannot, however, be presented from retreads of old lecture notes with little addenda; it will require effort to organize. Many lectures will have to be reconsidered, and old thoughts examined and synthesized. An interchange will have to be developed among colleagues from related but departmentalized disciplines. This is a small price to pay, however, to engage students. Too many professors feel obliged to augment the body of learning, and sometimes their efforts serve primarily to increase the area that must be learned, adding little that is important to seminal knowledge. The university is said to gain luster through their preoccupations, but the pressing needs of students are sometimes not met. Many members of the faculty must redistribute their energies and talents. These demands are not mutually exclusive.

Unfortunately, the great rewards of academia stem mainly from research and publication, not from giving time and attention to students. Professors consider themselves primarily responsible to their professional disciplines—their standards and requirements—rather than to any university administration, for it is the former that rewards them and thus shapes their incentives. The traditional slogan "publish or perish" must be modified to operate thus: "Publish and prosper; teach and prosper; teach and publish and prosper doubly."

I do not deny the need to recharge the academic battery, for nothing is worse than the teacher with an exhausted intellect. But such recharging should not deprive students by causing the absence or detachment of the scholar from teaching over an extended period of time. Moreover, as Whitehead pointed out, great scholarship is not always defined by research and accompanying publication:

It must not be supposed that the output of a university in the form of original ideas is solely to be measured by printed papers and books labeled with the names of the authors. Mankind is as individual in its mode of output as in the substance of its thoughts. For some of the most fertile minds composition in writing, or in a form reducible to writing, seems to be an impossibility. In every faculty you will find that some of the more brilliant teachers are not among those who publish. Their originality requires for its expression direct intercourse with their pupils in the form of lectures, or of personal discussion. Such men exercise an immense influence; and yet, after the generation of their pupils has passed away, they sleep among the innumerable unthanked benefactors of humanity. Fortunately, one of them is immortal—Socrates.[10]

Faculty tenure cannot be ignored in any discussion of university reform. Tenure produces rigidities and limits options, particularly in institutions that do not have the money to employ detours around existing roadblocks. Yet it would be unfair to suggest that any institution, be it a law firm or corporation, is free of *de facto* tenure. Nor should a university for many reasons (including that chief societal value, academic freedom) be without a basic tenure principle. But the present rules did not come down from Sinai and are not necessarily the best ones for these times. Too frequently young men are forced out of a university where they would prefer to remain for a few years more by the rigid "up or out" rule whose provisions may have better fitted another decade. It would be impossible in this article to do justice to the complex problems involved in the role of tenure at the modern university, but I do want to record my support of the Dunlop Committee's statement: "We do not believe that the outside period [established by the Committee of Eight from the Ph.D. degree to the decision on tenure, actually only six and one-half years], should be further reduced."[11]

The University and Society

Students have repeatedly charged that the university is the handmaiden of the Establishment. They assert, for instance, that the university is training them to fit into an existing and unjust social order.

Recently, a chemistry major at Brandeis announced to one of his professors that he was through with the subject because he did not

MORRIS B. ABRAM

"want to learn to make napalm." Aptly, the professor inquired: "Who is asking you to do that? Why don't you plan to use your chemistry in cancer research?"

Although the student had confused pure knowledge with its practical application, his impetuous indignation points up a pressing problem: Our society is not assigning priorities and resources so that knowledge may be applied primarily in what some of the best of our young people feel are morally and socially acceptable ways. Billions of dollars are consumed by war, while funds for cancer research dwindle. But by frequently directing his energies and indignation against the wrong targets—in the case of the Brandeis student, chemistry and himself—the sensitive student defeats his own ends.

The student often sublimates his outrage by demanding that the university become his instrument to reform society. Aside from the fact that the university is a weak lance, such efforts will, if successful, certainly further undermine its independence and objectivity. I say "further" because, as I have already stated, the university is not totally neutral.

Since the university operates in the world, there are forces constantly pushing it and pressures constantly exerted upon it. As Talcott Parsons has pointed out, there is a complicated relationship between universities and society. Universities depend upon support from society, but criticism of society is part of their basic role. In discussing "the underlying importance of strict observance of the *procedural forms* of intellectual discussion" and other factors, Parsons explains:

The above considerations concern an important "interface" between the academic system and the more turbulent aspects of society as a whole. They involve a kind of "dialectic" relation in that the academic system is differentiated from the rest of the society, and to a degree "withdrawn" from the more immediate social pressures, while the results of its activities constitute major influences on the society, not least on its processes of change.

The academic system is not primarily an "engine" of change (or reform) in the sense either that government strove to be in the New Deal or, more extremely, that Communist governments attempt to be in undertaking the radical restructuring of their societies. In a "lower key," however, a strong and prominent academic system is by no means a bulwark of the status quo, but very much a source, through many channels, of impetus to societal change. The development of the secular intellectual disciplines, which now lie at the core of the academic system, has been intimately involved with the three "revolutions" that have underlain the emergence of modern society—the industrial revolution, the democratic revolution,

130

and the educational revolution. Indeed, it is the focus of the present phase of the educational revolution.[12]

The university achieves continuity and sustains itself by changing. It is a social system, and, as is true of any social system, the boundaries of its concern change according to the forces that provide support and act upon it. At the present time, major constituent groups include students, faculty, administrators, alumni, trustees, parents, financial donors, government agencies,[13] private corporations, professional associations, and a number of other private pressure groups that may from time to time make their voices heard within the university community. University administrators, although they make demands themselves, are also involved as "conversion mechanisms" in dealing with the demands of the different groups. Responsible administrative authorities must take the demands of these various groups and balance them in accordance with political realities and the general operational ethic to which they adhere in running the university. That ethic must at the very least include a resolve to be objective and an adherence to an educational mission. Thus, despite well-intentioned student pressures, there is no justification for the financially-pressed university to give land or resources to the underprivileged unless an educational purpose is served. The university's service to the deprived should be education.

The University as an Operating Model

The existence of various constituent groups, autonomous to varying degrees, constantly making demands upon and supporting administrative authorities, makes the university a microcosm of the political world and unlike a business firm. The "theory of the firm" is not generally appropriate to university administration. The university should not be envisioned as a hierarchical business-like structure in which managerial techniques can be used to deal with the various political controversies that arise among constituent groups. Straight-line authority is not an appropriate method of university governance. Top authority should not and cannot designate all-inclusive goals. The process of university governance is one of negotiation, compromise, and adjudication. It is more legislative and judicial in nature than executive. This does not mean that executive techniques are not highly appropriate under certain circumstances. But during this year of campus turmoil, the most successful university administrators have clearly been those who understand the subtle processes of negotiation and recognize the need to build a viable university legislative system in which appropriate interests are represented and a judicial system capable of acting independently and rendering fair judgments.

Performance of the university's mission cannot, as in the firm, be measured by unit costs or formulae of cost effectiveness. Who knows the relative value of the isolation of DNA as against the education of a dozen technocrats? Who can be sure that one JFK was not worth one hundred average professors of political science?

Universities cannot be run by administrative edict, nor can they be ruled by majority opinions. A university organized to pursue scholarship in the social sciences on a theory preferred by the majority would always take the field against innovators who may discover and proclaim tomorrow's truth. In science, too, the majority is frequently wrong, and the man who refuses to believe what seems obvious may actually see more clearly than those who espouse and teach the obvious. Copernicus' theory, opposed by many scientists for over a century, was fought even by some of the Jewish communities which prohibited the teaching of the heliocentric system, and Galileo's telescopic observations were spurned by men agreeing with Francesco Sizi, the Florentine astronomer who declared that the satellites around Jupiter "are invisible to the naked eye and therefore can have no influence on the earth and therefore would be useless and therefore do not exist."

The Strengths and Weaknesses of "the Estates" of the University

A university has four estates with a close day-to-day relationship with the campus: faculty, students, administration, and trustees. (The alumni might be considered a fifth estate.) Even within the accepted traditions of the academy, the present structure of the university involving the powers and responsibilities of these estates is imperfect. No universities are ideal communities; all can and must change as the various roles of these estates are assessed and examined.

Faculties, for instance, have much power, albeit essentially negative power, but they do not have the accompanying responsibilities. Individual faculty members who see beyond their immediate personal and departmental needs and are "institution-minded" are a source of great influence and strength, particularly in these times of crisis. If numerous, faculty members who submerge individual preferences and act as adult role models for confused adolescents can stabilize the university in the midst of the new revolution.

The administration may also need to be changed in emphasis and approach. The basic problem of most administrations is that they have great responsibility without the accompanying power over the causes of discontent in the university community. These causes originate largely in the outside world; the university president can rail against them, but seldom has the capacity to change them. Not since Woodrow Wilson and Nicholas Murray Butler have governments shaken at the thundering of a university president. Nor does the administration have much control over many aspects of the internal affairs of the university—over the failures of teachers, over department heads, or over the organization of the curriculum. In relation to the faculty, administrators are restricted by tenure and because faculties are generally self-disciplined, discipline almost always being dispensed by the peer group. Moreover, disciplinary action from the administration is likely to be perceived, often unjustifiably, as an infringement on academic freedom. Nevertheless, administrations have a large role. The president who does not regard himself as a leader of the faculty, as a problem-solver, and as a source of innovation and renewal in academic matters is failing both faculty and students.

The power of university trustees is a vastly overworked subject. Trustees have all the trappings of power, yet they have even less power than the administration and little capacity to rationalize and control. In the statutes of the university, the power of the trustees appears absolute; in fact, it closely resembles that of the monarchs of England, without whose signature no bill can become law, but whose signature has not been withheld since 1703. The function of the trustees is, nevertheless, indispensable. They serve as a shield for the institution, guarding it against outside influences that could destroy it. They interpret the university to the community, which frequently is hostile to its aims, and nourish and sustain it with the resources that it requires in ever-increasing amounts. When the trustees function properly, they are the unsung heroes of academic freedom and excellence. There are too many instances, however, in which trustees in public institutions interpret their political appointment as the license to use the office for the exercise of political power; such efforts are bound to complicate enormously the task of university governance. The problem is different in the private institution where financial competence and communal influence must be delicately melded with the wise counsel so useful to the president. Not all boards can sufficiently furnish these abilities. The trustee who has expertise in solving the problems of the university, financial or otherwise, and who works hard within the self-imposed limits on his ultimate legal powers deserves every honor associated with such service.

Students today have become a particularly vocal constituency and must never be dismissed on the ground that they happen to be four-year transients. They form a group that has increasing power of persuasion, but is often unable to realize the importance and significance of that power. The power of persuasion within the university community is the primary leverage of initiative and veto, yet most students do not know this or will not believe it. They would be surprised to learn that in most institutions few decisions in the board of trustees are ever taken by a vote, but are arrived at after a modification of various viewpoints by the erosion of debate and the introduction of new elements into their consideration.

Both faculty and students should participate on boards of trustees. (Young people should serve not only on university boards, but on the boards of most associations and corporations where they should be turned out to pasture at age twenty-five.) Students add a new and essential perspective for university boards. The administration, for example, may look at the university through one end of a telescope; the students turn that telescope around, and the university looks quite different. With young people on boards, there will be a different chemistry. The discussions will be livelier; although when the facts are in, most decisions may ineluctably be the same. (Perhaps some of the decisions that really count will indeed come out differently. In any event, the change will have occurred not through coercion, but by consensus.)

The classic function of the university precludes student control of the curriculum, conduct of courses, appointments, and promotion. But students should participate in "educational" matters—the degree and mode depending on what the matter is and the extent to which student involvement is relevant. In no case should students be placed in a position in which they have a conflict of interest with the faculty that teaches and examines them.

Certainly, in such areas as parietal rules and control over dormitory life, systematic procedures for student involvement should be worked out that will recognize their legitimate interests. The rationale behind most parietal rules now is that the university stands *in loco parentis*. Today this position is ridiculous for a number of reasons. First, a substitute parent should enforce rules consistent with the standards of the actual parent—but then the university, as surrogate parent, should be strict with the students who come from strict homes and permissive with others who come from more permissive homes. A wide variety of rules could thus follow, creating confusion and exposing the university to the justified criticism of being one of the most arbitrary and inequitable institutions in society. There is another difficulty. In this day of the automobile and the open campus, the university cannot pretend that its effective writ runs much further than the classroom. It is ridiculous for a university to claim to stand *in loco parentis* to some young people while the Congress, representing national policy, makes all eighteen-year-old males in the country eligible to be drafted and sent to live away from home—with a first sergeant instead of a dean of students. First sergeants do not take the rules of parents as their standards for discipline—at least not the first sergeants I have known.

Some rules governing campus environment cannot be primarily the province of the students. Various elements of the university do, after all, share a common community. In certain areas, the interest and competence of each group must be made to meld with that of others. The rules governing demonstrations, for example, affect the entire community. To be effective, such legislation must have the presumptive legitimacy that comes from participation of all campus elements in the legislative process.

The University as a Free, but not Necessarily Democratic Institution

As a society, we have been able to agree upon fundamental concepts in government; we should be able to transfer some of these principles to the governance of the university, especially those Constitutional traditions that protect freedom of speech and press, freedom to assemble peaceably, and freedom to petition appropriate authorities for a redress of grievances. Freedom from religious domination over all secular institutions is another vital principle highly appropriate for the university world. (Another concept in the Western philosophic and political tradition—the democratic ethic—may also be drawn upon, but within the university it has more limited usefulness than the procedures that guarantee freedom of expression.) Some agreement must now be reached on what these great principles mean in a university setting.

The fundamental societal purpose of the university does not require—in fact, it may exclude—participatory democracy. The university does, however, need a strong emphasis upon the protection of the rights of individuals to operate freely within the boundaries of their responsibilities. In their governing of themselves, universities should advance, strengthen, and fortify those basic beliefs of society accepted as fundamental for the preservation of the free expression of ideas. There must be freedom not only from *external* forces—be they politicians, trustees, parents, donors, alumni, or members of any other group—but also from *internal* factions that seek to distort the processes of rational debate and discussion. The ideal university, where total freedom exists within certain boundaries and the learning process is responsibly conducted by all elements of the university, can never be realized, given the nature of the external and internal pressures that exist. It is to be hoped, however, that reasonable men will agree on the basic rules of operation for the university just as they must for the political realm and the community. By adhering to fundamental *procedural* principles, the conditions for substantive innovation will be established.

Basic to the university's mission is its commitment to the right of the professor to challenge orthodoxy and to express his views freely, regardless of their content or their unpopularity. The university can never be neutral about the concept of academic freedom.

Yet what should administrators do when faced with demands from constituent interests—radical or conservative—that a professor be fired for his actions? (He should never be fired for his views.[14]) This becomes a delicate political situation. How is it possible to reconcile the need of universities for "constitutional government" and procedures to advance freedom of expression with the reality of constituent interests that often make the implementation of such procedures extraordinarily difficult? There is a principle which should be followed, but which, if followed, may produce an explosion.

In this dilemma, the general principle must be upheld or the entire *raison d'être* of the university will be destroyed. Its societal function will be sacrificed to political exigency, and it will become no more than the political instrument of the most powerful external or internal pressures. (Unfortunately, the events of the last years indicate that professors are subject not only to outside investigation of their beliefs, particularly if they happen to teach in public insti-

136

tutions, but must now teach in an increasingly politicized *internal* university environment. As groups of all kinds make known their dissatisfactions with professors ranging from "racist" to "communist," it seems reasonable to assume that without tenure the position of the professor might become tenuous indeed.)

The University's Defense Against Forceful Acts

Clearly, every good university is a combustible mix. It contains not only bright kinetic youth who are disenchanted with society, but also small numbers of revolutionaries who—perhaps by deliberately co-opting their fellow students on the basis of contrived issues—may put the university in the position of having to determine how to defend itself against the attacks of extremist groups. In any constitutional democracy, this problem has always been one of the most difficult. The Weimar Republic, for example, was in part destroyed because of the unwillingness of democratic groups to take "undemocratic" action against nationalistic and fascist groups. Democracies have a responsibility to preserve their institutions, and universities have a responsibility to society to preserve themselves. The procedures for the acquisition and transmission of knowledge must be sustained and respected by all elements of the university. These must be set forth clearly by responsible authorities who have the courage to respect the procedures in the face of the most trying of circumstances. Although silent in times of crisis, the majority of faculty and students rely on the administration to uphold the rules of the community. They declare their views by teaching and going to class. When the administration wavers, they are disappointed and deprived of deserved protection.

I would propose that the university community adopt, with some modification, the doctrine of "clear and present danger" first developed by Justice Holmes. In the *Schenck* case in 1919, he stated in general terms that a government has the right to protect itself against acts that seek to destroy it. By the same token, radical groups must not be allowed to use the procedures of the university—especially the traditional freedom to speak out—to destroy it. Freedom of speech is not a license to shout a speaker down. The freedom to speak must not be allowed to encroach upon the freedom of speech. As Holmes pointed out in the *Schenck* case: "The most stringent protection of free speech would not protect a man in falsely shouting fire in a theater and causing a panic. It does not even protect a

137

man from an injunction against uttering words that may have all the effect of force." Just as the courts are used as independent judges to determine whether or not a clear and present danger exists in the broader political community, so also could they be brought into university conflicts. Injunctions and other appropriate judicial writs could be sought to curb action considered by the administration to be against the basic interests of the university.

The issue of "clear and present danger" should be taken to the courts only in the most extreme cases, and there administrative authority may be tested and judged. Internally, the university must, of course, develop an independent judiciary capable of rendering fair and reasonable judgments in disciplinary matters. The judiciary must not be a captive of political groups, and it must be so structured that it is capable of making independent decisions. This is difficult because if it is composed of various groups within the university, each will have an interest in the outcome of the case. Tenure of the judiciary is a fundamental principle, but it certainly cannot exist in any university's judicial body that has student and administrative representatives. Nor would faculty, regardless of whether or not they have tenure, feel entirely free to render unbiased decisions on such a university court. Nevertheless, in this all-too-imperfect world it seems clear that university judiciaries should be representative of major university groups.

Universities must be able to deal with destructive elements in the community through internal processes constructed in such a way that their legitimacy will be recognized, if possible, by all elements of the university community. Unilateral executive action should not be final in nature, although it might be entirely appropriate to suspend anyone who seems to present a clear and present danger to the university, pending judgment by an independent board.

The universities are in crisis because the society is in crisis. Activist students perceive the crisis in sharper outlines because it will affect them longer and they have had less experience with tolerating the unthinkable and living with the human tragedy that generations have shrugged off as "the human condition." These students feel the university is theirs. They wish to change it and to govern it, but not to be governed by it. They give obeisance to its mission of structured learning through frenzied efforts for admission, but once within its gates cry out against its intellectualism in a burst of romantic escapism. Although they reject the university as a moral tutor, they seek to use it as their moral instrument.

Yet these students are the nation's hope for tomorrow just as they are the university's troubled and troubling inhabitants today. We must understand them, engage them, and preserve for their own sakes the vital elements of the university. Finally, we must listen to what the best of them are telling us: We had better attend now to the dreadful problems threatening this planet.

The university must not be so pretentious as to think it can exorcise the looming disasters of nuclear war, overpopulation, pollution, and famine. But we must do all we can, as individuals and learned men and women, to resolve those problems we can in the time we have left.

As we look outside the campus, let us not neglect the university. If the university is ever distorted or converted into something else, we should still have to face the same problems, but our intellectual resources and skills to master these—if possible—would be fewer, our morale and commitment diminished.

REFERENCES

1. An America where Richard Nixon is elected President and George Wallace is given support (and the combined Nixon-Wallace vote totals over 56 per cent of the vote), where 88 per cent of whites and 76 per cent of Negroes express satisfaction with their jobs, is not poised to move in a revolutionary direction politically. (See report of the Gallup poll in *The New York Times,* May 11, 1969, p. 25.)

2. Alfred North Whitehead, *The Aims of Education* (Macmillan Co.: New York, 1929; Mentor Edition), p. 97.

3. Recent news reports describe "a party-throwing organization trying to create an atmosphere of revelry at New York University" which speaks of itself as a "radical political organization." Its activities, however, are remarkably similar to those of the trade-offs of the past, perhaps indicating that there may be an upswing in this group. See *The New York Times,* September 22, 1969, p. 25.

4. The find-out group is to be distinguished from the large percentage in college who are goal-oriented, with definite careers in the professions and academia already in mind. Find-outs are in college for the legitimate purpose of a liberal education, which will presumably help them in the choice of a career. Frequently, of course, find-outs discover what they seek during college. At Brandeis, about 70 per cent of all undergraduates eventually go on to graduate or professional schools.

5. Norman Birnbaum, "The Arbitrary Disciplines," *Change* (July-August, 1969), p. 20.

6. The influence of the find-outs undoubtedly is indicated in a recent poll conducted by Daniel Yankelovich in April 1969, which reports 63 per cent of college students strongly or partially agree that "what is taught in universities is not relevant."

7. It is interesting to note that in the last fifteen years, despite increased enrollments, the number of pass degrees awarded by universities in England and Wales has remained substantially the same, while the number of students receiving honors degrees has increased dramatically. In England, for instance, in 1953-54, the number of men and women receiving honors degrees was 8,676; in 1965-66, this figure rose to 20,019.

8. This has been well documented in a recent report issued by the Center for Research and Development in Higher Education at the University of California, Berkeley. See *The New York Times*, "News of the Week in Review," August 17, 1969, p. 9.

9. Birnbaum, "The Arbitrary Disciplines," p. 21.

10. Whitehead, *The Aims of Education*, p. 103.

11. *Report of the Committee on Recruitment and Retention of Faculty*, Harvard College (May 1, 1969), p. 65.

12. Talcott Parsons, "The Academic System: A Sociologist's View," *The Public Interest*, No. 13 (Fall, 1968), p. 195.

13. The increasing role of the federal government in education and in the expanding research programs deeply involves it in the determination of many of the research activities of the university. Some extremists, both of the left and the right, feel that there should be no connection between government and the university because the former corrupts the latter. A more reasonable view surely is that government agencies rightly exist and thus are entitled to fund research. Any attempts by government or anyone else to control the expression of ideas (including suppression of knowledge) and the content of courses must, of course, be firmly resisted. Students, faculties, and administrators should as citizens work within the political processes for increasing emphasis upon the funding priorities as they perceive them. As for financial aid, universities should be free to decide for themselves about it, always relating their decisions to the real purposes of a university.

14. Paradoxically, radical students, who may be the first to raise the banner of academic freedom at the stroke of an administrative pen, sometimes demand that professors be retained or promoted because of views associated with their own. There is the famous Daniel case at the University of Chicago.

RALPH A. DUNGAN

Higher Education: The Effort to Adjust

A COLLEAGUE of mine recently returned from a working visit to a number of European universities observed: "If you think we are having troubles, you should see them." Hard-pressed as he has been at his own institution, the solace that he found in the plight of others is understandable. At the same time, the reality of what he saw underscores two contemporary phenomena.

The first is the obvious world-wide dissatisfaction either with the character of higher education or with the role of the university in society, or both. The second is the confusion and contradiction among those most concerned within the higher education community about the central questions that need to be faced.

It seems important to recognize that the university is caught like other institutions in the maelstrom of rapid social change. This recognition should lead to an understanding that to some extent the pressures on the university are external and relatively uncontrollable. In the United States, because of its role as socializer, credentialer, producer of technicians, scholars, politicians, and soldiers, the university stands in a pre-eminent position among contemporary institutions. Because of the image it has projected and which often has been forced upon it, the university has become the church of a modern secular and technocratic society. It has been touted as the solver of all problems, the reservoir of all ideas, and to a large extent it has accepted these various roles. In fact, it often has assiduously and aggressively sought them.

It is no wonder in these circumstances that the university becomes a focus of social and political criticism, the object of attack by all who are dissatisfied with society as it is. This situation is not likely to change and probably should not, and universities are going to have to recognize that they are on the political stage, actively in-

RALPH A. DUNGAN

volved in the political drama with its unpleasant as well as its rewarding aspects. This has been true for some time, but, generally speaking, the reality has not been reflected either in the structure of the institution or in its mode of operation. For example, universities, unlike most other institutions, seem torn and indecisive when confronted with the basic issues of protection of life and property. Admittedly, universities have often had good reason to hesitate in such matters; the point is that there is a built-in reluctance to view such disruptions as at least partly political phenomena that need to be dealt with in political ways.

Colleges and universities were never intended merely to reflect the society in which they exist. Because the academic environment is properly among those most tolerant of ideas and behavior uncommon to society-at-large, it is not surprising that a good deal of the social protest has been concentrated on the campus. Nor is it surprising that outraged legislators (and some educators) are devoting a corresponding amount of energy to suppressing social protests on campus and elsewhere. No doubt ill-conceived legislation will be enacted in order to curb "the excesses of the disruptive minority." This sequence of events fits a pattern which has occurred over the past forty years.

But however great the similarities with the past, there are today at least two elements both new and significant. The first has to do with the confusion, conflict, and contention within the higher education community itself as to what the current discontent is all about and what should be done about it. The academic community has been rocked into asking itself the root (and therefore radical) questions: Education for whom and for what? At what cost and out of whose pocket? Who shall set the standards, and what do they or should they mean anyway? And, by the way, to whom does the college or university belong, and who should govern it?

The other major factor not present before is a kind of headlong, practically unplanned dash into universal higher educational opportunity. This kind of growth poses great problems for educators who must create new institutions and shape existing ones in response to the pressure of aspirations and numbers. The scale of resources required to support such growth will be enormous and will impose responsibilities heavier than ever before on those who must weigh the wisdom of such expenditures.

Obviously there are no definitive answers to the many questions —moral as well as educational, social, and political—that presently

142

occupy the minds of educators and their clients. Indeed, the identification of the most important problems is an awesome task in itself. To select one factor, such as governmental structure, and to place undue stress on it as a response to the unrest is to create a simplistic picture of an extremely complex question.

Role and Function of Higher Education

The most fundamental issue to be addressed is the role of the university. It is not uncommon today for many within the university to confess to not being sure what a university is or should be —the extent to which it should be devoted to the accumulation and transfer of knowledge or the degree to which it should be involved in providing services to the larger society. Historically, the university has had as one of its functions the integrative role of nurturing the values of society and transmitting them to succeeding generations. But in recent years the university has become part of the adaptive system of society and has assumed a more active role in determining the course that society will follow. The question now is whether the university can or should do both. And if it tries to do both, can the various clients be equally well served by the same type of institution? They probably cannot because the demands of some clients will conflict with those of others. One does not need to delineate the elitist tendencies of some institutions in order to spot the potential conflict between the demands of those who seek certain credentials or vocational training and those who desire specialized and advanced work.

This conflict between client expectation and institutional performance is widespread and will increase, traditional myths about higher education in this country notwithstanding. The university in the United States has long been described as multi-functional, but a candid examination of the distribution of resources within institutions and within the collectivity of institutions would show that there is a concentration in activities of interest to relatively few. Despite our protestations about pluralism and multi-functionality, we tend on the whole in higher education to do essentially the same thing with quite divergent degrees of quality. In general, we have not adapted either institutional structure or curriculum to the large and increasing varieties of needs of the individual or the society.

Although the argument is persuasive for a greater differentiation among programs or for a greater number of options for students in different kinds of institutions, it is a good deal more difficult to suggest exactly how such curricula or programs would look. But it is possible to set forth for the sake of discussion some functional objectives of a restructured or non-structured educational environment.

Certain objectives or elements of the higher educational experience should be common to any option or curriculum. Of these, the most important would seem to be cultivation in the student, the institution, and the society of a respect for learning; an appreciation and knowledge of the contemporary social and political environment; a facility in communication; and an appreciation of non-material values—religious and artistic.

If it is accepted that certain educational objectives, such as those noted above, should be common to any higher education program, the task remains to define the variety of vocational objectives or levels of preparation that are appropriate. Obviously there is no set list. The thesis here is simply that there should be greater variety and that not every student who pursues higher education should have as an objective the present baccalaureate degree or even the associate in arts or science.

In working toward this objective, we should start searching out the needs of potential clients and servicing those needs in a variety of institutions that are related to one another more systematically than at present. This approach offers at least two advantages: First, it would tend to decrease tension within institutions, especially the larger ones, which try under various pressures to be all things to all men; second, it would enable individual institutions to accomplish one goal well rather than many poorly.

What functions, other than those noted above, need to be performed by higher education today? Can they fit into the existing structure, or do significant changes need to be made? And, most important, who (how many) are to be educated for what? We assume that the vast majority of the relevant age cohort in the years ahead will be seeking some form of education beyond the secondary school. The goal of a majority of these students will probably be acquisition of skills or credentials that promise to lead to gainful employment and participation in a series of social and educational experiences that enhance their growth as individuals. A minority of students in formal higher education will seek more sophisticated intellectual objectives, and some will turn to professional training of one sort or another.

(Of course, the whole process is not so simple: A statement *about* goals does not tell us *how* goals are formed in the mind of the individual. For many, such a neat definition of goals does not occur at one point in time—it just happens; and institutions by their expressed sensitivity to the desires and needs of their students can help ease the difficulties that accompany the process.)

A large proportion of students should, within the stated goals, be able to fulfill their formal higher education within two years in a community college in certificate (less than two full years) or associate degree programs. Such programs can be designed to satisfy individual intellectual needs as well as to provide necessary skill training. For some, the two-year college experience will lead to the baccalaureate degree or more advanced training. Still others, more sure of their objectives, will begin pursuit of the baccalaureate education in a four-year college or university—at least as most universities are now organized. The most serious question of structure as it will be related to function in the years ahead involves the university as it has come to be. Although one would hesitate to prescribe uniformity, an argument could be made for confining the work of the university to upper-division undergraduate, graduate, and professional training.

Where an attempt has been made to devise structures related to function—for instance, in some of the community colleges—the value system of those who dominate educational policy and other forces external to the college (for example, transfer policies) have tended to pull the institution back into a conforming position. This is particularly true with respect to curriculum content and mode of instruction.

This raises the question of how best to develop institutions for higher education which, although functioning parts in a coordinated system, nevertheless retain a separate integrity of function and purpose. More concretely, the difficulty here is to guard against the possibility of institutions with more limited intellectual goals becoming inferior carbon copies of those with the highest intellectual aspirations. The most difficult task in the creation of such a system, of course, is to avoid attaching the label of inferior to institutions whose goals are different.

One thing more should be said of the functions of the modern university. Increasingly, the research function has become entwined with the adaptive function so that, especially in the physical sciences, the application of knowledge to technological problems

145

has become the dominant institutional orientation. The inseparability of theoretical and applied knowledge cannot be denied; in the social sciences, one would sometimes wish they were more closely allied. But concern with technology and applications has had a mixed, if not adverse, effect on the instructional function broadly conceived. To the extent that "teaching versus research" adequately described the tension problem in the university heretofore, increased concern with applied research has simply intensified the difficulty.

This suggests the need for new organizational forms separate from, but closely related to the university—what in other systems have been called research or technical institutes. Not only would such institutes or laboratories relieve certain strains now occasioned by direct linkages; they might also provide more responsive and organized vehicles for the application of knowledge to fields presently without a sound cognitive base. One thinks immediately of the major social problems with which we are faced. It may very well be that the state of the art in applied research is not sufficiently developed in certain fields to make a different mode of organizing effort attractive or useful. But surely effort at experimentation in this area is necessary, if only as a first step toward an alternative to the present trickle-down method of unfocused and basically irresponsible consultancies.

We are moving in the direction of a national system of higher education, a movement that is likely to be accelerated as public funds come to be an even more important part of the resources available to higher education. While not axiomatic, it is fairly certain that the various elements in a system are best assured the freedom to maneuver and change when the goals and functions of each are clearly defined. Regardless of how functions are cut or to which institution they are assigned, it is crucial that a greater differentiation of function be introduced into higher education and that individual institutions within a framework decide what they are going to do and then proceed to do it well.

Curricula and the Mode of Higher Education

Of equal importance and directly related to the definition of function in contemporary higher education is a critical examination of the way the education process is currently conducted. To a great extent, it appears that curricula and modes of instruction are inordinately influenced by the traditional regimes of graduate instruction. These may or may not be adapted to the particular educational function being performed and, at times, do not even reflect an understanding of the manner in which learning occurs. One wonders, for example, what the objective of a modern language sequence at the undergraduate level should be. For a few students, a detailed knowledge of the syntax and literature of the language undoubtedly is desirable because they will either become a specialist in the language itself or use it as a research tool. But for the vast majority, if it has purpose at all, it is as a mode of communication. A reasonable level of skill in speaking and reading is essential, but this is not reflected in most undergraduate curricula today.

The situation is similar in the sciences. The tendency is to stipulate a "lab science" as a requirement for an undergraduate degree whether or not anything is learned either about science generally or about the particular field. For the student, such a course often becomes a "credit hurdle" and not even an intellectual one; and for the professor, a burdensome and boring chore to be avoided if at all possible.

To argue for curriculum reform is not to advocate an unconditional surrender of standards or a facile reliance on warmed-over high school material. More serious attention must be given to presenting material and guiding study so that substantial and meaningful educational experience occurs.

While reference here has been made to undergraduate education, where the need is most apparent, there is no doubt that reform is in order at *every* level, including graduate and professional training. Here, too, curriculum reform should be evaluated in relation to the function being performed by the institution in question and to the contribution made by a particular academic regime to the professional growth of the individual.

Credential Madness

Probably the most serious barrier to a rationalization of the higher education structure as we know it in the United States today is the extent to which credentials—degrees, certificates, credits—have come to be accepted as a measure of intellectual or skill attainment. There is no doubt that any large and complex society will always require commonly accepted and meaningful measures of attainment. The difficulty now posed is the vested interest that present certificate holders have in retaining traditional requirements, whether or not they are relevant to contemporary needs.

This self-interest, no matter how understandable, carries high costs. In the short run, the student is frequently short-changed; in the long run, institutions of higher education find themselves unable even to ask, let alone act upon, questions concerning the most pressing needs of the potential clients of higher education and the adjustments that must be made to meet these needs.

The brunt of our concern should be placed on the "madness" of the present system, rather than on the existence of the "credentials." If credentials placed the professional stamp of approval on qualities that were important to the higher educational process, we would be delighted with them. The problem with credentials, in other words, is not that they exist, but that they are irrelevant in too many cases.

The present madness takes two forms, the first of which is the absence on our campuses of men who teach well. This can be due to any of several causes: pressures to obtain the next certificate, which make it impossible for aspiring faculty to spend adequate time either with students or preparing for classes; a general de-emphasis on teaching which convinces younger faculty that this is not an important goal; the screening out of those who have demonstrated a high capacity for teaching, but who do not measure up because such talents are not considered significant; and the willingness of those in power to overlook bad teaching when it appears.

The second form is the persistence of courses that do not speak to the needs and interests of students. Many courses have over the years simply grown irrelevant—if, indeed, they were ever worth offering in the first place. And yet for every course that should be stricken from the catalogue, there are many faculty members who see such a change as a threat to their livelihood and status.

Some professional groups have been notable in their efforts to modify or differentiate the kinds of preparation needed to perform certain tasks within the profession. For instance, among mathematicians there is a school which holds that not every teacher of mathematics in college need be prepared in the same manner or complete the traditional requirements for the Ph.D. in order to do a superior job as a math teacher. But for every profession that takes such an enlightened and rational view, there are ten that move in the opposite direction. Last year when the deans of graduate schools in the United States agreed upon the need for another professional degree different in its requirements from the Ph.D. for candidates who intended to pursue a career principally devoted to teaching, they also rapidly concluded that the strongest opposition to such an innovation would be encountered in their faculties.

Those within the higher education system are not the only ones perpetuating the credential mania. On the consumer side of the equation, one finds that employers of all kinds have taken the easy route and use the certificate or degree as a preliminary screening device. Although most sophisticated managers admit that a certificate establishes little in terms of adequate performance, they have contributed greatly to the present irrational scramble for what turns out to be the key to economic and social position.

This is indeed a problem, but perhaps the employer's role is less significant than it might seem. The employer has, out of convenience or the absence of a more valid screening method, taken his cue from the credentialers. If the latter were to start offering a range of credentials that made more sense, the former might be forced to respond accordingly. The employer will always seek those who appear to be the best candidates. But his reliance on irrelevant paper credentials would fade if other credentials were made more relevant.

People, Rewards, Tenure

This and other problems will endure until some change is effected in the attitudes and values of those who make the system work—the faculties. Little differentiation of function and no significant change in curricula can occur without at least tacit faculty support. And critical to an examination of their susceptibility to change are rewards and tenure.

It cannot be doubted that faculty members as individuals want what is best for higher education, but neither can it be denied that little within the system suggests much pressure for change. In most disciplines, higher education in recent years has been a seller's market. Faculty salaries have risen, although not uniformly at all institutions. Federal research funds have provided additional inputs, and reductions have been made in teaching hours. Improved economic conditions in the profession caused one university president to observe recently that if faculty salaries "continue to rise, we will be increasingly subsidizing a strange kind of leisure class." He went on to observe that he was not sure that this was to the social

149

good at all. Whether or not his observation has merit, it does raise the question of what would induce anyone to change the present rules of the game.

The academic profession is no different from any other in the need of its members to be well rewarded for the vital functions they perform. It also requires a system of tenure that gives its members job security as well as protection against ill-informed or unwise attacks on the freedom to teach and investigate. The question is how, within these essential borders, the system can be made to work so that it truly rewards quality and insures dynamic growth within the profession.

The difficulty of adapting the present mechanism of promotion and tenure to anything resembling an adequate system is great indeed and is made more complicated by the increasing bureaucratization of all elements of university life. Present procedures probably worked moderately well when the numbers involved were small enough to permit truly humane and personal evaluations, and when institutional and professional loyalties were important factors in the process. But this is not generally the case at the present time. Even in relatively small institutions where the number of faculty members is not so large as to preclude careful individual judgment, the feelings of institutional and professional loyalty seem increasingly to run less deep. And they will probably dry up altogether as the apparently inevitable trend toward unionization of faculties gains momentum.

What kinds of solutions can one devise to these problems? The major elements of a modified system are easy to sketch and terribly hard to sell. Most would agree on the need to develop a range of minimum salaries appropriate to various faculty ranks. There is no compelling reason why we need preserve the existing pattern of academic ranks, however, and one can bring forward good arguments for increasing by several the number within such a structure. This having been done, appointments and promotions could be made much as they are now with perhaps more emphasis placed on faculty-wide responsibility in decision-making and less on departmental and administrative judgment.

The important element suggested here is to append a flexible compensation mechanism to a basic or minimum scale, thereby permitting competitive forces to operate more effectively. Such a discretionary system of compensation would permit what is impossible in many institutions today—a discriminating judgment about the actual performance of individuals. The process of deciding when and to what degree to employ the discretionary power of rewards would involve faculty and senior academic administrators, but theirs should not be the final power of decision. The necessity to pinpoint responsibility and accountability is increasingly apparent in the modern university. In no area is such accountability more important than in the selection and rewarding of principal faculty members.

Closely related to the compensation system is the tenure or employment security arrangement. There is no doubt that academic tenure still plays an important role in insuring basic academic freedom. But by the same token it has—without any reference to academic freedom—assumed an equally or more important function as a guarantee of job security. It is this latter aspect of tenure that deserves re-examination. We need to devise alternatives to the existing tenure system that will continue to protect academic freedom and introduce more competition, thereby insuring continued vitality and productivity in the system.

One alternative might be a contractural arrangement granting tenure for a set period of years—say, ten—renewable at the option of the institution. In order to protect a professor who had given his best years to the institution, lifetime tenure would attach to the second contract. Under the present system the advantages all go one way, and the institution is powerless to protect itself or its non-faculty constituents.

Unless the present system of compensation and tenure is altered, pressures will continue to convert all colleges into universities, for it is research that is rewarded regardless of its quality or relevance. Similarly, the pressures within the present system—reinforced by bureaucratization, numbers, and trade union egalitarianism—will eventually price the academic out of the market or reduce the bulk of the profession to a relatively low level of uniformity. And of overriding importance is the threat that the present rigid system poses to real innovation in curriculum and modes of instruction and to the continued existence of the university as a dynamic institution.

How realistic is it to suppose that the university has within itself the capacity to examine itself systematically and rigorously and to make, in a timely manner, those adaptations that are reasonable and necessary? Posing this question does not presume that the university should be a great weather vane oscillating at the whim of one or another of its constituencies. But in order to survive in this period of change, the university will clearly have to make reasonably rapid responses to urgently needed reforms.

Faculties have been described as a collection of individual entrepreneurs who enjoy complete market control. While it pains one to extend the economic market analogy too far into the world of the intellectual, there is no reason to believe that academicians or intellectuals are any more or less selfish, conservative, or cantankerous than other human beings. It is difficult, in these circumstances, to imagine that faculties unperturbed by any force other than their own perceptions are likely to push for a radical change in the *status quo*.

Administrators, particularly those who view themselves or actually behave as agents of the faculty, find themselves in a weak position to exert leadership in situations requiring radical change, especially in a period of expanding faculty power. Students by and large are not and probably will not be strategically located in the decision-making structure of universities. Moreover, students as a group do not share so common a point of view on reform issues as is usually assumed, and their transitory status tends to militate against the development of a sustained and consistent effort.

While the foregoing is a vastly simplified picture of the major components of the university community, the fact that major reforms in education have occurred in the past predominantly as a result of external stimuli suggests that there is only limited capacity for internally generated reform and that such actions as are taken come at an agonizingly slow pace.

In the effort to focus attention on a few key issues that need to be addressed before progress can be made on subordinate questions, this essay has left a good deal unsaid about many important problems facing the university today. For instance, it should be a matter of great concern to all whether, apart from problems of curriculum already mentioned, the traditional modes of instruction facilitate or obstruct the transfer of knowledge. Obviously, no single answer exists, but it is clear that there should be more experimentation with directed self-study, off-campus instruction, interrupted instructional cycles, and the like.

We need also to be more forthright in saying that the university dedicated primarily to high-level academic pursuits is not, as such, the appropriate institution to make up for the frequently appalling deficiencies of the elementary and secondary public school system. But at the same time higher education as a whole has a most pressing responsibility to assist those who have been denied an opportunity to attain their full potential. If this means a shifting of resources and a slackening in other activities, or the creation of other institutional arrangements, so be it.

Institutional structures and mechanisms, informal as well as formal, must be adapted to the social functions to be performed. The undergraduate college and the research-oriented, graduate-training institute both perform distinct and honorable functions. Both deserve the best support we can give them. But it is clear that there are more functions to be performed in higher education than these and other institutions presently acknowledge, and that norms in certain key areas—compensation, job security, credentials, and curricula—should not be the same in each. We jeopardize the health of all educational institutions if we do not make the effort to match their functions, with adjusted modes of operation, to the most urgent social and educational needs.

ERIK H. ERIKSON

Reflections on the Dissent of Contemporary Youth

I

It is not without diffidence that one undertakes to write yet one more essay on youth. The literature on contemporary "unrest" is growing by the week, the day, the hour. Much of it reflects a profound unrest among adults—a traumatized state, in fact, that seeks catharsis in hurried attempts to reassert intellectual mastery over a shocking course of events. The conclusions reached, therefore, tend to become outdated during the very period of publication. At this point, then, only the double promise of some systematic clarification of the divergent phenomena of dissent and of some gain for the theory of development justifies writing about dissent at all. My reflections will concentrate on what we have learned about the place and function of youth in the human life cycle in all its historical relativity, and about the fateful role of childhood in historical change.

In writing for a professional audience, one can take the assumption for granted that there is, there must be, a pervasive irrational involvement in any attempt on the part of adults to reorient themselves in the face of youthful challenges; for youth, almost by definition, has a presence that defies theorizing. One may also assume agreement that a historical self-critique of psychoanalysis as well as other schemata of human development must include an assessment of the role that their discoveries are playing in the ideological tensions of our time. If rebellious youth in the second part of this fast-moving century must manage and transcend the revolutionary changes of the first part, the influence of Freud's insights into unconscious motivation are now part of that burden. True, some young people can accept the new depth only by displaying it, sometimes passionately and often mockingly, on the very surface, or by challenging it precipitously with experiences induced by drugs, as if the new generation had already faced up to all the inner dangers as well as the outer ones. But if in this stance—as also in that of much of modern literature and drama—we detect an attempt to assimilate the insights of psychoanalysis by means of overt enactment of previously repressed urges, then psychoanalysis is faced with new Hippocratic tasks.

One such task is defined by the fact that today we can no longer, not even in clinical literature, write *about* youth without writing *for* youth. And while a systematic critique of contemporary and controversial behavior is always beset with grave methodological problems, I do not see how we can take either our students or our field seriously without stating what *prophecy* and what *retrogression* we are able to discern with our methods in today's patterns of dissent. By this I mean that youthful behavior, where it arouses ambivalent fascination, always appears to be both prophetic—that is, inspired by the vigor of a new age—and retrogressive insofar as it seems to insist on outworn simplicities and to display astonishing regressions. I am speaking, then, of the emotional charge of certain patterns of dissent, not of their political utility or detriment. The young reader of a discourse concerned with such alternations, however, will always find himself responding to open or hidden indications as to whether the author seems to be for or against what he attempts to clarify; and if the methodology of the discourse is based on the application of clinical observation, every reference to developmental fixation or retrogression is apt to be understood as a suggestion of weakness, wickedness, or morbid pretense, and thus as an expression of a generational or political prejudice on the part of the author. These difficulties, however, cannot be shunned if and when we concern ourselves with contemporary phenomena, convinced as we are that psychoanalytic insight has a role to fulfill in the critique of the wasteful aspects of cultural and historical change, which mankind as a whole can ill afford. It would seem, in fact, that a few of the leading young revolutionaries of today are aware of some emotional regressiveness in radical undertakings which are already marked by historical retrogression.

In attempting to clarify the emotional roots of youthful dissent, we must concede from the onset that even psychoanalysis—like other once-revolutionary movements—has let itself be drawn into modern attempts to neutralize powerful inner and outer forces by making man more superficially and more mechanically adjustable.

Some of the more prophetic concerns of today's youth may, in fact, serve to renew—or, at any rate, to remind us of a liberating vision inherent in the beginnings of psychoanalysis.

II

Before selecting some circumscribed phenomena of active dissent for psychoanalytic scrutiny, I, too, must present a few speculations on the changing ecology of youth in the present stage of history. To the older generation, of course, historical and technological change always seems to be a matter of degree until many related differences have come to amount to a frightening change in over-all quality.

Adolescence has always been seen as an interim stage between an alternately invigorating and confusing sense of an overdefined past that must be left behind and a future as yet to be identified—and to be identified with. Even in a period of rapid change, adolescence seems to serve the function of committing the growing person to the possible achievements and the comprehensible ideals of an existing or developing civilization. In our time, the new requirements of disciplined teamwork and programmed rationality in organizations living in inescapable symbiosis with technological systems seem to offer a satisfying and self-corrective world-image to many, if not most. Most young people, then, see no reason to question "the system" seriously, if only because they have never visualized another.

In every individual, however, and in every generation, there is a potential for what we may call an intensified *adolescence*—that is, a critical phase marked by the reciprocal aggravation of internal conflict and of societal disorganization. Psychoanalysis, for obvious reasons, has primarily studied those more malignant kinds of aggravation that are the result of unresolved infantile conflict and of adolescent isolation. Yet, from Freud's patient Dora on, the case histories of neurotically aggravated young people have also demonstrated a relationship between the epidemiology of a given time and the hidden conflicts of the generations—and thus to history itself. If, on the other hand, another sector of aggravated youth becomes militantly agitated and sets out to agitate on a large scale, it often succeeds way beyond its numerical strength or political foresight because it draws out and inflames the latent aggravations of that majority of young people who would otherwise choose only

banal and transient ways of voicing dissent or displaying conflict—
and about whom, therefore, psychoanalysis knows so very little.
From this point of view, our patients often appear to be the inverted
dissenters—too sick for the modish malaise of their time, too
isolated for joint dissent, and yet too sensitive for simple adjustment.

What, then, are the quantitative changes that seem to change
the quality of adolescence in our time? It is said that there are
simply more young people around than ever before; that they now
generally mature earlier; and that more of them are better informed about world conditions—and informed both by a common
literacy and the common imagery of mass communication—than
ever before. But while these shared vocabularies and imageries
convey simplified ideals of identity, personality, and competence,
such promise becomes forever illusory because of the daily vagaries
of technological, legal, and bureaucratic complexities—themselves a
result of a variety of quantitative changes. Often, therefore, only to be
intensely "with it" and with one another provides a sense of individuality and communality in otherwise paralyzing discontinuities. This,
it seems, is expressed vividly and often devastatingly in songs of
shouted loneliness underscored by a pounding rhythm-to-end-all-
rhythms in a sea of circling colors and lights. Such active and joint
mastery of a cacophonous world can be experienced with an emotional and physical abandon unlike anything the older generations
ever dreamed of; and yet—especially where compounded by drugs—
it can also camouflage a reciprocal isolation of desperate depth.

III

But perhaps an observer learns most as he becomes aware of
what social change is doing with (and to) his own conceptualiza-
tions of youth. We have, for example, postulated within the stage
of youth a psychological moratorium—a period when the young
person can dramatize or at any rate experiment with patterns of
behavior which are both—or neither quite—infantile and adult,
and yet often find a grandiose alignment with traditional ideals or
new ideological trends. A true moratorium, of course, provides
leeway for timeless values; it takes the pressure out of time—but it
must end. If in the past young people (and creative adults) have
often mourned the end of the moratorium as an irrevocable loss of
potential identities, today young leaders, transient as they are, declare the world beyond youth to be totally void and faceless. But

a moratorium without end also disposes of all utopias—except that of an infinite moratorium. The large-scale utopias that were to initiate a new kind of history in the postwar period—the war that would end all wars, the socialism that would make the state wither away, the thousand-year Reich, or the advent of militant nonviolence— they have all been followed by holocausts as coldly planned as were the gas chambers and Hiroshima, or as shockingly planless as mass riots; and they have been superseded by bureaucratic-industrial systems of negligible ideological differentiation. Thus also ended the unquestioned superiority of the fathers whether they had obeyed and died, or survived and thrived. If then, as it always must, rebellious youth borrows roles from past revolutions, it must now avoid the temptation to settle for any previous consolidations. The mere thought of what form the world might take after the next revolution seems in itself counter-revolutionary.

A moratorium without some kind of utopian design, however, can lead only to an ideological promiscuity that both adopts and disposes of the old revolutions. There is, of course, the Marxist model. Some of today's activists like to resemble Marxist revolutionaries in appearance and in vocabulary, but cannot possibly share either their erstwhile hopes or, indeed, their intellectual discipline and political skill. They need a proletariat to liberate, but few groups of workers today could be led for long by intellectual youths with no blueprint. Thus, youth must appoint *itself* a kind of proletariat—and "the people" often comes to mean primarily young people.

Another model is the Gandhian one, anticolonial and nonviolent. There is hardly an item in the arsenal of modern protest—from card-burning to mass marching—that Gandhi did not invent as part of the revolutionary method of militant nonviolence. Originally a revolt of those who happened to be unarmed, it came through him to mean above all the method of those who *chose* to remain unarmed. Yet today's youth (except for such devotional groups as the civil rights marchers and the draft-resisting dissenters in America) has lacked the continuity that could elevate nonviolent protest to the level of national campaigns. Nor is there much likelihood that the remaining victims of colonialism care to count on the youth of affluent countries. Therefore, youth has appointed itself also the corporate victim of colonialism; and the mere dependence on an older generation comes to symbolize a despised colonial heritage.

Gandhi was by no means unaware of the cathartic function of violence; the psychiatrist Frantz Fanon was its spokesman. By emphasizing the therapeutic necessity of revolutionary violence, he forms an ideological link between anti-colonialism and the "Freudian revolution," which has counterpointed the methods of political liberation with a systematic exploration of man's psychological bondage. Some of our young people, combining emotional license with alternately violent and nonviolent confrontation and with both intellectual and anti-intellectual protest, attempt to combine the gains of all revolutions in one improvised moratorium and often succeed only in endangering and even mocking them all.

Out of the combined revolutions of the oppressed and the repressed, of the proletarians, the unarmed, and the mental sufferers, there seems to have now emerged a *revolt of the dependent.* That to be dependent means to be exploited is the ideological link between the developmental stage of youth, the economic state of the poor, and the political state of the underdeveloped. This, at least, could partially explain the astounding similarity of the logic used in the patterns of confrontation both by privileged youth and by the underprivileged citizenry. And has youth not learned from psychoanalysis to look at man's prolonged childhood dependence as an evolutionary fact artificially protracted by adults in order to subvert the radiance of children and the vigor of youth and to confirm the molds of adult self-images?

The revolt of the dependent, however, directly challenges all those existing institutions that monopolize the admissions procedures to the main body of society. These confirmations, graduations, and inductions have always attempted to tie youthful prophecy to existing world images, offering a variety of rites characterized by special states of ceremonious self-diffusion. All this, too, dissenting youth now seeks to provide for itself in newly improvised and ritualized self-graduations, from musical happenings to communal experiment and to political revolt.

I have now indicated a few aspects of the revolutionary inheritance which past generations and especially the charismatic leaders of the postwar period have bequeathed to youth. In the meantime, however, industrialization has changed all basic premises; and the majority of young people remain engaged in the invention and perfection of techniques that by their immense practicality could assure safety, rationality, and abundance, even as the exploration of space promises a new type of heroic adventure and limitless celestial leeway. But even technological youth respond at times to the prophetic quality of the two questions aggravated youth seems to ask: When if not now, in this post-ideological period in history and before cosmic technocracy takes over altogether, will man attempt to combine his timeless values, his new insights, and his coming mastery in one all-human outlook and planning? And who if not they, the young people assembled in the prolonged moratorium of academic life, will live and rebel for the sake of that outlook?

IV

Freud at one time stressed that society must of necessity act as a suppressor of individuality, genitality, and intellect, and that far from wishing to overcome human violence as such, societies merely insist on the right to control the means and to stipulate the targets of violence. Freud stood for the primacy of insight, but he took state and civilization for granted; he faced the specter of totalitarian societies only toward the end of his life. Since then, psychoanalysis has found a mutual accommodation with societal systems that can claim to offer a maximum of opportunity to the greatest number of their citizens and that promote, together with the comforts of expanding technology, the pursuit of learning and of health—even of mental health. Psychoanalytic ego psychology, in turn, has come to study those adaptive social processes that must protect and support ego development in childhood and give strength and direction to adolescent identity. But while the complementarity of individual and societal processes has been acknowledged and studied, questions in regard to the potential arbitrariness of all systems of power have remained. This questioning has, in fact, been vastly intensified in recent years with the increasing awareness of the use (or misuse) to which large-scale organization puts individual inventiveness and valor. Even the most affluent and progressive systems seem to thrive at the expense of individual values: Their costliness may become apparent in the restriction of spontaneity in the midst of a system extolling individual freedom; in the standardization of information in the midst of a universal communications industry; and, worse, in new and numbing denials in the midst of universal enlightenment.

Modern youth has grown up with the fact that an affluent civilization can learn to become relatively peaceful and neighborly in large areas of its existence and yet delegate the greatest destructive power that ever existed to nuclear monsters scientifically created and loyally serviced by well-adjusted experts and technicians. Not that most young people any more than most adults can keep this paradox in the center of attention for any length of time; but was it not, again, psychoanalysis which taught that man is responsible for what he represses or attempts to remain unaware of? Yet much as we have learned about the consequences of sexual repression, we do not yet possess systematic terms and concepts adequate to deal with the split in human awareness that makes the coexistence of consumer affluence and of minutely planned "overkill" possible, nor with the emotional price exacted for this split.

And yet we must realize that the specter of nuclear war changes the whole ecology of what we have come to view as the over-all instinctual economy of man. As long as wars can (or could) provide ideologically convincing reasons for the massive deflection of hate on external enemies, much interpersonal and intergenerational conflict could live itself out in periodic states of war. As communication makes the enemy appear human, and as technological developments make war absurd, unrelieved self-hate as well as the hateful tension in families and communities may well cause new and bewildering forms of violence.

No wonder, then, that the *legitimacy of violence* becomes the greatest single issue in the ideological struggle of youth today. It can come to sharpest awareness in those young men who must be prepared to see themselves or their friends inducted into a "service" that legitimizes what appears to be the senseless continuation of colonial wars. Most of them decide to fulfill traditional expectations of duty and heroism. Some object conscientiously, and—if they must also conscientiously admit that they do not believe in the prescribed kind of God—must face jail under conditions that negate even a traditional sense of martyrdom. A few turn furiously against the system; but if they seem totally committed to a negative utopia in which the existing world must come to an end before anything can live, one should remember that they have grown up in a setting in which adult happiness-as-usual did not exclude the minute-by-minute potential of a nuclear holocaust—and an end of mankind as we know it.

V

If I should now attempt to throw some methodological light on the range of reactions which youth exhibits in the face of the conditions just sketched, I must begin by clarifying some terms which I have used over the years. Instead of using *identity diffusion* (or ego diffusion) and *confusion* alternately, I would now wish to take account of the fact that the adolescent ego *needs* a certain diffusion. I would, therefore, use this term for experiences in which some boundaries of the self are expanded to include a wider identity, with compensatory gains in emotional tonus, cognitive certainty, and ideological conviction—all of this occurs in states of love, sexual union, and friendship, of discipleship and followership, and of creative inspiration. Such states can, of course, occur within culturally sanctioned affiliations or in self-affirming groups usurping a place on the fringe of society. The question is always whether the cumulative state of diffused selfhood adds up to a potent new vision or to a retrogressive delusion of acting meaningfully. *Identity confusion* would then characterize those states in which there is an impoverishment and a dissipation of emotional, cognitive, and moral gains in a transitory mob state or in renewed isolation—or both.

The difficulty of classifying such states and, above all, of assigning them to given classes of individuals with particular personalities or similar backgrounds is, of course, compounded where the same young individuals and the same groups seem to demonstrate an alternation of prophetic and retrogressive states, being at one time heroically committed and at another cynically disengaged, at one time devastatingly logical and at another quite deliberately irrational, at one time planfully affirmative and at another quite carelessly destructive. The defensive aspects of such alternation are inherent in the mechanisms described by Anna Freud in her classic characterization of puberty. But one could probably take up these mechanisms, one by one, and make explicit the complementary nature of the inner needs of the adolescent individual and the inducements offered not only by spontaneous group formations, but also by ideological movements. The cognitive facts established by Piaget make it plausible enough that youth *thinks* ideologically—that is, with a combination of an egocentric, narcissistic orientation determined to adapt the world to itself and a devotion to idealistic and altruistic schemes and codes, whether or not their feasibility can be proved or disproved with adult logic. Correspondingly, in ideological world images (and I am, of course, not speaking only of the totalitarian kind) such logic is rendered superfluous; the "self-evident" truth of simplistically overdefined

alternatives and the omnipotence promised in a radical course of action permit the young to invest their loyalty and to offer their very lives. At decisive moments in history and in the hands of leaders of genius, such prophecy, up to a point, fulfills itself; but in the long intervals of minimized revolutionary potential, youth is led into beliefs and actions in which the borderlines between prank and delinquency, adventure and political drama, are often hard to draw— even as it is often difficult to discern where in the personalities of ideological leaders, hysterics and histrionics blend with true charisma.

All this is well known; but there is much to learn about the developmental position of youthful enactments midway between the play of children and the ritualized aspects of adult society. Infantile play, among other accomplishments, re-enacts experiences and anticipations of a traumatic character in the microcosm of the toyworld, and the promises of its make-believe provide a necessary balance against the combined pressure of an immature conscience, a vague drivenness, and a bewildering social reality. The need for such a balance is multiplied in adolescence when the grown-up body, the matured genital equipment, and a perceptive mentality permit actions on the borderline of mere playfulness and utterly serious reality, of passing prank and irreversible deed, of daring pretense and final commitment. In negotiating these borderlines together, young people may be able to share transient conflicts that might otherwise force each individual to improvise his own neurosis or delinquency, but they obviously also can lead one another into permanent involvements out of line with their self-image, their conscience—and the law. Most "grow out" of this; but it is important to visualize how much the adult world, too, with its ceremonial habituations in areas of the greatest and most lasting relevance continues to express the need for ritual make-believe.

But we are concerned here with the retrogressive aspects of youth re-enactments. I avoid the term *regression* here because of its ontogenetic and clinical implications. Transitory regression can be part both of creativity and of development, as is implied in Kris' term "regression in the service of the ego" and in Blos' "regression in the service of development." Blos, in fact, considers the "capacity to move between regressive and progressive consciousness with ... ease" the unique quality of adolescence.

And, indeed, I would submit that some of the adolescent processes described so readily as regressive have the distinct adaptive function of reviving and recapitulating the fragmentary experiences of childhood for the sake of recombining them actively in a new wholeness of experience. Such unification must obviously count on the workings of the ego. But it is accompanied by a new sense of "I," as well as a new experience of "we." The fate and function of such a sense and such an experience in the sequence of life stages have so far eluded conceptualization in psychoanalytic terms. At any rate, that a specific wholeness of experience may be irretrievably lost once adolescence has passed is the fear which gives much of adolescent behavior a certain desperate determination. And this, too, is a source of identification with the underprivileged, anywhere, who have missed their chance and must be offered a new one.

VI

I will select for more detailed discussion one strand of development little discussed in psychoanalysis—namely, that of moral and ethical orientation. I will speak of *moral learning* as an aspect of childhood; of *ideological experimentation* as a part of adolescence; and of *ethical consolidation* as an adult task. But as we know from the study of psychosexuality, the earlier stages are not replaced, but—according to the epigenetic principle—absorbed into a hierarchic system of increasing differentiation. If the child learns to be moral, by which I mean primarily to *internalize the prohibitions* of those significant to him, his moral conflicts continue in adolescence, but come under the primacy of ideological thinking. By ideology, in turn, I mean a *system of commanding ideas* held together more (but not exclusively) by totalistic logic and utopian conviction than by cognitive understanding or pragmatic experience. This ideological orientation as well as the moral one are in turn absorbed, but never quite replaced by that ethical orientation which makes the difference between adulthood and adolescence— "ethical" meaning a *universal sense of values assented to* with insight and foresight in anticipation of immediate responsibilites not the least of which is a transmission of these values to the next generation. Such development guarantees to this whole value structure a gradual synchronization with economic-political realities, but it also results in a persistent liability that can always lead to partial retrogressions. In youth, this can be seen in an arrest on the ideological level or a backsliding to infantile conflicts over moral interdicts, wherefore aggravated and especially agitated youth alternately re-enacts a *premoral* position that denies any need for morality; in an *amoral* position that flaunts accepted norms; in an *anti-moral* position that militantly negates all authority; and finally, in an *anti-authoritarian* and yet *moralistic* position that condemns the adult world with righteous fervor—all in the context of an insistence that the stubborn vitality of youth must not be surrendered to the existing system.

To begin with the ethical orientation: On October 16, 1967, at the Arlington Street Church in Boston, Harvard student Michael K. Ferber was one of the leaders of an anti-draft ceremony at which he made a statement entitled "A Time to Say No." He concluded it thus:

> But what I want to speak about now goes beyond our saying No, for no matter how loudly we all say it, no matter what ceremony we perform around our saying it, we will not become a community among ourselves nor effective agents for changing our country if a negative is all we share. Albert Camus said that the rebel, who says No, is also one who says Yes, and that when he draws a line beyond which he will refuse to cooperate, he is affirming the values on the other side of that line. For us who come here today, what is it that we affirm, what is it to which we can say Yes?

If Ferber was speaking so ethically for the young who were acting like himself, there were at his elbows a most affirmative university chaplain and a famous pediatrician who had used psychoanalytic insight to make more people say Yes to more babies with more practical awareness than had any doctor before him. Such company, however, only emphasizes the fact that the most ethical sentiments of the young are often synchronized with the most youthful sentiments of concerned adults. Most of all, however, Ferber's statement must serve here as a motto for the ethical leadership of a new generation of *young adults* who, with exhortation by song or slogan, by dramatic action or quiet resistance, have in recent years introduced a new ethical orientation into American life—an orientation already well visible in the concerns of a new generation of students.

I have begun with the Boston Resisters because a group retrogression is least likely to occur where a disciplined civil resistance to a circumscribed nationwide grievance dominates action. I have heard an equally clear Yes by students at Capetown University who reiterated their and their teachers' determination to open the universities to black countrymen. If one should single out a retrogressive danger in this whole area of ethical dissent, it is the arbitrary choosing of rebellious gestures that do not add up to a sustaining Yes, and of methods uncoordinated with the actions of others.

In turning from a consideration of the ethical position to that of the re-enactment of earlier moral conflicts, I will follow the usual method of outlining the childhood stages first subsumed under the theory of pregenitality. In some analogy to the principles of that theory, we will proceed on the assumption that the process of adolescence includes a re-enactment of all the pre-adolescent positions, from infancy on, in order to integrate all the gains of childhood in an individual as well as a collective style of adolescence consonant with the needs of the historical period. On the way, however, each part position can make itself independent in conjunction with an adolescent subculture which specializes in some utopian promises of the position in question and attempts to contribute them to an emerging world order. Such a *totalization* of one set of human potentials can eventually become both regressive and destructive for the person, the "sect," and society at large.

Infancy contributes to all later life, together with some fateful vulnerabilities, an undaunted orality and an unbroken sensory eagerness. What in clinical discussion we have habitually called, for short, "oral" has always been more than a zonal or libidinal emphasis; the original modes of incorporating both food and sensations form a vital basis for an active acceptance of the world. Any clinical or developmental assessment, then, could begin with each of a number of themes and lead inescapably to all the others. I will emphasize here the infant's *mutuality* of responses with the *maternal person,* which leads to the introjection of a benevolent and reliable mother image and thus helps to appease primal anxiety. This, in turn, works for a favorable ratio of *basic trust* over *basic mistrust* that assures that *hope* becomes the fundamental quality of all growth. All this combines to form a first *developmental position* that will become a contributory element to all later stages as it reaches on each stage a higher level of differentiation. This developmental timetable is, of course, also a map of transient and partial regressions in states of crisis, illness, or fatigue, and of an irreversible withdrawal to delusional fulfillment in malignant states.

In adolescence, the quality of fidelity, the capacity to be loyal to a vision of the future, now incorporates infantile trust, while the capacity to have faith emerges as a more focused hope tuned to an ideologically coherent universe. The corresponding totalization we know clinically in the form of massive regression in isolated, addictive, or psychotic individuals. We know it biographically as the special state of a creative recapitulation of sensory awakening in some medium of artistic representation. And we know it sociologically as a utopian or revivalist community life of a markedly childlike, trusting, and mystical spirit.

Returning to today's patterns of dissent, it must be obvious that the group style generally subsumed under the term "hippiedom" is such a totalization of the first developmental position. In the midst of our technocratic world, young men and women encourage one another to live like the proverbial lilies of the field, with trusting love as their dominant demand and display.

In the scheme of moral stages, such a return to the logic of both infancy and paradise can be seen as a re-enactment of the *premoral stage*. These young people seem to convince themselves (and sometimes us) that the fall from grace and the expulsion from paradise were overexertions of divine rigor and that basic mistrust is superfluous baggage for a "human being." This return can be a reaffirmation of the indispensable treasure of experience that our technocratic world is vaguely aware of having sacrificed to the gods of gadgetry, merchandise, and mechanical adjustment; and, up to a point, the world is grateful to or, at any rate, fascinated by this tribe from "another world." But, alas, an existing technology has its own methods of absorbing and neutralizing utopian innovations, and the flower children, too, have suffered—precisely because of their repression of the necessary minimum of mistrust—from combined exploitation by microbes, drugpushers, and publicists.

VII

There could be no greater contrast than that between the ethical and the premoral positions just sketched and the amoral one to be considered next. And yet dissent unites, and the hippies and the motorcycle gangs have on occasion been seen to dwell together like the lambs and the lions. I have also heard of at least one instance when draft resisters linked themselves together around a conscientious deserter with chains handed them by a black-leathered gang. If the amoral position has more obviously sinister trends than the premoral one, however, it is because it champions a sincere belief in the goodness both of physical violence and of "obscenity."

The amoral position is clearly related to the second stage of infantile development (that is, about the second and third year of life). In dogmatic brevity, *anal-urethral* and *muscular* development had a psychosocial corollary in the sense of *autonomy* which in turn outweighed the danger of excessive *doubt* and *shame*. The new, rudimentary strength to emerge from this stage is a sense of free *will*—seasoned with the acceptance of a mutual delineation with the will of others. The psychopathological counterpart of all this is, in fact, a malfunction of the will, either in the form of inner *overcontrol* manifested in *compulsive* and *obsessive* trends or in that of a willful *impulsivity*.

Identity development in adolescence calls for a revival of the second developmental position too. Tested once more, will can then be subordinated to some order acknowledged as a higher will and willful impulse to communal experience, while blind obedience can become self-chosen discipline—the subjective emphasis always being that the individual chooses freely what proves inescapable. In totalistic rebellion, however, the negative re-enactment of this position can lead to a complete reversal of positions. Far from exhibiting any embarrassment, the dissenters sport shamelessness, obedience becomes defiance, and self-doubt, contempt. These deliberate challenges, in turn, arouse the worst in others, wherefore the militant amoralist finds himself, sooner or later, confronted by uniformed men, paid to do the "dirty work" for nice people, and apt to oblige the amoral phantasy-life by behaving like the externalized version of a brutal conscience while being at times—in terms of their task and training—amoral themselves.

It is well within developmental logic, then, that the retrogression to an amoral state recapitulates—no less compulsively for seeming so obvious and deliberate—such infantile patterns of protest as the deft deposition of feces in places to be desecrated and the use of excrement as ammunition. In this context also belongs the indiscriminate appellation of dirty names to authorities. In the case of "pigs," this certainly shows a strange lack of respect for an innocently muddy animal, and in that of sexual four-letter words, a blatant retrogression from sexual freedom.[1]

This may be the place to discuss briefly the often-heard simplistic assumption that such retrogressive acts on the part of privileged youth are simply overgrown temper tantrums due to their parents' "permissiveness." Authentic permissiveness can probably not be learned in a few generations. In the meantime, there is, rather, an excessive inhibition of parental anger and even of genuine indignation. This leaves the rage of both the parents and the children untested and untrained, and survives as a residual anxious expectation as to when the parents will dare to vent their suppressed rage and prove that they, indeed, can manage their own violence. But problems of child-rearing are always part of an intergenerational climate; and it may not be childhood experience alone that compels young people to test the limits of the dispassionate fairness claimed by authorities as well as by parents. Where such challenge is met with the deployment of a hired force that does not hesitate to vent all the frustrated anger shunned by the privileged, the ethical weakness in delegating violence immediately arouses the solidarity of those larger numbers of students who would not otherwise be attracted by amoral stratagems.

VIII

In the third stage of childhood—that is, the fourth and some of the fifth year of life—the imaginative *anticipation of future roles* is played out with toys and costumes, in tales and games. This, too, is recapitulated after puberty, when youth meets economic reality and historical actuality. What is reawakened, then, is the claim to the right to wield *initiative* of imagination and action—and this without the oppressive sense of *guilt* which at one time deepened the propensity for repression and made the child so amenable to moralistic pressure. In the boy this initiative was (and now is again) *intrusive* and *locomotor*, with an emphasis on invading the domain of the fathers; and it was (and is) for a while intrusive as well as locomotor in girls, sometimes with a competitive fervor surprising to the boys. If the repression of sexual and aggressive thrusts toward parent figures was the negative heritage of the third stage—and this with a marked fear of damage to the executive body parts—it becomes only more plausible that young people should be attracted by charismatic leaders and utopian causes which will sanction and give direction to the re-emergence of vigorous and competitive imagination.

To ward off the worst, the older generation tries, not without condescension, to assign to the young an area of boisterous, promiscuous, and rebellious re-enactment of phallic pursuits for the purpose of "sowing wild oats" or of "blowing off steam" before adult "reality" will force all sportive exuberance back into obedient channels. Higher education, especially, has always cultivated its style of

169

genteel boasting and sportive competition. But in the long run it has also conveyed the power of ideas as embodied in rebellious men and periods of the great past, and it has thus helped to thwart the readiness of aggravated youth to be made subservient to technical and bureaucratic regimentation.

Among the retrogressive trends associated with the revival in adolescence of infantile guilt, there is the *anti-authoritarian, hypermoralistic* stance which is sometimes even stranger to behold than the name I am here attaching to it. Here is a simple and mild example of what I mean. In a college paper, a student took a truly distinguished professor to task for an allegedly illogical and unethical point of view. The issue is not so important here as the stance. The writer scolded: "What truly bothers me is the quality and logic of your justification . . ."; "I find thoroughly naïve your attempt to distinguish between . . ."; "Still more ludicrous is the characterization in your letter . . ."; "Even if I were to grant you this point for the sake of argument . . ."; "What most . . . experts lack is a discernible sense of responsibility. . . ." This total kind of turning against the "authority" of a legendary schoolmaster's posture is typical of the tone sported by many self-appointed revolutionaries, who declare a given man or group to be "guilty" with a fanatic use of the "guilt-by-association" logic. Some young people with the clearest intelligence and the most ethical intentions can talk one another into such retrogression, unaware of the probability that they are hastening the time when they will use it against one another for reciprocal moral liquidation.

In the meantime, fanaticism "dared" by agitators can lead to dangerous confrontations precisely because they are staged in the center of adult male prerogative. Perhaps the re-enactment of the third developmental position is nowhere more obvious than in the emotional and behavioral side effects of those confrontations that center in the occupation of buildings as seats and symbols of established power. The acquisition of a *territorial base* in the heart of the Establishment is, of course, an old revolutionary technique which is as strategic as it is symbolic. In the occupation of a center in the alma mater, however, the retrogressive aspects are underscored because the conquerors claim and count on the protection of academic *extraterritoriality*. And, indeed, their subsequent moodswings seem to vary from an undoubted sense of having accomplished a historically valid communal deed to excesses clearly dramatizing themes of a degradation of father figures as guilty usurpers and of the right of the young to claim license and amnesty, almost before the deed is consummated. And, indeed, faculties tend to make family affairs of such revolts; so that it becomes equally ludicrous to demand or to grant amnesty or to insist on severe punishments for deeds that, in fact, do manage to arouse guilty doubts in the confronted adults and force them to confront one another in prolonged and overdue debate.

IX

We must now, at last, look at that majority of the young who, without such provocation, would be aggravated only latently and would probably never join a revolt. Not that the majority has not always cultivated periodic pranks, raids, and riots which in various cultures have come to be taken for granted. But even though in some countries occasionally lives are lost, these youthful disorders rarely assume the nature of a concerted rebellion, except where most students have reason to feel that the system does not give them their due place *within* it. Students are not necessarily alienated from an industrial world or even a military-industrial complex so long as their studies promise them active participation and advancement in it, and a style of leisure utilizing all the comfort of modern mechanization. It is difficult to ascribe to this majority a tendency to re-enact a previous developmental position, because their aspirations are to a large extent only an extension of the fourth stage, the *school and play* age, into a prolonged period of apprenticeship. In our continuum from premoral to expressly ethical orientations, this great middle range cultivates a post-moral and pre-ethical *pragmatism.* This dominates, above all, the students of occupational specialties which attempt to come to grips with the concrete complexities of modern life, be they production or distribution, transportation or communication, medicine or law: For them, *what works is good,* and it is man's fate to be in motion and to set things in motion in league with a divine engineering power. Teamwork justifies man's trust in the eventual manageability of all modern complexities, including poverty and race relations, war and the conquest of space.

According to this general orientation, morality, ideology, and ethics can all be fitted into the acquisition of techniques, problems of sin or salvation being delegated to a Sunday religiosity which is never in conflict with habit and reason and which rewards those who help themselves. The result is a new technical-cultural consolidation analogous to those that have dominated all previous periods of history.

If there is retrogression in this orientation, it is an all-too-early, all-too-complete adjustment to the dominant modes of production and of success; and while those who can feel at home in it are apt to escape the more disturbing forms of identity confusion, they also must live by a dissimulation of emotions, the cumulative and corporative fate of which in inner or interpersonal life is hard to gauge. The patterns of dissent displayed by those in tune with "the system" differ in countries of different degrees of economic development; and even where the pragmatists occasionally permit themselves to be aggravated or led by radical activists, the latter cannot always foresee whether their temporary supporters want a different system or a more profitable identity within the existing one; for the pragmatists are closer to the power struggles within the political structure than they are to ideological issues as such.

Do moral pragmatists, too, feel "alienated" in a technocratic world? It is hard to say. But increased contact with humanist intellectuality is apt to breed radical dissent. Otherwise, a retrogression within the logic of the school age takes the form of "dropping out" for the sake of doing "my thing." Such avoidance of an early submission to the narrow techniques of limited competencies can (where the draft laws permit) be of great value especially when joined to enriching experiences and exercises. But sooner or later dropouts are apt to erect a communal pretense of superiority over all those who work and serve—a superiority often only covering that exquisite *sense of inferiority* which is the stubborn shadow of the school age.

X

One could condense all that has been said about the various types of dissent by claiming that group retrogressions originate in the incapacity or the refusal to conclude the stage of identity on the terms offered by the adult world. But the generational barrier is always one between future adults and erstwhile adolescents. Today it is reinforced on the adult side by a pervasive sense of deficiency in ethical and religious orientation such as would be consonant with an identity development still promised a generation ago. In fact, many of the adults most effective in modern transactions have had

172

the least time to complete, or indeed to renew, their identity development—not to speak of their sense of intimacy or generativity—under the pressure of technological and historical change. (Is this the reason why some bearded young men and severe young women manage to look and act like veterans of life compared to their successful and boyish-looking fathers and their happy and girlish-appearing mothers?)

Some militants, of course, refuse to concede any need for identity; to them the very concept is only another attempt to force youth into roles prescribed by the Establishment. Whether or not this is partially true, it is important to realize that there is a hidden ideological connotation to all theories concerning man's nature; even the most carefully verified observations will prove to have been subject to the ideological polarizations of their historical period. This certainly has been the case with the theory of psychosexuality. Today, when (to paraphrase McLuhan) the mask is so often the message, we face young people who hide their true identity—in every sense of the word—behind dark glasses and ubiquitous hair, while flaunting a negative identity often way beyond their emotional means. This, too, can be part of courageous living; but it can also go together with a negation of the three developmental necessities marking the termination of adolescence: an identity tied to some competence; a sexuality bound to a style of intimacy; and the anticipation of becoming, before long, responsible for the next generation.

We should acknowledge in passing the advances on the part of many young people in making genital freedom a central aspect of greater communal honesty. A vigorous genital culture, however, depends among other things on contraceptive methods; and while their invention was fervently anticipated by Freud, it may be necessary today to be vigilant in the face of an all-too-ready belief that genital and procreative instinctuality can be divided so neatly without new kinds of emotional strain. On the other hand, the freedom of choosing parenthood with a fuller consciousness of what mankind can and must be able to promise each newborn child, *anywhere,* could well become the *sine qua non* of a future ethics equipped with a clearer knowledge of the all-around needs of a human being.

The future, so I would submit in conclusion, will force on young adults not only new styles of parenthood, but also the responsibility of being, indeed, their younger brothers' and sisters' keepers. After

173

all the remarkable service which some of our young people have rendered to the underprivileged and underdeveloped on the periphery of their lives, they may have to learn that to be a young person under conditions of rapid change means to assume responsibility for younger persons nearby, and this in ways impossible to perform by older people and least of all by parents. This, too, is prophetically anticipated in the transient brotherhoods and sisterhoods of today—even if such caring for one another is at times only a sporadic and romantic phenomenon.

In this mostly "diagnostic" paper I should like to make this one "therapeutic" suggestion which (luckily, as so often) relies on the prognostically obvious: If the older young people could find the courage in themselves—and encouragement and guidance from their elders—to institutionalize their responsibility for the younger young, we might see quite different images of both youth and young adulthood emerge than those we now know. New models of fraternal behavior may come to replace those images of comradeship and courage that have been tied in the past to military service and probably have contributed to a glorification of a kind of warfare doomed to become obsolete in our time; and they may come to continue the extraordinary work, both inspired and concrete, done in the last few decades by pioneering youth groups on a variety of frontiers. This, in turn, would make it possible for adults to contribute true knowledge and genuine experience without assuming an authoritative stance beyond their actual competence and genuine inner authority.

In the definition and defense of such a new generational bond I also see a new role for (well, relatively) young men and women with psychoanalytic training. Beyond their function as healers, they could well serve as interpreters of the conflicts that are aroused in those who—on either side of the barrier—cannot let go of the images and impulses of the "classical" generational struggle. But in supporting this trend, one must also emphasize the Hippocratic obligations implied in it: Diagnostic and therapeutic insights cannot, beyond a certain amount of professed partisanship, be subservient to ideological counter-transferences. In a post-Freudian world, psychological insight must assume a significance and an ethical power of its own.

For adults, too, retrogress under the conditions described. Or rather the manifestations discussed are already the result of acute and yet hidden adult retrogression. We who know so much about

the child in the adult know so much less about the fate of the adolescent in him; and yet it is eminently clear that adults of ethical
stature retain their irrational ideological involvements as well as
their punitive moralism and can fall back on both. That adolescent
remnants endure can be seen in quieter times in the ritualized retrogressions of such groups as alumni or veterans; and they are often
obvious in the peculiarities of people whose occupation forces (or
permits) them to spend their lives with and for youth, not to speak
of the adolescents-in-residence on every faculty. Acutely confronted
by challenges of aggravated and agitated youth, the adult is apt to
suffer a kind of emotional paralysis caused by acutely roused remnants of his own unfulfilled identity fragments and a certain irresistible—punitive or self-punitive—identification with the new brand of
youth. Whether the result is generational surrender or renewed generational isolationism, it must sooner or later lead to a display of
that brittle dignity which is supposed to protect occupational identity and status. To this, again, the majority of young people react
negatively; to them a career that is not worth sacrificing for professed ideals is not worth having.

To share true authority with the young, however, would mean
to acknowledge something that adults have learned to mistrust in
themselves: a truly ethical potential. To study the psychological
foundation of this potential may be one of the more immediate
tasks of psychoanalysis. As we have already passed the "century
of the child" and are now experiencing, with a vengeance, that of
the adolescent, we may well be entering a period in which we must
dare to ask: What, really, *is* an adult?

A new generation, for us, always starts again with Oedipus. We
take it for granted that King Laius knew what he was doing—for
could he not count on the authority of the Oracle when he left his
baby boy to die, taking no chances with the possibility that a good
education might have proven stronger than the oracular establishment? From what we know today, however, we might be inclined
to ask: What could you expect of a little boy whose father felt so
bound by phobic traditionalism? Yet theory has confirmed the
oracle: Each new child appears to be a potential bearer of the
Oedipal curse, and parricide remains a much more plausible explanation of the world's ills than does filicide.

And yet it must be clear that all puberty rites and confirmations
as well as all inductions and (yes, all) graduations, besides estab-

lishing a reciprocity of obligations and privileges, also threaten with an element of mutilation and exile—if not in the crude form of surgical covenants, then in the insistence that a person's final identity must be cut down to size: the size of a conventional type of adult who knows his place and likes it. Thus we continue to institutionalize generational identifications that serve as built-in solutions for childhood conflicts and yet also guarantee their recurrence from generation to generation.

The discovery of the Oedipus Complex made amenable to conscious critique a generational fate grounded both in phylogeny and ontogeny. Such fate does not become altogether relative through historical change. But it may well be that different periods of history and different epidemiologies open new aspects of man's tragic involvement and of his rare victories to psychoanalytic insight. In this wider sense, it may well be that some of the confrontations in actuality which rebellious youth insists upon and the inner confrontation which is the essence of our method are highlighting the inner and outer consequences of patriarchal moralism and the present necessity for a world-wide new ethics supported by the informed choices of young men and young women.

REFERENCES

1. I cannot discuss here the different significance which deliberate obscenity and profanity assumes among the militants of racial minorities, who for generations and all their lifetimes have been exposed to extralegal "law enforcement."

STANLEY HOFFMANN

Participation in Perspective?

IN ALMOST every instance, university crises in the United States and abroad have led to a quest for institutional reform. The *loi d'orientation* adopted by the French Parliament in the fall of 1968, the changes that have been carried out at Columbia and Princeton, and those being discussed at Harvard result from the following assumption: One of the reasons for the crisis must have been the inadequacy of the institutions of the university, for they have been unable to cope with the new pressures and strains, and indeed their flaws have often been the targets for, or the detonators of, the explosion. Structural reform should make the university more able to face its problems and remove some of the major causes of trouble.

It is, of course, true that the contours of each crisis are drawn by the peculiarities, including the institutional ones, of the university in trouble. But the diversity of institutions affected has been enormous, whereas the similarity in the students' revolts has been remarkable. Every kind of university government has been in difficulty. To look for even a partial solution in institutional engineering reminds one of those French politicians or political scientists who, throughout modern French history, have seen in constitutional reform the answer to France's problems. The result has been a rich and varied constitutional history and a fascinating demonstration of the way in which the underlying issues are affected by, yet survive, shape, and doom the institutional innovations. True, some institutions are better than others for dealing with certain kinds of problems. Discussions on governance, in a nation or a university, are therefore not only legitimate but necessary; for if the setup is both ineffective and drained of support, only chaos will result. Yet to focus too exclusively on "governance" is doubly dangerous. First, a new system of government must

177

be discussed in the light of those substantive issues that have led to the crisis of the institutions; "who governs" may well be one of the key questions of politics, but "what for" is the other one. The wrong "who" cannot reach the right "what"; but depending on the "what," the right "who" will not be the same.

Secondly, the discussion of "governance" risks becoming one more way of evading the substantive issues; it would thus not only breed dangerous illusions about how far structural reforms can go in solving the crisis, but also prolong one of the most important aspects of the crisis: the total lack of agreement on the "what." It is as if the academic Emperor had decided to build himself a new clothes closet so as not to face the fact that he has no real clothes to put in. He wears the tattered remains of his old, frayed, and shrunken garments and cannot make up his mind whether to buy new robes, or a business suit, or blue jeans, or a mod outfit, or a mixture. And while it could be argued that his old closet was so small, and dark, and empty of hangers that he was never forced to realize his plight, and while it is certainly true that the best closet would be one that could accommodate any combination of things, what good would a modern closet be if there were no clothes left to hang in it?

There are good reasons why academics flee from the storm of substantive disagreements on the future of the university to the (relative) shelter of structural reform. What is more unsettling than realizing that the institution to which one has committed one's life is adrift, that the foundations on which one built one's career are shaky, that the idea of a university which one thought common to most of one's colleagues and students has in fact been repudiated by many, that there are deep contradictions between resilient old ideals and irresistible new realities, or that grandiose recent ideals such as, say, Clark Kerr's "multiversity" breed their own quota of troubles? Most striking is the tendency to push such divisions and dramas under the rug or to deal with crises that result from the breakdown of the old order piecemeal—so that the underlying issues, untouched, keep producing new turmoil. To a considerable extent, it is the present generation of students that has, rudely, raised the questions, and we should all be grateful. But both the tactics they have often used and their tendency to be more critical than constructive or, when constructive, more utopian and confused than consistent and realistic (a tendency for which it would be foolish to blame them) have helped academics evade these issues or have diverted them into narrower debates on discipline or on "student power," which provoke strange alignments of men deeply divided on all the other issues.

It is not my intention to produce a capsule treatise on the crisis of the university; but I want to stress the seriousness of the problem of ends. The university is the place where some of the most important contradictions and tensions of modern society are at their most concentrated and explosive. The tendencies of this society, which has reshaped other institutions easily, meet special resistance here, both from the traditional nature of the university and from its constituents; and the university is especially vulnerable to the conflicts that this contest creates. Being the arena of greatest strain, the university becomes the stake of the deepest divisions. Depending on the purposes one assigns to it, different forms of government would be appropriate. The objective of institutional reform, therefore, cannot be merely the detailed realization of even so worthy (and universal) a catchword—or demand—as "participation." By itself, participation may fail to solve the bigger problems, or may even aggravate them if the wrong models are adopted. The key question of institutional reform remains—participation in and for what? As long as there is no agreement, the first order of business is to devise temporary institutions designed to provoke a great debate on ends, to facilitate an eventual agreement, and to keep the university going in the meantime.

Among the many features of advanced industrial society—features that transcend the diversity of political regimes, yet are of course affected and shaped by them—we can single out three that are of special importance for an understanding of the crisis of the university.[1] The first one concerns the form of social organization. In our societies, it is *bureaucratic*—that is, human activity takes place in large, hierarchical organizations, which tend to be run with general, impersonal rules, defined and applied by officeholders in charge of managing the organizations. The second feature concerns the method of recruitment of the elites: It is *meritocratic*—that is, access to positions of power is obtained through certified accomplishments, the certification being itself obtained through education. This is in contrast with societies in which the elites were recruited through heredity or wealth. The third feature concerns the basis of power: It is *technocratic*—that is, power tends to go to those who have the skill to apply modern science and technology to the practical problems of society. History has known bureaucracy and meritocracy without technocracy; but the latter is impossible to imagine without the first two features.

All three have been celebrated as liberating forces that enlarge the possibilities of human action far beyond what was conceivable in societies marked by scarcity, inequalities of birth, and rigid classes, or fragmented, small-scale, or relatively undifferentiated social organization. The combination of the three features has been hailed as the triumph of rationality applied to human affairs. Two sets of contradictions, however, have resulted in advanced industrial societies, especially in the non-Communist countries.

First, there is a contradiction between these features and the residues of the earlier forms of power and social organization. Sometimes the old perverts the new. Far from achieving a hierarchy based on skill, which would allow any competent person, whatever his origin, to reach a position appropriate to his talents, modern society often merely consecrates and hardens pre-existing inequalities, for it selects mainly among the reasonably well-off and well-placed. Far from assuring the broadest application of science and technology to human problems, modern society often merely concentrates this application in areas for which there is a strong market demand, determined by the vagaries of the government and of a capitalist economy—that is, by what is profitable to a few, or necessary for defense or prestige, rather than useful to most. Hence the revolt of underprivileged groups, who for economic or ethnic reasons remain shut out of the social elevators, and who see how the continuing power and concentration of wealth distort the benefits that the three features of social rationalization are supposed to bring forth. Sometimes the old and the new coexist incoherently. This is particularly the case in two realms: culture, where the old reservoir of general education, with its aristocratic background, profound individualism, faith in the possibility of synthesizing knowledge, and orientation to the past, stagnates surrounded by the mass culture of the present mass media; and politics, where institutions built in the eighteenth and early nineteenth centuries continue to operate in a world to which they are increasingly less appropriate, and where new institutions more adapted to the political needs of industrial society keep multiplying.

Secondly, there is a contradiction between what might be called the liberating potential of the three modern features and their oppressive implications. With respect to social structure, these features threaten to establish their own patterns of inequality and inequity—not only because the new elite, like all past ones, tends to protect its positions, to harden its hold, and to perpetuate its power by restricting access and renewal, but primarily because of the imperialistic tendency of the three features to extend to every segment of society. What made life bearable, and inequality breachable, in past societies was the diversity of forms of social organization, methods of recruitment, and bases of power. They varied from sector to sector (in seventeenth and eighteenth century France, a *roturier* could gain power through commerce, or in the state bureaucracy, or in the republic of letters). If the trend, first announced by the sociologists of industrial society ever since Comte, toward universal uniformity should prevail, not only in theory but in social practice, the relatively unskilled individuals at the bottom of the great organizations would find themselves, despite their affluence, at least as dependent and impotent as in past social systems, and even more deprived of remedies. Moreover, by themselves, the three features provide no clue about the kinds and degrees of accountability which the elites might tolerate as checks on their management and corrections of their abuses.

With respect to the political system, the combination of the three features risks spreading the myth of a "scientific" handling of political issues through techniques that may be adequate for the choice of the best means toward a given end (at least as long as "most economical" and "best" are equated), yet are unfit for the choice among ends or unable to determine the social validity and human value of any end. This pseudo-objectivity could squeeze out of political action not only one of the essential functions of politics—the assessment of social purposes, now taken for granted or deemed determined by the splintered drift of technology—but also the kinds of politicians whose only skill was the subjective and largely intuitive management of conflicts, a skill for which no formal educational process can provide the technical certification and whose essence is profoundly anti-bureaucratic, anti-meritocratic, and anti-technocratic.

Finally, with respect to the individual, the new social order enhances both personal insecurity and alienation (in the sense of non-commitment). The need to succeed in order to reach the top, to keep being a success in order to remain on top despite the challenge of the young (with their up-to-date education and training), the difficulty of rescuing one's own future if one is not on

181

top, the hardship of finding a new future if one's organization becomes a victim of technological progress—such are the sources of insecurity. The concentration of power at the top, the lack of a system of public values beyond the act of faith in science and in the social order itself, the relegation of ethics into the realms of privacy, emotions, or aesthetics (that is, social irrelevance if not irrationality), and also the difficulty, quite new in history, of finding a legitimate principle for revolting against a social order that claims to foster progress and rationality—these would be the sources of alienation. This is a problem which those prophets of the new order, Saint Simon and Comte, had anticipated; yet the only remedy they sought was one that this order undermines: a new religion.

Hence a fundamental conflict arises between the rationalizing pretenses of the new order and what might be called its multiple irrationality. The new society is one in which, supposedly, the hierarchy is based on individuals' differing skills in applying their reason to modern science and technology. Collective social organization is said to oblige men to calculate the consequences of their actions—that is, to behave as responsible citizens and not as capricious masters or hapless subjects. The combined resources of science and large-scale organization are assumed to multiply man's choices and free him from the inhibitions and constraints of traditional or early capitalist societies.[2] On the other hand, it is easy to point out that the application of methods of rationalization to complex choices among conflicting ends and rival systems produces pseudo-rationality. In areas as important as the world political and military competition, the "rational" logic of the contest leads, at best, to the mad momentum of the arms and space races and, at worst, to the recurrence of wars. The very size and complexity of modern organizations, by depersonalizing decisions and by making immobility, or minimal changes, or ambiguous compromises easier than imaginative or drastic measures, often entail irresponsibility, generalized impotence from top to bottom, and a lack of sufficient regard for long-range consequences. It is the clash between, on the one hand, the engineer's and social engineer's hubris, his vision of an increasingly conscious, controllable, and planned society, run by "the most effective techniques for the rational exploitation of social talent,"[3] and, on the other hand, the increasing lack of control over one's individual and collective life, the accumulation of waste and the destruction of nature, the replacement of the old oppressions of personal dependence and misery with the new oppressions of impersonal dependence and life in urban blight, the disappearance of any yardstick of value above and beyond technological innovation, the triumph of instrumentalism. For new reasons, the old human dream of a society allowing for individual self-fulfillment is once again being frustrated, this time in a context of material fulfillment.

The protest against the three features of modern society is made both more bitter and more futile by the irrelevance of the solutions applied to earlier injustices. In the capitalist societies of yesterday, the assault on the inequalities left over by the feudal order or created by the accumulation of industrial wealth proceeded through two concepts: equality of opportunity and fair treatment. The hierarchies of status and wealth would be, if not eliminated, at least partly corrected by a legal order of equal chances and minimum standards and by the myth of the rational, self-governing individual. Man as citizen and as *homo oeconomicus* would be a free participant in the political and economic market, thanks to the legal order that would remove the obstacles to his full participation, and to a representative system of government that would establish and protect this order and define the standards of fair treatment. Thus, there was a close link between a horizontal view of the legal order—an order of competing equals— and a view of the political system, which was essentially legislative and whose purpose was the promotion of equal rights and the redress of those injustices that could have invalidated them and closed the market. The legislature was both a delegation from the legal order and a reproduction of it: a small assembly of equals. Self-government was equated with the opportunity to participate in the open market and in elections to the legislative bodies. Political and economic activity could be theorized, paradoxically, yet without any deep contradiction, both as a bargaining contest of rational individuals and as a balancing of group interests—for these groups were seen as mere sums of individuals.

The solutions of the old political liberalism and state-regulated capitalism have become obsolete, given the evolution of industrial society, the increasing differentiation of the social order, the dynamism of the economy. The present problems emerged once equal chances and humane treatment were no longer at stake. In part, the solutions of yesterday have even contributed to the difficulties of today. The attempt to correct injustices has meant the growth of centralized public bureaucracy and the gradual shift, in Daniel Bell's terms, from a system of distributive power in which all interests are represented to a system of aggregative power dominated by the executive.[4] Today's central issue is not participation in an open market and essentially legislative political system, but participation in the control of the specialized, hierarchical organizations that make up most of the government and the society. Everyone (or almost) has an equal chance to become a subordinate agent of such an organization; the legal right to go all the way to the top is not in doubt. Fair treatment, such as a minimum wage, was essential as a means to the end of allowing each individual to enjoy his legal rights; but today's problem is that of the ends of the organizations in which fair treatment is assured.[5] Self-government today would mean participation in the determination of their ends and in the control of their activities. The old conceptualization of political and economic activity has no leverage for the present: *homo politicus* and *homo oeconomicus* are not organization men. The large interest groups of yesterday—employers', labor, and farmers' unions, even the political parties, all horizontal associations cutting across the vertical lines of territory and work— seem irrelevant to the problem of control of hierarchical organizations. In a totalitarian system, the issue of participation does not even arise; in a non-totalitarian one, the central legislators seem incapable of doing more than ordering paper solutions, and the executive is in many ways the first and biggest organization in need of control. It is this inadequacy, and occasional nefariousness, of the traditional method of seeking remedies at the center which explains why today's rebels often look for them in schemes of community control. But notions of complete decentralization and disorganization inherited from Proudhon or Fourier are no answer: They merely consist in wishing the problem away.

The critique of modern society, in words and in acts, tends to come from three sources only. Yesterday's proletarians, the workers, having won the battles of equal rights and fair treatment, seem usually far more concerned with increasing the range of material benefits which the new social order can bring them than with exploring new possibilities of participation: Their concerns are quantitative rather than qualitative. Their place has been taken by today's underprivileged, those who have not yet gained equal rights, or who feel that they are not receiving fair treatment in a social order that tends either to treat them as an unskilled manpower reserve or to work toward their total elimination: America's blacks, the foreign and migrant workers in America's and Europe's industries, the peasants, shopkeepers, artisans, small factory workers who do not fit the "post-industrial" world. Then there are those intellectuals who look with dismay at the three features described above. They represent what Michel Crozier calls the "aristocratic intelligentsia." They see themselves as the guardians of cultural values; they are anxious to serve as prestigious critics and moral guides of society rather than as engineers and managers of limited social change. They are found, here and abroad, mainly in the humanities and in some parts of the social sciences. Finally, there are many students, on the verge of being absorbed into the new order. This rebellion against it is waged by its potential leaders and beneficiaries.

The university has been deeply affected by the three features of modern society. It is, of course, presumptuous to speak of *the* university, given the bewildering variety of institutions of higher learning. But we can take as our subject the traditional communities of scholars devoted both to undergraduate instruction (based on the classical conception of general education) and to graduate training for professional work in an established discipline (aimed at communicating a certain branch of knowledge rather than at teaching techniques with little intellectual content). In these universities, until recently in fact, and even until now in the minds of many academics, the three features had either no place or only a qualified one. Their introduction has turned the university into a battlefield.

The universities of the past were not heavily bureaucratic.[6] Indeed, they all prided themselves on the decentralized self-government by the faculty. This does not mean that there were no traces of authoritarianism, no distance between professors or students, but it was the distance and hierarchy of a feudal order rather than those of a modern bureaucratic, impersonal organization. Of course, within the university, student and teacher progression was largely "meritocratic"—hence the whole network of grades, examinations, and promotions; but as long as higher education in elite universities was essentially the privilege of the sons and daughters of the wealthy and well-born, the meritocratic principle was merely subsidiary and operated without the psychologically unsettling rigor which it has when a whole life's course depends on a few performances. Moreover, even when meritocracy played a large role (as it did within the faculties), the skills demanded and displayed were those of basic learning and research. In the pecking order of prestige, the more "disinterested" branches, the disciplines of pure science or the humanities, came before the applied sciences and the vocational fields. Power in the university itself either reflected the internal hierarchy of prestige or else was divided between academic internal self-government and a limited control by representatives of society, politicians if the university was public, or men from the world of business and the professions if it was private. (The structure of American private universities thus resembles a compromise between a mandarinate and an industrial enterprise.) As a result, there existed a curious relationship between the university and society. On the one hand, the university played an important social role, both in giving to the children of the elite a higher general education and specialized training which would enrich, mature, or mellow their future performances, and in providing a limited number of children of the less privileged with access to the elite. On the other hand, the university was a separate universe, largely autonomous and apart from society. Indeed, in order to conquer its autonomy from previous controls—religious, political, or economic—the university secreted a kind of ideal or mythology of itself as a temple of learning, far above the market place, distinct from the political world, both neutral as an institution and devoted to the normative function of evaluating human achievements. The professor was seen not as an employee of society, but as a high priest of truth, knowledge, and reasoned discourse; the student was there to learn from him, and the outside world was to finance and ask no questions.

Modern sociologists have characterized the university of today as if it were the equivalent of the church in the feudal order, of the factory in capitalist society. If knowledge becomes the basis of power, and education the condition for acquiring certified knowledge, then the triumph of the meritocratic principle in society should allow the university to cast its net far more widely than in the days of numerically and socially limited admissions, and the advent of a scientific and technological order should make of the university a key determinant rather than a mere reflection and gentle civilizer of society. "Knowledge becomes a tool of power," and the university is the knowledge factory. But there is a heavy price to pay for becoming "an intensely involved think-tank, the source of much sustained political planning and social innovation."[7] By turning from the myth and partial reality of the sanctuary to the myth and partial reality of the social laboratory and executive basement, the university has lost both its distance and its innocence. On the one hand, it is the microcosm of the contradictions described in the previous section. They are heightened by the strength of the contrast between the old academic order and the new: Here the new destroys the old, rather than merely coexisting with it or being subverted by it. On the other hand, by allowing the new features to reshape its structure and activities in a haphazard and unexamined way, the university legitimizes the new social order— hence another contradiction between its new mission and its old role and ideal.

The impact of technocracy on the university has been described and deplored frequently. The "knowledge explosion" has meant the fragmentation of knowledge, the triumph of specialization under the guise of professionalism, the undermining of general education, the subversion of the hierarchy of prestige, the establishment of a new pecking order that privileges what appears, rightly or wrongly, to be directly useful—that is, usable.[8] It has also meant a growing dependence of the university on the "knowledge market" outside, that is, both the industries and the government. It has turned the academics away from the university, made them over into men of affairs and entrepreneurs for whom the university is merely a base, a part-time employer, and a focus of partial allegiance. Whatever greater direct impact on social affairs may thus have been achieved by individual academics or teams, whatever strengthening of disciplines and of professional research cutting across university lines may have taken place, such functional gains have been made at the cost of a vital loss of substance for the university as a community, and of weakening its structure. The priorities are now set outside. The tradition of decentralized faculty self-government, the repugnance of old-style academics to grant full status to what many see as insufficiently scholarly and disinterested activities, have resulted in a proliferation of technical institutes, centers, programs on the margins of the old university. Hence there are uncertainties about who is truly included in the faculty, competition for time and allegiance between the old university and the new, and reluctance of old traditions and institutions to accommodate the new developments that is paradoxically responsible for that very splintering and disintegration of knowledge which they deplore and which technocracy fosters.

One of the consequences is, evidently, bureaucracy. The new

187

research outfits and public or civic affairs enterprises of the university can function properly only if they have an extensive and hierarchical division of labor, and the management of their relations with the outside world—particularly the government—requires a growing administration. The multiplication and growth of the regular departments and the increasing number and heterogeneity of students recruited by the university have also contributed to turning it into a bureaucracy, especially in the United States. Here, as elsewhere, size and differentiation entail the need to develop a corps of administrators—professionals, or faculty members turned bureaucrats. The old core, teaching and scholarly research, is dwarfed and eroded by all the time spent on rulemaking and executing, planning and adjudicating. The great advantage of bureaucracy is efficiency—but bureaucratization has not improved academic decision-making. It has contributed to the decline in the autonomy of the university as a social system, through the transfer of power from within the university to agencies outside: Administratively, the university's faculty and governing boards may propose priorities and allocations, but the decisions are often made by the bodies that actually sponsor and finance. With respect to the university's internal government, the old, largely pre-bureaucratic structures are being gradually undermined in two ways. The decentralized, faculty-ruled process of yesterday, with its limited functions, is being made more formidably complex and rigid by the increasing number of activities only marginally related to teaching and research with which the traditional units now have to cope. It is also being increasingly emptied of importance by the new bureaucracy, which grows either centrally, above those units, or peripherally, in the well-staffed research centers. The result is frequently paralyzing. The older units deal with trivia, at worst, or parochial subjects, at best; the new bureaucracy is either highly specialized or deprived of any coherent impulse, for the governing boards are not equipped to provide direction in a period of rapid and general change. The combination of time-eating processes that absorb the faculty, of bureaucracies that give the (false) impression of usurping decisions, and of central decision-making bodies that are good only at expediting run-of-the-mill affairs and bad at taking initiatives leaves the university with little or no capacity for concerted innovation, and re-enforces the sense of drift. Finally, for the individual student and teacher, bureaucratization means the intrusion of anonymity. For the tenured professor

188

who used to see himself as the university, this is a fall from grace; for the student or untenured faculty member, it means the addition of impersonal distance to the personal hierarchy of academia.

The impact of meritocracy is more complex, but no less divisive. Universities are making a valiant effort to open their doors to young men and women selected exclusively for their previous achievements—that is, to apply the meritocratic principle not merely within the university, but as a criterion for admission. As a result, the scramble for success, both among students and in the junior faculty, has become more intense, for more is at stake. Hence a paradoxical consequence: Yesterday, the meritocratic principle at work within the university served as a corrective for the prevailing principles of access to positions of power—birth or wealth; it was, literally, a humanizing and equalizing force. Today, it often serves as a brutalizing force of harsh selection—which may explain both why tensions between students and junior faculty, on one side, senior faculty, on the other, have on the whole increased, and why the revolt against this permanent competitiveness has often received the endorsement of otherwise standard-conscious humanists.[9]

The university is a battlefield between rival meritocratic principles. A meritocracy is an elite recruited through certified achievement, but this does not tell us what is supposed to be achieved. There is a tension between what might be called a *mandarine* meritocracy, whose criterion of accomplishment is "cognitive rationality"—that is, a prowess in demonstrating, in acquiring, or in communicating knowledge—and a *technocratic* meritocracy, whose criterion of merit is one's capacity to contribute to the application of a certain body of knowledge to human problems or what might be called "pragmatic" or "service" rationality. The latter, of course, is a mark of the interpenetration between society and the university and of the domination of the former over the latter. It is also far more vague, at least in the sense of not being easily measured by the kinds of tests that have traditionally evaluated cognitive rationality. Thus, not only do we find a battle between young and old—the tested candidates versus the established testers—but also a debate among testers on the nature of the test and a dilemma for the tested as to which course of merit to select. In this contest, the new meritocratic principle has many assets, for the test is intellectually easier and success delivers more—not just academia but the whole world.

At a time when bureaucracy and technocracy raise the problem of governing so large an institution as the sprawling modern university, all the uncertainties of the meritocratic principle, when applied to the political sphere, trouble the university. For what may be a fine principle of selection into, and of advancement within, the university may not be an adequate criterion for the recruitment of academic "governors." The best mandarins are often the most reluctant, and least competent, to serve in such jobs. The best technocrats—even if their field of expertise is public affairs, and even if they serve not on the faculty, but on the university's governing boards—are not necessarily masters of the very special art of handling a university: an art that is both new and elusive. Mandarins know a lot about academic politics—the C. P. Snow world of appointments and allocations; and technocrats tend to be best at the specialized politics of their particular branch. Ideally, the task requires men of character and imagination, two attributes not necessarily connected with certified achievement. Nor are the character and imagination required to survive in the bureaucratic jungle of the government necessarily those for which the very different world of the university cries. Men who have the necessary qualities exist, but are normally discovered only in a crisis, when it is fairly late. Meanwhile, by another paradox, the meritocratic principle contributes to what might be called the governance vacuum of the modern university. Leadership, now essential, is obstructed.

As a microcosm of modern society, the university displays, consequently, the baffling but familiar feature of a loss of control over its own fate. For lack of a principle of integration and discrimination that could guide its growth and order its activities, it exhibits fragmented, low-level, instrumental "rationality," which usually consists of the rationalization of demands for more of everything, but no over-all rationality. This is particularly scandalous in a university, both under the old ideal of providing its members not only with knowledge but with standards of judgment for mastery and self-mastery, and under the new ideal of providing the locus and the tools for the "integrative planning" of modern society. Nor is the university's structure any more rational: a mixture of yesterday's oligarchy (academic self-government); yesterday's non-bureaucratic, church-like hierarchy (shown both in the powerlessness of students and in the key role played by a small number of influentials who are important less for their formal positions in the university's organization chart than for the personal authority they derive from the president's or governing boards' confidence); and, finally, today's bureaucratic hierarchy, growing capriciously in the interstices of the other two modes.

There is one final respect in which the university serves as a microcosm of society. The three features of modern society all tend to reduce politics to management, to concentrate decisions into the hands of "those who know," to neglect the definition of and choices among ends, and to reduce the selection of means to a choice of techniques—whether the ideology that covers the method be called global planning or incrementalism. As a result, established political parties become increasingly interchangeable and irrelevant, or else (like Western Europe's Communists) bloated collectors of protests condemned to perpetual and ineffective opposition. Those who oppose the whole system and want to fight it actively, whether on the far left or on the far right, in their fear and suspicion of being co-opted (or, as the French say, recuperated), tend to resort to an activist version of Marcuse's great refusal—to the politics of total challenge and direct action. Thus, between the prestigious and smooth managerial nihilism of piecemeal drift and the noisy and destructive nihilism of *contestation*, the political horizon shrinks. Even the tried and tested axioms of traditional "group theory" politics fail—in situations where those who accept the new social order tend to be disdainful of the time losses involved in consultation, log rolling, and group adjustment, and those who reject the present society refuse any adjustment or compromise.[10] The university seems to be the laboratory of so bleak a political future. In recent years, it has displayed the bizarre dialectic of countless, reactive, and inevitably contradictory responses emanating from faculties and officials—"disconnected discussions of discrete demands, i.e. . . . the kind of pragmatism in which what is truly important gets subordinated to what appears urgent"[11]—and of disruptive tactics focused on symbolic issues, yet unappeasable by specific concessions precisely because of the global discontent and totalistic aspiration that move the militants.

This discontent would perhaps not have taken the university so directly as a target had the university not appeared as legitimizing what is obnoxious in modern society by letting the outside world invade its own inner sanctum. Here, there is a contradiction both with the university's past role and, even more, with its past ideal. Yesterday's university could not really be accused of sanctifying the feudal or the capitalist order. It did not challenge it directly,

191

and the restricted nature of the student body indicated a kind of tacit acceptance. But this limited access was the result of things beyond the university's control—inequality in society, consecrated by the secondary school system. Moreover, the university, as we have seen, did its best to temper the privileges of birth and wealth, both through scholarships for pure merit and through a scholarly selection based on merit among the privileged. The whole ideology of knowledge as virtue and power had a revolutionary impact. The university, by virtue of its distance from society, succeeded in being both "integrative" and "adaptive": integrative directly, in transmitting a cultural heritage and in helping recruit an elite; adaptive indirectly, in providing a critical examination of society— that is, in laying the intellectual groundwork for a slow change of its cultural base.[12] Today's university, by becoming more like industry or the government, and through its very efforts at direct social innovation, acts as if it endorsed the way in which such innovation takes place in modern society (whether this way be called gradualism or tokenism, progressive or repressive, foreign aid or imperialism), especially as its new role can be carried out only by accepting external financing, priorities, and controls. An ideology of neutral and critical detachment blurred the inevitable connection between university and society (and helped isolate the university from the battles between defenders and challengers of the social *status quo*). The ideology of service developed by the champions of the multiversity helps turn the university itself into a battle-ground between the moderates (conservatives or reformists) and the *contestataires*. Yesterday's claim to neutrality was hailed as the protection of a sanctuary; today, the same claim is often resented both as a Pilate-like acknowledgment of the established order's rightness and as a hypocritical demand for immunity from criticism of the university's overt activities as a promoter of that order. The modern universities' expansion and the resulting urban problems symbolize the clash between the "ins" and the "outs" of the new order and demonstrate both its inexorable march and its human costs. In other words, knowledge, instead of being celebrated as the explosive force that destroys Bastilles through enlightenment, is often denounced as a corrupt force that consolidates the power of the educated few at the direct, physical expense of the others. It is still power, but more visibly for evil than for good (whereas in yesterday's society, power for evil was associated with wealth or birth); and it is certainly not virtue.

The university is not just a good place to study the impact of the new social order. It is also particularly vulnerable to the tensions that follow. Solving its problems would, in any case, entail nothing less than straightening out all the kinks of modern society. The claims presented, imprudently perhaps, by the celebrators of the post-industrial age on behalf of the university should allow one to expect it to try for nothing less. But it is not realistic to be too hopeful.

The university is vulnerable, first of all, because of all the institutions of society it is the only one that has both deeply submitted to the new forces described and is least naturally made for them. Some institutions, like the family and, to some extent, the churches, have not yet been deeply affected. Others have been, but they are single-purpose institutions, openly at the service of society—such a service being their *raison d'être:* I refer to the professions. The debate among their members is about whom to serve rather than about whether and how. Other institutions have been greatly helped, revived, perpetuated, expanded by the three contemporary features. For instance, the large modern corporations have revolutionized industry, and the armed forces have been given the most advanced gadgets and the most appealing glamor by technological modernization. Some institutions have, in fact, developed in response to the new features, such as the modern state bureaucracy and many of the services of the so-called tertiary sector. But the university, whatever its past ideology, was never a single-task organization with simple ends. There was, to be sure, a hierarchy of functions (and of prestige), but there were always enough vocational aspects, especially in the United States, to explain why contemporary proliferation and fragmentation could occur so easily. Despite the attempts by defenders of the new order to show how it grows out of the old and continues an old tradition of service, however, there is a hiatus between the new activities—multiple involvements and involvement with multiple co-workers—and what used to be the quintessential educational relationships: the dialogue (unequal, to be sure!) between teacher and students, the lonely confrontation of the scholar or apprentice scholar with his material. A thorough remodeling of the university along the lines of a technocratic bureaucracy and meritocracy might literally destroy what has been its traditional core; a partial remodeling perpetuates the inner conflict.

The university is vulnerable, in the second place, because it shelters the three groups most opposed to the new order. True, it admits very few children of this order's underprivileged, and many of those who get in prefer, to the buoyant pleasures of *contestation,* the absorbing demands of trying to make it, so as to escape from their background and to enter the elite (thus choosing the new and more vocational features of the university instead of the old, humanistic ones). But this does not apply to America's black students, representatives of an ethnic minority that (like the European workers of the early nineteenth century) opts for collective ascent rather than ascent through individual escape. As the perpetual proletarians of the social order, old or new (at a time when the workers, yesterday's proletarians, have become largely integrated and—sometimes in fact, although not in theory, but at times most emphatically in both ideology and practice—opt for individual ascent through "the system"), they challenge the new order. They try to pressure the university into letting more of them in, thus attacking its meritocratic aspects, and try to divert it from consolidating the established elites.

The same is true, of course, of the sons and daughters of the affluent, who question the values, or lack of values, of the social order which they will be asked to lead. For the young blacks the university is both a powerful elevator and an instrument to be used for radical change. The behavior of the more privileged young *contestataires,* on the other hand, is difficult to explain by their social background, but understandable in terms of the conflicting psychological pressures to which they are subjected while at the university. During those years of protracted adolescence fostered by industrial society, they are in a state of suspension from society; yet they are being, so to speak, prepared for it. Adolescence has always been a period of reluctance toward adulthood, a time for the "redefinition of internalized culture."[13] This reluctance used to take the form of antiparental rebellions. With more permissive parents and in universities that have lost their distance from society, it is normal that the rebellion turns against society itself—and against the university, insofar as its emphasis on fixed curricula, grades, concentration, and specialization seems to force the young to make decisive commitments, to narrow their perspectives, and to limit their experience long before they are ready for such closure. The drive of adolescence is one of integral spontaneity. It conflicts with what they feel to be the multiple sterility of much of their education. The language of adolescence is easily that of liberation—through "imagination, direct perception and fantasy"[14] or through political militancy. It clashes with what they feel to be society's overt or covert repression, manifest in and sanctioned by the university. Moreover, at the same time as the students are being trained to become self-reliant, self-directed, and adapted to society, they are also kept in a situation of dependence within the university. They rebel both against the contradiction between their status and the purpose of their presence in the university, and against a dependence that is easy for them to interpret not merely as the reflection of academic hierarchy (the traditional relation between novices and initiates), but also as the translation within the university of the hierarchical relations of modern society. Placed in the position of underlings while they are trained for mastery, they are led to reject the very notion of hierarchy and the criteria on which it is based.

Thus they react because both their thriving for being treated as adults and their clinging to adolescence (which today means also their solidarity as an age group, distinct from the adult world and distrustful of the de-energizing procedures invented by the adults) are being thwarted by the university. Nostalgia and impatience merge in the grand fantasy of a counter-adult world, in which they would have the same rights the adults have now, but so as to reject what the adults have done to the world. They would not enter the adult's world, even as equals; it would be up to the adults to get admitted into the world remade by the young. It is not surprising if they do not, on the whole, show much enthusiasm for the old notion of the ivory tower, for they know it to have been highly hierarchical, and the mass media, from which they have learned so much, have blasted all the tower's walls. Moreover, brought up in a climate hostile to enclaves and oases and favorable to social integration, brought to a university that has become penetrated by society, their natural reaction is not to return, but to overturn—to turn the university both into an instrument of social change that would save the world from bureaucracy, meritocracy, and technocracy, and into a laboratory of non-directive relations. With few models in the real world, they have to improvise life styles or to draw from the real world not examples but mythic approximations such as Mao, Ho, or Che.

As for the academics dissatisfied with the new order, some of them are self-professed revolutionaries whose goals are similar to those of the rebelling students. But most of them, in the humanities especially, have in the back of their minds the model, often highly idealized, of the university of the past—what might be called the Barzun model. Theirs is a protest against the fragmentation of knowledge and the cheapening of the university through "servicing." Theirs is a plea for restoring the unity of learning and upholding the principles of humanism. Insofar as contemporary meritocracy has contributed to fragmentation, cheapening, and dependence on the outside market, they are often willing to soften its rigors with respect to grades or exams. But precisely because of their attachment to the old ideal, they are sharply critical both of student demands for "relevance" (which strike them as the mirror image of the instrumentalism they deplore) and of student claims to power. In their eyes, students come to learn, not to rule; considerations of power are already a mark of intrusion of the outside world into a sanctuary that should deal only with matters spiritual; and problems of curriculum and appointments should remain in the hands of the wise. It is an aristocratic notion, not devoid of noble and self-serving delusions. Rebel students want to turn the university into a counter-society; dissenting academics would prefer it separate from society. They agree on the condemnation of the new order, but their agreement is not the outcome of identical analyses: It is the momentary convergence of a basically anti-elitist, communitarian, anti-institutional radicalism, and of an elitist and slightly parochial defense of a threatened institution (both from outside enslavement and from inside student disruptions).

Thus, the number of dissenters is great, but there is really no common front among them. The university appears doubly condemned to remaining the battleground of a protracted war. The young children of established parents object more to the notion of the university as a service station for the Establishment than to the idea of the university as a service station, which appeals to their idealism. The academics who criticize the present state of affairs object to the notion of the service station, partly because the Establishment it works for is one in which the traditional ivory tower intellectual becomes an uninfluential relic. The convergence against the present Establishment is not sufficient to eliminate the profound divergence about the status of the student within the university. Indeed, since most of the university crises have been initiated by student activists, it is around the single issue of reacting to their disruptions that alignments have been formed in the university. One finds on each side of the barricade men otherwise in deep disagreement over all other issues. In particular, resistance to student agitation and to demands for student power has often thrown together humanists or historians deeply hostile to the modern multiversity and pragmatic managers who are its spokesmen. All they have in common is the desire to defend authority, while they disagree as to where it should reside and how it should be organized. On the other side, impatience with obsolete institutions and irrational hierarchies has often thrown together student militants, who want a counter-multiversity, and academic reformers, who play with the tantalizing notion of a more communitarian (although not necessarily fully democratic) ivory tower.

There is a third reason why the university is vulnerable. It is a delicate machine that can be paralyzed by a grain of sand. "Our social Waterloos are being fought out in match boxes."[15] A handful of disrupters can "close it up," simply by forcing all the constituencies into turmoil and through the agony of choosing between equally unsavory courses of action. It is easier here than almost anywhere else for a very small group to move. In a factory (as was shown in France last year), a disruption has a chance of succeeding only if it is endorsed—willingly or reluctantly—by the unions, which provide a kind of disciplining straitjacket. There is no equivalent in the university, whose members have never thought of themselves as part of a political institution (hence the pitiful weakness of student government in those times when it ought to be most effective). In a city or in the countryside, would-be terrorists hesitate to launch a campaign unless there is at least an incipient network of support; in a university, they can count on provoking such support by acting first. A campus is a better trial ground for Debray's theories than Bolivia. On the side of "law and order," a university—again by contrast with industry or with cities—has no secular arm. The commitment to "reasoned discourse"; the reluctance either to develop an internal police or to call on the external one; the physical difficulty of protecting every possible building, classroom, or facility against harassment or guerrilla tactics; the slowness and frequent (and inevitable) arbitrariness of disciplinary procedures—all of these make it difficult for the university to find a middle ground between the peace and order of self-discipline, the voluntary practice of commonly accepted rules of civility (barely breached by a few individual violations), and the return to the state of nature, whereas most institutions have found some way, Hobbesian or Lockean, to live in the middle.

True, the university is not the only institution vulnerable to conflicts. But it is uniquely unfit to manage them, for several reasons. It is probably the only institution that recoils before the

197

notion that it is a political system. To me, an institution is a political system as soon as there is a conflict over ends and over how power should be arranged to reach them. Yet most academics and university administrators reject the idea with indignation (and thus resist the notion and practice of leadership), partly because of the hallowed but false notion that the business of the university is truth, and truth and power are incompatible; partly because of the fear of external manipulation and internal chicanery which the word politics evokes. Knowledge, alas, has not only its sociology but also its politics. As long as there is unwillingness to recognize reality, there can be no realistic way of preventing the conflicts from wrecking the university; for the task ahead is not the suppression of conflict, the achievement of the seductive dream of total harmony in community, but the management of conflict and its channeling in such a way that it can gradually be resolved.

As anyone who has lived through a university crisis knows, the university tends to be a total institution that absorbs not merely part of the personality of its inmates, but most of it; students, often denounced as transients, behave as totally committed occupants who, even when they attack the university, do it as if it were "their" thing and from an ideal of perfection. Professors, it is true, increasingly play various public roles (which is part of the trouble); but for most of them, all the other roles are rooted in their academic status. As theories of cognitive dissonance would make one expect, they convince themselves that there is no conflict among their roles, so long as the university is redefined in a way that embraces and enshrines them all. There are divergences as to what the total commitment entails, but not as to whether it is total. As their physical involvement shrinks, their psychological one grows—and it is intensity, not quantity, that matters here. Now, it is easier to devise a workable political system when it involves only certain roles, functionally *and* psychologically. (This also allows the participants to select representatives who will defend their interests and who are, so to speak, more or less full-time delegates of those roles.) In the political system properly so-called, elected representatives and executives look (supposedly) after the people's interests *qua* citizens; in factories, workers' efforts have consistently aimed at minimizing the impact of the work relationship—that is, at limiting their stultifying role as workers, short of being able to realize the early dreams of a total take-over of the workshop by the workers. Only military services display a total commitment comparable to that which exists in the university—but for obvious reasons the problem of conflicts in the armed forces does not have the same urgency, except in times of split loyalties and civil crisis, and the problem of managing such conflicts is a problem for the over-all political system.

There is a final reason for the university's plight in handling conflicts. At the turn of the century and almost until World War II, the industrial world was the focus of maximum tension, largely under the impact of ideologies (both economic liberalism and all the varieties of socialism) that pointed to the factory as the center of decisive power in society. Moreover, there was considerable, although not exclusive, truth in this. Today, academics and *contestataires*, heralds of the dawn of the post-industrial age, believers in the university as the guardian of culture, *gauchistes* who see in it the linchpin of the industrial-military-scientific-Establishment complex—all elevate the university to a symbolic height at which compromises become degrading. Hence an unleashing of hyperbole and hysteria ensues whenever trouble begins, helped by the flocking of mass media hipsters to the trouble points. But here the analogy with factories stops: A general strike or even a strike in key industries can bring a nation to *its* knees, whereas the disruption of universities only closes *them*. Society can find ways to have those functions they perform directly for society carried out in extra-university research centers or laboratories, and as Japan has been showing with a fine mixture of savagery and indifference, the indirect service that the university performs for society by promoting knowledge and educating its elites can be disrupted for years without any noticeable collapse of society. For those who want to learn the tools of the trade which they will need either just to earn a living or to succeed in positions of technical expertise *and* social influence, there always are other channels.

Thus today's university stews in the heat produced by passionate involvement on behalf of conflicting beliefs. If each member's commitment to his notion of the university were more limited, a resolution of the conflict would be easier. But its intensity is equal to, and aggravated by, its scope: There is a most extensive disagreement on ends.

There is a basic antagonism between those who think that the university can be an adequate instrument of social action and those who remain skeptical or suspicious of the new functions unrelated to teaching, basic research, and training through the communication of substantive knowledge. In one direction, this disagreement extends into a debate on the relations between culture and praxis: on the degree to which what a university offers ought to be determined by its own ideals of education, or by society's often conflicting vocational needs, dominant demands, or minority claims. In another direction, this disagreement carries over into a conflict over the proper size of the university, which the skeptics would like to cut back to the core functions. It also leads to a conflict over structure, which one group would like to adapt so that the new functions could be fully integrated or absorbed into the old ones, and the other group would like to disconnect—partially or totally— from the university.

Among those who favor an activist university, there is, of course, a clash between those who would like the university to be the agent of society (so as eventually to improve it), and those who would like it to subvert society (so as to transform it radically). There are tensions within each group—divisions in the second over the degree and direction of activism (should it aim at a radical reorientation of the university or at a preliminary, purging destruction?); there are divisions in the first group over research priorities.

There is discord over the degree to which the university should be made into more of a community. The alignments are not the same as over the first issue. Those who see the teaching-research relationship as the essence of the university, and as fundamentally noncommunitarian (so that all efforts at community-building are seen as anti-intellectual diversions or perversions) are skeptical or hostile. But they are joined by those who favor the trend toward diversification, promote functional rather than university involvements, and believe that decisions ought to be made in "a broad systems context" rather than on a community basis. And they are also joined by those student activists who see in the idea of an academic community an elitist and parochial distraction from drastic social change.

There is a disagreement over standards of admission. For example, should there be a special effort at accommodating minority groups? Alignments here cannot be predicted in the light of attitudes taken over the first three issues.

There is also a complex disagreement over curriculum reform, which involves both a debate on the nature of the subject-matter appropriate for academic teaching and research (here one finds, of course, a reflection of alignments over the first two issues), and a debate on the best methods of learning. Thus, *what* is to be taught and *how* one is to learn are the issues at stake; and through those issues, the relations of teachers and students are being questioned.

There is a disagreement over the usefulness of preserving the notion (or myth) of academic neutrality. Those academics who rebel against the new order are divided: Some see this idea as a delusion that facilitates degradation; others raise it as a banner against further involvements. The whole concept of academic freedom is being scrutinized in this debate, which raises the question of how far the corporate will can regulate and curtail the activities of individual members.

Finally, there is a bewildering range of discord over every aspect of governance: the role and composition of the governing boards, the nature of the presidency, the appropriateness of a more representative system, the respective virtues of formal versus informal channels of authority, of larger versus smaller or professional versus amateur bureaucracies, the proper role of and institutions for students, and so forth.

The crisis of the university is thus far more than an institutional crisis. But institutional reform is essential and cannot wait—not only because one cannot afford to keep the present procedures until a new agreement on fundamentals has somehow been reached, but also because no such agreement can come out of discredited procedures. The task ahead can be defined as follows: to devise broadly acceptable institutions rapidly enough so that energy shall at last be focused where it should—on ends—rather than diverted to the poisons and delights of constitutional arguments, and so that the university may cope with the continuing crisis. It looks like the search for the formula to square the circle.

There is a crisis of legitimacy, which has undermined the existing institutions. No amount of muttering about a mere handful of youthful demagogues and willful faculty fools (or tools) can make reality disappear. A crisis of legitimacy develops in any political system when its members feel that the institution is no longer effective and that part of the reason for inefficiency is not just technical miscalculations or ignorance, but also insufficient responsiveness to the needs or desires of the members, even if those needs and desires are widely different. In the case of the university, the piecemeal way in which issues have been raised and handled, a consequence of substantive discord and procedural deficiency, has weakened the institutions further. A coherent approach to the crisis has been made impossible by two kinds of institutional fragmentations: horizontal and vertical. On the one hand, there has been a rather rigid separation of constituencies along status lines, resulting in a large amount of authoritarianism—each stratum is partly ruled by the one above it. The students' government has usually dealt with trifles; what most affects their lives in the university—studies, discipline, even extracurricular activities—has been largely determined without their participation. The faculties have enjoyed considerable autonomy over educational matters, but the financial framework of their freedom is established from above, and the transformation of the university through direct involvement with society has mainly taken place as the result of decisions made by the governing boards, whose main concern, indeed whose constituency, is society at large. These boards, in turn, have often reacted to initiatives and pressures that come from society and the government. On the other hand, there has also been a vertical fragmentation along the functional lines of departments, institutes, and established schools.

The consequences have been destructive. Fragmentation has bred misinformation and distrust. The governing boards are theoretically the only bodies empowered to deal with the whole, but their composition, priorities, and fitful mode of operation—"absentee government"[16]—also made them less than effective. The student constituency, long treated as irresponsible, has often tended to behave irresponsibly, by taking apocalyptically vague and sweeping positions, of great peril to the delicate balance of the university, or by showing no concern above and beyond their academic performances. The faculty, having enjoyed considerable but parochial self-government, has tended to behave parochially, digging in for the defense of its traditional trenches or splitting under pressure along every conceivable line. Moreover, each of the constituencies below the top of the pyramid could not help but feel victimized by those placed above it, since the latter had a part in determining their fate with almost no input from below. This was a perfect recipe not only for trouble, but also for the kind of conspiratorial mythology that worsens it. Those above are resented as powerful and malicious groups, not as fragmented or haphazard assemblages of men. At the same time, the paternal existence of the bodies above removed from each group below the necessity to think through, and do something about, the problems that affect it, but over which it has no legal authority.

Given these tensions, an impossible burden has been put on those unfortunate men who, formally or informally, were supposed to be the links between constituencies, especially the deans and the president. Like hinges in a burning building, they became unstuck, unsure of which piece of the carpentry to fall with. They find it hard to rule and often impossible to lead. A dean is supposed to be able to report to the president and to the governing boards what his faculty wants. But if he considers himself to be first of all the president's administrative aide, both his influence over the faculty and his effectiveness as a spokesman for it—that is, as the president's chief of intelligence—will be impaired. As for the president, if he feels closer to the internal constituencies (students and faculties) than to the external ones (alumni, government, and foundations), he may end in trouble with his trustees. If he tries to represent or to appease the external constituencies, he risks losing the support of the internal ones. The present setup makes any kind of over-all leadership unlikely in normal times and impossible if matters come to a crisis. But it thereby contributes to bringing about a crisis, for the men who have to make the key decisions are isolated, which partially blinds them; they are overworked, with little time left to anticipate and to listen, which largely numbs them; yet they are endowed with extensive powers over their subjects, which makes them easy targets. It is hard to imagine a more bizarre melange, although it was perfectly "functional" in the days when the university was seen primarily as a center for learning and scholarly research. How often do we find, in the history of institutions, that the bodies most appropriate for one particular phase were also quite incapable of preventing—indeed they sometimes accelerated—the passage to another phase in which they would prove both ineffective and illegitimate?

Efficiency and legitimacy today go together. Efficiency requires the capacity to take an over-all view of the university's problems so as to redefine its purposes. Legitimacy requires a less authoritarian and oligarchic structure, in which the constituents have a greater sense of responsible involvement (by contrast with mere emotional commitment without corresponding responsibilities). Broadening and democratization should not be separated. On the one hand, given the need for a new global view, there is a growing recognition of the need for bodies that cut *across* the existing lines of division, horizontal and vertical. Democratization *within* each of those lines could easily make the university more rigid and paralyzed than it is now, just as "community control," even if it is genuinely democratic and not merely the control exerted by local elites or special interests, can often result either in stultifying conservatism or in a chaotic mosaic of conflicting experiments. On the other hand, without responsible involvement of all the parties, the present mixture of parochial fragmentation and over-all irresponsibility would persist, the new bodies becoming mere arenas for the paralyzing confrontation of vested claims. Democratization is the precondition for a true raising of sights that will result not merely from a breaking up of the barriers within each constituency, but also from the mutual prodding of delegates from all.

The notions of broadening and democratization give us a direction, but not much more. They indicate only that the university must now be studied and handled as a political system; and in advanced societies that are not run by totalitarian cliques, a political system cannot be governed from the top down. But what are the democratic procedures adequate to so complex a system—one so different from other institutions and also so diversely divided over its goals? Can one even find an adequate scheme of governance to facilitate the debate on ends as long as the range of discord is so huge? The truth of the matter is that the notion of participation—which implies both democratization and, logically, involvement in the making of decisions affecting the university as a whole (that is, *more* of a voice on *more* issues)—this notion, which has been embraced both by students and by faculty in their revolts against decisions from the top, runs into obstacles and objections that cannot be dismissed.

Albert Hirschman has studied the two ways in which ineffective organizations can recover[17]: They can be forced to do so by the *exit* of their members or customers, who leave in order to join or patronize more efficient rival organizations; or they can be improved by giving a *voice* to their dissatisfied clientele. The university is both a further example of his theory and a very special case. In the university, as elsewhere, the demand for voice grows as the possibility and the attractiveness of exit diminish. Academic mobility, especially among the top universities, has lost some of its appeal; and the students, of course, all want in, not out. In the university, as elsewhere, the effectiveness of voice is increased if exit, while not so easily available to the discontented as to be deemed by them preferable to voice, is still usable as a threat: It is, in fact, still available to many academics and effective as a threat if they are of considerable reputations. But there are some very special circumstances here.

First, there is the phenomenon of conflicting clienteles within the same institution. The professors are often hostile to giving students a voice, even while they claim more of a voice for themselves. Should the students gain too much voice, many professors would prefer to exit. Should students and faculty gain too much voice, it is the alumni (or the legislature) who might exit—that is, drain the university of resources. The students' demand for voice is to a large extent a protest against what they see as a partial exit of the faculty—that is, the part-time absenteeism of the consulting academic. Secondly, there is a division within some of the clienteles. Hirschman notes that when one has paid a high price for entry into an organization which one then finds disappointing, either one will protect one's investment by self-deception, or one will try to vindicate it by active demands for reform. Some students react in the former way, others in the latter. The same is true of the faculty. There is a notable reluctance of many professors toward voice even for themselves, precisely because they have had the opportunity of *partial* exit—not only to raise their salary and status, but also to rise above academic parochialism. As Hirschman points out, the greater the number of involvements, the smaller the appeal of voice. Their reluctance is, of course, also due to their impatience with the costs of voice—that is, with the diversion from scholarship and teaching which participation implies; one might call this a preference for *internal* exit from the vicissitudes of management. Rather than gaining voice, many faculty members would rather exit completely, toward research institutions other than universities where the problem would not arise. Hirschman has noted the power, in organizations, of those who have nowhere else to go— that is, those who cannot exit and who often prevail precisely because of their capacity to spend all their energy on controlling the organization, even at the expense of its long-term interests (for instance, the most doctrinaire members of a party in a two-party system). In the university, those who have nowhere else to go, both in the faculty and in the administration, are mostly the enemies of voice.

Thirdly, it is particularly difficult to obtain in a university that correct mix of alertness and inertia, of loyalty and dissatisfaction, which Hirschman deems essential to the recovery of damaged organizations. He points out that loyalty is functional (that is, contributes to reform) when it prevents the premature exit of worthy members or clients to similar organizations; dysfunctional when there is no similar organization to which one could flee (that is, when abstaining from voice means thwarting improvements, as is frequently the case with national loyalty). Now, the university resembles the nation-state in this respect, for the kind of exit that is still most easily available and attractive to academics and university administrators is exit toward different organizations: not from Harvard to Yale—if only because no university is really safe from conflict—but from Harvard to Rand or to an industrial laboratory. Those kinds of exits, when they do take place, as well as many of the demands for voice, may be counterproductive from the viewpoint of university reform: the former because they are less jolting for the university than the increasingly rare exits to rival universities, and the latter because, when they take the form of violent protests, they are clearly nefarious. In one case, one never reaches reform; in the other, one courts destruction.

Hirschman has incisively commented on the general American reluctance toward voice. This is a nation where success has been based on exit—first from Europe; then, through individual ascent, from one's own milieu. What is true for this largely democratic people is even more true in nations whose neglect of voice is due not to any cult of exit, but simply either to a preference for authoritarianism (as in much of Europe) or to a preference for non-involved independence (as in France). These attitudes toward voice are reinforced in the case of the universities not only by the special circumstances just described, but also by the weight of traditional authoritarianism and by the burdens of academic participation. Those burdens are not inherent in the notion of participation. They result from a double mistake. We tend to think of a more democratic university as if the job consisted of transplanting into it the institutions of political democracy, without reflecting whether they are at all appropriate. Just because the university is *a* political system, the institutions we have devised for *the* political system are not necessarily relevant. Moreover, the members of the university tend to base both their judgments on new academic institutions and their estimate of their fitness for these institutions on their estimate of and performance in the existing ones, thus forgetting how deeply behavior can be affected by new institutions, as long as they are well devised.

There are three models of political democracy. None of the

three is suitable. One is the model of so-called participatory democracy, whose intellectual foundation remains Rousseau's *Social Contract*. It assumes that one's interest as a member of a community is qualitatively superior to all one's other interests and cannot be delegated: Each member must contribute to the general will. It is a fascinating ideal-type, but it does not work. True, the present generation of students leans toward participation in the sense of total involvement. But in real life, participatory democracy means, at best, the triumph not of the will to the common good, but of sheer majority rule and, at worst, not even the victory of "the people," but the rule of the manipulators—those who have the vision to define the general will and the energy to coax and coerce assemblies into "recognizing" it. In real life, it also means not, as Rousseau wanted, the discovery and declaration of a general, legislative will, but the improvisation of *ad hominem* and special measures, often either partial or fatal to minorities. The model of the small nation is especially useless for the university. On the one hand, the university has the special problem of its relation to society. Is its general will to be that of the university members *qua* citizens, in which case any university autonomy disappears; or is it to be that of its members *qua* participants in academia, in which case we will return to the ivory tower? Surely not all of its members, when they want the common good, agree on whether it is the first kind of will or the second. On the other hand, whatever the answer to this question, the notion of the single and homogeneous legislative will—general in origin and essence, but limited in scope "to impersonality and to fairness toward all"[18]—while helpful in underlining the need for a common spirit and a minimum of corporate rules, provides inadequate guidance for a complex system in which the joint commitment grows out of highly differentiated enterprises and constituencies. The "governance job" is to reconcile and balance their interests rather than either to fuse them or to leave them out of the body politic. The general will either leaves the problem of university government unsolved, or else it means the usual perversion—in this instance, the destruction of the university through total politicization—and hence the demoralization, sooner or later, of all of its members and their withdrawal from the general will.

A second political model is that of nineteenth century representative government: government by parliaments and boards or councils or committees, in which the diverse interests of the constituents are represented by delegates. Two kinds of objections arise instantly. On the one hand, in order to function properly, representative government everywhere requires political parties that offer competing programs to their constituents. Politics being a specialized activity, the citizens, while split along party lines, can ordinarily cooperate in their other activities or else, in those activities, conflict in non-partisan ways. This is much more difficult in a university. If there is to be not merely corporate representation along functional lines, but also representation based on general opinions about university purposes, what will prevail will be not a genuine consideration of the issues over which people disagree—that is, a political resolution in the highest sense—but the political game itself: the arcane intricacies of caucuses, elections, jobseeking, and bargaining, a mixture of ideological polarization and personal accommodations in which the basic issues will be lost. The advantage of representative government, when it works, is that it relieves the citizens of the necessity to be full-time politicians; the disadvantage of such government in a university is that it might turn students, professors, and alumni into politicians. In a total institution, parliamentarism, instead of allowing for the representation of political views, risks degenerating into the politics of representation; and the definition and enhancement of the university's specific functions may get drowned in the all-pervading function of politicking.

On the other hand, even in the state and its subdivisions, parliamentarism has not worked well. Nothing would be more paradoxical than the adoption by the university of a method of government that has, in effect, become obsolete where it started. There has been a marked shift from legislative to executive preponderance. Whenever a constitution has tried to interfere with this evolution by preserving legislative supremacy, as in France's Third and Fourth Republics, two sets of disastrous effects appeared. One was paralysis through sheer inefficiency. Large bodies of men simply cannot cope with the overwhelming number of essentially executive decisions which any modern government requires. The other was paralysis through corporatism—the conservatism of log rolling, of compromises based on the mutual protection of established positions. Translated into university terms, one can easily see what might result: There would be a continuing absence of leadership, dissolved into a multitude of anonymous committees. There would be so much government that, as one university president has put it, there would be none[19] (or rather there would be innumerable conflicts without adequate resolution, splintered impotence but no center of power, energy lost on jurisdictional contests but missing for the important issues). Only the most unimaginative outcomes would result, for even in committees of broader scope than the present ones, accommodation might most easily be reached not on innovations or around the university's critical function or by a transcending of departmental or functional interests, but on the basis of a kind of pan-protectionism that would consecrate the reassuringly vocational aspects of the university.[20] Bureaucracy would triumph, given the amount of paperwork involved; and technocracy at its most capricious would triumph, since each technique would be enshrined, and each unit's own idea of "service" would be endorsed. The necessary redefinition of ends would elude us once more, and the incremental or immobilist approach of so many committees would feed the impatience and apocalyptic tendencies of the *contestataires*.

A third political model is that of most contemporary democracies: a powerful executive, based on the consent of the public, and operating between elections with very few formal checks, although under the control of the legislature and the obvious need to keep the trust of his constituents. There are evident advantages over the previous formula in terms of initiative and leadership. But there are, again, two drawbacks: This model entails the growth of a very large and autonomous bureaucracy, which ends up not merely initiating and executing decisions, but also actually making them, and thus limits considerably, in fact, the margin of freedom of the men who are theoretically its political leaders. In a modern state, while the disadvantages are well known, the social services often performed by bureaucracy tend to be sufficient to stifle protest, and the capacity of the constituents to do something about it short of costly, negative insurrection has so far remained limited. The bureaucracy, as Tocqueville had foreseen, is anonymous and distant enough to discourage revolt. In a university, however, the presence of a bureaucracy responsible only to the president and governing boards (whether its members are professional administrators or faculty "in-and-outers") would provoke shrill demands for voice or accountability—especially as such a bureaucratic outcome would appear to thwart the hopes for democratization. The administration would be close and visible enough to become the target of all the tensions and conflicting demands, and at least some of its accomplishments would always be judged contrary to the "true purposes" of the university or to the goals some of its members would like the university to serve.

The second drawback of this model lies in the fact that both the representative and the executive model require a large, full-time political class in the broadest sense—legislators, governors, judges, or bureaucrats: more or less closely controlled, more or less directly representative delegates from society for the handling of its collective affairs. The citizen recognizes that he can be only *indirectly* and *partially* involved, and he chooses men who will be directly and completely involved for him. But the student or the faculty member is directly and almost totally involved. The management of the university is the management of most of his life at the moment, and he does not want someone else to handle it full-time for him. Neither professors nor students would respect or trust a specialized corps of academic or student governors; they would quite rightly see these as an inferior or at least external caste, alien to all the (contested) purposes of the university and threatening to at least some of those ends. The qualities needed for full-time political management are not those on the basis of which students and professors are recruited. Moreover, a full-time legislator, cabinet member, or party leader usually still manages to preserve the kind of perspective that come both from being a professional in politics and from working for a distant or general public. A full-time academic politician risks putting into his performance the peculiar passion and acrimony that comes from seeing himself on a mission rather than in a profession (his profession is to be a professor, if he is a faculty member) and from his immersion in his "public." The politician's involvement is full-time, but (fortunately) not complete psychologically in most cases; the academic governor's involvement would be full-time and total in intensity. To sum up, the division of labor between the political class and the citizenry is essential to the existence of a nation, but a division of labor between a political class and the rest of the university is antithetical to the existence of a university. Being a complex organization with conflicting aims and diverse constituencies, it needs political institutions—institutions that serve, rather than detract from, those purposes for which the organization exists.

The university is *sui generis.* On the one hand, it is an organization with limited, special purposes, and thus is distinct from the national community. What those purposes are, how far they reach, is presently in doubt. But there is a core that, vague as it is, represents the essence of the university—an essence that has to be redefined and made precise and operational from time to time: The essence of the university is the accumulation and transmission of knowledge. To be sure, the university has no monopoly either on the creation or on the communication of knowledge; nor does this description of the essence tell us what constitutes knowledge, how it is to be passed on, or whether transmitting it entails all that the enthusiasts of the university as social laboratory would like to see the university undertake. Were there a consensus on what the essence means today, there would be no crisis. But were the essence to disappear (were it, for example, to be submerged by the attempt to apply knowledge to the solution of current problems; by the attempt to limit the knowledge to be transmitted to what is immediately and thus passingly relevant; or by the attempt to turn the university into a soapbox from which students and society are to be indoctrinated), then there would be no university. This notion of a core provides us with both a point of departure and a thread; at the end of the labyrinth, we hope that the meaning of the essence for the future will have been discovered. But there will be a future only if the essence is saved.

On the other hand, the members of the university have been and are being trained for intellectual mastery and personal autonomy. By virtue of its striving toward the ideal of an association of educated men, and by virtue of the commitment of its members to this ideal (without which, as we have just stated, there is no university), the university is unfit for the kind of voluntary (or implicitly accepted) and recurrently renewed abdication that is the lot of the citizenry in, and the mark of, the all-inclusive political system. Although the ideal is assumed to be shared by all, the nature of the involvement in the university is different for each constituency.

The boundaries of structural reform are thus clarified. Its purpose must be to preserve the essence and to facilitate the great debate on ends which has been avoided so far. "One of the real lacks in our institutions now is . . . a matter of never saying what they are really about."[21] The function of the new ones would be to remedy this lack and to define what the university will be about. If the new functions kept proliferating haphazardly, the university would risk destroying whatever autonomy it still has, both by drowning its core functions and by ditching the ideal (and possibilities) of self-government. Becoming undifferentiated from the rest of society, it would have to develop a specialized political system, like the all-inclusive society, and it is easy to guess that between the political system of the nation and that of the university the relation would be uncomfortably close and hierarchical. But if the goal of the enterprise is to give a new, clearer, and more coherent meaning to the essence of the university, then the institutions to be set up for the debate must be such as to maintain the university during its present time of troubles. Total commitment entails the participation of all the constituencies; but the limited purposes of the university and the different forms the commitment takes oblige one to define carefully what participation should imply.

The general nature of the institutions needed today can be deduced from their functions—to reconsider the aims of the university and to keep it alive in the meantime. This means that the institutions needed now will be temporary. A final, grand exercise in "restructuring" makes sense only once the debate on ends has been held and resolved. (Resolution does not mean a full substantive agreement, but a consensus on a broad range of substance and on procedures for channeling remaining disagreements.) Institutions must be flexible and open. They must be flexible for several reasons. The behavior and beliefs of the various constituencies have been shaped by the responsibilities, roles, and institutions they have had in the past. These attitudes are doubly dangerous: insofar as they are conflicting and insofar as they are (for different reasons) non-participatory—that is, badly prepared for cooperation and compromise, torn between apathy, parochialism, desires for exclusive control, impatience, and the itch of total *contestation*. The new, temporary institutions must be capable of coping with and accommodating these unpromising but unavoidable attitudes. Moreover, only if the institutions are flexible enough will the attitudes change fast enough. Most importantly, since the debate on ends has barely begun, rigid institutions would become an overwhelming, diverting, and irritating battle stake. They must be open because the outcome of any debate on ends is largely determined by the nature of the participants. If one wants a full and thorough debate, the only way to play fair is to have all viewpoints expressed. This means, at one end, that student voices must be heard, however crude or shrill, and, at the other end, that not only the viewpoints of the rich, the successful, and the established should be present in the governing boards which try to bring society's concerns into the university. The underprivileged too have their claims, and there is no reason to leave them or their spokesmen out, either because they represent "failures" or because introducing them would add to the demands that pressure the university. Those demands are made anyhow and might as well get full hearing.

Finally, there can be a true debate on ends only if procedures are established. The present generation of students and many young faculty members see in procedures either a form of "repressive tolerance" or an alibi for inaction. This is often the case, but a debate without procedures and rules of discussion and resolution is an instance of the state of nature. The respect for orderly procedures is a substantive requirement of any civilized society and quite particularly of an educational institution. In a democratic society and in an institution devoted to the ideal of individual autonomy, those rules should be based on broad consent, but they must exist and be enforced.

Concerning the basis of authority or principle of legitimacy, participation will have to be a compromise between democracy and other considerations. That a university cannot and should not be a full democracy, with all members equally sharing in all decisions, has been often and persuasively asserted. But that assertion, by itself, does not consecrate the *status quo*. Because the nature of economic activity rules out total democracy in a factory, boss dictatorship is not thereby the only form of rule. Many of the arguments against democracy in the university overshoot the mark and are not valid against a large measure of democratization. In matters of broad, non-professional judgment, it is legitimate to state that continuity and experience must be somehow weighted, but impossible to argue that students are incompetent to participate in decisions on subjects that affect them or incapable of knowing what their true interests are. Any university crisis demonstrates that the capacity to lose balance and perspective is not any more widespread in the student body than in the faculty.

Full democratization, in the sense of either an exclusive or a shared power to make the final decision, is impossible in two areas. First, there are issues in which professional judgment must remain decisive. (This does not rule out compulsory consultation insofar as non-professional judgment may be relevant, such as on teaching talent.) Appointments to faculty positions and the granting of degrees must remain a faculty preserve not because existing spe-

213

cializations and credentials are sacred cows, but because education is a serious business. Professionalism has its claim, for it means disciplined culture. (This is not synonymous with culture in a discipline, but it distinguishes the professional from the amateur and from the demagogue.) With respect to curriculum reform (which often extends to changing the way in which knowledge is being sliced or the way in which it is acquired), while the professional expertise and experience of the faculty must carry weight, the claim for exclusive decision-making power by the faculty is excessive. The faculty is entitled, indeed it has the duty, to see that whatever subject is taught and whatever method is used to teach it have intellectual substance, for the purpose is learning, not happiness or direct utility. But exclusive power only breeds sterility and *rigor mortis*. Secondly, the power of the purse will inevitably claim respect, and while there is little to be said for trustees thoroughly divorced from academic life setting all the priorities by themselves, faculties will have to remain within the often frustrating limits of financial responsibility.

Concerning the organization of authority, a great deal of imagination is required. Each of the constituencies—students, faculty, alumni, administrative staff—has its own separate interests and must therefore have its own institutions. But there are many decisions that affect several constituencies. Insofar as the conduct of one of them (or rather of its members) has an impact on the others and on the university's capacity to perform its essential functions, there is a need for joint institutions in which decisions on such matters can be either prepared for submission to the constituencies or actually made. Thus, there is no need to put students and faculty members on boards of trustees or students with voting rights into full faculty meetings. But there is a need, especially during the crisis period, for a minimum code of rights and duties—a sort of sketchy social contract—listing the freedoms and the responsibilities of each category of university members, so as to protect its essence from destruction either through the activists' disruptive "voice," or through faculty "exit" to more profitable or less demanding side-jobs, or through administrative highhandedness, or through a governing board's inroads into academic freedom. This legislation on matters of concern to all, even if they are initiated by one segment only, should be devised by joint procedures cutting across all constituencies.[22]

The temporary institutions to be devised will have to be a mix of limited direct democracy and limited representation. Some direct democracy is indispensable—in the form of occasional student referendums (such as on social rules and on extra-academic services provided by the university, for example, for future employment) and of regular faculty meetings for legislative purposes—precisely because of the differences between the over-all political system and a university. No student nor faculty member can, by entering the university, be assumed to have abdicated his right to take a direct part in basic university legislation. As for representation, it must remain part-time. No member of the university is competent to be a "ruler" (except in administrative positions that are not truly policy-making ones) unless he is still, primarily, a student, a faculty member, or an active alumnus. A violation of this precept can only perpetuate the crisis of legitimacy. Thus "the administration"—this recent product of the exuberant growth of bureaucratic activities—would mean either student, faculty, and alumni part-time delegates to executive decision-making functions or full-time professionals of office management. To be sure, it will continue to be difficult to recruit able students and faculty members for "governance." But one should not judge the future by the past. Student distrust of student government is tied not only to the anti-leadership bias of the present student generation, but also to the folkloric functions meagerly granted to such government in the past. The more responsible the positions made available to the students, the more likely it is that they will attract not "campus politicians," but responsible students—especially if their new functions are neither so time-consuming nor so dull as to conflict with their desire "to live and learn up to the hilt and to . . . develop their capacities by trial and error in pursuit of personal enthusiasms."[23] Faculty reticence toward "voice" is based either on the utter sense of waste induced by the proliferation of committees on trivia or on the legitimate fear of becoming (or developing) a special permanent caste of academic politicians increasingly divorced from teaching and research. But if the institutions are flexible enough and aim at broadening the professors' horizon, those fears should wane.

Nothing is more important in this connection than restoring the distinction between general rule-making and executive decisions There has been both a tendency to entrust the latter to "a quasi-legislative process in the name of representation"[24] and a neglect of rule-making in the name of academic freedom. As a result, obsolete rules are still being maintained on paper (and honored in the breach), whereas in important matters, especially those concerning relations with society at large (such as guidelines for the faculty members' research and outside consultancies, and sometimes even for discipline) decisions are made *ad hoc* and case by case—or result from the very absence of formal decisions. Participation should mean the involvement of the constituencies, through direct legislative consultation, in the adoption of general rules prepared by representative bodies. But the application of those rules must follow two precepts: It must be thoroughly decentralized, so that valuable time stops being lost at higher levels on subjects that could be settled at lower ones; and it must be entrusted to specific individuals with clear-cut responsibilities. Large committees cannot play executive roles. Since so much of modern political action is of an executive sort, these individuals must be representative—that is, selected by, or at least with the formal consent of, the legislative bodies. For even if ultimate power rests with these bodies or the constituencies from which they emanate, both instant and intermediate power is in the hands of the executives; and short of wanting a caliphate, in Daniel Bell's phrase, one must see to it that the men who exert power are both entitled to and responsible for its use. But participation here cannot mean more than selection by and accountability to; the executive agent is obligated to listen, to disclose fully his decisions and his reasons, and to submit himself to the judgment of his constituents. Only in this way can democratization be reconciled with leadership. Given the need for flexibility, the multiplication of formal procedures of mere consultation (that is, advising) can only be harmful. When a decision is of great importance (for example, on how to handle a disruption), the man in charge obviously has a stake in consulting broadly with the representative, rule-making bodies. But, on the whole, the setting up of purely consultative committees with no genuine responsibilities either for rule-making or for execution only breeds those twin calamities, radicalization and disenchantment.

These suggestions are certainly neither original nor far-reaching. But their object is limited: It is to force all the constituencies into a re-examination of their relations and of the goals of the university, and to allow for the kind of leadership that is indispensable both for short-term survival and for the resolution of the debate on ends. Should fragmentation and the present mix of authoritarianism and oligarchy persist, most of the energies will be wasted on the battle of legitimacy, and the university will remain trapped in the vicious circle of incremental paternalism and mock revolutionary nihilism —two forms of self-indulgence it cannot afford. Broader, more democratic institutions geared to action will not only have the chance to face the bigger choices; they will also have the duty to handle the specific issues (or demands) as they arise over the relations of the university and its professors with the government, over its duty to the local community and to the blacks, over curriculum reform, discipline, or the governance of a particular unit. The main point is to make it possible for those issues to be discussed in relation to a deepening debate on over-all purposes and handled with a minimum of institutional congestion and emotional upheaval.

The present crisis is both a warning and an opportunity. It tells us that what might be termed the unguided university explosion of recent years leads indeed to internal explosion, to an outburst of all the tensions that had long been contained under a crust of civility and professionalism. But the crisis is not merely the outcome of centrifugal forces at work; it also shows that all the participants—except for tiny groups that would rather close down the university than improve it—are eager to have a fresh look at the institution, to take stock, to examine at last what has happened to it, and to suggest new designs. It can therefore be seen as a crisis of growth, on condition that the conflict of designs be channeled, that the confrontation be orderly, and that, through debate, the contours and consequences each of the designs be clarified—an indispensable prelude to accommodation. For much of the current debate is strikingly unrealistic. No society ever tolerates a university dedicated to its subversion—indeed, to the making of its future elites into grand agitators. No university can be the commune; nor, in George Kelly's apt phrase, can it be either Mount Athos or the Hotel de Ville. Many of the critics of the technocratic university have only offered us, as a substitute, a "new cultural synthesis" that would restore the unity of learning, a "resurgent humanism" left undefined and abstract. Many of the champions of new university trends have denounced this vague program as intellectual *poujadisme*[25] and its proponents as modern Luddites, but they, in turn, have failed to see how the contradictions between the ideals and practices of the multiversity and those of the old university could tear the university apart. They have often talked with the overconfidence of men who, projecting present trends at their happiest into the future, offer as a forecast what is in

217

fact a preference, thus forgetting that "the profile of the future, drawn merely with those technical lines which intuition, even associated with mathematical models, can forecast with maximum plausibility, is thoroughly informed by today's values: the options inspired by tomorrow's technological imagination are inseparable from today's ideological realities."[26] Between a humanism of angry nostalgia and the cheerfully overextended drift of scientism, there is little to choose from.

The normative concern of the "Luddites," however, will have to be saved and made useful by applying it not to the denunciation of modern society, but to its reform—by which I do not mean *ad hoc* tinkering but, literally, giving a new shape. Only in such a way can the claims of humanist rationalism and the pretenses of scientific and technocratic rationality re-enforce and correct each other. There can be no return to the ivory tower; but there will be no university if it gives up the greatest service it can perform: that of questioning and challenging the very knowledge it creates, collects, and communicates, of clarifying values, of showing how value choices do indeed lie behind not only the ways in which we apply scientific knowledge, but also the way in which we acquire it. At a time when the vocational graduate schools themselves recognize the need for this function, it would be absurd for the "humanists" to yield to bitterness and to strike poses. If the university cannot serve as the normative light of a society that staggers in the dark, if it merely provides each traveler with a flashlight for his own stumbling course, it will be of little use—especially if the indifferent production of flashlights for any purpose as long as it is in public demand keeps being sanctified, and the corporate attempt at occasionally throwing the light of moral standards for action on vital issues keeps being shunned, all in the name of academic neutrality. A university as distant from society as that of the past could invoke neutrality as a defense against dependence; a university as inevitably tied to society as today's should not use neutrality as an excuse for not performing the normative function this society needs most.

This function is hard enough to perform. The reinjection of standards of value into technological society is no easy task. It will be performed only if the university is first capable of putting its own house in order and of ceasing to be the microcosm and legitimizer of society's own drift; it must do the kind of imaginative, creative, long-term thinking that has been lost under the pounding pushes of the crisis and the permanent pulls of daily professional work. The students with vocational blinders and the students intoxicated by *contestation,* the humanists at war with the modern world and the scientists or social scientists too much in love with it, the professors who ask themselves no questions beyond their specialty and their servicing of it, the administrators concerned only with managing the unmanageable, the alumni whose loyalty to the university of their idealized youth obfuscates how they see the very different university of their present indignation—all must be forced to reflect together on the shape and destination of what, even in their most hostile moments, most of them still see as a common enterprise. They must all be forced to become, at least for a while, social philosophers, as a first step toward restoring, if not the "unity of knowledge," at least a sense of purpose in the university. Participation is necessary, both because the future university *cannot* be built without the involvement of all its constituencies, and because the society of the future *ought not* to continue to be one in which the gap between material choices and self-mastery, affluence and influence, keeps getting bigger. Whether one wants the university to shape the society of the future or wants it to stay apart from a world beyond repair, it ought to be there as a model, or as a recourse, or as a remorse. But since in any organization there can be a pluralism of chaos as well as a pluralism of conciliation, and since the sheer procedural mechanics of making sure that it be the latter risk becoming all-absorbing, the institutional modesty recommended above should be observed.

Given the purpose of the enterprise, and the danger for any executive or any rule-making body of becoming trapped by the short-run, by the pressing rather than by the essential, nothing would be more useful than the selection of a small council of what might be called futurists from among the university's executives and legislators (for their practical experience in "governance" is needed to prevent this from becoming a disembodied exercise of "imagineers" without either baggage or impact). Their role would not be to forecast, but to clarify choices; not to plan, but to propose; not to project trends and call them the future, but to remember that "the spatial language of probabilities does not give one a more rigorous vision of the long range than the intemporal language of preferences."[27] They would attempt to define common preferences and their implications; to show how

219

STANLEY HOFFMANN

probable trends could be turned toward preferred outcomes, and
to see how new trends could be made possible by the determined
promotion of essential values. They would be concerned centrally with the long-range future of the university; but precisely
because it is inseparable from that of modern society, their normative role, essential for the university, would be useful for society
as well. We know more and more what we do not like, and we
know rather well what we are likely to get. (For many of us this
is the same.) The time has come to think about what we want,
about how to achieve it, and about how the inevitable evils that
accompany any good can be kept limited. For every possible
reason, it is in and with the university that we should begin.

REFERENCES

1. For two different discussions of the problems of modern society, and
incidentally of their impact on the university, see Raymond Aron, *Progress
and Disillusionment* (Basic Books: New York, 1968) and Norman Birnbaum, *The Crisis of Industrial Society* (Oxford University Press: New
York, 1969).

2. This is a constant theme in the writings of Michel Crozier, the most convincing of the "optimistic" sociologists of post-industrial society. For a
counter-argument, see John McDermott, "Intellectuals and Technology,"
The New York Review of Books (July 31, 1969). See also, for a balanced
and skeptical view, Victor Ferkiss, *Technological Man* (George Braziller,
Inc.: New York, 1969).

3. Zbigniew Brzezinski, "America in the Technetronicage" (Occasional paper,
Columbia University School of International Affairs, 1967), p. 9.

4. Daniel Bell, "Structural Changes in the U. S." (Paper for the Princeton
Seminar of the International Association for Cultural Freedom, December,
1968).

5. America's blacks, however, are waging a triple battle for equality: (a)
the "old" battle for equal rights and fair treatment—they are only now
beginning to achieve the former and are far from having obtained the
latter; (b) what might be called the "new" battle for participation in
the control of those bureaucracies (schools or corporations or executive
agencies) that control their lives; (c) a more purely ethnic battle for
identity, which, to many blacks, entails the opposite from either "horizontal" or "vertical" participation: separate, all-black institutions.

6. In the case of France, one should not confuse the centralized Ministry
of Education and the almost pathetic lack of administration of the Faculties themselves.

7. Brzezinski, "America in the Technetronicage," p. 9.

8. For a recent blast, see articles by John H. Schaar and Sheldon S. Wolin,
"Education and the Technological Society," and Christopher Lasch and
Eugene Genovese, "The Education and the University We Need Now,"
The New York Review of Books (October 9, 1969).

9. See, for instance, Robert P. Wolff, *The Ideal of the University* (Beacon Press: Boston, 1969).

10. For an analysis of the Columbia crisis along these lines, see Daniel Bell, "Columbia and the New Left," *The Public Interest,* No. 13 (Fall, 1968), pp. 61-101.

11. Interim Report of Harvard's Committee of Fifteen (June, 1969).

12. Cf. Talcott Parsons' analysis, "The Academic System: A Sociologist's View," *The Public Interest,* No. 13 (Fall, 1968), pp. 173-97.

13. See Kenneth Keniston, "Youth as a Stage of Life," in J. Zubin and A. Freedman, eds., *Psychopathology of Adolescence* (Grune and Stratton: New York, 1970).

14. Kenneth Keniston, "You Have to Grow Up in Scarsdale to Know How Bad Things Really Are," *The New York Times Magazine* (April 27, 1969).

15. George Kelly, "The Future of the University," *Interplay* (October, 1969), p. 4.

16. Gerald Holton, Proceedings of the Conference on Governance of Universities, Sponsored by *Dædalus* and the Danforth Foundation (November 14-16, 1968), p. 5.

17. Albert Hirschman, *Exit, Voice, and Loyalty* (Harvard University Press: Cambridge, 1970).

18. Judith Shklar, *Men and Citizens: A Study of Rousseau's Social Theory* (Cambridge University Press: New York, 1969), p. 191.

19. Edward H. Levi, Proceedings of the Overview Committee on Governance of Universities, Sponsored by *Dædalus* and the Danforth Foundation (April 5-6, 1968), p. 84.

20. This has been one of the more unfortunate results of the "co-management" bodies set up in French law schools since 1968.

21. Hanna Gray, Proceedings of the Overview Committee, p. 52.

22. The minimum code referred to above would have to insure the protection of minority rights. For instance, should this code rule out certain activities from the teaching and research curriculum of the university, it would be necessary to make sure that interested students and professors were allowed to pursue such activities outside the curriculum, unless they belonged to a small category of occupations deemed, by broad consent (that is, not the mechanical application of the rule of "the half plus one"), incompatible with membership in the university.

23. Kingman Brewster, "The Politics of Academia," *Boston Sunday Globe,* October 5, 1969, p. A-23.

24. *Ibid.*

25. See, for instance, Nathan Glazer and Seymour Martin Lipset's articles in *The Public Interest,* No. 13 (Fall, 1968).

26. J-J Salomon, "La politique de la science et ses mythes," *Diogène* (November-December, 1969).

27. *Ibid.*

DANIEL BELL

Quo Warranto?—Notes on the Governance of Universities in the 1970's

QUO WARRANTO?—"By whose right"—is an ancient legal challenge to authority. The controlling problem of the governance of universities in the 1970's will be the resolution of a crisis in legitimacy, in the definition of authority which justifies any use of power or command. Clearly, in the last two years, there has been an enormous erosion of authority. The cry of the angry student has been, "By what right—who gave you the right—to say so?"

To govern is to exercise authority. In *The Social Contract* Rousseau wrote, "The strongest man is never strong enough to be always master unless he transforms his power into right and obedience into duty." No institution can live free of the daily shadow of coercion without the freely given consent of its members. A university cannot rule by power. In fact, it has no power other than the reluctant threat of expulsion; and if besieged it has to resort to civil force, an action that serves merely to confirm a rupture rather than resolve a conflict. The lack of power makes the problem of winning assent much more a question of agreement than of vote, for if a minority finds a situation immoral, or intolerable, being outvoted will not convince them to comply. The problem then is twofold: accepting the challenge to deal with the morality of specific actions; and recreating a generalized trust in the institution. The first involves the willingness to debate established, and often unquestioned, judgments. The second means that one has to strengthen a belief in the worthwhileness—in short, the character—of the university.

The older authority of the university (and therefore a definition

222

of its character) was, in Max Weber's sense, of a "traditional" kind. It was rooted in the past and sanctified by its attachment to the central value system of the society. Its role was to exemplify and express those values. Those values were not, however, the ideology of any particular social body, but the maintenance of a tradition of free inquiry and of a consensus about what constituted civility. Recently, particularly during the past twenty-five years, the university has sought, again in Weber's sense, a "rational-legal" authority—namely the assertion of a particular expertise (as the source of rational authority) and a willingness to serve society in its pursuit of socially defined goals (the basis of its claim to legal support). These rational-legal claims as well as the traditional authority are being challenged today—first by the students and now in a growing voice by the faculty.

To say that the university must regain its authority is simply to say that the university must live. But live as what? True, there has been an erosion of authority in the society and, to the extent that the university is part of the society, it is subject to forces beyond its control; but there has been a loss of trust in the institution itself because something has happened to its character. I would suggest that the crisis of legitimacy in the university (to the extent that it is specific and not just societal) derives from its assumption of many new and contradictory functions and from its evident inability to fashion a structure appropriate to its purposes. For twenty-five years the American university has been a vast "dumping ground" for tasks that society could not fulfill elsewhere. The university did not resist—in fact, it often welcomed—the intrusions; but it failed to adapt its structure to these new tasks. Now, the major question is whether the university should fulfill these functions; and if not, what tasks should it legitimately assume.

Thus, we have a double problem: to redefine the character of "the university," and to create a system of governance appropriate to that character. Universities have become part of a new system of higher education—yet that system itself has had no central authority to raise questions about the direction of the university, its division of labor, and its acceptance or rejection of specific functions. The irony is that the universities, which have been accused of being an Establishment, lack the first requisite of an Establishment—the readiness and the ability to provide authoritative leadership.

DANIEL BELL

The Societal Context

Any forecasts of problems facing the universities in the 1970's inevitably derive from a set of judgments about the relevant issues, and sources of tension, in the society. Some of these are obvious, some less so; but five factors seem to me to be central.

The Vietnam War

The war is morally dubious to a large section of the society, particularly the youth in the elite universities. But beyond the question of an immediate settlement of the war or the withdrawal of American troops is a deeper question of credibility. Was the decision to extend the American presence in Vietnam, and to undertake a leading role in the fighting, a mistake in judgment, an aberration of foreign policy, hubris about American power and omnipotence, or an integral extension of the character of the society? A significant portion of American youth questions American power and asks whether similar kinds of intervention, overt or covert, will be made in the 1970's. The nature of American foreign policy, the definition of national interest, the role of the United States as a world power, are all problematic today; and these ambiguities affect the judgments and commitments of young people. A significant number are wary or skeptical about the nature of America's intentions as a world power; a smaller number are already actively hostile (because of their vague allegiance to the idea of a *tiers monde,* to anti-Yankee and anti-colonial sentiment among the Latin American intelligentsia, or to pro-Maoist or pro-Castro sentiment), and translate this into campus action. The question whether the Vietnam war was "integral" to the American system, whether this country is or is not imperialist, will be one of the great ideological debates in the universities—and among historians and political scentists—in the seventies, particularly as the New Left generation moves up into the professoriate. This question surely will affect the debates on the nature of the university's service to the society (for example, the appropriateness of government-related and military-related research).

The Blacks

In the last two years, the blacks have become the most explosive issue on American campuses. Although the tensions will continue and even, intermittently, increase in the next year or two, I think

224

that insofar as the universities are concerned, the situation will ease off by the early 1970's. This prediction is based on the observation that, even now, in spite of some heavy rhetoric, the blacks want to be included, not excluded from, society. Particularly in the universities, there is every disposition on the part of the authorities to accommodate those claims. What we are now witnessing is the familiar sociological trajectory of every dispossessed group that has suddenly been enabled to move into a society from which it had been excluded: the ability to express hostility that has previously been suppressed; the reach of subjective expectations far exceeding objective gains; and the psychological need to assert a new group identity. Black studies and black control of segments of the curricula, it seems to me, are not, in the long run, fractious issues.

The last point needs some elaboration, particularly about the college blacks. It is a familiar sociological phenomenon that a second generation that has not experienced the travails and humiliations of its elders often will become more militant and assertive in its expression of its claim and right to leadership. This is an "expressive" phase that is often necessary for consolidating group pride and group progress (witness the *sabras* in Israel). The crucial variable is the *objective* change in circumstances: so long as gains are real, visible, and *steady* (it is the abrupt halt or reversal in social advance that tends to precipitate revolution), then subjective expectations and psychological manifestations eventually become congruent with reality.

In all this, there is a useful analogy with the labor movement of the 1930's, which also had its sit-ins, its militant left-wing leaders, its wild rampages, and the like. But once the mechanisms of advance were institutionalized (in the labor contract), a process of accommodation developed. For the society as a whole, particularly in urban affairs, there is a need to create mechanisms of political bargaining (community control of schools is one such example) analogous to those of economic bargaining in the 1940's and 1950's.[1]

The Multiplication of Social Problems

The most fractious and frustrating dilemmas of the 1970's will be the multiplication of domestic social problems: the environment, urban policy, housing, health, education, and so forth. These have come to a head for several reasons:

The growth in numbers. Since 1945, ninety million babies have been born in the United States; the net addition to population has

225

been about 60 million (or more than the total added from the founding of the republic to the Civil War). These individuals have demanded a level of services and amenities higher than that of any previous generation, owing to our rising expectation of a minimum standard of life, at a time when the costs of services have risen more rapidly (particularly in labor-intensive areas like health and education) than any other economic sector.

The creation of a national society. In the last thirty years, the United States has become, for the first time, a national society. We have always been a nation, yet not, until now, a national society— one in which change in any one part of the society has an immediate and obvious repercussion in every other part. Social issues are thus more visible, and their impact more coordinated.

The growth of "externalities." Externalities, as economists define the term, is the unintended and often unplanned impact, in short the "fallout," on Third Party C (and D, E, and F, as well), of a private transaction between private parties A and B. The result is a social cost (though sometimes a social benefit, too). The most obvious example of a social cost is air pollution which is the result, in part, of the larger number of private automobiles. Externalities often call for public action and lead to the expansion of public, as opposed to private, goods. As the national society becomes more interconnected, we can expect the growth of more externalities.

Yet all this comes at a time of triple failure. One is the failure, or the lack, of social knowledge. We just do not know how to cut into the system, how to decide which expenditures have a greater social-multiplier effect than others. We do not know how to organize an effective medical-care delivery system. We do not know how to design an effective low-cost housing project (witness the extraordinary disarray of such projects as Pruitt-Igoe in St. Louis). Nor do we know (see the Coleman Report) how to organize a meaningful educational system.

The second failure is that of government. In the decade of the New Frontier and the Great Society, we have had many ideas and many programs (several hundred in the Great Society alone), but several of these (for example, the housing program and the welfare program) have been failures. In part they have failed because there is a shortage of capable administrators; because there are political pressures which distort the programs; and because there is a simple lack of social knowledge.

Governance of Universities in the 1970's

The third failure is the unwillingness to support a tax program adequate to social needs. The Vietnam war has only masked (or exacerbated) this failure. But in truth, as the present political agitation reveals, there is a great public cloudiness about the meaning of taxes, and the successive administrations have been unwilling to educate the public about the benefits of taxation. Most people view taxes as money taken from "me" by "them," as a subtraction from income, although actually taxes are the use of money for the necessary purchase of public services that individuals cannot buy for themselves.

In one sense, these are the failures of liberalism, of the easy pieties of liberal platitudes about "government planning" and, "social change." These failures have contributed to young peoples' disillusionment about the ability of the society to provide social amenities and a livable environment.

All of this will come to a head in the 1970's in a major respect. A society that has become a national society must necessarily become self-conscious about its goals, and the means of reaching them. We know that while we can clean up the environment (at a cost), provide more houses (at least in quantity), spend more for schools, and underwrite ballooning costs of medicine, we cannot do all of these at the same time (see the National Planning Studies of Leonard Lecht in "costing out" the Eisenhower Commission projections on national goals). We must choose. The great political debates of the 1970's clearly will turn on the subject of national priorities. And the big problem, if we are not to yield simply to organized political pressures, or to the exigencies of the moment, is to try to specify why one or another set of needs must take priority, and for what social reasons. Otherwise we simply multiply the frustrations and the loss of faith in the ability of the system to function.

The Post-Industrial Society

Whether one calls our future state of affairs a "knowledge society," or a post-industrial society, it is becoming increasingly clear that the future urgently requires a highly educated population. I have argued previously [2] that the post-industrial society will increasingly depend upon the university for the codification of theoretical knowledge. But largely, this is the role of the elite universities. It is also true that there will be a greater occupational need for college-educated persons of all kinds. But in the headlong expansion of higher education, the university has become a gatekeeper, issuing credentials that regulate entry into the places of privilege in the society; indeed, it has almost assumed a quasi-monopoly position in this respect. And like any other human institution that assumes a monopoly position, the university inevitably has become a target for attack.

To a considerable extent, this attack comes from the students themselves. They fear, as the German poet Hans Magnus Enzenberger has put it, "the industrialization of the mind." The metaphor is not too far-fetched, so long as one remembers it is a metaphor. The industrial revolution brought with it a new discipline and a new rhythm of work, imposed on the recalcitrant bodies of a rural artisan and farm-labor class. Between 1814 and 1840, the reaction to this imposition took the forms of machine-breaking, wildcat strikes, pastoral romances about the superior and idyllic virtues of times past and an elaborately conspiratorial image of "The Thing"—William Cobbett's word for the Establishment. Recent student outbursts are, to some extent, the early class struggles of the post-industrial society, against the imposition of an "organizational harness" and the discipline of a particular kind of intellectual training and professional expertise. Over the last several years, this organizational harness has been dropped on young people at an earlier and earlier age. The anxiety about admission to college begins early in high school; pressure to choose a major starts in the freshman year; the following year, anxieties about graduate school appear. And the pressure to remain in school in order to avoid the draft foreclosed any possibility of a moratorium, a breather between college graduation and graduate school. (Perhaps the recent influx of college graduates into secondary school teaching as a result of the draft will be productive.)

The recent agitation to depreciate the importance of college degrees, to eliminate grades, to have freedom in curriculum, to seek interdisciplinary work and the like, reflects all this pressure. I argued in *The Reforming of General Education* that much of this is logically and educationally unsound and that we need a greater degree of coherence and training in disciplines already in the curriculum. But one has to recognize the latent reasons and anxieties underlying the agitation.

Most assuredly as the student cohort of the late 1960's moves into teaching positions in the 1970's the attack on the established curriculum will gain force. This can be a source of enormously fruitful debate, if it is conducted in positive terms; but, if linked, as it may be, to the larger political issues of the day it will certainly be one of the major problems facing university administration.

The New Sensibility

The most diffuse, but in the long run the most potentially disintegrating force in the society is "the new sensibility" in American culture. The relationship between social structure and culture is perhaps the most complicated problem of all social analysis. A change in the economy or technology, constrained as these are by resources and costs, has a determinable time sequence in a society. But changes in expressive symbols and values, in statements about the meaning of experience, and in the codes for the guidance of behavior—the dimensions of art and imagination—are unconstrained. At times, as Ortega has said, they foreshadow the social reality of tomorrow because they are played out in the mind; but at times they remain only in the realm of imagination. Thus it is difficult to specify the exact consequences of experiments in sensibility.

For the last hundred years the culture of the Western intelligentsia has been largely anti-institutional and even antinomian. In the celebration of the self and the individual it presented a polarity of the individual versus society. It exalted the idea of the genius, or the artist, above social convention. But these impulses, as expressed from the romantic poets to the surrealists, have been contained by the shaping discipline of form in art. Today one encounters a double movement: an attack on form itself and on any effort to find meaning in art—the breakdown of boundaries and the end of genres; and what Karl Mannheim called "the democratization of genius," the idea that self-expression and self-fulfillment are open to all without regard for boundaries and limits. In the "cult of experience" all realms of experience must be open and explored. Everything is under attack: authority, because no man is better than any other; the past, because learning tells us nothing; discipline and specialization, because they constrict experience.

Primarily, what has been added to the anti-institutionalism and antinomianism of the past is anti-intellectualism. What is celebrated is expression rather than idea, improvisation rather than text, sincerity rather than judgment. The psychedelic experience and the drug culture, the search for the "high" and for extended awareness, are the mass manifestations of this phenomenon. In this fierce anti-intellectualism, feeling and sentiment, not cognition, are considered more important. Education becomes not the transmission of learning but a search for "meaningful identity" to be gained by "dialogue," "encounter," and "confrontation."

As the political issues recede, it is likely that this cultural radicalism, which preceded the political, and has deeper roots in the past, will be extended. The cultist aspects of these movements (the Living Theater, Susan Sontag) may fade from fashion, but it would be a mistake to assume that the deeper impulses will pass. For the time being, all this is restricted to a relatively small number, yet they are the culture-bearers of an age. Just as Rimbaud, less than a hundred years ago, prefigured the beat and hippie cults of the past two decades, so do the Beatles make waves for the decades ahead.

Any cultural movement is multifaceted, and some interesting new areas of creativity will probably emerge from the new sensibility. But the *social* question is not the character of the next kind of high culture, but the fact that, for the first time, a sensibility of this kind has permeated a larger mass which by itself is not creative, yet which presumes that its experience, its search for "the true self" is as relevant as all art.

For the universities, the problem will swell in the 1970's, particularly as the large upcoming high-school generation, in which many of these attitudes have taken a strong if inchoate hold, enters the colleges. The situation will be particularly explosive in the humanities where these new impulses find their widest expression.

What does all this add up to for the next generations of college youth, and for the New Left now coming of age? In any immediate sense, the ability of young people to act in an organized, disruptive way will depend, in large measure, on pressing political questions such as the settlement in Vietnam. The SDS itself is in disarray. But if one wants to assess the possible consequences for the 1970's of these attitudes, then one can identify three responses, though not, perhaps, the actual extent and influence of each of them.

1. *Urban guerrillas.* Some small portion of the New Left, completely hostile to the society, has psychologically taken the steps toward becoming "urban guerrillas," ready to act as a revolutionary force.[3] Tom Hayden and those who acknowledge his leadership typify this position. In Uruguay and some other countries, these

urban guerrillas have already organized "hit-and-run" raids in their effort to disrupt the society. These cadres will be mobilized to exacerbate problems, maintain conflicts, and incite disruptive actions.

2. *The Crazies.* As mass frenzies recede, some small groups of *enragés*, becoming ever more frustrated at their inability to shape reality, will break out in nihilistic, sometimes senseless behavior. This has been the history of ebbing movements, from the Anabaptists to the Anarchists. One sees now, in such movements as the Weathermen and the Crazies, similar types of action. In any large sense, these are not serious. In a few specific places (Berkeley, Boston, New York), they may be responsible for serious incidents.

3. *The Alienated.* A large group of young people, puzzled, angry, alienated, constitute the "mass" for the radicals. While unwilling to act in a disciplined fashion (like the urban guerrillas), or in wild fashion (like the Crazies), they will find particular issues (the Columbia gym, the People's Park) which will be both symbolic and inflammatory.

How many young people are we talking about? We have little way of knowing, though the *Fortune* polls give us some clues—in all, the three groups may reach as high as 30 per cent in the elite schools. A more important consideration, however, and a crucial one for all our problems, is less the percentage than the *change of scale*. In an arena of a thousand students, the 5 per cent who are active radicals adds up to only fifty activists, and they may have little impact. In an arena of ten thousand students, 5 per cent comes to five hundred, and these can form a powerful striking force when the situation is favorable. Our problem for the 1970's is that we are living through a new change of scale.

The University System in the 1970's

The problem of governance is tied up with the question—increasingly an ambiguous one—of what a university is and, more broadly, what *a university system* is in the society. One can, for the purposes of analysis, identify four functions which have been and are being performed today by the university:

1. Custodian of the traditions of Western culture and the evaluation of claims to membership in this "great chain of learning." This is the oldest function, and it centered in the humanities. But

231

this function is in process of dissolution. Ten years ago, a serious debate could take place about whether Nietzsche belonged in the canon of great works to be studied in a Humanities course—it actually took place at Columbia. Today, almost anything goes. During one of the sit-ins at Duke University, a student complained (on camera, during a TV news program) that his modern literature course only went up to the 1950's and did not include the 1960's.

2. The search for truth through inquiry and scholarship: the effort to assert the philosophical foundations of certified knowledge, the discovery of the laws of nature, the explication of the norms and rules that govern human behavior. These inquiries still go on, though they have become, necessarily, more technical and specialized.

3. The training of a large number of people as professionals in specific fields. A hundred years ago, one learned on the job. Now, with knowledge increasingly dependent on theory, one learns in a school and then takes a job. This function has been combined in recent years with mass higher education and technical training on the junior college level.

4. The application of knowledge to social use. This includes, in earlier years, aid to agriculture; more recently it has been service to military technology and to economic planning.

Since World War II, the third and fourth functions have expanded enormously, for many reasons: the fact that theoretical knowledge has become more intimately entwined with applied research and development; the needs of government and industry; and so forth. Whatever the reason, one sees the fruits of this in the multiplication of research institutes, centers, and programs in universities, the expansion of research and the service functions.

But all this brings us back to the root question: What is a university? It is startling to realize that we have not really had any adequate definition of a university. The university is ordinarily likened to an extended family, a secular church, a corporation, a community, or it is simply described as a microcosm of the society. And the multiplication of functions in recent years leads to increasing ambiguity and amorphousness about the nature of the beast—and this is one of the central reasons for the failure to define adequate governance. If it is like a family, then one kind of standard applies; if like a political community, another set of standards; if like a corporation, a third, and so on. But the very fact that all these metaphors and analogies are possible only multiples the confusion and makes more difficult the question of asserting some justification—and therefore legitimacy—for authority in the university.

There are, it seems to me, two distinct justifications possible, each (as ideal types) representing markedly different roles for the university.

The first might be called the classical model. This is to say that the university is that institution in the society endowed with the special function (and the extraordinary immunity) of searching for truth and evaluating the culture of its times. In this sense, it is free to question everything—*in theory*. If it is to be true to its purpose, nothing is exempt from its scrutiny. But if it is to have the immunity from reprisal that goes with this power, it must obey the self-denying ordinance of remaining at the level of theory, of speculative discourse. The question whether anything is to be put into practice is a question, not for the university, but for the society. In this model, the university stands outside the society, and contains within itself all varieties of creeds and beliefs, and all kinds of persons, subject to the one qualification of competence in the world of learning and scholarship. These qualified individuals, scholars, are free to explore any question, and test all areas of human experience—in theory.

The second might be called the pragmatic model. Here the function of the university is primarily one of service to the society: service in training large numbers of persons, service in the application of knowledge, service of the members of the university in government and elsewhere, and so forth.

The legitimacy of each type is clear: the first, knowledge for the sake of knowledge; the second, social benefits. But the limitations of each view are also apparent. If one chooses the first, then one is barred, in the role as scholar and researcher (though not as citizen) from political advocacy and active partisanship. If the second, the question becomes: "Who shall decide?" Should the universities serve the military? Or the urban poor? Or the radicals? Should the criterion be national interest, social need, the command of money, the influence of power groups, or what?

Although my formulation of the types is extreme, and somewhat abstract, the division is nonetheless real, and some choices will have to be made.

One answer can be to continue what we have at present—in effect, a form of *laissez faire*. Those individuals who want to work in an ivory tower can do so; those who want to serve one or another group in the society are free to do what *they* want. This is possible, perhaps, from the point of view of the individual professor in the university. But what of the administrator, the foundation, the alumni, the government, and the various public claimants, those who give the money or make the demands. What choice can they make?

One way out of this difficulty is to realize that there need *not* be an either/or choice. If we are to fashion, as we must necessarily do, a national *university system*, then we can allow the different choices to exist within a differentiated system.

The difficulty, hitherto, has been that every institution of higher learning has sought to be, with few exceptions, like every other. What we need is greater variety, serving different aims in a differentiated division of labor. There is no reason why some institutions cannot be primarily in the service of scholarship and learning, with little need to take on added responsibilities. Some institutions can be oriented primarily to research, and others to training.

But in addition to differentiation we also need divestiture. The university has become a multipurpose institution taking on all the chores that a society cannot take care of elsewhere. When the military could not find disinterested sources of advice in industry, it created the Lincoln Lab and MITRE Corporation at MIT. When the Ford Foundation wanted to extend a system of public broadcast laboratories, it asked Columbia University to accept the responsibility, which at first it did, and then declined. When the AEC needed a manager for its Argonne Lab, it turned to the University of Chicago. But why should the universities take on all these functions? The problem for the 1970's, I would predict, will be the effort of the universities to divest themselves of many of these tasks; and this is as it should be.

If there is to be a national university system, then we need to initiate more sustained thought about its desirable shape. Should graduate schools and their research preoccupations be linked with large undergraduate colleges? Should one not have two kinds of graduate schools, one for detailed research training and one for broader education? What is the optimal size of a single campus? What kind of division of labor can be created among universities as regards concentrations in different fields? Should some kinds of research be detached from universities and lodged either in govern-

ment, in non-profit institutions, or in some kind of academy structure (as in the Soviet Union)?

These are questions about structure and function. But if one
goes further and links them to the question of legitimacy, one should,
perhaps, grasp the nettle and make some further, broad distinctions.
Can one give all universities—private and state, small and large,
elite and mass, liberal arts and junior colleges—the same cloak of
immunity and privilege that is worn in the classical model? What is
"academic freedom" in a junior college and how does this differ from
the citizenship of a corporation employee to speak his mind politically? Does membership in a "faculty," with all its privileges, extend
to teaching assistants and librarians? In the present "idea" of a university, we have a hollow ideology that is contradicted by a complex
reality.

For the sake of argument, what would a national university
system look like, if divided along the lines of legitimacy that I have
proposed? In effect, we would have three different systems:

1. An autonomous system of elite universities and liberal arts
colleges whose justifications would reside in their allegiance to the
classic pursuits of truth and scholarship and who also would receive
the traditional immunities of a university so conceived.

2. A large-scale system of state universities and junior colleges
whose functions would be professional and technical training.

3. A large-scale research and service system which would be
client-oriented—to the government, to industry, to the various minorities—and whose function would be primarily that of applying
knowledge to technological and social problems.

The system I have outlined so schematically is open, of course,
to the charge of elitism. It is subject to the more serious accusation
that in the character of knowledge and its application such distinctions are false and unreal. Perhaps. Each of these arguments is de-
batable. But the simple point is that these issues have never really
been debated. If one is to think seriously of a national system of
higher education, serving various purposes in a meaningful division
of labor, surely we must initiate this kind of debate.

The Immediate Issues

This discussion has dealt largely with deep-rooted structural
problems of the university system. Yet there are some immediate
problems of governance ahead.

DANIEL BELL

The Containment of Disruption

Before the invasion of Cambodia, the student protest had been ebbing, and while outbreaks of violence had occurred these were sporadic. The problem before the university is not the existence of protest, the nature of student extremism—the altered character of the chief organizing force, the SDS, and what this portends for the universities.

The character of the SDS has changed. Early studies of student activists, such as those by Kenneth Keniston, Richard Flacks, and M. Brewster Smith, portrayed them as passionate, idealistic youngsters who, looking at the evident imperfections of the society, sought to redress these evils at a great personal sacrifice of time and even of careers. Whatever the truth of these characterizations—and I believe they were on the whole accurate at the time—the picture is vastly different today. What these earlier studies have failed to take into account is a situational logic. For one thing, the kinds of action employed—militant, boisterous, disruptive, personally aggressive—have attracted to the movement many unstable personality types for whom the attack on authority is a sanction for their own obsessive rages and the acting out of hostile impulses. The "paranoid style" has become a feature of the SDS. More important, we see here the repetition of what Frank S. Meyer has described, in a Fund for the Republic study, as "The Molding of a Bolshevik," a "hardening" process which has also been graphically pôrtrayed by Bertolt Brecht in his play The Measure Taken. The SDS organizational form has been transformed from its early open, spontaneous emphasis on participatory democracy to a closed, manipulative cadre form of organization, ready to use deceit and violence in order to gain its ends.

This trajectory of change is a product, in part, of being a harassed and hunted minority; more to the point, it is inherent in the political logic of a group that has become more determinedly revolutionary and finds that its older, anarchist mode is inadequate to its new aims.

The SDS picture is further complicated by a split in the organization that has now produced three groups claiming the use of the name: one, the faction whose headquarters are in Boston, controlled by Progressive Labor, the Maoist wing of radicalism; the other two, wings of the Revolutionary Youth Movement. The PL faction emphasizes the need for a "working-class alliance," and tends to be anti-drug and anti-pornographic. The Weatherman faction of RYM, which controls the Chicago national office, thinks of students as the adventurist spearhead of a revolutionary movement. RYM II has become an old-fashioned radical youth movement, with overtones of Castroism.

Both aspects—the splits and the change in organizational character—will reduce the size and effectiveness of SDS. Sectarian wrangling drives away many individuals, and is a diversion of energies. The kind of commitment now demanded by SDS is too extreme for most students. Yet the rivalry between the various factions, plus the desire of both to "prove" themselves, may in the short run provoke more disruptions, as the SDS groups seek to inflame existing issues and find new ones.

How can such disruptions be contained? We must realize that the issue of disruption and of the character of the university are one. The authority of a university is not a civil authority but a moral one. It can deal with disruptions—or the threat of disruption—not by invoking civil force but by rallying an entire community to establish common rules of common procedure. Disruptive students can only be contained by a faculty and other students, not by police.

This is not to say that police should never be used. But calling in the police is not a last resort or a first resort, but one that may be used only after an administration and faculty and students have been mobilized on the issues. The failure of the Columbia administration in April 1968 was its aloofness, not from the SDS, but from its own faculty and students. It was the SDS which initiated the violence at Columbia by insisting that the university was the microcosm of the society and challenging its authority. After some confusion, the administration, in its actions, accepted this definition and sought to impose its authority on the campus by resorting to force. But in a community one cannot regain authority simply by asserting it, or by using force to suppress dissidents.

Authority, in this case, is like respect. One can only *earn* the authority, the loyalty of one's students, by going in and arguing with them, by engaging in full debate, and, when the merits of proposed changes are recognized, taking the necessary steps quickly enough to be convincing. During April 1968, the Columbia administration never explained its case on the issues, and it had a good one (as Roger Starr has shown in his article "The Case of the Columbia Gym," *The Public Interest*, Fall 1968). The following year, when the SDS made wild allegations about the role of the university in community evictions, they were quickly answered in a White Paper, and the agitation collapsed. At Harvard, it seems to me, President Pusey drew the wrong conclusions from the Columbia example by moving to call in the police soon rather than late, instead of first mobilizing the Harvard community to condemn the seizure of University Hall.

In short, the point at issue is not SDS, for SDS is not concerned any longer with redress of specific evils or with genuine reform, but the confused allegiances of the moderate students. Without the support of the moderates, the SDS actions begin to crumble, as they did at Columbia and Chicago in the spring of 1968.

On the question of containing disruption, a crucial variable is the *style of leadership*. In situations of conflict or stress, the university, like any institution, needs a rallying symbol, and this is, necessarily, the president of the institution. Clark Kerr's conjecture (in *The Uses of the University*) that the president of a university has to be a mediator is not so. The president needs to be active and cool, and aware of the ideological currents that are running so swiftly in the schools.

Structure and Representation

One of the immediate reforms that must take place in many of our institutions of higher learning is the creation of juridical and representational bodies to deal with policy issues of the university. The university, today, faces a special problem. The idea of a small community of scholars (with senior common rooms and junior common rooms to mark the differences in rank) on the Oxbridge model is clearly inapplicable in the United States. Given its size and varied functions, the university today mingles a political model (as regards faculty self-governance and self-selection) with a.bureaucratic model (in the relation of an administration to the students, often in the organization of research, relation to the community, and so on). The clarification of these differences—how far the university must go in being a political community, and how much bureaucratization is necessary—is one of the most pressing problems in the explication of university governance.

Clearly the university must become, more formally, a political community.[4] The making of policy decisions must be open, subject to debate, and to some form of confirmation by the relevant constituencies in the university. There are, it seems to me, three major areas which require exploration:

1. *The structure of representation.* The problem will vary from school to school. In some unitary colleges there might be some kind of proportional representation between faculty as a whole, administration and students; in other, federated institutions, there would be representation by federated unit, and so forth. So far as I know, there are no studies of the range of representational structures and the rationales for each.

2. *The relevant constituencies.* Who is to have a vote, and of what kind (with vote or without), in university deliberations? The librarians are pressing for faculty status. The teaching assistant wants to be considered as having a faculty role, though usually he is also a graduate student. Do non-tenured and tenured personnel have equal voice on all issues? Again, there is here a major area in need of research and clarification of principle.

3. *The division of powers.* What decisions, if any, are reserved for the trustees, who are often the legal custodians of the corporation? What kinds of administrative action are subject to review, and by whom? To state these questions is to indicate again how little discussion there has been of these most crucial issues of university life.

Beyond all these problems, one crucial consideration—which most people accept as metaphor, yet rarely explore in practice —has to be observed: that all these problems take place within a change of scale unprecedented in the history of the university. A change of scale is not simply a linear extension of size. As Galileo once defined it in his square-cube law, a change of *size* is a change in *form*, and consequently in institution. Most of our older discussions of rights and responsibilities, the allocation of powers and the devolution of responsibilities, are modeled on an organizational form whose size is of a vastly smaller magnitude than our own. It is this change of scale, in all its dimensions, and for all its consequences, that still has to be explored.

REFERENCES

The essay was written originally as a memorandum for the Carnegie Foundation for the Advancement of Teaching in the summer of 1969. It was published in *The Public Interest,* No. 19 (Spring, 1970), 53-68, and is reprinted here with the permission of the editors.

1. For an exploration of these problems, see Daniel Bell and Virginia Held, "The Community Revolution," *The Public Interest,* No. 16 (Summer, 1969), especially pp. 173-77.

2. "Notes on the Post-Industrial Society," *The Public Interest,* No. 6 (Winter, 1967) and No. 7 (Spring, 1967).

3. Witness, for example, the following argument for "resistance" by an SDS leader: "The institutions our resistance has desanctified and delegitimatized, as a result of our action against their oppression of others, have lost all authority and, hence, all respect. As such, they have only raw, coercive power. Since they are without legitimacy in our eyes, they are without rights." From a paper given at an SDS meeting in November, 1967, "Toward Institutional Resistance," by Carl Davidson, Interorganizational Secretary.

4. I speak of the university as a political community only in relation to its internal structure and internal governance. I do not mean that the university should become a political entity, acting as a unified body or with a common voice, in relation to political issues, other than those that affect the life of the university and its pursuit of knowledge directly. For if the university became a political entity, seeking to influence events as a corporate body, it would have to enforce discipline over dissidents, establish restraints on recalcitrant members and opponents, and, in short, destroy the very quality which gives it its unique position in the society—a sanctuary for truth.

PART II

Dialogues on the University

Preface

THERE IS constant talk today about the need for "dialogue." The term is, in most respects, ambiguous. It may mean almost anything —the establishment of new forums to encourage the exchange of opinion; the development of new political instrumentalities, even in non-political institutions, to alter the distribution of power; the creation of new communities, with a promise of their being guided by higher ethical standards. Each of these prospects will seem compelling to the individual who is persuaded of their need; each will seem unnecessary (or even dangerous) to those who are satisfied with existing forms. When, as in the present climate, strident and angry voices are raised on every side, it is difficult to know what the intent of any radical proposal is, or whether any deserves to be taken seriously. New terms like "participation" become clichés almost as soon as they are uttered; old terms like "authority" are simply vulgarized. Rhetoric and passion take the place of common sense and reason, and we no longer know whether we are seeking new forms of representation, new rules of political procedure, new devices for airing grievances, or new ways of living together. The art of debate is lost; the convention of discussion is threatened; and rational discourse becomes the casualty of intemperate demagoguery.

The mass media (television, press, and radio) do their best to record and reproduce these "happenings" for audiences whose taste for such news would appear to be insatiable. Another generation, chancing on this "record" and having access to no other, might well conclude that men in this time were indeed mad, made so either by the gravity of their problems or by their obvious incapacity to cope with them. It is precisely because the mass media are so addicted to the sensational demanded by the consuming public that there is a special obligation to tell of events which suggest another temperament in our society, one no less concerned with truth, social justice, and moral improvement, but one somewhat more restrained in its expression. Ours is indeed a time of "dialogue," but not only of the kind that is angry and agitated. There are today unequaled opportunities for the exchange of opinion. If, as many of us believe, these opportunities must in fact be strengthened and multiplied, there is good reason to look

STEPHEN R. GRAUBARD

closely at what is presently happening in certain of those places where discussion still thrives, where differences may still be expressed without offense being given. The American Academy of Arts and Sciences offers hospitality to such possibilities.

Some will say that Academy discussions, as reproduced here, are too academic and too tame; that they do not sufficiently touch on the more fundamental grievances of our time. This situation may indeed obtain, though there is reason to think that Academy conferences in fact reflect diverse opinion to an extent that is not at all common when the decibel is higher or when protestations of concern are more insistent. There are no rules of debate in Academy conferences; no principles of representation; no pretense to preparing a record that will go straight to persons in the highest places. A more modest ambition insinuates itself, creating the civility and tolerance that is so essential to good talk. The conferees are interested in one another's thought, expecting to derive pleasure and profit from it; they share with the Editors the hope that out of good talk may come a better publication that will in time reach an interested public and have its influence there. Academy conferences are intimately tied to plans for publication, in *Dædalus* or elsewhere. These are indeed "dialogues," but in the best sense; they express appreciation for the spoken (and the written) word.

Those who participated in these American Academy discussions understood that their remarks were being transcribed, though it was not expected that these comments would then be circulated widely. Our practice in the past has been to mimeograph conference transcripts, making them available to small numbers and using them to assist in planning publications. The warm and enthusiastic reception of these hastily prepared transcripts— and the constantly repeated suggestion that they be made available to larger numbers—led us to decide to experiment with their publication in the present volume. Participants have been asked to review their contributions; some have made minor stylistic changes; the greatest number, however, have permitted the record to stand as originally transcribed. These are, then, the spontaneous and unrehearsed comments of men and women, seated around a table, speaking for themselves to others who were in precisely the same situation. They did not attend as representatives of institutions or professions; they did not imagine that their words carried weight except as they might persuade some individual in the room who found them challenging. The Editors feel a deep gratitude to those who have agreed to have their contributions made available in this form.

The American Academy's interest in the problems of higher education is of long standing. On many occasions in the last three years men and women from all the major constituencies of universities—trustees, administrators, students, faculty, alumni, legislators—have gathered to discuss the problems of university goals and governance. These meetings generally took place at the House of the Academy in Boston; selections from two conference transcripts suggest how advantageous it is to bring together informed persons from many different kinds of institutions and, also, to give thought to including some from outside the university. A great debt is owed to the Danforth Foundation for making these meetings possible.

Finally, we publish the first sessions of what is to be a continuing seminar on the problems of higher education in industrial societies. These sessions took place at the House of the Academy in Boston. A second meeting has since been held in Paris. Again, the object was to bring together people who do not normally meet one another to discuss problems that have great concern for all of them. There can be no question about the importance of such international debate, carried on in an environment where each seeks to liberate himself (if only for a few days) from his more parochial concerns. The Ford Foundation is to be thanked for making this "continuing seminar" possible.

The Governance of the Universities I

Participants
Daniel Bell
John Brademas
Jill Conway
Martin Duberman
Robert J. Glaser
Stephen R. Graubard
Hanna H. Gray
Carl Kaysen
Edward H. Levi
Martin Meyerson
Robert S. Morison
Talcott Parsons
Bruce L. Payne
David Riesman
Neil R. Rudenstine
Preble Stolz
David M. Wax

Historically universities have been part of an integrative system of society because they hold the values of society and pass them on. The universities have now become part of the adaptive system of society in terms of its innovation. Can they carry on both burdens? Can they be both integrative and adaptive? Logically, it seems to me, one would say that they cannot be both because the strains become too large in those terms. Should the whole research organization be re-examined so that something like an academy system, which the Russians have put forward, is the model? I am not making a judgment one way or the other; I am merely proposing that these are the kinds of questions to raise. Should there not be more and more government laboratories to take over the problems of science, rather than simply not-for-profit corporations which are attached to universities? You have a variety of models of which the university is only one: the academy system, government laboratories, university laboratories. All of these questions must be answered in reference to the framework of the purpose of a university.

To try to focus upon the function of the university and the new shape of the university, I would formulate the problems in this way. Since 1945, although one could date it earlier, a whole series of new functions has been thrust upon the university which raises the question: To whom is the university responsible? Practically without question, new functions were assumed by the university. It was almost taken for granted that the university would be the place for these tasks to be done. There was in part, I suspect, the sense of the tragedy of World War II and the continuing strain of the protracted conflict with the Communist world. There was also a sense of a mobilized posture. Because of a whole series of processes, including this mobilized posture, the university became expanded. You had the growth of various institutes, for example, to train people for Russian studies, Chinese studies— things which had never been considered as being intrinsically scholarly functions. But we needed Russian experts, Arabic specialists, and so forth. As part of the whole aura of science, the emphasis on research, you had a series of functions related to the design of defense—missile systems and questions of this kind. A great many of these functions were not just thrust upon the university, but were in some sense accepted as a social responsibility. By and large, there was a sense that scientists had to be involved in military problems and the science gap. M.I.T. became the center of a large political thrust against SAC. A huge bureaucratic struggle took place in the labyrinths of Washington in terms of setting up a

Distant Early Warning Line, a continental air defense, and various other measures. In large part, these programs were initiated by scientists using the university as a base. There was a great self-consciousness that the university would be an important political base in this regard. A whole series of things began to develop out of these elements. There was a feeling that mass higher education was needed. Professors considered themselves a new class and self-confidently accepted the argument that they were a new class.

Partly in jest, Mr. Kaysen asked whether, if the business corporation in a sense encompasses all the profit functions in society, the university encompasses all the not-for-profit functions. To some extent, this is quite truly happening. I thought it was quite interesting that Mr. Kaysen approves of this, although he runs a nineteenth-century institution. But Mr. Meyerson, who runs a twenty-first-century institution, retreats from this. Each is obviously searching for what he does not have in this respect.

In the last four or five years, there have been some very interesting reactions to the transformation the university has undergone during the last twenty-five years. The two major reactions have been in part because of the growth of a semiskilled intelligentsia who are, in a sense, the graduate students and the graduate assistants. They have suddenly discovered bureaucracy in the university. Bureaucracy is a dirty word, and to some extent it has been a bad situation for them, particularly in terms of the teaching conditions at the large state universities. Even in a place like Berkeley, something like 15 per cent of all classes are taught mostly by graduate assistants.

RIESMAN

What is so bad about that?

BELL,

It is bad not so much because they are teaching, but because of the ambiguity of their status. By and large, they do not seem to have a feeling of being respected; they do not know exactly where they are going to go.

The university used to be a collegial institution, although it was never wholly that. It now becomes a bureaucratic institution, although it never wholly becomes that either. The second reaction has arisen in large measure because of the Vietnam war: the charge that the university has become part of the social system, part of the military-industrial complex in particular. If one looks at the figures, although they have been changing very radically, it turns out that more than half the research money comes from N.I.H., rather than the Defense Department. This reaction is symbolized by the campaign against the Institute of Defense Analysis and university ties to the military-industrial complex. It is quite clear in retrospect that I.D.A. was a very ambiguous thing. I.D.A. was set up by the Army to do weapons evaluations, and twelve universities were asked to lend their names to create a respectability for the undertaking. It is quite interesting that universities were asked to lend their names to a project in which they had no role. It was not as if they were in Brookhaven where they are really part of management or actively managing it the way they are, let's say, at Argonne. They were to provide window dressing.

One finds three different kinds of reactions about university activities; all are contradictory in a way and pose a series of problems. On the one hand, you get the extreme left-wing attitude that the university is corrupt, and you have got to destroy it because it is now a part of a rotten social system. This has become almost a universal reaction. Students toppled the city administration of Berlin after one boy was shot during demonstrations over the visit of the Shah of Iran. There were riots in about fifty German cities and a great sense of instability in the political system suddenly being introduced by the extraordinary tactic of student activism. The effect has not been so great in this country, but universities have been shaken—particularly Berkeley—by this kind of intense negativism, nihilism, reaction, romanticism, or idealism.

There is a curious second contradiction which is allied to the first and yet has an independent source: the plea for a new activism on the part of the university—namely, that the university get involved in race and urban affairs. There is a polarization between good activities, such as those related to urban affairs, and bad ones, related mostly to the university's ties to the military-industrial complex. Sometimes students and even faculty talk in terms of wanting the university to become tranquil, a place to teach; at the same time, they suddenly say that they want the university to undertake these good activities. Thus, you get the same kinds of pressures, but in terms of a good cause. To some extent the universities again, oddly enough, have not scrutinized the situation, but have gone along. Columbia is now setting up a large urban study center because Ford is putting up ten million dollars. There is nobody of real competence or interest in the university on this problem; we have gone outside now to bring in about ten people, all of whom have no relation to the university and many of whom are political figures. People at Columbia have suddenly decided that the university must be involved with Harlem. We have organized remedial classes and helped to organize small businesses.

The very same process which took place in the forties allied to defense and the Cold War and which created certain reactions has suddenly been brought forth again under the pressure of the urban situation and has been accepted without real forethought as to whether such activities are a part of the university's role.

The first reaction has been the one of destruction and nihilism; the second has been a new activism for good things; the third has been a mixed notion of retreat to teaching—to recapture somehow the old nineteenth-century ideal of the university. The old pastoral romance has now become a slum romance with the university as a great center of communion in which teacher and student come together. Here too, of course, you have the visions. You have those who talk about restoring the old student-teacher relationship and those who talk about destroying it so that the university becomes a place where everybody goes around touching and feeling one another and expressing joy. The latter becomes a form of group therapy with the implicit notion that a teacher is not a competent person who knows more than a student and enters into an adult relationship with him. The assumption is that one cannot learn from another person; one can only learn together.

If one wants to define the purpose of the university, one must reach this definition by deciding whether the university should accept a whole series of activities which have been thrust upon it simply because it has been the one institution available to carry on these burdens.

DUBERMAN

I am surprised at Mr. Bell's terminology and at some of his specific examples. Some of the things that he labeled "romantic" would from my point of view require more definition. I am not sure that this is one of the two main camps on any given issue.

KAYSEN

I wanted to comment on two of the things that Mr. Bell said. I do not differ with his description at all; I do think, however, that some details of this picture are worth mentioning. First of all, I see the origin of all this in the World War II experience, especially that of two, perhaps three, institutions. The two most striking ones are the Manhattan Project and the M.I.T. Radiation Lab which did radar work. There were also some smaller projects and lots of committees—the National Defense Research Committee, for example. Perhaps the most significant aspect of the Manhattan Project and the Radiation Lab is that they were probably the first seri-

Governance of the Universities I

ous interdisciplinary efforts on a large scale. They put together
people who normally did not work together in the ordinary structure of the university. Bell Labs achieved this only to a moderate
extent, and it was departmentalized. Bell Labs changed its structure a lot after the war, in part by learning from this kind of experience. The people involved were not dragooned; they were
eager to do it for two different kinds of reasons. One, of course,
was political. We have to think back not to 1945, but to 1939, to
the Nazis and the war in Europe, and to the significant element
of refugee input into American science, which had a lot to do with
the spirit of many of these enterprises. Einstein, Leo Szilard, and
many others came here after they had been driven out of Europe.
The problems they worked on were intellectually difficult. The
natural scientists and later the social scientists discovered for the
first time that things which ordinarily would have earned their contempt as engineering, as applied science, were technically and
intellectually quite interesting. George Kistiakowsky, a very good
abstract physical chemist, found that it was fun to be an engineer
and to design a particular device—namely, the first nuclear
bomb—and to show that the theoretical physical chemist was a
better engineer than all the engineers.

RIESMAN

European baseball.

KAYSEN

Yes, that is right. There were other organizations in which this
kind of thing went on. One of them was the O.S.S. which had
many qualities of an interdisciplinary character. It was the first
interdisciplinary social science venture; this was Harvard's march
on Washington. Aside from General Donovan, what you had was
a group of Harvard professors in history, in economics, in political
science, in certain languages who were put together to create the
country's first intelligence analysis organization. This amateur organization—and this may be a parochial view—was much better
than the professional civil service organizations. Just as George
Kistiakowsky and Ed Purcell and Isadore Rabi turned out to be
much better electrical engineers, mechanical engineers, chemical
engineers, factory managers, than the engineers and the factory
managers, professors of French and Renaissance history turned out
to be much better intelligence agents than people in the intelligence profession.

Another organization important to this history is RAND.

RAND was set up outside a university context, but it had this same approach—interdisciplinary problem-solving. Its first administrators were quite bright and followed a basic academic rule. They said that RAND should not care about the problems it was going to solve, but should create a situation so attractive that lots of bright academics come, regardless of what they do. Thus, Tjalling Koopmans, professor of economics at Yale, a very theoretical person and, incidentally, a pacifist, went to RAND and wrote theoretical papers on the general characteristics of economic equilibrium systems, and RAND was smart enough to pay him to do that. And because Koopmans was there, young men came there and got involved in more concrete projects, so the institution became inventive.

If you look at the university during the postwar period for comparison, you see a substantial shift in the disciplinary composition of the status order and numbers in a faculty. In the twenties, the professors of languages, literature, and history would have been the people who were heads of faculty committees at any of the great universities. Now the natural and social scientists carry the heavy weight. Part of this is statistical change; these are the departments that have grown the most. The social scientists are drawn to the kind of work we have been talking about because, in a certain sense, it is field work for them. If you get involved in a city's problems and are an urban sociologist, you have access to data that you would not have in the university context. You actually generate data which you would have a hard time generating in an academic setting. Many natural scientists cannot do science full time; it is too intensive, too intellectually demanding. So much applied activity is recreation; it is baseball, as Mr. Riesman remarked. One of my colleagues who is a most theoretically oriented man, Freeman Dyson, designs rockets because he enjoys it, although he is really interested in quantum electrodynamics.

The phenomenon to which Mr. Bell rightly calls attention represents not only society pushing functions on the university, but the university reaching out to repeat experiences which its active constituents—the faculty—enjoy. If one looked carefully into the history of most of these enterprises—and this is a conjecture—a faculty member, rather than a dean or an administrator, would appear as the active entrepreneur, as the person who has made the bridge between the foundation, the government department, the corporation, and so on. The Carnegie Corporation and the State Department thought that it was a good idea to have a Russian research center, but without the entrepreneurship of Clyde Kluckhohn we would not have had one.

I would round off these perhaps rambling observations by saying that this activity will be bounded in some dimensions; unless you find some correspondence between the natural intellectual interests of some group of faculty members and what they feel professional competence is, it will tend not to take root. On the other hand, that may be small consolation, because what we define as the legitimate intellectual interests of professors has widened enormously. There is a general belief in the society that there is nothing to which intellectual expertise is not relevant.

PARSONS

May I add a footnote? The Russian Research Center at Harvard and the Russian Institute at Columbia were established at the beginning of the Cold War. The people who came into them had a dual orientation with respect to public service. They thought knowledge of Soviet society would be extremely useful in case of serious trouble, but were, on the other hand, disposed to hope that institutes of this kind could help in achieving a *rapprochement* and an easing of the conflict. In other words, these were not warmongers who, having knocked the Nazis out, decided they were going after the Russians. I doubt very much if people on the left are willing to give the professoriate that kind of credit. Some of us have been in contact through Pugwash and other channels with a major effort of American natural scientists to work with the Russians on disarmament problems and to go quite far in that connection.

MEYERSON

Mr. Bell mentioned that his university had accepted a large grant of money to establish an agenda for the university, an agenda which did not derive from the interests of the members of the university. When we talk about the ethic of the university and the governance of the university, are we talking of the university as an environment that enables a great many intellectual activities to take place, or are we talking about a hierarchical organization in which there are central decisions on how resources get allocated and to what purposes? Mr. Levi said earlier that, in a sense, the best university is the least governed one. If that is the operating principle, there would be little opportunity to make these central decisions; the decisions would essentially have to be made on a decentralized basis. Are we talking about different kinds of decisions? Are there decisions that can appropriately be determined centrally, while others ought only to arise from the members of the institutions? And if we talk about membership, are we talking only about the current membership, or about a future membership as well?

BELL

A university plays a crucial role in society not only because of the problems of service that are all evident and real, but for a latent reason. One of the aspects of any modern society is the breakdown of any notion of ritual, a breakdown of a place—call it transcendental place, call it symbolic place—which is meaningful to people and provides some sense of something of importance that goes beyond the immediate self-interest and the notion of the person *per se*. Increasingly one finds, particularly among middle-class people, the notion that there are no places which mark out the passages in one's life. We all talk about the breakdown of religion and about the search for religious things. For most people there are no distinctive places any more; patriotism does not provide you with a sense of identification; religious rites no longer give you that sense of anchorage. To some extent, for a lot of people the university has become, without this being explicated, the transcendental institution in society because it seems to promise the notion of a community. It is a place in which people feel an attachment to something beyond themselves—scholarship, learning, books, ideas, the past. The university has some sense of reverence attached to it; it is a place where you have colleagues and engage in activities which are satisfying to you in a very emotional way. A lot of student agitation about the university comes out of the fear that they want the university to be such a place, but feel that somehow it is not living up to their expectation. In terms of a long-run structural feature of the society, there is a sense in which a long time ago people thought that the corporation would perhaps become a community, an occupational community replacing the family. This idea broke down quickly because the corporation was not that kind of institution. The university, however, does have that kind of resonance as a community, but this raises a real question—namely, what are the limits of a community in this sense? The university cannot be a total community because it cannot be the whole of one's life, but it has to be a large part of one's life.

When the university becomes more and more a center for culture in society—not just for science or for social science—theaters become part of the university, as do the little magazines. It is accepted somehow that the university will take such things under its wing. More importantly, as universities grow, they should provide places wherein people can spend a large part of their lives. Lectures, theaters, music supply a sense of attachment.

If one asked what the university is for, I would say it is for more than scholarship, although it is for that; it is for more than teaching, although it is for that. It is basically for a sense of a community. One of the great attractions of the University of Chicago has always been its sense of being a community. It provides a place where people live near one another without necessarily becoming conformists, without necessarily becoming small-towners. It engenders a sense of attachment which makes you feel that a large part of your life is being lived in a meaningful way. All of us still hold to a certain extent the Western ideal that work and home and place ought to have some sense of unity; that somehow the sundering of work and place, and work and family, and work and emotional attachment is wrong. The university is the one place that has been able to recapture the feeling that work and place and home and colleagues and friendships do have this kind of unity. If the university does provide such a sense, you have certain baselines for identifying what you want to take out of the university and what does not belong in a university atmosphere.

RIESMAN

When Mr. Parsons and I were involved in filling a chair in social ethics at Harvard, we found it very difficult to find nonschizophrenic, disciplined, cogent academicians who connected their work and their emotional concerns in a way that was not metaphorically simplistic or methodologically trivial. When I consider this in light of our discussion, it seems to me that the ethical, human, and integrative problems look different in different fields of knowledge. I cannot imagine most social scientists being so brilliant as most natural scientists, getting their work done and then wanting to play around. Social scientists and certainly most people in the humanities are just too dumb; moreover, their work is too involving, and they are too narcissistic about it. I have perhaps an idyllic image of the natural scientists as being more sanguine, more team-prepared, less concerned with small status struggles. Theoretical physicists have more prestige than metallurgists, but still do not hesitate to associate with them and indeed they enjoy these opportunities. As Messrs. Meyerson, Kaysen, and Bell have suggested, the social scientists enjoy downward social mobility— in other words, slumming. They are perfectly willing to go into Harlem or the urban center; that is moral or that is legitimate.

My experience in teaching, both at Chicago and Harvard, suggests that it is almost impossible to get students not to consider themselves corrupted if they go upward. If I tell a student to go and work in the Federal Government to see how problems of disarmament are really discussed, I meet the feeling that that is corrupt. When I say he has got to know the language in which these problems are discussed in the government if he is to have any impact, I encounter the same pastoral romanticism to which Mr. Bell referred.

This makes for enormous disparities among the different academic guilds. How does one's affective life get touched in one's work? What is the impact of that attachment on the relations to one's colleagues and to general society? What contacts are regarded as field work or educative? The answers that the natural sciences do not give, but that many of the concerned people in the social sciences and humanities do give are precisely illustrated by the Bell-Duberman exchange. In the humanities and the social sciences, the growth of "total individuals" is regarded as a perfectly legitimate, if dangerous, academic concern. In the natural sciences, bringing along colleagues who are par for brilliance is, on the whole, the only kind of teaching which has legitimacy. One of the problems of our discussion reflects the disparities in intelligence, ease of playfulness, locales of preoccupation as these change and as these reflect the way people get differentially drawn into different fields.

GRAUBARD

Messrs. Bell, Riesman, and Kaysen all see roles for the faculty in the university which they have been able to find for themselves or have been asked to assume. What is really interesting in these accounts is that there has been no such opportunity for the student. Despite the change in the character of the institution and the community in which the student is temporarily a member, it was assumed that he would be willing to go on with somewhat less attention than he had received simply because his professors had so many other competing interests. It is the students, however, who are saying in effect that they now want to become more active. In short, the student no longer accepts the idea of the university as a moratorium; he resists the notion that his university experience should be a waiting period during which time he acquires certain capabilities. At a meeting *Dædalus* recently had, very able graduate students, who could go on doing "their thing" the way that graduate students did in the 1950's, expressed a firm resolve no longer to do so. They felt the obligation, the need, to get involved, but the university has not been able to resolve the question of how to involve them, nor is it at all clear how the rest of the university community will react to their involvement or what the university will be like when they are involved.

BELL

It seems to me that two different things are happening here. Students resent faculty, and yet faculty help them; both are valid reactions. The important question is whether the student is searching for an identity or for an education. The two are very different things. In many cases, involvement in activism, which is poignant and real motivationally, is more a search for an identity than for education. Education is a confrontation not so much with events as with a teacher and a tradition. You have no way of holding or judging events. Although you do get a sense of emotional satisfaction that relates to these events, I am not sure you educate yourself through them. You would have the ideal process if a highly motivated and activist student followed these inclinations and afterward had a chance to spend two years as a Rhodes Scholar or as a fellow. He would then have had a sense of experience, of finding himself. When he came back and confronted a tradition, he could relate himself to it this way. I am not saying that the two are necessarily antagonistic, but in most cases you do not have the opportunity to do both. Then the question is what do you want to do. Are you asking a student to say education is a tradition; that it is a coherent notion of a rationally defensible body of learning to which he has to relate himself? Or are you asking him to find himself in terms of some antipodes? It may well be that something is wrong with the whole university system if it cannot trust itself.

KAYSEN

Obviously the more advanced graduate students, those writing dissertations, become apprentices within the system. There is, however, an important qualification here. In the natural sciences and to some extent in the harder social sciences, professors are allowed to play with applied problems, but their graduate students are not; they must do their proper, methodologically correct academic business. With that exception, the more advanced and better graduate students are allowed to participate in the academic process. The undergraduate is not, primarily because that would be too expensive; it would take too much of the professor's time and so on. There are exceptions to this. In the bursary system at Yale, a student has to give a certain amount of time working as a research assistant to a professor in return for a scholarship. This is the way it is formally defined; in fact, of course, it is a great opportunity, and the bursary boy obviously gets a much better educational experience than he would if he did not have this opportunity. On the whole, a Harvard professor who tutors students treats them a little at arm's length, while at Yale the same man with the same student might involve that boy in his own work and therefore teach him in a much more serious and effective way. These are, of course, terrifically expensive educational devices which cannot be widely used. Thus, you return to the question of the economics of this whole process, to the cost structure of such educational arrangements, and to the scale at which it might be possible to provide them.

PAYNE

One of the things that ought to be noted, and has not been, is that while students are at an institution, they are very often more involved with and more committed to it than is the faculty. The faculty is off on the kinds of projects that have been talked about, it is off to Washington, it has its own methods, and so forth. The difference between the search for identity or for education is not the real problem. If students at a university are offered a chance to get an education, if they find a teacher, most of them will discover their identity there. Most of the time the students that I run into, even at Yale, do not find teachers. I agree with what Mr. Kaysen says about the bursary system; it can work well. Some tutorial systems have also worked well. Nevertheless, not many people have that kind of experience. If you are going to confront the teacher and the tradition, the teacher has got to be there—at least through intermediaries. I think that graduate-student teaching makes sense if it is part of a cooperative enterprise in which some of the best minds on the faculty take part. I went into political science because I found two honest men at Berkeley in my sophomore year who both happened to be in the political science department. I was able to confront them not in a situation divorced from student activism, but in an educational process. I find very few models for that kind of teaching. I do find an academic culture in which people are involved in a great many other things and have a great many interests beyond the boundaries of the campuses, interests generally opposed to teaching. It distresses me that at Yale, where you have got these people around, the teaching does not happen because there is a reserve, a backing off from it. The possibilities for this kind of teaching exist on most campuses, but are seldom used. There are not many people in academic positions who are concerned enough to teach in this way.

DUBERMAN

There are, perhaps, some basic disagreements here about what education is and, therefore, about the function of the university. I am not clear, for example, as to what Mr. Bell meant by distinguishing education and identity. In terms of what he did say about education, I am not convinced that his definitions are mine. He defined education as the student's confrontation with a teacher and a tradition, or, as he alternately put it, the way in which a student relates himself to a rational body of learning. It seems to me that this is one part of education, but I would prefer to define education more broadly as the student's confrontation with himself. This can be aided by a confrontation with a rational body of learning or tradition, but the latter, taken alone, is not all there is to the process of self-confrontation. Indeed, I am increasingly convinced that the content of university work has little to do with self-confrontation. Other things that go on either in the classroom or outside it contribute more to self-awareness and individual growth than the actual discussion and transmission of information.

PARSONS

Does this mean that the intellectual content is completely dispensable?

DUBERMAN

No.

PARSONS

This is a crucial point. It is a very defensible position to hold that confrontation with a teacher and a tradition is not all there is to education. Higher education without intellectual content, however, has never made great cultural history, just as religion without a theological tradition has never made great cultural history.

DUBERMAN

If the function of the university should be the accumulation and transmission of knowledge, and if a great deal of emphasis is put on that function, the students' needs must be and traditionally have been almost entirely ignored.

PARSONS

I do not think either Mr. Bell or I said that.

BELL

I think there are differences, and I would like to explore the lines further. If you are talking about education, I would emphasize the intellectual content as being primary. This does not mean that there is only one body of thought or one tradition, but at some point you have to put your thoughts together in a coherent way that is rationally defensible. I also said, however, that this confrontation can only take place within a community, a community which makes the acquisition of a body of knowledge a satisfactory process. I do find a little distressing the tendency to consider feeling and emotion and the notion of individual growth as an end, because the phrase "individual growth" becomes intransigent. You live for something; you do not relate only to persons. A teacher is a model who embodies something; he is not just an abstract person who is satisfactory in terms of his learning, his style, the way he has mastered a body of thought. He has lived a satisfactory life in his way. The old word *magister*, or master, carries with it an important concept; you master *something*. To use a Jamesian idea, you do not have a state of consciousness; you have a consciousness of something. You have a consciousness of an intellectual tradition—with all the emotional content that learning or recognizing this implies. This may be a very personal statement since I grew up in a highly Talmudic way of life in which you mastered with your thumb, one way or the other. You get a large thumb this way; you may not get a green thumb, but you may get an enlarged calloused one from turning book pages. That may be a special kind of bias, and yet it is one that is central to the history of Western culture. You cannot throw out the whole Western culture in the unthinking way that is now being done. You must have standards to make any kind of judgment, and thus you must have something that is rationally defensible as to what a standard is.

LEVI

Very strange things have happened over the years. We used to put facts against theories. Theories were good; facts were bad. Now theories have become facts in the lexicon, because they stand for the rational. Thus there is a kind of disrespect for the theoretical structure, which in itself mirrors the problem that we were talking about before—namely, the scope of the university. It is a great mistake to say that one of the jobs of the university is to provide a place where people from eighteen to twenty-five are to be kept while they grow up. That never was regarded as the best way to put it, and yet that is often suggested today. Another mistake we have made is to overemphasize the academic role as the sole way of learning. Moreover, the notion that the university should pre-empt all of the student's time in the sense of community or whatever is also a great mistake and contains elements of snobbism. One would hope that a sense of community could be developed without imposing all the operations upon the university. One of the tragedies is that universities exist in communities that do not themselves stimulate the kinds of operations which would be desirable. These operations are, therefore, put into the universities, and as soon as you do that, you get an extraordinarily peculiar kind of tension.

One of our problems is to cut down the size of the university at the same time that we increase the importance of the community. We must free the student from the notion that the university is the only path, or from the idea that when he elects to follow this path, it must be his total preoccupation. I do not want to belittle the problems of teaching. This is a constant struggle. There is, however, little to show that teaching and education are more difficult or less successful now than they used to be. I am not sure that education should come easily to anybody. The report that one or two or three faculty strive for stimulation is, I think, quite natural. Books can do that. Other things can do it as part of growing up.

As we talk about these things, the cost element should be regarded—not for the sake of universities, but for the sake of the society. From an educational standpoint, the tradition of large first- and second-year classes, particularly in the state institutions, and then more individual attention in the third and fourth years is absolutely wrong. If you had all the resources that you wished, you ought to be able to turn it the other way around. You cannot look at this question only in terms of universities, because the great problems of this society deal with primary and secondary education, and we should not forget that. The universities should not be hogs about educational resources. There is an enormous selfishness in pouring money into universities where it is not essential.

MORISON

I just have a couple of footnotes on the two-culture problem. There are some real differences between scientists and people in other parts of the university. I do think Mr. Riesman is right in saying that natural scientists have more time to go down to Washington and to engage in social things, but it may not necessarily be because they are brighter. It may have to do with the structure of science. In science a person can be assured ,of a long career by having done one brilliant piece of work. In physics, they very frequently do this when they are twenty-eight or so and then get a Nobel Prize when they are thirty-two. They feel satisfied at having done one or two or three things. Historians, on the other hand, take on the job, say, of understanding the nineteenth century, and there is no end to it. The structural differences are also important. A physicist or even a biologist has a lab with several people in it, and so he can reach the stage fairly early in life when his principal job is to talk with these people and get things set up, and then go to Washington. Thus he leads two different lives. Also, he has become rather deliberate in separating the second life from the first life, partly because of our worries about having classified projects on the campus. We deliberately separate graduate students from the secret things we engage in because we think it is bad education to have them do secret things. Many universities have now said that they are not going to have any classified research on the campus. Faculty members who want to do that go out and consult with industry, or work with RAND, or do something of that sort, and then come back to the university. This does not separate them from their students, although it does separate students from secret work.

When the scientist is on campus, he may have a fairly intimate relationship with his students, because he can bring them into his lab in a way that the professor of history does not bring them into his carrel. In science, the tutorial relationship is almost automatic, at least in the junior and senior years with the good student. The teacher welcomes that relationship because the student actually produces something for him. Consequently, students in the sciences begin to identify themselves as scientists relatively early and feel fairly satisfied. As far as I am able to observe in my institution, science students do not become activists in the political sense. The number of biologists who are picketing is extremely small. I worry, however, that they may become prematurely mature, so to speak. They never confront themselves as political people or as scientists or as emotional human beings. They get their emotional satisfaction out of identifying themselves with their profession, and I do not know whether that is good or bad. I do not know whether we are really educating our people or not. They seem to be happy, and they get happier as they go through college. By the time they are seniors, they feel great, but I am not sure how much they are going to contribute to society.

MEYERSON

In talking about the distinction between the search for identity and the search for education, Mr. Bell was urging both in his nostalgic approach to the University of Chicago. At least it was able to provide both ventures for faculty and probably for very many of the students there.

There is a conventional wisdom today which suggests that the private universities, with the exception of a handful, will cease to be: that Boston University probably cannot survive; that Northwestern will have the greatest difficulties; that Washington University in St. Louis will probably move in the same path of economic demise; that despite various efforts to provide some public compensation to students or to institutions, there will not be enough funds to enable the private institutions—apart from the Harvard's, the Yale's, the Stanford's, the Columbia's, the Chicago's —to exist in the future. As a result, in this view, there will have to be more and more public higher education, which will almost inevitably carry with it certain kinds of controls.

The concern about controls is relevant to a point Mr. Bell made: Can the university be both integrative and adaptive? Can a university that is to be a transmitter of the social values of a culture also be an innovative agent for radical change in the state of that culture? Again and again we see that there are great constraints upon such innovation where there are public controls. These same constraints also exist where there is private control through donors and other means, although they are more marked in the public sphere than in the private. These constraints run counter to the tradition of the opportunities for an innovative social role for universities, which is one of the reasons why I think that for many kinds of innovation we would be well-advised to look elsewhere. In the case of universities, we are dealing with institutions that are very fragile. Throughout history, they have been the transmitters of the existing social order—whether it be a religious social order or the kind of landed gentry aristocracy that the British universities had maintained. I would question whether the university can both obtain the level of resources that the future will require and be socially innovative. It can be educationally innovative in areas that people do not care about, but can it be the instrument of radical social change?

CONWAY

People have spoken of education as confrontation with a body of learning and as a process of self-confrontation. It has been generally accepted that the essential factor in achieving both confrontations is the teacher as model. I would like' to point out that a large part of the student constituency of state universities and many private ones, too, is feminine, and that these students do not have many women teachers as models. This is an important educational problem, one which leads at present to a misdirection or inefficient use of educational resources. The amount of money that is invested in educating women today on the undergraduate and graduate level does not produce the kind of service to society that it could. One reason for this is that there are very few models in contemporary society for educated women to follow.

RUDENSTINE

The idea that the teacher is a model is probably a new one. The teacher used to be rather despised. Certainly in the twenties and thirties, the last person a great many people on campus would have looked to for their model would have been a teacher. Now the teacher is a professional model and an idealistic model in a way he has not been before. That role suggests an inordinate burden on the teacher and the university, and we are suffering from the strains of it.

Mr. Levi's idea of demythologizing the university and the teacher's role is a healthy one, but how we go about doing that is another problem. Part of the reason for this is that the career options open to students are no longer so secure, so acceptable, or so predictable as they once were. In the thirties somehow you could take your education for granted because you could take your career for granted. You did not have to fight every inch of the way with your teachers or their courses. You did not make those kinds of demands, because somehow education was what it always was and then you went off to your career. Now most undergraduates are puzzled about what they should do. The government is unacceptable; business is unacceptable. This is to speak hyperbolically, but most of the "ordinary" careers are no longer the place to go. People think much more now in terms of high-school teaching, inner-city projects, the Peace Corps, or Vista. Careers are in such flux that there are no clear options as to what would integrate one's ideals and one's work. Somehow the burden of integrating ideals and work got transferred to the university and university careers during the fifties. Students are still looking to the universities, but they are now beginning to be disillusioned. They are discovering that the teachers are not all they thought they were, that the universities are not all they thought they were. It would be good to demythologize both the teacher and the university. It would also be good if there were other career options so that this enormous burden would not be placed on a university.

When ritual and the order of your life break down, you look for some definition of reality and a confirmation by significant others. People need some sense of confirmation in this respect; somebody confirms you as to what you are in terms of whatever statuses you achieve. This is why people turn to the university. Lacking the various other kinds of persons who would be the significant others to confirm them, the teacher becomes the model. Mr. Rudenstine wants to demythologize this role; I, however, think it is a valid role simply because a university degree does become a valid model of an acceptable life.

RUDENSTINE

If you are an academic.

BELL

No. For a period of time, most of the young people in this country and certainly the brightest ones are going to be spending a significant part of their time in the academic world. It is important for that very reason not to demythologize the professor. That does not mean that you put him on a pedestal or anything of this sort. You need an aesthetic distance in order to be yourself and not be swamped by students. In order to be a confirming other for them, you must maintain this distance. To that extent, I go against Mr. Levi's plea that this role be restricted. I think one should enlarge it because there is perhaps no place other than the university in contemporary society where a confirming other can be found.

KAYSEN

In taking up Mr. Duberman's point, I have to ask myself the old question: Compared with what? He has in mind presumably some alternative ways of growing up, some alternative places to be between eighteen and twenty-five. In an earlier stage of social organization, growing up usually took place in an apprenticeship context where one combined the learning of some body of knowledge—not necessarily a traditional body of knowledge, but sometimes a body of knowledge with considerable abstract content—with the mastering of nonintellectual techniques: physical skills, interpersonal skills, whatnot.

A politician in the seventeenth or eighteenth century came to be a politician by being drawn from a certain class—in most polities, the aristocracy. He went to Court as a page or had some relation to the political establishment; in some context he would read and associate with learned men; he would also learn all kinds of interpersonal skills and some technical military skills, because every politician was expected to have some share of them. He did this in a way which was mostly highly concrete. There was little reflective discussion about political life, although there was some. Today you learn to be a politician in the university.

More and more skills have become intellectual skills. Again, let me draw some samples from science. A fellow named Fieser at Harvard used to dazzle students by doing an organic analysis very quickly using a lot of brilliant manual techniques. Now there is a spectrometer that does the whole thing more or less automatically. Thus, rather complicated manual techniques have been replaced by purely intellectual ones.

A particular element of the apprenticeship relation has to do with the physical handling of things in a community enterprise. I remember when the first synchrotron was built at Tech. It was a pretty sloppy thing; you would go down there, and somebody would be tinkering with it with a screwdriver. You cannot do that now; you have to call in the engineering department. The university, as well as the general society, has increasingly substituted intellectual techniques and bodies of knowledge for these other techniques. What is going on in the university is also going on in the society.

Most of the jobs that most college graduates will undertake are undergoing this transformation. That means that the university and academic work provide two kinds of role models and techniques: intellectual techniques and interpersonal techniques. If you accept this projection, although it is clearly exaggerated, the existentialist anxiety that we are being provided a role model only for a tiny fraction of the world which goes into the academic profession misses the point of what is going on.

Business is going to absorb for some time to come the largest number of people who get degrees from colleges. These graduates will go into jobs where they must be able to absorb a certain amount of information and translate it into a decision. They will operate in a context in which they must have some skill in interpersonal relations. All that they learn at the university, whatever they study.

DUBERMAN

I might be making reference to a rather narrow group of students—those I have seen in the humanities and the social sciences.

It may well be that students in the natural, physical, or biological sciences do not react in the same way. Nevertheless, the students I have known do not feel that their four years in college are a growth experience, nor do they feel that they are a learning experience. I could not agree more with Mr. Bell that growth and learning come from confrontation with significant others; most of these students, however, feel, as Mr. Payne has already said, that they do not come into contact with significant others on the faculty. What they come in contact with instead are specialists in academic learning; they absorb a body of knowledge about a particular field. Often in the humanities and the social sciences, that body of information does not appear to them to be noticeably relevant either to their needs or to those of society.

I am not at all clear about what can be done to correct this situation, but from my experience I am sure that it poses a real problem. From the point of view of most graduating seniors, the university has not been the best place for them to have spent the preceding three or four years. They do not feel that the university structure has met their needs. They often would agree that they had been educated in terms of Mr. Bell's definition. They have been put in touch with a rational body of learning or a tradition, but they doubt the relevance of the tradition; they doubt how relevant or how rational the body of learning is; and they also doubt whether they have been put in touch with whole people. They see their professors only for an occasional hour or so; they see them dealing with specific matters in terms of the mastery of a particular subject. They do not see, as they used to in certain progressive colleges like Antioch or Black Mountain, whole people performing in a large variety of areas. It seems to me that until they see such people and such variety, they will not have had confrontation with significant others.

PARSONS

I should like to come back to Mr. Meyerson's remarks. The question of whether the university can or cannot be innovative is an important one. I am speaking, however, more in terms of the university's cultural and social impact than of its effect on the individual student, which is a somewhat different problem. The greater need for public support and the general differentiation of the academic world from other sectors of society clearly mean that the university is developing a new combination of independence and dependence. I myself think that the university's structural autonomy is exceedingly important. If it is specialized in its traditional functions, teaching and advancement of knowledge, it cannot in itself be politically powerful. It cannot itself produce wealth on a big scale. It inevitably becomes dependent on non-academic agencies for its position in the society. Cases where this has not been true are largely those where higher education has been closely bound up with some special elite—as was true, for example, of Oxford and Cambridge in the late-nineteenth and early-twentieth centuries.

In this situation, only in generally revolutionary eras can the academic world be a spearhead of what is often referred to as fundamental social change directed, explicitly and in the short run, against the dominant institutions of the society. Over a century or two a university may deeply undermine the authority system of an earlier time, but it cannot directly challenge it and overthrow it. This is not the nature of its function. If it is to be innovative, it has to change the cultural base of the society.

We have to a degree institutionalized an important balance between constancy of pattern and innovation. The prototype is the advancement of knowledge, but carried on within a relatively stable, though changing, institutional framework. Beyond that there is obviously the dissemination of the implications of these changes through the education of people in a variety of ways. The distinction between being innovative in the sense of being essentially a political source for relatively immediate change and being innovative through these more indirect channels is extremely important. Doing something about the urban ghetto is an intermediate thing, but I quite agree with Mr. Meyerson that universities and students will not be the primary agents in the mitigation of ghetto and poverty problems. They can be an important stimulus, symbolically showing the way, but if there is to be a big push, it will probably have to be governmental.

RIESMAN

I want to pick up the financial and demographic problems on which Mr. Levi touched, and then try to link both to the demanding ideal of academic responsiveness to constituencies. I keep asking state university people: "How many on your faculty earn more than the governor? And how long can this go on?" In the case of the private universities, faculty are only beginning to get more than the trustees. How long can that go on? There are only a few places where it can go on at all. Faculty are more and more in demand because of the social needs we have been talking about. The resultant pressure from students is likely to create a faculty power backlash which will seldom manifest itself in formal counterattack, certainly not in support of Reaganism, but very likely in personal flight from demanding to less demanding settings. Yale, Princeton, Stanford—places like that can afford the luxury of having some concerned faculty because by and large those people do not want to go anywhere else. I do see a potential flight of faculty from places like Antioch because they share the Duberman ethos in some degree—the feeling that the students' claims are just. I know I feel this. The model I see for myself is that of racial integration—that is, student integration has some of the same problems of tipping the neighborhood. Negroes spread from the Black Belt of Chicago south-vard to the University of Chicago because this is liberal, non-violent terrain; they do not go to Cicero or westward against the Polish or the Italian communities. Similarly, the vulnerable faculty go to the place where they will be cannibalized and not to the slightly more guarded gates where less is expected of them vis-à-vis demanding students.

On the one hand, universities seek faculty to do less and less for more and more; on the other, students ask faculty to do more and more for fewer elite students. This leaves the great bulk of institutions, many of whose faculties come out of the ethic of wanting to teach high school. Although I find many more of my students wanting to teach at Tugaloo or other Negro colleges than in a commuter urban poor-white college with some Negroes, nevertheless there is some effort to character these institutions with the ethic of total involvement and commitment. I do not have an answer to the issues I raise. How does one put together what I, along with Mr. Levi, believe to be a declining luminescence of the university with the increase in what is being asked of that fraction of academic men who have been socialized to want to teach? Such men find it hard not to respond, and yet (as in the case of racial integration) they feel that they are paying a personal price for previous cultural neglect.

PAYNE

It is clear from Mr. Kaysen's remarks that skills are imparted; it is also clear that we are in trouble when we risk meeting students even less than we are meeting them now, when we risk professors and students doing less than they are doing now about things they care about. How good is the educational community? What determines its quality? I am opposed to demythologizing the university. I want to remythologize it—professors, presidents, and students. There is nothing wrong with casting things in a more heroic mold. Disagreements like those between Mr. Duberman and Mr. Bell are fine. We need both kinds of teaching done with that kind of feeling in the university, but there is little of either.

Few people are actively building the kinds of communities that we want to see, and we are crucially lacking leadership. It does seem to me that for the universities to back out of a lot of activities is exactly the wrong way to proceed, precisely because the one great advantage we have is that students want to be whole people and to meet whole people; they want to be involved in lots of different things that challenge their minds and their feelings. That means there ought to be theater, music, and such things around. In regard to the problem of the university acting as an umbrella, it seems to me that the university can act more effectively if it shelters some things that the surrounding population is more happy with as well as some things that they may not like very much. We may be able in a pluralistic society to do both these things, whereas doing one and not the other would either be unsatisfactory ethically or simply impossible politically.

I think we should talk later specifically about such questions as: What do you do in terms of student life? What do you do in terms of making it possible for professors to teach, for building some kind of community on a commuter campus, on a campus where students are not involved in any formal organizations?

GRAY

I am impressed by the constant harking back to the past as a time when things were different. This is a nostalgia, a utopianism, that sees the past as having somehow incorporated values which we have now lost. In many ways the academic community did not possess those values in the past either. For example, the notion of a faculty that was once individually concerned with students as they are not today is wrong. The notion of a past in which there was a community of faculty and students that no longer exists is wrong. In the past, the criticism of a university that was being made by students was far less radical than now, but the students expected a good deal less of the university. Students became alumni; they then thought of the good old college days, of the professors who stimulated and inspired them, and translated these notions into the community that they had experienced. They then thought of that as the totality of what their university experience had been.

Although teaching roles have declined, although teaching is a lesser part of many faculty members' activities, the teaching that is done is without doubt better—better in terms of the standard and rigor of the courses. This is the consequence partly of the greater attention given to fewer courses, but also of real developments that have occurred in various academic fields. On the other hand, it is also true that teaching has become somewhat of an underground activity in the universities. Those who see many students on an individual basis are a part of what is a really new academic underground—the underground of teaching and of contact with students.

The quality of teaching has not declined, nor is the world of students more alienated than it had been in the past. The student feels that alienation, and his expectations as to what he is to derive from the institution have changed. That seems to me as important as the actual change which these institutions have brought about. These also seem contradictory desires. The desire to have a total community in which every kind of experience is open is directly counter to the notion of having an integrated community in which the members of that community are as one. It is like wanting to have a life of the village in the midst of a city, yet both students and faculty seem to be demanding just that. They want the whole city within the university and then complain when it turns out to lack the values of the smaller community.

There is an enormous gap between the rhetoric about education and the reality of the institutions which assert that rhetoric in their catalogues, in programs which they announce, and so forth. Universities are in a sense competing for students as well as for faculty. The gap between the rhetoric about what is to be made available and what the student actually finds is growing all the time. It does not just grow because professors are away in Washington; it grows because there is a real contradiction between the increased sophistication, the felt complexity of academic work and intellectual discipline, and the easy clichés in which all this is quoted. Not only does the institution promise the students something which it will not give them and which, if it is a good institution, it ought not give them, but the student is caught between the emphasis on education and the importance of professional training. One of the real lacks in our institutions now is not simply their structural difficulties; it is a matter of never saying what they are really about.

I am always amazed that students believe that so many of the faculty are on their side. The faculty is on their side; the administration is their enemy. To a great extent, these conditions are the product of faculty and of tensions that exist in the professional life of the faculty. Some faculty members are very good at seeing students in their homes, but that is not the solution to anything. Contact between faculty and students has to be made on those things with which faculty are most concerned within their own professional work, within the academic discipline. That contact has to do with the nature of the work that they are jointly involved in.

There is so little rational discussion of the complex issues that are involved, issues that cannot be simply absolved and where the conclusion of the discussion ought to be a further awareness of intellectual and academic integrity.

RIESMAN

Why in order for people to say that what is going on now is bad do they have to say it was once better? I have never been able successfully to combat this prevailing nostalgia. It exists not only about the university, but about the country as well. I have found no talk about the childishness and ham-acting of earlier academia. Students lapse back into the assumption that there were once great days.

GRAY

This clearly seems to be a repetitive pattern.

CONWAY

I think I can explain why those who are discontented with the modern mass university today do hark back to a golden past. Although it is true that what is taught in the modern university is conveyed with more intellectual rigor and discipline than, let us say, it was in the average college lecture room in the late-nineteenth or early-twentieth century, students today have many expectations concerning their university experience besides intellectual ones. Historically American institutions have been expected to serve a democratic end—namely, to multiply the options for academic and vocational advancement for all those who study or teach there. This function is, I think, still discharged well. What is new about the expectations which students bring to university is that they expect to find there the kind of environment for personal development which in the past was to be found at an elite college which followed the Oxford and Cambridge tradition. This expectation is not being met by institutions of higher learning today anywhere in North America. Yet I stress that this expectation is at the root of much dissatisfaction among students. I teach in Canada where most of the reasons for disenchantment with contemporary society to be found in the United States are not present, and yet we face the same kind of angry criticism of the university. Why this revolution of rising expectation should occur in the 1950's and '60's is difficult to explain, although one can sketch in the broad outlines of causation. Ours is a society in which affluence does permit for the great majority of students a concern with personal adjustment and self-development which was once possible only for an aristocracy. At the same time our culture is one in which there is a rising level of awareness of psychological thought. Philip Rieff has pointed out that just as nineteenth-century man was economic man, his twentieth-century counterpart is psychological man. One consequence of the incorporation of much popular psychology into our culture has been a change in the expectation of students about just what will be a good learning experience, and I think a corresponding change in the pedagogical goals of teachers. Many of us, I think, do see ourselves as teachers working to create a situation in which students will become self-aware and develop insight into their potential powers—not just, say, as students of history, but as whole human beings. We may not do very well at this, but to the extent that we do succeed in the context of a modern mass university, we are creating a situation in which students catch a glimpse of the possibility of self-development, while at the same time they realize that the existing occupational and economic structure of society is bound to frustrate that development outside college. Indeed to pass on to graduate school often means that the search for a fully elaborated consciousness must be abandoned for a personality structured to function well in some professional role. I think it is this profoundly disturbing awareness which is different from the past and makes people look back to a time when either the educational process was not consciously invested with such psychic significance, or when at least in some elite institutions the goal of personal development was a realistic one. The search for community is essentially a search for sharing of more than rational experience, and because of this it is not addressing the whole problem to discuss only the intellectual rigor of what is taught today.

PAYNE

In general, I think the hardline approach to the past is right. It seems to me, however, that the hopes of the students are the best thing we have, and we ought to be capitalizing on them. That we do not do enough. Of course, it is impossible to have the village in the city; the village has been gone for a long time. Nevertheless, it is not impossible to have a series of communities where graduate students, undergraduates, and occasionally professors talk together about the things that matter. That kind of community exists in places in Berkeley, so that it may be impossible to hire some Berkeley professors away, even though their academic situation is awful and the political situation worse. They stay at Berkeley for those communities. Those kinds of possibilities are clearly open. Students are not looking for the past, but for something that we have not had very much of yet. It is not just honesty nor just intellectualism. There are other parts of life, and those are not being met by universities now.

STOLZ

There is no better way to build a community than to have a generally approved riot. Everybody loves everybody else, and you get to know them; that's splendid. I am not sure that this a solution.

One of the mythologies of American higher education is that it has provided equal access to everyone as a way up through the community—a new route, a leveling technique where character and quality rather than wealth are the determinants of a person's capacity to get ahead. Going back to something Mr. Levi said earlier, secondary education is the place where we should be spending more money if our mythology of higher education does include this element of upward mobility. That mythology is sufficiently important and sufficiently a part of the tradition of American higher education to render silly the question: Should we have mass higher education or should we concentrate on graduate institutions? Politically that is not even a sensible question. We are clearly dedicated to the idea that anybody who wants a higher education and is capable of receiving it should get it. The problem is how do we do it, and how do we do it most efficiently. That is where I bump into what seem to me to be the critical problems— the economic ones. Where are we going to find the resources? The public sector is being squeezed hard, and there does not seem to be any reason to suppose that the situation is going to get any better in the future. Where are we going to get the resources to devote to mass higher education? Can we afford to indulge in some of the luxuries that we presently have? I do not know the answers to these questions, but I do feel confident that *we* are not going to make those decisions. They are going to be made outside the university. Unless we can build a persuasive case to the authorities of the public sector, we are not going to get the resources.

BELL

This raises a question which puzzles me. About four years ago, there was a fiscal drag because the growth of the economy was such that taxes were accumulating at a faster rate than the government could spend them. Now suddenly we find there are not enough resources. Which level is one talking about?

Governance of the Universities I

STOLZ

Jesse Unruh's Joint Committee on Higher Education in California obviously focuses on the resources of the State of California rather than the tax resources in the government as a whole, but it is very clear that the lush period in California's higher education was attributable to a certain accumulation during the war and the extensive utilization of credit in the period following the war. We have now run out of credit, and the demands of other portions of the state government are increasing, as are the demands within the educational establishment—including secondary and primary education. There is simply a squeeze on.

KAYSEN

This is partly a question of what perspective you wish to adopt at any moment. My own view is that there is a lot of money for education in the sense that the political process can easily and probably will provide a sufficient flow of money to do quite a lot. I think the acute questions are those Mr. Levi originally raised and Mr. Stolz has elaborated on. What particular packages for what kinds of things will look attractive enough to spend tax money on? In my own political perception, it is a mistake to compare this with the need for prisons or mental hospitals. The thing you compare it with is roads. We spend money like mad for roads because everybody uses them. More and more, higher education is coming in under this line. It will be used by a high proportion of the politically effective population of the United States. The people who do not use higher education are the objects of the political process and not actors in it.

RIESMAN

What about Negroes in the city?

KAYSEN

It is a mistake in proportion to emphasize Negroes in the city if we are trying to have a broad perspective. The parts of the political apparatus that deal with these things are completely different even though the programs and the agencies that hand out the money may be the same. In the one case, you are talking about a great political crisis and how we react to it. In the other, you are talking about how the government provides for something that everybody in society wants.

275

In 1945, there was not one analyst shrewd enough to predict the extent to which people in this country would want automobiles —not just one, but two or three. If this had been foreseen, we might have been able to come up with a better resource allocation. We built lots of roads because this was the easiest thing to appropriate tax money for; everybody liked it for a variety of reasons. I would guess that the whole education business is going to be that way. Whether it is fair or unfair (and Mr. Levi's observation that it is unfair is probably one I would share), the distribution of funds between higher education and primary and secondary education is going to be in favor of the former. We already have a set of institutions and tax processes that determine the resource size for the primary and secondary sectors. We do not yet have these for higher education on the scale that it looks to be growing. We will have to develop them, and it is always the new boy that gets treated the best. That is the way our political structure seems to work.

The question is not whether there are enough real resources in this country to buy this kind of higher education system, but how much the consumer will be willing to pay for it. And, of course, the consumer in this case is a most complex and curious congeries of state legislators, federal legislators, the executive branch, and various pressure groups. Trying to predict the outcome of this process is fairly difficult. One can, however, make some obvious predictions. It is going to be hard to say to a state legislature that a professor of Iranian manuscripts ought to be paid more than the governor. If the state is paying a man more than the governor to study old Iranian manuscripts and not to teach anybody anything, that fact has got to be buried in such a way that they do not notice it. It is not hard to persuade a legislature that a man ought to be paid more than a governor to teach us how to go to the moon, and because it is not hard to do that, you can pay people to read old Iranian manuscripts at these rates.

PARSONS

One of the most important conditions of the growth of the American academic system has been that the interests in it reach into wide sectors of the population through different functions, through different classes of institutions. Thus we have escaped the sociopolitical isolation that an elite system is likely to be exposed to.

KAYSEN

Competition alone was tremendously important; it is not an accident that the best university system in Europe was in Germany where you had the competition among separate sovereignties during the whole period of that system's formation in the first half of the nineteenth century. Competition among the sovereignties generated the competition among universities for people.

LEVI

A minor caveat—if you divide education between undergraduate and graduate, I am not sure that we do not have a good deal of an elitist student body. Most of our graduate students as opposed to our undergraduate students are very much like their fathers were when they were in college.

PARSONS

The undergraduate part of the system has been so strong and so viable to a great extent because there is by far the broadest base of interest on the undergraduate side.

KAYSEN

I disagree with Mr. Levi's caveat. He is in a law school, which is elitist. But in the natural sciences and to a great extent the social sciences, the affluence of government has had an enormous effect. Graduate students in these fields represent a much wider social spread than you would see in a law school because of National Science Foundation money. In the natural sciences it is relatively objective exercise to determine who is bright; the same is true in physics and economics. In a sense, by the time people are at the end of the first graduate year, you already know who is going to be a professor at M.I.T., Yale, Berkeley, Harvard, Chicago. On this level of the graduate system, I would say that there has been a great increase in the degree of egalitarianism; in the professional schools, practically none.

RUDENSTINE

We may be in this difficulty at the moment in part because the universities have managed during the last fifteen years to level compelling criticism at much of American society and indeed Western culture. This is certainly true politically. When a student arrives on the campus, he learns that we are in some sense an imperialist country, that our farm policy is out of phase, that our democracy is not precisely what he thought it was, and so forth. His educational experience is apt to be a fierce questioning of many of the values, political and otherwise, that he has accepted up to that point. The university criticizes our society and, therefore, gives students the impression that somehow the university and academics are better than the society.

This breeds extravagant hopes on the part of the students. They are inevitably disappointed when they discover that their professors may not act any better than the rest of the world. An issue like Vietnam makes that all too clear. Students discover—whether accurately or not—a tension between what the university says collectively in its books and lectures and what it seems to do at a moment of national or international crisis.

PARSONS

A large number of the people who demythologize the society hold out what I think many would regard as unrealistic hopes for the readiness with which society can be fundamentally changed. In other words, if they said what was bad about it, but also made clear how difficult it is to change it, their comments might have a different effect.

KAYSEN

If what Mr. Rudenstine is saying is the correct diagnosis, it is the result of some very bad teaching. Intelligent, responsible social scientists do spend a lot of time pointing out the way in which institutions and society do not function properly, how they fall short of their ideals, and so on. After all, that is what makes social science interesting and what attracts a great many people to it. But the same people, if they have any sense at all, point out that on any reasonable comparative standard this is one of the more flexible, humane, and open forms of social organization.

RUDENSTINE

I cannot help feeling that the emotional thrust of much of the work that has been done in the last ten or fifteen years has been deeply critical of America and its culture.

PAYNE

Students are always going to be fired up about issues of social justice, and it is not the teaching of the universities that has lighted those fires. In fact, it has in some ways been quite the opposite. A great deal of social science is devoted to justifying this political order, and, by the way, I think that is a decent task for social science. Students become activists partly because of the lack of a political understanding. The first time you face an issue of social injustice, you are going to be shocked, as people were shocked by what happened in the Montgomery bus boycott or during 1963 and 1964 in Mississippi. Those first political experiences are their first real perceptions of the extent to which the social order does not measure up to what they were taught by the Boy Scouts or in the first grade. That is where the ideas can be traced back to, although they are reinforced all the way through the system. When those ideals come up against harsh realities, the confrontation produces that kind of student feeling; it does not have much to do with what goes on in the universities.

GLASER

I attribute part of the difficulty to Mr. Kaysen's scientists who have inculcated us with the notion that truth is simple. Students get to college and, thanks to our educational system, learn that few things are simple. As a result, they find great comfort in the issues of social justice in which right or wrong can be clearly delineated. The issues of Vietnam and civil rights are simple ones for the students, as they are for most of us; there is a right and a wrong. In addition, numerous other matters, including the rebellious feelings that many current students have toward their parents and toward their elders, contribute significantly to current student unrest.

RIESMAN

I have been auditing courses at Harvard off and on for ten years. The audiences at Harvard are slightly different from those even at Yale, Stanford, and Princeton because Harvard students come from the sixth grade already slightly more cynical. The neighborhood is more tipped in that direction than it is in places that until recently have been slightly more square and are therefore more susceptible to activism and disillusion. In these classes, I constantly hear the refrain: Most of my colleagues are idiots; most of the books in this field are not worth reading, and yet you have to read them; most of the things that are believed in this field are not so. This tone obtains regardless of the professor's political position on the larger social issues.

In the general education class I direct, a colleague asked students who their heroes were, and they came up with, among others, Humphrey Bogart and Adam Clayton Powell. Although this is a coed class, there were no females. The feeling I have is symbolized by a talk I had with a Radcliffe student. She said: "The first thing I learned as a freshman in history here was that you got ahead by attacking the book and the professor. This defeminized me, and the problem of being a girl and being an intellectual was hopeless for me." This half of the university population is in a setting in the elite and potentially elite places where what they learn has a destructive undercutting element. It reflects the ambivalence of academic men—perhaps especially younger ones, but not all the younger ones—about what they do as well as about the society. One of the reasons why young women do not connect so much to the intellectual life is that they are both more responsive and more responsible than men, otherwise none of us would be here now. There is a real incongruity between the world in which they respond to people as well as to books and ideas and the one in which men respond by the narcissism of small intellectual differences.

KAYSEN

I have only been away from Harvard for two years after spending twenty years there. I do not know how Mr. Riesman goes to other people's classes; I cannot imagine anything more against the Harvard ethos than that. I must say, however, that in the department of economics, with a few trivial exceptions, you never heard a professor criticize his colleagues. If two colleagues had sharply different views, as they often did, you heard a lot of fairly serious discussion.

RIESMAN

Economists are, I think, more like natural scientists.

KAYSEN

Economists *are* more like natural scientists. I cannot imagine such comments in the natural sciences. The most I can imagine is conversations which say: "Oh, yes, X thinks thermodynamics is fascinating; I can't understand why he thinks it more interesting than field theory." It does not get any stronger than that. A few people are a little more passionate, but they are generally looked down on as being rather childish to talk that way. You do hear this kind of comment in a faculty of literature where there is an awful element of personal style. This is not just a sidelight that is personally interesting to us because we are professors, but something fundamental to what the academic enterprise is supposed to be doing.

One would be far less likely to hear this among historians.

From the point of view of one who has been a student over the last eight years or so, the kind of thing that Mr. Riesman mentions is not the universal experience, but it is the most common. It is the most common subject of graduate student discussion. I have heard it very solidly in history departments and throughout the social sciences and the humanities.

Wouldn't you rather agree with me now, Mr. Payne? The thrust of my statement was that students are taught to repudiate. The implication is that somebody who teaches you to repudiate somehow ought not to be repudiated.

I think this is true at the academic level; I was only questioning it as a political explanation. I do not think it explains much about student politics.

This nostalgia versus hopes or hopes versus nostalgia is a critical issue. At our college, maybe 15 per cent of the people come with hopes which are frustrated, and they take it out in activism and so forth. So purely from that standpoint, it does seem worth thinking about. I think they are hoping for specific sorts of techniques and information, and universities are far better able to give them that sort of thing now than they were when I went to them. You can be better prepared for a profession; you can be better prepared and discover truth on your own. Those hopes seem to be satisfied. The hopes for some meaning in life are not being satisfied, but in my opinion they never were and the university was never designed to answer such needs. The question is whether you redesign the university so that it can take the place of the other mechanisms which man has had in the past to make life a meaningful experience.

In the twenties at Harvard, there was no personal criticism of colleagues on the faculty, but there certainly was a great deal of skepticism. The whole purpose of the enterprise was to shake the beliefs students came with; we did not feel so upset about this. Somehow we were quite pleased to discover that there were people around who would question those rather rigid value systems in which we had been brought up. The Boy Scouts were very real for us in those days, and many of us went to church. Our parents were quite clear about what they thought life ought to be like and what we ought to be like, much clearer than parents are today. Consequently, we found this skepticism refreshing. I have a feeling that the students who are most upset now are the ones who do not come to a college with values—either from their parents, their church, or the Boy Scouts—and are looking to the college to give them a set of values and beliefs and meaningfulness which universities simply have not been designed to do for a very long time.

RIESMAN

We are the gods who failed.

MORISON

Yes, and I am not sure that I want to do anything but fail.

PAYNE

There are going to be more and more of those students coming.

MORISON

It is really a question of whether a university is a good mechanism for erecting a positive value system to which everybody can tie themselves.

PAYNE

But there is a second question: Is a university a good place for getting a hold on that kind of framework?

MORISON

Since the discussion about the role of the teacher as a role model, I have been jotting down certain thoughts. It seems to me that there is a hierarchy in this. I would say that the biologists, chemists, physicists, and literary critics, in about that order, are pretty good in supplying role models. There are creative artists around universities, but they do not show what the role is in that line. We do a poor job of providing a role model for businessmen and political and government figures. We tend to deprecate those to the extent that the student feels that that cannot be the way to engage in society. The difficulty is that most of the things that go on in society are carried on by either businessmen or politicians. We do not seem to have been able to give any dignity to that very large sector of society which is engaging in society's problems directly. The student rejects these roles and tends to feel that the university ought to engage itself directly in social problems. I am not sure that that is quite the thing. The university is perhaps failing to show that the people who do engage directly in society have something to be said for them; that it is not so bad as it looks on the outside.

PARSONS

When I was an undergraduate, the business community was very much debunked. I was partly concentrating in economics at that time, and Veblen was the hero of my principal teacher. He did not give a damn for Alfred Marshall or anyone like that. Veblen was his hero, and Veblen was about as destructive a social critic of American business as you could find.

MORISON

Few of my classmates thought business was a good thing to go into.

WAX

Although very few of your classmates thought very much of business, it seems they went into it.

MORISON

Right.

WAX

My impression today is that the bright people who are coming out of good universities are not only opposed to business, but will not go into it. That is why Motorola has this big advertising campaign in the Harvard *Crimson*; obviously there are people who go into business, but the larger percentage of them do not.

KAYSEN

Does somebody know the facts? My own impression was that the proportion of college graduates going into business is about the same now as it was in the twenties.

PARSONS

No, it is decreasing at the elite colleges.

LEVI

I am terribly skeptical about information about students. There was a time, however, when it was not so upsetting to have students upset. Today, the notion that somebody is frustrated or upset seems to demand some kind of response. I am not sure that it warrants that kind of response. Being upset is probably a good thing in the educational system. A lot of the criticism of the kind of education given obviously comes from those schools where the education is very much the best. There seems to be a lack of urgency, a feeling of boredom, a grasping for even greater luxury, and a very peculiar value system. A foundation made a study of the present college situation, and part of the grief they discovered arose because the rooms for college students were not very nice. When one thinks of the pressing problems of our society, it is immoral to center on this kind of thing for a luxury class.

I do think that the university should stand for something. But what? I do not think it should be deceptive. It should stand for intellectual truth as it sees it. I completely disagree with Mr. Duberman. There is a sense in which finding one's self intellectually is a part of the whole thing; you do not have a disembodied intellect sitting there anyway. It seems to me that the important service, the real task, of the university in this country is to provide intellectual truth. I do not believe that it is fulfilling this role very well. The social scientists are very much to blame for this. They have inculcated the notion of deception, rather than rationality, which is extremely dangerous. The humanities, philosophy departments, and divinity schools have added the notion that intellectual honesty is impossible for a lot of reasons. If the universities do not stand for intellectual integrity, they are not properly communicating with their students. The judgment I would make on a university, then, is whether its size and the activities that it takes on are such that they defeat this basic conception of the university's purpose. I realize that what I have said is very foolish, because there is not one kind of university. Part of the problem is the terminology; we ought to have different words for different institutions. We ought to separate them out. There is a whole variety of institutions. One of our problems is that we keep talking about things over one ball of wax, and we do not separate out the talk about universities within the university from the talk in *Life* magazine and over the television.

It is terribly important that the institutions find their own integrity. If it is not the rational intellect as the main focus for some institutions, let it be something else then. Nevertheless, this problem of purpose has to be met head on. Part of the problem of undergraduate education is the problem of graduate education. You cannot justify a great deal of graduate education. We have much too much of it, particularly in the humanities. We have erected an enormous structure in this country, and we find ourselves discussing whether there will be sufficient financing to keep it going. I doubt whether there will be, and, furthermore, I think it is improper to ask for that financing. Many other needs are much more pressing in this country, and it is wrong to have this enormous structure of education which cannot refuse the challenge to take on everything and loses its identity as it does. The kind of university that I am talking about would have to keep its size down to a basis where it can have an intellectual mode and mood and candor which go throughout the place; there can be other kinds of institutions. Not only would this be good for the institution, but it is imperative for the society.

The whole urban redevelopment field is a dramatic illustration of much of what I have been talking about. Social scientists do not know how to write about it, but they write about it, and generally speaking with enormous inaccuracy. They remake history gladly and happily, because they know that that is what history is for. They do not have a professional sense of responsibility. Quite apart from that, they are not the people to do it. There is the notion that we turn to the universities because that is where you can tuck the problem. What has been done is to blunt the charge of society on these points.

It is curious that we maintain this elaborate graduate center when there are enormous jobs that could be done on the outside. We lock students into graduate activity for years on the theory that everybody has to get the doctor's degree. Not only that, we have told them that they have to do it in order to make money, in order to be trained. There are other ways of training, and adult education is very good too. Moreover, we have locked *ourselves* into a multilithic-monolithic structure of what we think a university is. This is the problem.

BELL

The important prior question is who should be educated and how far? What standards do you have to determine this? How does one create such standards? One of the things which has bothered me is that about 50 per cent of the students in most state universities drop out by the end of the second year. These universities have the habit of taking everybody who maintained a C average in high school—and in many cases not even a C average. Madison, Wisconsin, has been blown up completely out of proportion because it now has forty thousand students and will probably have forty-eight thousand in a few years. This has literally wrecked the university; half of the students are deliberately dropped by the end of the second year, which is an enormous waste of resources.

DUBERMAN

If you reduce student discontent to how large their dormitory rooms are, of course you trivialize that discontent. I, however, contend that this discontent is so important that it weighs equally with what is happening to our cities or to our Negro population. This generation of students is not content at age eighteen to be told that somebody else has the right to make the essential decisions in their lives. They feel more mature than that, and from my observations they are more mature than that. In other words, they are protesting the whole super-structure of *in loco parentis*, their lack of control and involvement in basic decisions that have touched their lives.

In asking that we consider or re-evaluate the role of teaching, I was not necessarily implying that the re-evaluation would involve an increased amount of time or work or expenditure. Such an implication would come very badly from me, as I teach at Princeton and live in New York City. We need not so much to expand the number of contacts between student and faculty, but to look at the quality of the contacts that already exist. We need not to add ten hours to the teaching load of each professor, but to re-evaluate what is going on during that initial ten-hour period. Our investigation might in fact lead to a reduction in expenditure. By a variety of definitions, student-initiated and student-run seminars are often a better form of education. This would mean an actual reduction both in faculty teaching levels and in expenditures of faculty time. We might want to do away with certain kinds of classes altogether, whether or not they were run by students or faculty. We might think that certain kinds of material are best dealt with outside the university structure.

GLASER

Should students be intimately involved in appointments and promotions?

PAYNE

Yes.

GLASER

What expertise do they bring to the selection of a professor of biochemistry or of Latin?

PAYNE

At institutions where teaching makes a difference, where there are standards that say teaching is important in terms of the appointment of a faculty member, students want to know whether those standards are being followed. At Yale about three years ago, we were not sure that the official standards of the university were being followed. A student who sits on that committee during the course of a year can say, in general, whether a person's teaching ability has been taken into account. There are lots of sources for information about teaching ability. For example, at Yale some of the top seniors and the top freshmen are asked to describe their educational experience. The question that is raised is whether those opinions get into the discussion. If they are not getting into the discussion, something is wrong. In some departments, in some tenure committees, they do not because people try to maintain an objective stance and shy away from the evaluation of teaching. Students do not need to have a veto power nor a controlling power of any kind. They do need to see the process as it goes on. There is no reason that representative students cannot know about confidential matters. The more confidential information that students have, the more responsible they are likely to be; and conversely.

GLASER

I gather Mr. Payne believes that students will not accept the assurance of the faculty that these matters are considered critically and thoughtfully. If they did, they presumably would not be concerned. Assuming that one student was on an *ad hoc* committee of five people to consider the promotion to tenure rank or the appointment of a professor, how long do you think the students would be satisfied if they found that their criteria for this appointment and those of the faculty did not coincide? Inevitably in many areas there is going to be great stress put on productive scholarship. How long would the students be satisfied with that system and not want to take over the whole thing?

RIESMAN

At Harvard, and the same may be true at other leading institutions, the students internalize faculty values very early. They make judgments of faculty harsher than the president, certainly harsher than the trustees. I would worry about their conservatism.

PAYNE

The suggestion that there would be an *ad hoc* committee on questions of tenure or appointments is probably not a good one. I would want to institutionalize that kind of committee. If a department discusses appointments, students ought to attend each of those meetings. Over the course of a year, you would find that the disagreements would probably be fewer and fewer. If there were serious disagreements, however, they ought to be aired. If students sat in on more departmental discussions, in a great many institutions their fears would to a certain extent be laid to rest. If it turns out that a problem is one of personal clashes within a department and not a question of teaching and research, it is not bad for responsible students to know that. These things have to be discussed; eventually they are discussed and known in any case.

DUBERMAN

The problem often is not whether standards are being followed in regard to teaching, but whether such standards exist. The value of having student representation would be that perhaps for the first time in the university we might get a general discussion as to what good teaching really means. Students can tell us better than anyone what strategies and techniques do or do not succeed.

PARSONS

I would question the assumption that students are the best judges of teaching. There is the old legal principle of not making a man judge his own case. The student has a definite self-interest in the teaching, but it need not be wholly objective.

PAYNE

I would not say that students are the best judges, but they do provide the information on which the best judgments can be made. Students understand perfectly well that if a professor is a good teacher for 20 per cent of his students, he may be very valuable to keep around even if he is not a good teacher for the rest. Channels of communication might get much better with student representation on such committees.

DUBERMAN

Many of the suggestions that some of us have made have been regarded in the nature of "instead of" suggestions; they ought to be seen as "in addition to" suggestions. I am not saying that students by themselves are proficient to judge teaching, but neither are professors by themselves. I should like to see student opinion added to that of departmental representatives.

MEYERSON

The etiquette of American colleges and universities is such that we have no source of knowledge about teaching other than students; it is the rare institution where we attend one another's classes or in any other way have a sense of how our colleagues teach, what they teach, and their effectiveness. In that kind of unfortunate etiquette, if we do not lean upon students, we are being foolish. By saying "lean upon them," I do not necessarily mean that they have to have the fifth seat on an *ad hoc* committee.

It is critical that we provide ways for student opinion about teaching to be heard. We must make sure, however, that we weigh that opinion. Max Planck never had a large number of enthusiastic students, but he should not have been dismissed because he did not succeed well in that particular popularity contest. Such cautions have got to be built in, but we also have to establish some channels whereby student opinion can be heard. Few universities have those channels today.

KAYSEN

The distinction between an organized way in which student opinion can be taken into account and student participation in a decision is quite important. The arguments for an organized channel are interesting and worth considering. Systematic ·attention to teaching ability has merit.

I should also like to say something which will not be received sympathetically, but is still important. It is extremely difficult to make an appointment, which is why it is difficult for a good department to remain good. Students can be trusted. They would be no worse as sources of gossip than faculty. Nevertheless, it takes a long time for the sense of shared values to grow up among a group of people which permits them to talk with some candor and to expose their foolishness. I have heard my distinguished colleagues say things which I would never quote back to them because they are so stupid. They say them in the heat of discussion, because they do not want a particular man appointed.

If a student were on the committee, the discussion would not proceed. The faculty are not going to trust him. He is around for three years. Faculty contemplate spending on the average twenty-five years with their fellows. They adjust their thoughts, feelings, and interpersonal sentiments to make that possible. It is hard; often it does not work. Many good departments tear themselves to bits.

One of my colleagues at the Institute says that there is an exponential law of faculty: First-rate people appoint only first-rate people; one second-rate person leads to a fourth-rate appointment which then leads to an eighth-rate appointment. He exaggerates a little, but this process is extremely complicated and difficult.

I once tried to explain to one of my colleagues in Washington why Harvard professors were so reluctant to resign when they came into government service. I pointed out that anybody who has been through the appointment process once knows how difficult it is. This is not a process which can be exposed to an essentially unserious influence. The great work of a university is intellectual. No one who has not made that commitment—and very few graduate students have made it—is entitled to participate at this level. That issue is quite different from the question of how you get intelligent and organized student opinion about who is a good teacher. Universities do this very badly.

PAYNE

Having a student on a committee ought not to make it impossible for the discussions to proceed. I admit the difficulties of keeping a first-rate faculty, but students today would be willing to put that amount of time in. They are serious about what they know. Harvard and Yale make a lot of bad appointments, occasionally on the basis of teaching and particularly at the lower levels. Sometimes they appoint a professor who is supposed to be a good teacher when his teaching is not that good. As Mr. Duberman said, we are asking to add something to the process. The difference between having organized channels to discover student opinion and having a student sit in on the deliberations is that in most places students simply are not going to trust the organized channels unless the channels reach to the top. They may at Harvard; they do at Yale. I have been in many difficult discussions, and I do not see why one other person, even if he does not understand what is going on in some ways, makes it impossible to say certain kinds of things.

KAYSEN

I predict that if students come on, the faculty will go off.

DUBERMAN

What is being said is indicative of the basic failure of student-faculty relationships today. Faculty feel they can be vulnerable, make mistakes, and expose parts of their personality only in front of their peers. Students are human and, in most cases, mature—often as mature as their counterparts on the faculty. If faculty have trouble saying certain things in front of students, they should be forced to confront their trouble. There is so little communication between faculty and students today because faculty members will not permit students to see them other than as masters, as perfect creatures.

CONWAY

In our discussion, we have been talking about stable institutions in which the informal power structure has been legitimized by custom and habit, where informal consultation could go on, and where it is perfectly clear with whom you should consult. That is not true of most state institutions that are growing rapidly. I think benevolent despotism is wonderful if it is really benevolent and genuinely efficient. You have it at Harvard, and it has functioned marvelously. But I should like to examine the analogy in a little more historical detail. Benevolent despotism worked well in the small German states, but when the attempt was made to apply the methods of enlightened absolutism to the Austro-Hungarian empire, those methods were disastrous. Despotic methods cannot be applied to the government of a large lumbering institution, particularly one which is undergoing rapid change.

We have not talked much about the question of instability and growth, but I think it is very important to do so. At the University of Toronto I have become involved in all sorts of decision-making processes simply because the administrative structure there was designed for a small college, but the institution has now grown large. When a university is expanding rapidly there are many power vacuums; there are many instances in which administrators are simply not there to make appropriate decisions, and so many administrative tasks fall back upon faculty committees. A faculty member at such a growing institution is in a political situation whether he wants to be or not, because power is thrust upon him. Another problem of institutions experiencing rapid growth is that they do not possess an informal power structure known and accepted by the whole university community. It takes time and familiarity for such a structure to establish itself. We should view the question of participation in terms of developing some new kind of legitimacy for the decision-making process, and remember that it is critical to develop this legitimacy in new and rapidly growing institutions. We might also ask ourselves how fast institutions can grow and remain viable, because I think there is a point in institutional expansion where change is so fast that it becomes impossible to define a stable power structure or establish any basis of legitimacy for authority.

GRAY

Obviously universities are oligarchies; the question is whether they are restrictive or open oligarchies. Even if there can be no question of absolute democracy in a university, there can be constitutional monarchy. One is essentially talking about how this oligarchy becomes more or less democratic.

Although we constantly use the analogy of a political system, the representation characteristic of political systems is not possible in a university. A professor's professional commitment is such that he is never going to let himself be represented by somebody else. A faculty representative asserts his own views, sometimes taking the trouble to find out whether these are also the views of the people whom he represents. On the whole, however, he argues a case as he sees it in the same way that he would argue a case in the abstract or if he were simply individually asked. Thus, the notions of democracy and representation in a university have to be qualified by these obvious differences between the university and a political system. These differences come out of the structure not only of universities, but of intellectual life as well.

Furthermore, the ways in which the political structure at universities has grown up are such that it looks like a rational matter. Everybody knows exactly what the pattern is and is able to suggest the way in which one could tinker with it and make it still more rational. Most questions then become procedural ones. But underlying this passionate rationality is a structure which is traditional, which has grown up in a Rube Goldberg way.

How does one preserve the individual emphasis which is part of the intellectual life of a university together with the belief in the need for some kind of consensus, for majority rule, for a stricter representation than is possible within a university?

While faculty at some institutions are clamoring for more participation, at others where faculty participation has always been great, they are withdrawing. It is difficult to get people to sit on committees at such places. They are withdrawing in those institutions, but wanting at the same time to be consulted on matters of individual interest to them. There cannot be, obviously, any solution to the division of functions within a university. Universities are reluctant to abolish anything. They build theologies all their own.

RUDENSTINE

The primary question is whether the oligarchic leadership can be good enough to establish a regime of trust and confidence that will make students believe that they do not need to take part in selecting tenure faculty.

LEVI

You cannot go through a situation such as the one at Berkeley without making mistakes. I am not impressed by the predictions. It may very well be that universities will be ruined. There is no reason, however, for us to be on the majority side, no reason for us to participate in ruining them. Many universities may not be ruined, but they may become even more mediocre than they now are.

It is odd that people say that universities have the capacity to change society, but do not have the capacity to resist the evil influences within themselves. I am not impressed with these arguments, nor am I impressed with the claims of the seriousness of the situation. A university president is used to resisting pressures. I do not understand why he should not resist them.

There is a great danger due to governmental involvement in the universities. It might be assumed that because government is the all-embracing thing of life, every part of life should be in the same model as the government, that everybody should participate in all the decisions.

I am most serious about the university and its purposes. If you change those purposes sufficiently, you change the institution. It might go on, but it would be much less interesting to many of us. The consequence would be the creation of other kinds of institutions.

If the politicization goes to these extremes, I assume that institutes will develop and that the graduate and undergraduate areas will become separate. I am not sure that would be bad, although it certainly has not been the direction that many of us thought we should go in. Nevertheless, it is a likely outcome if Mr. Payne's predictions prove to be true.

The civil rights tactics have been adopted by students, and the response of younger faculty who have their own problems is important. There is a group of students who want to destroy the university; they have written documents pointing this out. The most important thing that a faculty does is to make determinations on appointments and promotions. It is difficult to force someone to speak critically about these issues. If these become public confrontations, the process would entirely change. The only consequence is that more mediocre people would be appointed. The institutions that allow extreme student participation will become mediocre; maybe all institutions will, and others will have to be created.

I do not like the language which says that it is quite all right to speak about the intellectual purposes of a university, that all we want to do is add other things. That is very seductive. If you add on things, these additions change the university's purpose. There is an enormous amount of participation in a university. In many institutions the choice of a dean involves formal faculty participation. Nobody is opposed to turning over to students a variety of things.

The younger generation may, as Mr. Payne predicts, radically change the universities; it may also have to explain to its children how it happened to ruin these institutions. If such is the case, I would expect other institutions to grow up, other institutions which are interested in intellectual strength.

MORISON

I should like to add a few footnotes to Mr. Levi's comments. Since I have had my present job, we have lost five tenured people, and four of them went to nonteaching institutes. This could be coincidence, but I am not at all sure that it is. They left because they did not want to participate in all of the things one presumably has to participate in these days. They did not want to do so much teaching as we thought they ought to do, even though this was not very great.

This flight from the university is disturbing, and I was thinking of it earlier when Mr. Payne commented that knowledge about teaching is not taken into account enough in making appointments. It is not purely a question of information. I can tell you quite accurately the teaching ability of at least seventy of the seventy-five people in my group. I interview about two hundred students a year to see whether or not they want to major in biology. I ask them informally how they are enjoying their courses, and they tell me. We started a new course last year with four of what we thought were our best teachers, and it turns out that they get standing ovations at the end of every lecture. These people are people I want to keep.

The question is how you use this information to get something done. Many people at Cornell know that certain elementary subjects are badly taught. These courses infuriate the students. I do not have to have students on a committee to know this. Nevertheless, it is extremely difficult to persuade a department to include some people in it who can teach elementary courses. This becomes an administrative or management problem.

It takes a lot of time to use this information. It is easy to find out what is lousy in an institution, but it is difficult to do something about it. I do not quite see how students can help in this. Students have legitimate gripes. I do not think our teaching is so good as it should be. We rely too much on graduate students and do not get the best team in the first-year courses. It requires infinite tact to get first-rate people into the first-year courses. If you put too much heat on them, they go to an institute. Most administrators are scared to death that they are going to lose the people they have. Anybody on my staff who is any good at all is getting between two and five letters a year. The amount of heat you can put on a faculty member to do what you know has to be done is limited. If administration gets any more complicated, it will be increasingly difficult to get anyone who will administer.

PAYNE

I am sure that Mr. Levi is going to be able to resist almost any kind of pressure. That is not the question. My suggestion was that we could make a few creative responses to the student anxiety beyond simply resisting. There are adaptations that can be made. I was not suggesting that students ought to be involved in all the difficult tasks of administration. I made a specific proposal that on one of the questions that bothers the students most—the question of tenure appointments—they might have some guarantee that the information that ought to be coming up through the channels is coming up and is being heard. I do not know any way to get that guarantee other than a feeling of confidence in the administration and faculty, so I opt for a structural innovation. Structural innovation is possible; it has been suggested not only by myself at Yale, but by the dean of the graduate school at Harvard. I find faculty at Yale not nearly so frightened about it as Mr. Kaysen.

KAYSEN

It will not do any good.

PAYNE

It may very conceivably do some good in terms of the crisis of trust and confidence that I was talking about. I grant it probably will not result in the appointment of many more people who are that much better.

BELL

The words "student participation" always bother me, because you tend to think in terms of numbers. Is this supposed to be a symbolic gesture or an actual participatory gesture? You have thousands and thousands of students, and only a few are going to participate even if you succeed in all your structural innovation.

PAYNE

If those students are talking to one another and are involved with a group like the Student Advisory Board at Yale, which is concerned primarily with educational policy, these checking mechanisms are probably adequate. If something seems to be out of line, that issue can be discussed not necessarily in terms of specific people, but in terms of the general direction in which the university is moving.

KAYSEN

Are these undergraduate or graduate students?

PAYNE

I am thinking primarily about undergraduates, but my argument would apply equally to graduate students on certain other issues.

Governance of the Universities I

DUBERMAN

I am interested in the university continuing to serve the function which theoretically it has always served—a devotion to intellectual pursuits. The university is not now succeeding in these pursuits; it is certainly not communicating enthusiasm for those pursuits to its students. It is not succeeding mainly because of the separation that exists between faculty and students. Rather than student participation corrupting the current aims of the university, it might for the first time help to fulfill those aims. All kinds of inhibitions against understanding could be broken down by an increase in trust and confidence between students and faculty.

PAYNE

The question is not whether a single decision is made on which there is disagreement, but whether there is a pattern of such decisions. In many instances, students do not have any recourse until an extreme case develops and they can blow it up publicly.

RIESMAN

I served for a year along with Dean Monroe on the Harvard policy committee, an educational group selected by the residential Houses, therefore violating student power groups who wanted campus-wide elections which would allow political parties to form. Mr. Payne should be more familiar than most of us here with the agony of such meetings. There was seldom a quorum, people came late and left early. They were frustrating meetings, and yet it was an enormously worthwhile group. It took its work very seriously, negotiated with departments about curricula, and got through a pass-fail system. In working with this group, I was constantly caught between the faculty right and the student left. The student left regarded this group as a co-opted body. Even at Harvard, which is relatively small in terms of the Houses, there was not much communication between the student body and this group, who by and large took their task very seriously both in the sub-committees working with individual departments and in the committee as a whole. They got little support from fellow students; they were, in fact, much attacked as stooges.

One of the things that this group could potentially do if this is an area of concern would be to try to free the vision of arrangements from the parliamentary model. This mechanism at Harvard would have worked better if people had not thought it evil *per se*.

MEYERSON

I should like to second Mr. Riesman's comments. They are extremely important.

BRADEMAS

What troubles me about this discussion is that a choice seems to have been imposed on us between student participation or no student participation. The same point could be made, for instance, with respect to the role of the trustees. It may well be that students have no business expecting their voice to be taken seriously with respect to the choice of a new president or a new dean, but perhaps in respect to other decisions something can be said for listening to what they have to say.

Nobody has as yet addressed himself to the question of who speaks for the students. I turn your minds to the community-action programs and the poverty war wherein we had written into law a requirement that there be participation on the part of the poor. The problem of trying to decide who speaks for the poor is a much more difficult problem than we had anticipated. Do the students have elections on campus? Are their leaders self-appointed? Are they the heads of the local university student associations? What if there is a fight among the students as to who speaks for the students? What kind of mechanism for deciding do you develop? Who decides the issues on which student opinions are to be taken seriously? It ought to be possible to have informal mechanisms as well as highly formal ones for enlisting student opinion.

The Federal Government is getting into this act. If I am going to be voting, as Mr. Pifer suggests, for 50 per cent of the monies that a college president is going to be using, what about my participation? What do I have to say about what goes on at a university since my vote is going to determine, in part, 50 per cent of the money that the institution may get? To turn this question around, since the universities will be directly affected by congressional legislation, ought they not to have something to say about that legislation and about the mechanisms Congress develops to ensure that Congress hears accurately and effectively from higher education in the United States? What, in fact, does it mean to say "hearing from higher education"? If you are talking about a national policy for higher education, how do you decide which student leaders or which university presidents are going to be heard? Think of the proliferation of individuals and institutions in American society that are directly affected by what higher education does. How will their voices be heard if we are writing legislation that will have such a tremendous financial impact on American higher education? This discussion has not yet addressed itself to what may be a far more serious problem than student participation in terms of policy-making for American higher education—that is, what does the government have to say?

GLASER

I want to illustrate what Mr. Brademas said. Because the curriculum at Stanford is changing so radically, we decided to have student representation and discussions. We asked that the students give us two people to participate in a group of eight or ten. We left it entirely to the students to determine how they would do this. I was soon visited by a small group of students, representing perhaps 5 to 6 per cent of the total student body; they announced that they did not approve of the representatives who had been selected and that they would consider any participation by them in the curriculum discussions as invalid in respect to their own personal interests. They are not prepared to accept anything in which they themselves are not involved. If their classmates do not decide to make them representatives, they say the procedure is invalid.

RIESMAN

I am much in sympathy with what Mr. Brademas said, having watched the land-grant and the private colleges battle these issues, and having felt the appeal of institutional grants to almost all administrators. These grants are not in the interests of students, but in those of the going concern. This is one of many reasons why I favor the Zacharias plan. It seems to me to be a counter-weight to the institutional grant. The institutional grant involves the university in on-going, but not always happy, momentum.

BRADEMAS

I was in Iowa the other day talking to a group of presidents of small private colleges. Their conversation started off with an attack on the large land-grant institutions. This attack was not, in my view, a particularly useful enterprise. One of the ways in which the dilemma has been put is this: Assuming that there will be a substantial increase in federal support, should that support be provided in the form of general institutional grants or in the form of a variety of categorical aids, as is presently the case? There is a similar battle going on at the elementary and secondary school levels. I happen to be militantly opposed to the general grant approach at the elementary and secondary school level for a variety of reasons which need not be aired here. I am not honestly sure, however, whether or not the same kinds of arguments obtain at the level of higher education. As one prejudiced in favor of categorical grants, what does concern me is that if we were to provide general monies to every institution according to formularized percentages, the grants would not amount to much. You might see an inflationary consequence financially, rather than an increase in quality in respect to the purposes for which categorical aid is supplied. At the very least, higher education in this country has not thought through the problem of financing higher education.

Within the last several weeks, I have begun to hear university presidents and others saying that their institutions are going to go under financially in about ten years unless something revolutionary occurs. These comments are, I suppose, triggered in part by the proposed cutback in facilities money under the higher education bill and also by the cutbacks in money for research. You can normally predict a land-grant college president's response in respect to student-aid proposals. A private university president, for example, is likely to opt for some tuition tax credit approach, where the other fellow is not happy about that since tuition is not his major headache.

I strongly agree with Mr. Pifer's suggestion that we develop some kind of mechanism for shaping a coherent and national policy for higher education. I am not suggesting a highly centralized mechanism whereby Congress dictates what universities do and do not do. Nevertheless, with so many different institutions of higher learning of so many different kinds in the country, all of which will have an increasing stake in the decisions taken on federal money, we must develop some way of deciding who gets what and for what purpose. If we do not do that, we ought to at least consider the issues involved. If we cannot establish some kind of procedure, we ought at least to talk about the critical issues. At the present time, it is a nonsystem in which everybody goes his own way in some general *laissez-faire* approach.

KAYSEN

Mr. Brademas, at what level would you judge that the situation will get so rough that the Congress will be willing to do some unpleasant things? We have a large number of small colleges. They do not educate a great proportion of the student body, but they do educate a not trivial proportion of it. They are inefficient, and, with few exceptions, they are terrible. Haverford is suboptimal in size, but it is quite good because it happens to be rich. How much money would you have to be spending before you could write into a bill a statement that says no dollar of student aid could be used in an institution that does not have X thousand students, assuming that you had competent testimony that X thousand was the reasonable floor for an efficient institution?

BRADEMAS

There is a certain unstated assumption in your question: namely, that you close up the small colleges rather than make the small ones good enough to survive. That is an open question.

KAYSEN

Let's assume that you cannot make the small colleges good enough unless you have fewer of them, which would, in effect, make them larger. What do you think is the point at which Congress will get tough in the sense of demanding a show of resource? The present programs, even though they are fairly large, are not big enough to exercise that kind of pressure. Every special interest group can get in and get something in the program because it is reasonably sized.

BRADEMAS

Your question illustrates the point that I was trying to make earlier. When you have two or three thousand colleges and universities of every size, shape, and description devoted to different kinds of educational purposes, what does the phrase "to get results" mean? Some qualification is necessary before one can make an intelligent judgment on how much money would have to be spent.

There are other policy questions that at least ought to be thrown into the cauldron. In the South there are a number of struggling Negro colleges, and there are also barely viable institutions in Appalachia. On a cost-effectiveness basis, I have little doubt that you could make a case for closing those places forthwith. But what do you do then? Perhaps in some cases it is better to have second-rate universities than none at all.

KAYSEN

Suppose you were to conclude that a few of these places should be closed so that the others, especially the ones that are in or near cities, could grow. You might let the country community college, the country Negro college, and maybe the country Appalachian college just die in order to provide not fewer total places, but a different institutional distribution. When the defense budget got so big, we became less sensitive to certain kinds of pressure groups.

BRADEMAS

I do not know the answers in monetary terms, but I should think that we are going to be getting to that point within four or five years.

KAYSEN

There will be a point when it is no longer possible for Congress to accommodate whoever comes in with the combination of a plausible program and a constituency.

PARSONS

Let us hope it is not an across-the-board formula, but a highly selective program.

BRADEMAS

Who is going to make the selection?

PARSONS

I think it has to be a collaborative governmental and academic body.

BELL

I do not see how Congress can escape making categorical judgments on higher education. The Zacharias plan, although useful in providing flexibility, does not take into account the total picture. It does not face the primary problem of the categorical judgment. The educational plants in this country are largely in the hands of the states because of the distribution of constitutional responsibility. The states have become increasingly inadequate as an instrument for carrying on education.

If you begin to look at the whole federal scheme, at what might be called regional institutions and regional needs with cluster arrangements, the policy of giving monies to states makes no sense. They simply follow existing lines and probably reflect the political weights of the different states. If there is going to be some distributive justice, one cannot wholly concentrate on the state unit. One would have to take into account certain kinds of regional distributions.

Perhaps a different kind of cluster arrangement might be viable in which you begin to distribute certain kinds of strengths or insist upon the distribution of certain kinds of strengths. A regional cluster might allow for distributive strength so that people in the area could share resources in a particular range. In that case, there would be a great responsibility on universities themselves to begin to think in terms of sharing their resources rather than in terms of the higgledy-piggledy pattern which is now in existence. Presently, universities simply grab faculty and follow the free market at its worst in this regard.

One would also want to get a clearer sense of resources. We do not know what the complete demands are, but we do have a fairly clear sense of what the resources are in terms of specialists in Latin, in Russian, and in various other areas.

BRADEMAS

I agree. I want to endorse thoroughly what Mr. Bell has said. One of the parts in the higher education bill which we are probably going to finish up next week is the so-called "networks for knowledge" title which is aimed at encouraging precisely that kind of inter-institutional cooperation. Although we have not got any money yet for the International Education Act, it has at least had the value of encouraging a number of institutions to make an inventory of their libraries, students, and faculties.

MEYERSON

I am worried by Mr. Bell's last comment and Congressman Brademas' agreement with him. Most efforts in which the Federal Government manipulates coordination have been dismal. We have seen such difficulty in federal stimulation of metropolitan planning, and I can see some of the same failings occurring in higher education. We have seen problems in the national systems of education in other parts of the world and in the state systems of our country. In California, as an example, the decision was made that African studies were to be concentrated in Los Angeles even though most of the students interested in African studies might prefer to be at Berkeley.

This tendency for federal coordination may come up with extremely conventional approaches. A safer approach is the one that

Congress has traditionally followed. Congressionally the United States has favored a series of competing claims and different viewpoints. We may even have had contradictory programs running side by side. I do not demand coherence.

I would hope we would have not a carefully worked out national Cartesian scheme for higher education, but rather a series of competing and even contradictory programs. We would thus avoid the problem of imposing a pattern that may not be a good one. It is also important to have the source of financing going through the students so that the student as a consumer of education can make his choices. The existing programs ought to be continued and amplified. There ought to be other programs too. I can, for example, imagine branches of the Library of Congress throughout the country serving the academic community; instead of asking for two copies of a copyrighted publication, the Library of Congress might ask for two dozen. This would be simple to do, and the Library of Congress could put the other copies in large regional depositories.

There are many approaches of this kind. It would be far wiser to diversify the sources of support than to try to rationalize them. In diversifying these sources of support, it is important for universities to make sure that they have private as well as public support. We ought to try to develop a mixed economy for colleges and universities.

BRADEMAS

You exaggerate my point greatly if you assume that I am in profound disagreement with a great deal of what you have said. Nevertheless, one must still come up with a generally intelligent national approach to legislation supporting higher education. This does not necessarily entail a centralized Cartesian rationale being imposed from on high.

BELL

I agree with the second part of Mr. Meyerson's comments, but not with the first part. With the second part, he ends up with a mixed economy; with the first part, he wants *laissez faire*. This is a crucial distinction. Clearly none of us want patterns; we have all had enough experience with that. We may, however, want to have some sense of the guidelines, some sense of planning, without patterns.

Society, as Mr. Meyerson remarked earlier, has made a decision that everybody should have the opportunity for some higher education. Society did not make that decision because there was a conscious plan wherein somebody said X number of persons a year will be allotted to higher education. There was a *laissez-faire* situation and a rush in terms of aggrandizing in many states. California had some degree of planning; many states did not. Along the way, many institutions became wrecked or are in the process of being wrecked because there was no notion of how many students a year they could absorb, no conception of the costs of such a pace.

The Governance of the Universities II

Participants
Landrum R. Bolling
Peter J. Caws
Sarah E. Diamant
C. M. Dick, Jr.
Seymour Eskow
Edgar Z. Friedenberg
Stephen R. Graubard
Andrew M. Greeley
Jeff Greenfield
Eugene E. Grollmes
Gerald Holton
Willard Hurst
Dexter M. Keezer
Clark Kerr
S. E. Luria
Jean Mayer
Walter P. Metzger
Martin Meyerson
Robert S. Morison
Henry Norr
Talcott Parsons
Bruce L. Payne
Roger Revelle
Philip C. Ritterbush
Neil R. Rudenstine
Edward Joseph Shoben, Jr.
John R. Silber
Charles E. Silberman
R. L. Sproull
Kenneth S. Tollett
George R. Waggoner

With these few caveats, the following agenda was proposed for the discussions on November 14-16, 1968, at the House of the Academy.

American colleges and universities are today, as in the past, immensely diverse in their organization and purposes. To pretend that the problems of the public junior college, concerned with the "career programs" of nonresident students, are fundamentally like those of the great private or public university, with its continuing commitment to undergraduate and graduate instruction and to the advancement of research, is to ignore substantial differences in favor of superficial similarities.

Still, to see no similarities in their situations is to forget how much the United States is becoming a "national" society, subject to common pressures. Greater numbers of young men and women expect to be accommodated in colleges or universities. There is a prevalent belief that a high-school diploma does not provide sufficient training for the most desirable kinds of employ, and that a thirteenth, fourteenth, fifteenth, or sixteenth year of schooling ought to be made available to high school graduates. No one seriously contests the "right" of young people to these additional years of education, and the sentiment in favor of making places available for those who wish to fill them is not likely to diminish in the near future. There is an analogous opinion that advanced training in the professions is another obligation that cannot be turned away from without seriously harming both the individual and the society. The "right to higher education" is seen very differently today than it was even a few decades ago.

The increase in the number of students, independent of any other variable, guarantees that higher education will remain a heavy charge on the nation. Although institutions may seek additional funds partly from private sources, both public and private institutions will certainly require vast new appropriations, and these will come largely from public sources. As both private and public institutions turn increasingly

*to state and federal agencies for support, they must
be prepared for a type of public control and audit
that has rarely existed heretofore. Arguments about
appropriations and curricula, not to speak of those that
touch student and faculty conduct, will almost certainly become the subject of public political debate.
The old "independence" of higher education will be
seriously affected by these new public pressures. The
conflict between a public demand and a university's
own sense of what it ought to be doing may become
very intense. Each may be interested in innovation,
though each may wish to define that possibility differently. Within the university community itself there
may be real differences in the definition of appropriate service.*

*In recent years, universities have substantially in-
creased their research activities and dramatically revised traditional nineteenth-century definitions of university "service" to the community. The prospect is
for society to look increasingly to the university for
various kinds of assistance, thus perpetuating the
current stress within the university over the priorities
assigned to teaching, research, and "service." The contemporary debate about the university's role as a critic
of society will certainly continue. The guaranteeing of
certain rights in this area and the fulfilling of certain
obligations become matters of urgency if criticism is
an essential function of the university, and if, as some
suggest, the intellectual authenticity of the university
is tied to its capacity to protest.*

*The ambiguity that has long existed about whether
the university ought to be viewed as a sanctuary,
isolated and protected from the general society, or as
a microcosm of the larger society, responsive to its
needs and pressures, is debated more passionately
today than at any time in recent history. If the university is seen as a monastery, one set of relations may
be expected to prevail; if it is viewed as a small city,
other kinds of relations will be valued. Perhaps the
university ought to resist all efforts to make it appear
analogous to other kinds of institutions; it is neither a*

309

church, a city, nor a business corporation, though it may bear superficial resemblances to each. The need may be for a more fully formulated expression of what, for lack of a better term, might be called "university law."

This "university law" would seek to establish the rights and responsibilities of the various constituent elements of the university. It would aim, among other things, to describe the kinds of authority that ought to subsist in the university and to create principles of accountability that would protect all who have a stake in the university.

The American Academy's effort, if it is not to traverse too many fields, might reasonably address itself to the following five topics:

1. *The rights and responsibilities of trustees;*

2. *The rights and responsibilities of university administrators;*

3. *The rights and responsibilities of faculty members;*

4. *The rights and responsibilities of students;*

5. *The rights and responsibilities of the general public, as expressed particularly through the state and federal legislatures, but also through alumni organizations.*

There is a hazard in a too formal distinction between the rights and responsibilities of these various constituencies. The discussion ought certainly to be informed by a precise consideration of the kinds of issues that presently preoccupy university communities. Thus, for example, one of the crucial problems of any institution is whether or not it ought to take on additional functions. These are various and may include anything from service to the federal government in the field of defense to involvement with local communities in urban planning or secondary-school curricular revision. Who is to decide whether or not the university becomes involved in such matters? Until

*recently decisions of this kind were generally made
by administrators in consultation with trustees. Should
the faculty have a voice in such decisions? Of what
kind? Ought students to be consulted? On what principle?*

*Clearly, the purpose of the Academy study is to
ask: How are important decisions made today in
higher education? What are the sources of dissatisfaction? What might be done to resolve these dis-
contents? The conference ought to direct its attention
to the larger policy questions presently agitating universities—whether they touch on the draft law, the
use of university facilities by other than university
members, investment policies, or the like. It would be
a mistake to neglect the more strictly university issues
that have to do with course offerings, housing arrangements, and the regulation of student activities.*

*In thinking about each of the five constituencies,
one ought always to have in mind specific examples.
The conference must think not only of the issues that
presently "make the headlines," but also of those that
are likely to confront universities in the future. Some
of these have not yet become urgent, but they may
soon figure prominently in public debates on higher
education.*

AGENDA

I. *Rights and Responsibilities of Trustees*

A. What ought their appointive power to be? In most
colleges and universities, trustees have for all practical purposes abdicated their traditional right to
veto the appointments of faculty (when voted by
departments and approved by administrations).
They retain large (sometimes, exclusive) authority
in the choice of presidents. Should this authority be
shared? With whom? On what principles?

B. Their fiscal authority, legally and actually, remains
substantial everywhere and is sometimes absolute.
Should it be limited in ways not common at this
time?

311

C. What other powers inhere in boards of trustees? How should these other obligations be defined? Is there a hazard in boards of trustees assuming that every matter affecting the welfare of the university (issues ranging from student discipline to the acceptance of architectural plans for new buildings) properly falls within their competence?

D. What kinds of administrative regulation should not be considered the responsibility of trustees?

E. Is the principle that trustees ought to act as a buffer between the university and other bodies in society a reasonable representation of their proper role?

F. To whom ought trustees to be accountable? How can such accountability be provided for? What moral and ethical considerations ought to guide trustees?

G. Is it possible that the concept of the "trustee" is outmoded and should be set aside? What would be gained or lost from such a change?

II. Rights and Responsibilities of University Administrators

A. If the administration, particularly the president, is accountable to the trustees for the governance of the university, what kind of audit ought to be instituted so that the exercise of authority is not judged simply by how the administration comports itself in time of crisis?

B. What relations ought to subsist between administrators and faculty members? What controls may the former reasonably have over the latter? What restrictions may faculty members reasonably impose on deans and presidents?

C. What relations ought to subsist between administrators and students? What sharing of authority ought to be provided for? How can this be institutionalized?

D. Can the responsibilities of the administration be effectively discharged when so many in the administration are faculty members who hold office for relatively brief periods? Ought there to be a larger career opportunity for those in universities who permanently choose to be administrators? How can they avoid being thought "second-rate citizens" in the better universities and prevented from appearing to be "the controlling force" in the lesser universities?

E. What rights ought administrators to claim vis-à-vis state legislatures, alumni groups, and other public and private bodies that have reason to be concerned about the university?

F. Are there any areas where administration ought to claim exclusive authority? Where ought administratration to be ready to share authority? How can systems of accountability be constructed that will not hamper effective action, nor stifle initiative from constituencies outside administration, both within the university and without?

G. What values ought to enter into the administrator's decisions?

III. *Rights and Responsibilities of Faculty Members*

A. What are the obligations of a member of the faculty to his colleagues? What are the faculty member's obligations to students? Is the idea of the corporate faculty disintegrating, giving way to a too exclusive concern with professional and other allegiances? What hazards are posed by such developments?

B. What rights ought faculty members to enjoy with respect to the appointment of their own colleagues and the creation of suitable curricula? Are departments, as presently constituted, a barrier to educational innovation? How serious is this? Does departmental organization provide positive benefits? What are they?

C. What examining prerogatives ought faculty members to enjoy? Ought these powers to be shared with others? On what principle?

D. Ought there to be any boundaries governing intellectual dissent? Are the foundations of the university jeopardized by attempts to impose such limits?

E. What concerns ought faculty members to have with the "needs" of society? Should these be reflected in a willingness to alter curricula to serve those needs? Also, does the present commitment to accept extra-university appointments imperil in any significant way the freedom of universities?

F. What are the research obligations of faculty members? What liberties must be guaranteed if those obligations are to be discharged?

G. To whom ought individual faculty members to be accountable? Are there special obligations that properly inhere in the role of professor and need to be acknowledged? Is it possible that the socialization of young men and women into this role is happening too quickly and too haphazardly? What obligations do older (tenured) faculty members have to those who are younger (presumably, serving term appointments)? How can faculty members express and communicate faithfully the personal as well as the academic values of their profession?

IV. *Rights and Responsibilities of Students*

A. Is there some area where students ought to enjoy exclusive authority? What ought that to be? Where should students share authority with others? On what principle? Are the present conventions governing student rights in respect to curricula outmoded? What control, if any, ought students to have in this regard?

B. Does the status of student impose obligations? What ought they to be? Who is to judge whether or not they have been transgressed?

C. What political freedoms ought to be guaranteed to

students? Ought they to be different from those granted others?

D. Have young people a "right" to a university education? Does this mean that the traditional methods of student selection and admission are untenable? How ought they to be modified? By whom?

E. Should the fact that students are still overwhelmingly adolescents or young adults, passing only a brief time in the university, be given any weight in determining their rights and obligations? Ought differences to be established between undergraduate and graduate student rights? Why should all not enjoy the rights that might be granted a postdoctoral fellow? What ought those to be?

F. What claims may students legitimately make of their professors? What may they reasonably demand of university administrations? What, in turn, may professors, presidents, and deans ask of students? Does the status of student carry with it certain rights? What are they?

V. *Rights and Responsibilities of the General Public, Federal, State, and Local Governments*

A. As major benefactors (and beneficiaries) of the university, what are the legitimate rights and obligations of government—federal, state, or local—and of alumni organizations? What kinds of control must they explicitly forswear if the university is not to be deflected from its purposes? What kinds of accountability may they reasonably demand?

B. What budgetary decisions ought to be made in the political arena? Is it possible for this decision-making process to be institutionalized in such a way that it is not directly tied to politics? Is it desirable that there be a separation between the two?

C. What restraints must the general public accept in respect to its right to interfere with the criticism made by faculty members and students of institutions (and, often, of themselves)?

D. Does the existence of the university in a democratic society, pledged to giving opportunity to all, impose special kinds of obligations, both for the university and for state and federal legislatures? What are these?

E. What information ought the university to provide about itself so that those outside may be in a position to gauge accurately its needs and its performance?

F. Which of society's needs must the university be ready to acknowledge and serve? How can this service be guaranteed? What respect must the university be prepared to give society's opinions? What is society's responsibility in defining the demands it makes upon the university?

MORISON

I have a predilection for thinking about what a university is for and whom it serves. Indeed, I am not sure how far we can go inside the university without thinking about those on the outside. But before my prejudices show too clearly, let's turn to the agenda and begin to discuss trustees.

HOLTON

I wonder whether we should not perhaps first define the framework. The subtitle of this conference is "Study in Academic Ethics." We do not want to lose sight of that aspect. What, then, is the role of the trustee not with respect to day-to-day things, but with respect to the main theme of the conference?

DICK

Perhaps my experiences as a trustee will help start off the discussion. Three years ago, I became a trustee of a liberal arts college with an enrollment of about five hundred. A friend asked me to come on the board, and I agreed to serve because I am interested in education. My friend had been chairman of the board; when he resigned, I took over the chairmanship. A lot of important things were going on at that college—problems with the students, faculty, and president—and I got an extraordinary education in a short period of time.

Speaking from my own experience, I would say that the primary responsibility of the board of trustees is to keep the institution going. Our particular board came up against this point time and time again as the future of the college became the principal issue. The second responsibility of the board of trustees is to provide guidance and policy to the administration. The president, to whom the board has delegated operational responsibility, should expect this contribution from the board. The third responsibility is to try to insure that the financial resources are available to enable the college to carry out its program.

MORISON

To whom do you feel yourself responsible?

DICK

We certainly are not responsible to any particular body that comes to our meetings and says: "You are responsible to us." We say on

317

various occasions that we have responsibility to the students, to the faculty, to the other board members, to the president, to education in general. The thing that keeps the board together is that all its members want to see the college keep on going and improve. I cannot think of a better way to define the responsibility.

SILBERMAN

I wonder if there is anyone here who is a trustee of a state university or municipal college. It seems to me that the agenda itself betrays the initial bias of the steering committee—a tendency to think of the university as the elite, private university. The representation here is very heavily from the private universities, although the great majority of students are now attending public institutions of one sort or another. In a sense, the dichotomy between the trustees and the public is broken in public institutions where at least formally, if not substantively, trustees are assumed to be the representatives of the public. If you ask the trustee of a state school to whom he feels responsible, he would answer that he is responsible to the public or the legislature. It might be useful in terms of bridging these few items on the agenda and perhaps of dealing with the question of purpose if one could get some sense of how trustees of public institutions view themselves and how this view differs from that held by trustees of private institutions.

KERR

I am not a trustee at the moment, but for a period of time I was a regent of the University of California in an *ex officio* capacity. I could make a distinction between what trustees should be and what they really are. What they really are varies enormously, depending upon the nature of the institution, its history, its traditions, and the particular composition of the board at a moment in time. Trustees also change depending upon the issues with which they are faced. I do not know whether we should discuss what trustees should be or what they are.

Charles Silberman raises an important question. Are trustees representing the public to the institution or are they representing the institution to the public? When the chips are down, that question is absolutely central. In the case of the University of California, when the trustees and regents were not under pressure, they thought that they were representing the university. When they were under pressure, a lot of them decided they were representing the public.

PARSONS

There is a group that, curiously, does not figure in the agenda. You might call it part of the not-so-general public—namely, the alumni. Alumni figure rather prominently in the affairs of many institutions of higher education. The extent to which trustees or administration or faculty are responsible to the alumni raises complicated questions. The alumni ought not to be left totally out of the picture.

FRIEDENBERG

I wonder if it might be helpful to try to be slightly more functional in drawing inferences about what trustees do and to whom or what they are responsible under what circumstances. It has come to be customary to select trustees from within a relatively narrow and familiar range of other social roles, which may provide a reasonably valid clue to the questions we are asking. The trustee's task is almost always a part-time and usually unremunerated one in this society. Trustees are primarily drawn from either successful business ventures or in some cases the bar. Very rarely are they drawn from scholarship or the arts, which are more usually the main concern of the university's curriculum. I take it that the selection process has to do with the trustees' having a kind of alarm or fusing function—that is, they are expected to remain inactive and do remain inactive until certain kinds of interests, generally upper-middle- or upper-class interests, come to be frightened. Surely it is proper for a trustee to be devoted to the continuity of his institution. The ease with which we accept that premise may have much to do with what we have been calling the crisis of the university. Indeed, one of the questions very much before this meeting is whether it is desirable that the university be kept going if it is to have such a preponderance of the legitimate social roles of young adults in the United States. If the only way you can keep the place going is to have a system where the final panic button rests in the hands of such people as normally become trustees, then I rather think I should like to see funds going elsewhere. Some of us yearn for an irate public that would throw us out into experimental colleges that could not grant degrees, could not contribute much to vocational education, and therefore would not be besieged by the lower-middle classes simply because these settings could not do them very much good. We might get the equivalent of the suburban shift in education where we have to build our own poor utilities and live less lavishly to begin with in order to have certain kinds of freedoms. If we look to the charter and ask what a trustee is supposed to do, then I think we will be way off. University people are not any different from any other segment of the population when they start talking about law and order.

HOLTON

We must distinguish between governance and representation. Absentee governance seems to me an ethical problem whether it is in slum housing, in a family where the mother is not at home, or in those universities where the governors are essentially absentee landlords. In the latter case, faculty might be regarded rather like tellers at a bank.

Indeed, much depends on the models that exist in the minds of a university's governors. In the modern governing board of a university, physically and professionally distant from the real "business" of the university, the model for running the university may well come from some more congenial activity such as the local bank, the law office, or whatever other field of enterprise the trustee is engaged in. In such cases, there is a premium on keeping the thing going more or less in the same way year in, year out. On the other hand, in my laboratory the whole object is to terminate an experiment successfully and in an orderly manner to go to something entirely new and different when a brighter line of research opens up. The Cambridge Electron Accelerator is not going to be kept going at all costs and through all crises forever. Some day a quite different facility is going to be put in its place when its present usefulness is over. Also, in the internal governance of a lab, the voice one has in the long- and short-range decisions is much larger than the voice students and faculty have in the governance of most universities. The danger I am pointing to is that the governance of the university by predominantly business-enterprise-oriented groups may impose upon the university institutional models which will inevitably get the institutions out of step with a changing situation.

Neither the lab by itself nor the business corporation by itself may be the best model for the governance of a university. The trick is to produce the right model intermediate between both to assure stability and change.

RITTERBUSH

It seems to me that the central problem of competently functioning trustees is to guarantee that the university stays governable. We should bear in mind that in the corporate sector there are well worked-out procedures for going through transitional phases—such as bankruptcy proceedings—which do not serve to extinguish the array of talent that has been assembled to do a job, but do establish it on a new footing. Institutions should not necessarily fear entering a spore-forming phase to knit themselves together in some new way. If universities and other institutions do face a time when major change is needed, it may be desirable to shut them down for a year or two, indulge in a period of patient reconstruction, and then open them up again. If there were somewhere in this society where a group of conscientious trustees, for there are many such, could turn for advice and help as to how to go through this almost clinical experience with their institution, many of them might be encouraged to try it.

BOLLING

One of the threads running through our discussion is a tacit assumption, which you find on many college campuses, that the trustees are a necessary evil, but unmistakably an evil, and the less they are heard of the better. The concept that a significant group within any institution is only a window dressing—a tolerated nuisance—means that you do not get the best possible results out of that group of people. We have not given nearly enough thought to the question of how you select trustees in the first place. What kinds of people ought to be on boards of trustees? We have not given sufficient attention to how to inform trustees and keep them involved. One of my presidential colleagues once said he thought he had an ideal board of trustees because they only met once a year for a half day, heard him make reports, patted him on the back, and went home. He did not want any more involvement than this. I think that is nonsense. I think also the question comes up as to what the real role of the trustees ought to be. This again is not clearly defined. We do not want them meddling and trying to overrule the administration and prying into the affairs of the faculty, and so on. Yet they must have a significant role in the over-all policy-making of the institution, or they are going to be frustrated. Otherwise, you will only get people who are collectors of titles or honors to do this kind of job.

GREENFIELD

Why don't you want them meddling in what the faculty is doing?

BOLLING

The trustees ought to be informed and involved and selected from a sufficiently wide range of competences in our society that they have useful opinions about the total operation of the college. It seems to me that one of the most critical difficulties about educational institutions today is that we have not gone beyond the concept of just keeping things going the way they are going. We are not taking a hard enough look year by year at what we ought to be doing. Who is going to do this? As a one-time faculty member who now has the prejudices of administrators, I would submit that the faculty are jolly well not going to do this. Some group that has the over-all view of the institution and of the society, one that can break loose from its departmental hangups, has got to take on the job and keep the pressure on the institutions to reform themselves.

There is a mythology in our society today that the teaching faculty is the great fountain of reform and change. This is just nonsense. You have got to have an informed board of trustees and a sensitive, informed, and determined administration, at times backed up and allied with the students, to change the educational institutions so that they will be what they ought to be in our time. Here the trustees have got to be an important participating element within this total effort to rebuild and renew.

The question of institutional renewal is certainly one of the most crucial issues that we face. When you talk about governance, you have got to talk about not just governance in terms of keeping things going, but governance in terms of making the institutions relevant to the needs and problems of the times. I think this is where the trustees can be very useful—if you pick them correctly, if you inform and educate them, if you give them significant things to do. Then I think they can be a very creative force; otherwise, it is going to be terribly frustrating for everybody.

MORISON

Are you and Mr. Greenfield ganging up to say that the real engine of reform and change in American education should be the boards of trustees as such?

BOLLING

No, but if they are properly selected and informed and involved, they can interpret to the public, to the donors, why reform is necessary, why it should be supported.

GREENFIELD

We have always thought of a university as something like a corporation in that it is separate, in the private sector. If universities are going to get more than half their funding from public institutions, if they have the kinds of public effects that we know they have, it may well be that there are going to be constitutional requirements—much like the one-man, one-vote decisions of the Supreme Court—demanding that universities, both public and private, have effective, meaningful representation from all sides of the community. I am talking about judicial decisions based on the Fourteenth Amendment. I am saying that if Columbia University, located in the heart of Harlem, does not have a single black man on its board of trustees, that comes close to an unconstitutional use of power against the community.

RUDENSTINE

Mr. Greenfield is right, I think, up to a point. Boards do have to be democratized for many reasons. At the same time, he is a bit sanguine. It is clear that when "democratization" happens, there will be many practical implications and repercussions. It will certainly mean that black people and other kinds of people will come on to boards, as indeed they ought to have a long time ago. But as a result there will be new cleavages, tensions, and important changes in universities. Many people will resist such development, and that will create even greater tension. I fear that the academic community as a whole is simply not looking at certain problems that are going to be with us in much more chaotic ways very quickly. I am dismayed, for example, that many universities do not yet have people in the administration who work on community problems. It seems to me that until universities face up to their public roles, they will continue to be in great trouble.

At the same time, by abstracting the role of trustees and either hoping for too much from them or blaming them too much, we are overlooking the problem of the academic profession itself. Mr. Greenfield suggested over coffee that the trustees should tell the faculty that they could not expect any further salary increases or special kinds of privileges. But the problem of high career expectations—financial and otherwise—is clearly a national cultural one and the faculty cannot be held entirely guilty for its particular expectations. We will not solve such problems by having the trustees tell faculty that there are not going to be provisions for housing and other fringe benefits or any more salary increases.

LURIA

It seems to me that the basic issue is who ultimately will set the purpose of the university. It is certainly not the trustees who set the purpose. The point that Mr. Rudenstine and Mr. Greenfield made is excellent—we are visualizing a dynamic process in our society in which the purposes of the university are being reviewed actively under the leadership of both students and special community groups. The only way that we can expect universities to respond to the situation is by creating, within the university, machinery that continuously re-examines the question: What is the purpose of the university in this specific situation, in this community, in this state, or in this type of technological demand? I should like to propose the following: The best function of the trustees, if they continue to exist, is to steer the machinery of the university by responding to the community. A board of trustees should be a plastic group maximizing the inputs and providing the machinery for the response. One of the problems has been that trustees in the past inevitably have acted as instruments to slow down processes of change. On the one hand, they have represented the need for efficient, financially sound operation and, on the other hand, they have been drawn from a part of society that traditionally has not been actively interested in change. If the trustees are to continue to exist, they must take the leadership in making the university extremely responsive to new pressures from within and from without.

GROLLMES

I would suggest that the role of the trustees is going to vary depending on the particular kind of institution. A trustee at a large state university is going to have significantly different concerns than the trustee of a small Catholic liberal arts college. It is important that the trustees understand not only what adjustments the school must make in order to make its contribution to contemporary society, but also the purpose of that particular school, especially in the sector of private education. Private education, it seems to me, is based upon a presupposition that private institutions offer a particular kind of education that you cannot get at the secular, state institutions. Thus, one role for the trustees is to insure that the institution be true to itself as well as to its public. In being true to itself, if Shakespeare is right, the institution will serve the public.

One of the recent phenomena in Catholic higher education is precisely in the area of trustees. Formerly, with very few exceptions, the top executives in Catholic colleges or universities were also the trustees. There really was no distinction so far as personnel were concerned. As they have brought in lay people and religious people from other institutions, they are finding that the trustees can serve as a check on the executive. When the executives were the trustees, there was no one to say that the institution was not doing what it said it was going to do. I think it is fundamental to the success of higher education that the trustees not only have an understanding of society and what is needed today in the whole realm of higher education, but that they also evaluate the precise function of their particular school.

NORR

It seems to me that our analysis of the functions of the trustees—the ways and means by which they should have a role or whether indeed they should exist at all—has to be seen in light of an issue that has been mentioned, but not really dealt with here: that is, the sociological and constitutional source of the authority of the trustees. If the trustees are to continue to represent primarily businessmen and corporate lawyers—and not the students and faculty or certain members of the communities around the universities—then most of us would feel that the thing to do with the trustees is to ignore them or minimize their role or, best of all, abolish them. Their abolition would involve looking toward the creation of new mechanisms by which the interests presently not adequately represented in the governance of the university could be represented. If, on the other hand, we admit that we can amend the concept of what a board of trustees is—sociologically and constitutionally—then we can indeed talk about ways in which the trustees can and should act. If we talk about the kinds of changes that would be necessary in order to make the trustees into a body that would represent the community, the students, the faculty, the general public in a broader sense, the issue of how the trustees can act as a check on the selfish interests of other elements in the university becomes more meaningful. But I do not think it is worthwhile for us to talk about the rights and responsibilities of the trustees without asking who they are, where they come from, what the source of their authority is, what motivates them to devote their time, energy, and resources to the university, and what interests they in fact serve in running the university.

PARSONS

I think Mr. Norr raises a central set of questions. I know the faculty is not our current topic, but Mr. Rudenstine brought up that constituency in the context of the professional role, as individuals and corporately, at several different levels. If it is correct (and there may be a good deal of discussion on this) that the primary functional focus of the system of higher education centers on knowledge—the advancement of knowledge, the transmission of knowledge, and the maintenance and use of the cultural traditions of knowledge—then from one point of view the key role of responsibility is in the academic profession. We are all well aware of the extent to which the professional privilege can be abused. Mr. Greenfield called attention to one type of abuse; but the pressure exerted by faculty for improved conditions is not a simple one. Faculties have had too much of a "stand pat" tendency to preserve the status quo. If, as Mr. Bolling suggests, trustees combine with administrators to put pressure on faculties, if severe pressures develop to force faculties to change their ways—especially in directions that deviate from the primary concentration on knowledge—then I would join Mr. Kerr in predicting the large-scale unionization of the academic profession. Faculty could become very obstreperous indeed from the point of view of their relations with trustees, administrators, and possibly students. I do not think, therefore, that you can leave the professional concerns, standards, and traditions of the faculty as a secondary aspect of the general problem.

WAGGONER

I am struck by the readiness with which we, in our closed system of higher education, accept the board of trustees and then start tinkering with the system in a pragmatic way, as if that tinkering were all that is necessary. Clearly, the public university stands in a somewhat different relationship to organized democratic society than does the private university. Mr. Dick described a concept of the role of the trustee in a private university: to make policy for the university and delegate the administration of that policy to the president. In most of the public universities those are exactly the legal powers of the board of regents or the board of trustees. On the whole, this system has probably not worked too badly in the United States, but I should like to take a few minutes to relate an anecdote that I think leads to a generalization. A couple of years ago I entertained a group of foreign rectors and deans for six weeks. I asked them to evaluate the State University of Kansas in the method of our U.S. accrediting associations. They observed things that normally we do not observe and focused on things that normally we do not. First, they wanted to read the statutes of the university. They observed the legal role of the regents and were shocked. How could a university community turn over policy-making powers to a group that was completely nonacademic? This seemed absurd to them. The American concept of a board of trustees in public universities is a rare thing in the world. It is not the traditional method of administering a university. They went on to say that even though shocked, they were compelled to admit that it seems to work pretty well. How could this be true? Obviously it can only be true because there is total unity between the governing group of society and the aspirations of the university. When no conflicts arise, university autonomy is not a significant matter. I met a Canadian Communist on his way back from Cuba a month or two after that. I asked him about university autonomy in the University of Havana. He said that was a silly question: When you have an absolute unity in society and an absolute purpose, you do not have to bother about a university being different. Instead of a board of trustees for a public university, why not put it under the state office of education, an agency of the people and its processes, or under the ministry of education, as has been done in the Communist countries?

I balk at comparing boards of trustees to board of directors of corporations, administrators to corporation executives, and faculties to the production-line workers in a factory. The student, of course, is the fabricated product. This does not work very well. The evidence is that the student does not behave like an automobile coming off the production line. A traditional view of the university in the whole history of Western education would be that the university has a special kind of role in society and that it demands independence and autonomy. The last thing that one would want would be this constant nonacademic definition of the purposes and policies of the university. I would speculate that the board of trustees is probably an anachronism carried over from the private, small liberal arts college of the nineteenth century where one board of clergymen had to supervise another group of clergymen who were teaching and were not really much to be trusted in their dealings with students.

MORISON

Are you *for* or *against* the autonomy of the university?

WAGGONER

I am for it. What I am arguing for is a concept of the autonomy of the university as a community made up of students and scholars and teachers which does not need an external policy-making body and cannot accept one over the long run and fulfill its function as a university.

MORISON

Would you say that the Latin American and European universities have more or less autonomy?

WAGGONER

Many Latin American universities have much more. They have problems which are sometimes blamed upon their autonomy, though I myself would not accept that reasoning, and would attribute their problems to other factors.

LURIA

Is this not a critical issue? If a board of trustees has a representative role in the sense that the society has a real voice—whether it be the internal society of the university or the larger society—could the board effectively mediate so that the problems the Latin American universities meet would not be encountered? Cannot the trustees play a buffer role? Performing that function, the board would not prevent shock so much as mediate between the university and the society. It would determine what the university thinks it wants and test those proposals for feasibility within the university. An intermediate body of people can play such a role as long as it is not representing only one small sector of the community.

CAWS

As Mr. Holton predicted earlier, the discussion has kept pretty much to structural considerations with a few moral interjections now and then. But we are commissioned to talk about ethical questions. Meetings like this are called, I think, because of a sense of moral crisis in the community at large. It is important to realize that one of the unclarities in this situation is who, precisely, is the agent. Moral questions arise when people do things that affect other people or fail to do things that affect other people. If we are to talk about morality in the university situation, we must have some conception of who is acting. I do not find it helpful to use simple collective terms like "the faculty" or "the trustees."

Mr. Bolling said a little while ago that change is not going to come from the faculty. I certainly do not think it is going to come from the trustees as boards are presently constituted. Thus, the question is: Is there a recognizable collective agent? There is one obvious sense in which the corporate model is appropriate: The trustees originally constituted the legal entity that was empowered to receive funds, own real estate, and have responsibility to some constituency or other. They were collective agents. The issue confronting American higher education and perhaps higher education around the world is whether these entities as presently defined are fulfilling their moral obligations. Are there actions that the university performs or fails to perform vis-à-vis the society at large that it ought to be performing or not performing? The Columbia trustees are a case in point. If one asks a moral question about agent, action, and consequence at Columbia, it appears that there has been something lacking in that situation. Should some sort of evolutionary descendant of the present board of trustees continue to be the agent that has responsibility toward the internal and external community? Or are there other models of the collective agency of the university that might be just as good, if not better?

Mr. Waggoner also said something which struck me. There is a well-known tradition in certain places that faculty members and students are in fact members of a collective, members of a community, with legal standing. They are not simply clients or employees; they *are* in some sense the institution. I do not see why one should not explore seriously the conception of the university as a collectivity having certain members. I should myself wish to restrict membership in the university to students and faculty, who would then hire the administration. The administration would be a service, not quite on the level of the janitors but having a rather similar relationship to the body itself. Students and faculty together might very well elect a body that took on their behalf the collective stance of responsibility toward the society.

I thought that Mr. Greenfield's remark about the adversary role of the trustees was admirable. The faculty has never been tried in this connection. Within faculties, some of the best ideas are very often generated; yet the present governing arrangements do not make it easy for those members of the faculty to be heard. We have not yet even begun to explore alternative structural possibilities in the light of the moral challenge that confronts higher education at the moment. I must align myself with Mr. Friedenberg's demurrer to Dr. Morison's summary in this respect. I do not think we can assume that a reformed board of trustees will do this job. We may have to turn to a collective agent of an entirely different nature.

BOLLING

I suppose I was playing devil's advocate; I frankly shrink from neat categories and any attempt to approach these issues by separating out the faculty and the administration and the trustees.

You cannot brush off these problems in terms of a bureaucratic tidying-up or a slightly reformed board of trustees. We need a new concept of ultimate authority within the university community that will embrace more fully than it has in the past the teaching faculty and students. You have also to bring in some representatives of the general public to look at what we are doing. I do not think there is any special virtue in any category of people. We all partake of original sin in a sense. I would not trust the faculty and students any more than I trust the administrators or the board of trustees to have the exclusive authority. You have various interests that have to be looked at, and there is something to be said for bringing together people who will have influence upon one another in weighing what is being done. They must work together to produce devices, mechanisms, and policies for renewal. I would not for a moment suggest that the trustees should be put into adversary roles, although indeed they sometimes are—just as administrators and teaching faculty are often put into adversary roles. This is a childish game we sometimes play that the students and faculty—many of whom shift from institution to institution—are going to hire the administrators as a bunch of janitors. I do not think this will work.

CAWS

I specifically said *not* as janitors.

GREENFIELD

I think universities have tended to posture themselves as something divorced from the community and have asked the board of trustees to protect the university from the Yahoos without. The problem is not the trustees' holding on to the status quo against the push for change; it is that universities, like labor unions, have been perceived by some people as what they are not, as necessarily beneficent institutions. Certain people never cross picket lines even though labor unions are racist at home in a lot of cases and colonial abroad. Some faculty members have been in the forefront of a kind of change that has worked for the worst. They have pursued active fundamental far-reaching technological change that has adversely affected people here and around the world. What we have to do now is let the technological mechanism work itself out so that everyone is happy. The point is that the trustee should have a concept of being an outside force checking an institution that frequently does harmful things. That is why the notion of a student-faculty union is appropriate only if we restrict its influence to what happens on campus.

I would suggest there is a two-level construct that applies to this problem. One would want the trusteeship check to look into problems of exploitation on the campus. The notion that the university charges $100 for two people to share a room which is nothing more than a slum is disgraceful. Providing a check through the use of advocacy planning is the kind of thing that the trustee concept ought to take into account. The second is to prevent the university from going outside itself to effect fundamentally inappropriate, undesirable, or immoral change in the community at large, whether it be through supporting Project Camelot, an increase in the power of the military-industrial complex, or destruction of neighborhoods in ghettos. We must ask whether the board of trustees is going to assert a constitutionally valid, effective check on the activities of a university that harm other people.

CAWS

In some other parts of the world what you describe is called a board of visitors.

GREENFIELD

We must discuss with some specificity the notion of what the constituted mechanism is. Obviously the absentee problem is serious. I have been to board of regents meetings at the University of Wisconsin and they are simply a joke. The expertise is all on the side of the administrators. There is no way that the regents can provide an effective check because they do not have the information. The regents are as vulnerable as any welfare mother in a ghetto trying to confront some white-collar planner who has all the facts at his disposal. The result is downright immoral.

MORISON

You are now looking at a university as an agent of social change that, by making an investigation such as Project Camelot, is changing the world in a deliberate fashion.

GREENFIELD

It is more than that, however. I do not have a conspiracy theory, but I do have a performance theory. The same constitutional requirements that would require greater representation would, in my view, effectively prevent, for instance, the dismissal of a professor who spoke out for or against the war in Vietnam. The same con-

331

stitutional checks that require some boundary of the university influence, in my judgment, would also vastly increase the freedom of student journalists and faculty members to probe actively into conditions of the university without reprisal. This is why I was so annoyed at Jacques Barzun's book. Look at Columbia's activities: cigarette filters, real estate, and IDA. It is hypocrisy for the administration to say when the pressures begin to mount: "We are an institution divorced from greater concepts and it is not our concern."

MORISON

I am interested in how far a mechanism within a university can go in telling its faculty what it can and cannot do. Is this the role of the trustees, or the faculty, or the administration?

CAWS

An academically responsible body ought to exist; I agree with Mr. Greenfield entirely on this point. But it cannot be at the same time the legal embodiment of the university. It has to be something different. Nevertheless, the university has to have a legal embodiment of some kind if it is going to own real estate, have money, be responsible, and so on. Thus, I think we are talking about two separate bodies, and part of the ambiguity of the whole situation is that one body has traditionally been supposed to fulfill both these roles.

HOLTON

I have just had the illuminating experience of being at the University of Rome for eight months. It was in turmoil almost every day I was there—often shut down either by students, by the police, or by the authorities. The slogan on the walls on the first days was "Why do we not hear more about Vietnam in the classrooms?", but by the end of the eight months the students painted the walls with a new slogan: "Let us abridge capitalism." They found themselves moving from certain local issues—why are there no political science professors in Italy except for one or two who seem to think that political science stopped with Machiavelli—and they ended up asking questions about the foundations of their society.

I believe a large proportion of those young people, and some of the faculty, wish to commit themselves to a different ideology than the one that has been ruling trusteeships and the faculty's relationships with their students and with their funding agencies. There is a rather general ideological rebellion against the current models—be they the models from the far left (which certainly are in disrepute) or the models with which we find ourselves in our own situation. If one foresees the constitution in the year 2000, it might very well contain additional provisions: It is the right of every person to have the education that he feels he ought to have to lead a meaningful life, to be a unique individual to a degree that is not now granted in any meaningful way. We are seeing, particularly among the young, a reaching out for different models, a different constitution.

We all seem to agree that some modification is necessary. But that body of wise people who will govern the modified university, who see the future clearly and have the world at heart instead of their own small concerns, will not be solely the members of the faculty; they usually have been selected for other reasons, for narrow self-centered achievement aims. We are all groping for a mix that will educate the different parts, so that we can have the kind of informed dialogue out of which governing policy would arise.

KERR

There are two questions I want to raise. One is a question of fact; the other is a question of policy. First, the question of fact. I was rather surprised when Mr. Waggoner said that there is more autonomy in Latin America and in Europe than in this country. I just do not think that observation is true at all. I think it is rather basic whether or not you think we have more or less autonomy under our system.

Second, we have not got to the question of whether we want autonomy in the United States. There are some people here who are arguing for no autonomy in the university and others who would favor a great deal of autonomy. It seems to me that this question is central with respect to trustees. Have they in the United States been a mechanism to give more autonomy to universities than they had when they were under the control of the church or the state? Is it desirable to have more autonomy, or should we be working toward less autonomy?

It is not only a quantitative question. What kind of autonomy and for what purpose? In Germany, the individual full professor has more autonomy than the American full professor, but I do not think you can say that about the university as a whole. You cannot say that about France nor about Russia nor even about England today. It seems to me that for better or for worse we have more autonomy in our institutions than those in any of the major developed countries of the world. The American system of lay trustees has contributed to this greater autonomy and diversity. One must ask whether it is desirable to have this additional autonomy.

SHOBEN

I find a troublesome drift in the way that we have been considering this general problem of trusteeship and, by extension, the primary social leadership of the university as an institution. Mr. Greenfield has argued for values that, in general, I thoroughly share; yet I worry about the extent to which we may be a little time-bound in giving a somewhat hurried and possibly too strong assent to particular ways of achieving these values. When I think about some of the techniques now being considered for promoting greater internal democracy in universities as well as for generating an enlarged concern among academic people for institutions in the larger society, I wonder if we might not attend with profit to the ghost of that prototype of fanatics, Oliver Cromwell. Never expecting to lose the battle of Shrewsbury, but worried about the possibility that his troops would loot the city after their conquest of it, he rode through his ranks, admonishing his men, "Be mindful in the bowels of Christ that ye might be wrong." In the present groundswell of enthusiasm for universities to become highly serviceable in direct ways to the American community, we may indeed be wrong in a fashion that does real harm to the very groups to which the academy should be responding much more positively and constructively. For instance, we might keep in mind the sheer fact that the official personnel of our colleges and universities differ in some fundamental and distressing dimensions from the great majority of minority-group members. Consequently, although any decent-minded man will applaud our attempts to cope more humanely with what Clark Kerr has called "the ghetto clientele" by more open admissions policies, I hope we can at least think seriously about the possible outcome of merely increasing educational access. Until we learn better how to define and provide bona fide educational experiences for people with whom our institutions are too little acquainted, I am not at all sure we will be serving the black community or the university by a more open admissions arrangement. As a matter of fact, that arrangement strikes me as implying a promise that we cannot fill (and that may look as if we have no intention of filling it) until we have worked out proper and creative modifications in our programs, our instructional staffs, and our standards of evaluation to insure that Negro, Puerto

Rican, Mexican-American, and other students, new to our campuses, really have *de-facto* opportunities for self-development and the acquisition of the skills and awarenesses that are most relevant for them. Such changes simply won't be easy to bring off in our institutions, and we do not know what the cost—in intellectual and educational coin as well as in dollars—will be even if we manage somehow to get the changes instituted. I certainly do *not* mean these remarks as a plea for a series of studies that will postpone our meeting what for me is a clear and urgent responsibility. I am certainly pleading that we recognize much more clearly than I think we have so far some of the complexities in issues of this kind. They are pretty harrowing for all their sharp moral imperatives.

GREENFIELD

Did anybody even ask those questions ten years ago?

SHOBEN

I suspect none of us did, but I see little advantage in wallowing in either our own or somebody else's ten-year-old guilt.

GREENFIELD

No, but the point is not guilt so much as responsibility. A pretense that we can remain at the status quo while we decide whether or not to go out from the boundaries of an isolated institution is simply not supportable. The question is whether the universities of this country bear complicity not for indifference, but for active participation in activities that have harmed groups that should not have been harmed by what they were doing.

SHOBEN

Quite right. Again, however, even though my values are yours, the issue of community involvement in university government strikes me as enormously complex. It is extremely difficult to argue for the notion of a high degree of internal institutional autonomy, which has its own calculus of dynamic expansion, and at the same time espouse the thesis that there are certain kinds of common and widely accepted social constraints that can be responded to only selectively. Can we really have institutions that respond only to those community influences that the university itself invites or approves of? If a university subjects itself to the kinds of review procedures that Mr. Greenfield mentions—procedures serving purposes that I heartily endorse—then it puts itself in some degree under the jurisdiction of interests quite external to itself. When you begin to get the representation of these other kinds of interests in reviewing a university's program, then it is going to be very hard to keep out those interests that would be less welcome than those to which we presently feel warmly receptive.

GREENFIELD

Yes, it would. But I am arguing for the necessity of making that effort, not for the ease with which it can be made.

SHOBEN

I am not all that sure that the case for necessity has been convincingly made; but in any event, the argument is a matter neither of ease nor of necessity, but of entailments. If we begin to think seriously about community review as an alternative to conventional concepts of trusteeship, then we must ask what we are going to be letting through our gates that we have not yet considered very carefully. I see little basis in this arrangement, for example, for screening out a variety of right-wing influences or of determining on educational or intellectual grounds those kinds of contradictory interests and conflicts of opinion to which universities can productively react. At the moment, we are generally willing and even eager to hear: "You have no business being involved in classified research. You have no business being such a foul neighbor to a poverty-stricken neighborhood from which you get real estate. You have no business serving the ghetto clientele as badly as you do now." But although these are messages to which our ears are now wide open, they are not the only ones we are going to hear if we adopt the procedural alternatives that are being advocated.

GREENFIELD

I think that is misreading what I said. I do not share the view that we should participate in everything that is left and progressive, but shun everything to the right. Is it not odd that SDS, George Wallace, and many people who are not Wallaceites, but lower-middle-income whites are saying the same things about the influence of foundations and the influence of academia? That does not necessarily mean that one can sit back and say: "Aha. Both

extremes are wrong. We have to continue to occupy the middle."
Both those groups may have legitimate complaints, and we must
listen to both of them. I am arguing not only that we have not
listened to black people and radical students, but also that we
have not heard the factory workers and the Wallace constituency.
They are citizens of this country too, and we may have overridden
their legitimate concerns as well.

TOLLETT

Their concerns are really a desire for universities to facilitate
their own socialization. Their concerns are primarily vocational:
They want to get an education that will equip them to earn a
salary that enables them to move to the suburbs. I am not sure
that you can expect progressive reform to come from the democratization of the educational process. Indeed, I think an important
question that should be raised is just what kind of institution a
college or university is. Is it a democratic institution simply because it is in a society that is democratic? We automatically
think that the university will be better if it is more representative
since ours is a democratic society. Yet no democratic implications
flow from the premise that a university is concerned with cognitive
rationality, as Mr. Parsons says in his paper in the fall 1968
issue of *The Public Interest*.

ESKOW

I should like to struggle publicly for a minute with my bewilder-
ment, because I can no longer connect the cure with the disease.
I cannot trace any of the ills of the modern university to the trustees at all, nor can I see any longer how the multiversity would
be any different today if there had never been trustees. If the
market mechanism is the protest and the protest is listing the
diseases, which of these diseases were created by trustees? Were
our prescriptive and elitist policies for admission the doing of the
trustees? Is the irrelevant and fragmented curriculum a reflection
of the value system of the trustees? It seems to me that the university as it exists today is a projection of the wishes, dreams,
and aspirations of the faculty. The trustees, in a sense, had almost nothing to do with the design of the institution. I think we
are creating an elaborate mythology that suggests that this institution has become an expression of the value system of the trustees—of the military-industrial complex that they have organized
with the aid of captains of industry turned administrators. That
is a mask that hides the truth. If we have become knowledge

factories, it is not because the trustees have wanted to generate knowledge. If we have lost community, it is not because the trustees do not have a sense of the college as a community. If we have been indifferent to the factory workers and the blacks, it is not because of the trustees.

CAWS

Yet the existence of boards of trustees has had the effect of removing from the faculty the necessity of thinking about some of the questions we have been talking about.

GREENFIELD

You cannot at one point say, "We have to be very careful about going into the ghetto," when you have an active, encouraging, free-wheeling, eager participation by many of the faculty in the damaging activities that now go on. You cannot consult corporations, the Institute for Defense Analysis, send missions to Vietnam, study pacification of insurgencies abroad, and at the same time say you shall discourage or be very prudent about going into the ghettos, about encouraging anti-war protests because, after all, you are an isolated community. You cannot have it both ways.

SILBERMAN

It seems to me that we are blurring two rather separate questions. One is the question of whether the university should be an agent for change or a body for the accumulation of knowledge. The other is the unintended consequences of what we normally think of as the search for new knowledge. We are now discovering that many university undertakings have rather large consequences for change outside the university, and that we must take these into account. Columbia may be buying property on Morningside Heights only to permit its own expansion, but this expansion may have detrimental consequences for the community in which it is located. To talk simply about the university as a place where knowledge is sought and not as a service station ignores the large consequences for society implicit in many of the things a university does. We cannot get away from that question.

Much of the discussion so far does not bear much relationship to my understanding of the history of the American university. As I understand it, the trustees did not take away from the faculty the power to choose the administration. More often it was the other way around. The primary academic freedom at Columbia, certainly, is the freedom from any responsibility for administration. In the past, the Columbia faculty chose deans and department heads. At the turn of the century when the university was expanding, the faculty pounded the table and said: "We are not going to be burdened with these administrative chores. We are scholars. The problem of picking deans and department chairmen is a function of the trustees and not something a real scholar ought to be concerned with." Much of the growth of the administrative apparatus at Columbia has been the result of the refusal of the faculty to have anything to do with administration. Faculty may have changed their mind, but the experience at Berkeley suggests quite the reverse. The faculty response to the first crisis was to insist that student discipline ought to be in the hands of the faculty and not the administration. But the faculty then responded to the Dirty Speech Movement by saying: "Do not ask us scholars to be concerned with things of this sort." I think we at least ought to be candid in recognizing what the historical movement has been.

Also our talk of the autonomy of the university seems to exist in a historical vacuum. From the Middle Ages on, the university has not been autonomous; it has been, as Mr. Kerr suggested, a service station for society. Those who are arguing that the university recover its autonomy and search for scholarship are really asking for a return to the ancient role of the servicing of the clergy, the aristocracy, and the elite rather than for the dirtying of its hands with servicing other groups in the society.

Perhaps the question that is most useful here is one Mr. Riesman posed at the April meeting: "Who are the customers?" The suggestion that the students and faculty ought to make all of the decisions and hire the administrators implies that they are the only customers. Yet if we recognize that the university has rather large effects on the rest of society, it is hard to deny that other groups in the society are customers also. The question then becomes one of balancing conflicting claims. At what point do ethical questions merge with administrative questions? What groups in the society is the university supposed to serve? Autonomy is a will-of-the-wisp in any absolute sense.

MORISON

This question of the customers is clearly an important one. Are the objectives of the university truly internal ones? Is the university autonomous in that sense or is its autonomy a procedural thing in order to meet the needs of the customers? This morning we have reached a consensus that there are customers outside the universities as well as inside for which the university has some responsibility. But how much autonomy does the university have in deciding how to fulfill these obligations? I think of autonomy as meaning that the internal part of the university as an institution has a right to choose its own faculty, defend its faculty against outside criticism, and not bow to outside pressure. This is quite different from what happens in Latin America. The university should also have considerable autonomy in selecting its students and research projects. It probably should have some autonomy in determining how it goes about extension activities since many of our universities were set up with extension as one of their main functions.

KERR

I should like to discuss the idea of autonomy in choosing students. Oxford and Cambridge had autonomy in their choice of students. It took a couple of Royal Commissions to get them to take anybody who was a Methodist, or a Jew, or a woman. In Mississippi and Alabama there was also autonomy in the choice of students.

RITTERBUSH

May I offer a statement that might help to resolve the difference of opinion on autonomy? I should like to propose a hierarchy of governance. At the top and most important is the adoption of institutional objectives drawn from the range of available alternatives. This is really the most important function of governance. Subordinate to it, at a second level, is the setting of intellectual and other goals derived from those objectives. And then, on a lower level still, are questions of strategy relating to the mode of pursuing those goals. It seems to me that Mr. Kerr has been saying that the American university has been autonomous at the highest of these levels, freely altering and adopting objectives, and what Mr. Caws seems to be saying is that the university should be so stable an institutional type that there need be no uncertainty or outside intervention in setting objectives, which would leave only questions about intellectual goals, which could best be left to students and faculty. The degree of autonomy desirable within and for universities seems to me to depend upon which level of choice is being discussed: objectives, policy, or strategies.

CAWS

All I mean by autonomy is self-regulation.

HOLTON

It is not self-regulation if you keep on doing what everybody cheerfully lets you do.

CAWS

But from the point of etymology, autonomy *means* self-regulation. Self-regulation is not inconsistent with being held accountable by some sort of body.

HOLTON

An operational definition of autonomy that makes sense to me is that you can engage in a qualitatively new venture with fairly good expectations that you can carry it out. It may turn out to be a bad venture, but at any rate you can change things rather than keep doing what the matrix already has been set up for you to do. At most colleges, we cannot suddenly give credit for a course that a group of students wants to force into the catalogue. Our lack of autonomy comes from the structure of the faculty and of the student body as it is set up. Harvard cannot (and I believe should not) suddenly turn around and give credit for courses that are in fact being widely attended—1,100 students are attending courses under the auspices of the Kennedy School, but as extra-curricular activities. When there is a group that wishes to do an experiment, then we have a test of whether this group is antonomous, and of the limits of its autonomy. For example, those students are autonomous within extra-curricular activities, but not autonomous within the framework of college credits.

MORISON

The individual is autonomous in a university in that sense. But the university itself has an autonomy in the sense that it does not always have to check its procedures with some external body. You are just hung up on your faculty.

HOLTON

No. I am interested in understanding the mechanism for changing the rules in order to make a new venture possible. Within a small framework we can make some experiments. We can, for example, suddenly have a freshman doing independent study instead of a specific college course. It is not necessary to go through a major re-examination of the university to let this happen. But I think the operational test of autonomy is how far you have to rediscuss the whole purpose of the organization before you can make a new experiment.

MEYERSON

We were talking over coffee about the financing of higher education, and I should like to relate the problem of the financing of higher education to the problem of student rights, responsibilities, and behavior. The adult backlash running through the country is such that I strongly suspect that within the next few years those institutions with a strong financial base will be those institutions whose donors are dead: namely, Harvard and a few other universities or colleges for which past bequests provide both the capital and the income for a splendid or potentially splendid ongoing program. I suspect there is going to be a tremendous reluctance to provide money through the means that we have known heretofore for the support of conventional kinds of collegiate and university programs and, I fear, even less inclination to support unconventional programs. I say this with great sorrow, but I think, for example, that what we see currently in the State of California is not due to Governor Reagan alone. When we find a political leader of great subtlety, such as Jesse Unruh, saying much the same thing, we begin to see a pattern in which funds will be sharply reduced—not absolutely reduced, but reduced in terms of the needs that come both from an increase in scale and from the increasing desire on the part of the faculty, students, and others to have far more flexibility.

Let me proceed to discuss certain possibilities that exist before us. The next few years will see gigantic debates on the financing of higher education. The public institutions have formed a coalition with the aim of getting funds from the federal till. For the most part, the private institutions have concurred in the aims of that coalition. The result will be the greatest educational pablum that the nation has seen. Every institution will have a basis of support quite apart from its competence and quite apart from the imagination of its programs. There is an alternative suggestion that we single out a handful of institutions as national institutions, making sure that they get the most significant kind of support. Such a proposal would freeze into the system a pecking order and would reflect past achievement rather than potential. If one were to single out a dozen institutions, who would say that Columbia should not be on the list? Yet from many points of view, it might still have to prove itself.

All of this leads me to the proposal that Zacharias and others have framed. I think their proposal has the greatest merit. They suggest that it ought properly to be the student who receives the financial where-with-all—the token, if you will—to enable him to go to the institution of his choice. Let me proceed to indicate some of the virtues of that proposal. I can imagine few things that will give the students a greater influence over colleges and universities than their control over the dollar. If a student has through a grant or a loan—and in most cases, especially in the near future, it will be a loan—the funds to pay for his tuition, his living arrangements, and probably some kind of cost-of-education allowance to the institution, the vote of the student would determine the financial viability of many of our institutions. This would not be true of those institutions where the donors are dead, but it would hold for most other institutions.

I also support the efforts to do away with large numbers of required courses—almost a return to Charles Eliot's university—because natural science and other fields will be put on their mettle. A chemistry department may now get five hundred students in beginning chemistry simply because the students have to take a set number of science credits. If the students do not have to take beginning chemistry, you may get a significant intellectual advance in the teaching of chemistry. A chemistry department will be most reluctant to lose five hundred students.

Similarly that institution that cannot appeal to the student who comes with his token for tuition and board will lose him. In some cases, the student will choose the institution that is the least rigorous and the least demanding, but I am far more hopeful that students today instead will choose subtle kinds of educational experiences. They will go to the institutions that are trying to improve themselves and are trying to develop a level of educational excellence far superior to that which we now know. Many institutions will "suffer" if we permit the use of that rhetoric. I think people rather than institutions suffer. Institutions ought not to have human characteristics applied to them. They can come into being, and they can go out of being. If they go out of being, there may well be some good reason why they go out of being. This past Congress passed legislation encouraging universities to punish students who have engaged in disruption. Such legislation will, I think, quickly become standard for all federal aid programs to higher education, and I suspect it will become the standard for legislation on the state level with even more alacrity. State legislatures in all the states are much more subject to the adult backlash than Congress is. One of the safeguards against the results of that reaction is an approach that provides money to students. It is a very minor safeguard, functioning much the same way that the

G.I. Bill functioned a generation ago and has functioned to some extent since then. I mention this last point in passing and tentatively; I am not convinced that such a program of aid to students will have the political character that I have suggested.

The main reason in favor of this proposal is a very simple one; it is a crude form of economic control. Those who in the past have had economic control over our institutions have had many other kinds of control over them as well. Let us not deceive ourselves into thinking that they have not. The controls may have been direct or more likely indirect. It is a rare meeting of the governing board of any state university, for example, that is not constantly concerned with what the legislature will think of its action. It is a rare meeting of the board of trustees of any private or public institution that is not deeply concerned with what the alumni donors will think of the actions of the students, the faculty, or the trustees. I am not disputing the pattern of trusteeship at this time, but I am saying that giving students the money to provide for their own education will produce a greater responsiveness to student needs on the part of the 2,200 colleges and universities in the United States than we have ever had before.

I am not willing to predict what the outcome of this redistribution of resources will be. It might well carry the worst features of camp existence. We might end up with the same kind of collegiate institutions that made Mencken wince in the 1920's. Yet I believe that this process would encourage a set of colleges and universities to be more responsive to a different and important set of educational requirements and to be intellectually far superior to anything we have ever had before.

MAYER

I could not agree more with what Mr. Meyerson has said. But there are certain colleges and universities that will not lose public support to the extent that Mr. Meyerson suggests; these are the colleges or parts of universities that are devoted to technology and to the professions—colleges of agriculture, engineering, nursing, public education, home economics, and so on. For these, support is going to continue to increase because this increase is necessary for the operation of our society. Furthermore, students in colleges other than those of liberal arts, by and large, seem to have had far less difficulty in finding the meaning of their education than have liberal arts students. Yet all of the non-liberal arts colleges as well as some of the graduate schools—medical schools, for example—have given insufficient attention to the arts, the history of their own science and technology, the philosophical and ethical aspects of their profession, and indeed the place of their profession within the over-all context of the nation. Reinforcing the liberal arts content should not necessarily take the form of additional courses. Rather it should be a change in the general atmosphere. This is very much needed, particularly in this time of increased specialization, and the liberal arts college could make a much greater contribution than it now does to those other schools of the university where the public expenditures are not going to decrease and may perhaps even increase.

MEYERSON

We tend to forget that the overwhelming majority of American undergraduates are in professional programs, because most of us are from universities where that is not so. But the great bulk of undergraduates are in business schools, in engineering schools, in teacher training programs, and in a whole series of other vocational programs. Indeed, depending on what definition you choose for narrowly defined professions, as many as two thirds to three quarters of the undergraduates in the country may be in such programs. At many universities the great bulk of the so-called graduate students are in fields that have been designated as professional.

An astonishing change has taken place between the events at Berkeley and Columbia. At the time of the Free Speech Movement at Berkeley, there were no professional students in the Free Speech Movement—almost no engineers and no architects, for example. At Columbia the students in the school of architecture played a critical role within the series of spring events. The involvement of law students in dissent has grown enormously during the past several years throughout the country (and incidentally at far greater risk to themselves than almost any other group of students because it is a rare bar association that will admit a member who has a history of dissent or especially a history of arrest). For the first time you find medical students expressing disdain at their curriculum, their program, the conditions under which they study, and so forth. If somehow we could create the financial mechanism whereby students are granted levels of choices that they have not had before, we will find a tremendously impelling force for the remaking of these curricula. It is madness to assume that a student who is convinced at the age of twelve that he wishes to be a physician must go through a rigid four-year undergraduate program in which the closest experience to being a physician he has is with a test tube in organic chemistry. He has no exposure to the opportunities that such a calling provides. He is so removed from humanistic training in medical school that by the time he has completed his medical degree, his internship, and his necessary residency, he has ceased to be the educated man he may once have been. Even in their admissions policies, medical schools still tend to favor the boys who did well with their test tubes in organic chemistry. But the students are resenting this more and more. A student in our medical school came to see me in June. He had been at Columbia as an undergraduate where he had had a brilliant record. He then went to work in a psychiatric clinic in Harlem for a year. In his first year of medical school he was near the head of his class in half of his program and in the other half he was near the bottom of his class. He was asked to leave the medical school and is now at another university studying history. But he came to see me before he decided to leave medicine. His argument was that there is something terribly wrong with medical education if a student can do well in part of his program and so badly in another. No program should be so rigid that it cannot recognize that the physician cannot be all things. His plea made me feel dreadful. This man could have made a tremendous contribution to medicine. If you give the students opportunities for choice, I suspect that many of the difficulties that we are talking about would alter.

SILBER

Would you favor a system that would differentiate the amount of financial aid made available to students from families with incomes of less than $10,000 from the remuneration provided for students from wealthier backgrounds? Under such a program, how would one protect the educational system from the application of Gresham's Law? Would the colleges not start competing for students by means that would be contrary to the interests of higher education?

MEYERSON

If we expect large-scale financial support of the kind I am talking about, it is far more likely to be on the basis of loans rather than grants. If it is largely on the basis of loans, then I would worry far less about the social origins of the student, because the loans would be repaid through some linkage to future income and earnings. Nevertheless, many problems arise. What happens to the woman in such an arrangement? In Sweden where such a pattern existed for many years, through the Swedish insurance companies, there was a joke that by the time a woman had paid off her university loan she was past the menopause. I am also assuming that although a large part of the income of institutions of higher education would come from the student tokens, a significant part would come from other sources as well. Those other sources will help to provide a leavening agent.

When we follow through on Mr. Silber's Gresham's Law problem, there is much confusion. Suddenly we see de Gaulle possibly being forced to devalue the franc, having just conducted a campaign to force the devaluation of the dollar. Which was the bad money driving out the good? Was it the pound, the mark, the dollar, the franc, or what? It just is not clear. Of course we are all concerned about bad educational money driving out good, but which is the bad money? It may very well be that the student token system will drive out what may now be highly valued currencies. We have got to assume that in the history of university life we must have a certain continuity. How do we make sure that there are certain programs that persist even though tokens are not used for them? This question is, of course, one we constantly face in our own institutions. Obviously classical archaeology these days attracts relatively few people, but it is a rare one of us who proposes the abolition of archaeology departments. We would have to make sure that we do not let the students, through their choices, fully determine the history of higher education.

GREELEY

I am inclined to agree with your recommendation, but I wonder about the mechanics of it. Would you permit the tuition to reach its natural level, or would you subsidize the schools to make up the difference between tuition and cost per student?

MEYERSON

I do think the question is a little more technical than we probably ought to get into. It is a very rare service in our society on which we place a single charge. This includes public services as well as private ones. And yet for some unexplained reason we have assumed within universities that we have got to have common charges. There are people who do not hesitate to pay a surgeon a huge fee, but assume that in universities there ought to be a common denominator—not only among universities, but within a university as well. There would have to be a variety of checks in this financial plan, and there ought to be a vast difference in the amounts of money provided for particular kinds of programs and educational experiences.

METZGER

I agree with Mr. Meyerson that the Zacharias plan probably offers

347

us the best answers. It seems clear to me that across-the-board subventions to institutions would finance mediocrity, that selection of certain institutions for institutional aid would reward past performance or present reputation—both unreliable guides. The Zacharias plan does raise some problems, however. First, it appears that giving the student the right of choice would reduce the residential cost advantages that certain institutions currently enjoy. This might have an adverse effect on community politics, or polities, or institutions. You might say that those that cannot survive are victims of the market place, but that is also an argument for the reduction of diversity in higher education, and whether we want to have institutions that are in every way national would be a question. There is another question—quite the opposite of the Gresham's Law fear—the fear that the good and the bad will be all right, but that the different will go under.

One other issue that I think we must recognize is the possibility that the giver will lay down behavioral and attitudinal tests for the receipt of funds. Is it not possible to penalize an institution that deviates? Is it not possible to penalize the students? Those that have been aware of the pressures of loyalty oaths and disclaimers are aware of this danger. The question of whether it is or is not a certainty depends on the degree of legitimization that the university manages to secure. The question of legitimization and all it implies must be explored. There still would remain a need for categorical aid to finance the expensive research equipment that modern science and scholarship require. I take it that for the Zacharias plan to go into operation current modes of financing and all the problems they involve would automatically disappear.

Then finally I should like to raise the question of whether or not the Zacharias plan would truly equalize access to educational opportunity. I have no doubt that it would go a long way in that direction. That was not a reason you gave for the program, but it surely is an important one for financing higher education in this way. It makes it possible for the poor to get an education. Yet, on the other hand, one must not forget that there is a problem of foregone earnings. Individuals bear much more of the cost of higher education than is represented by their tuition and their residence expenses. They forego the money they do not earn while they are in school, with the exception of their summer earnings. I wonder whether it would be possible to imagine a Zacharias plan that would take that into account; I assume that the costs would be astronomical.

KEEZER

What has been the rate of repayment of the student loans thus far?

MEYERSON

As you know there are mixed histories. A number of loan programs have had substantial defaults, but others have been administered in such a way that repayment raises few problems.

In answer to Mr. Metzger's point on the reverse of Gresham's Law, I would count that as one of the benefits. Let me use for examples the case of the two-year colleges and the needs of the Negro colleges. The two-year colleges are disparaged around the country. Some are marvelous places for educational experiences, but in many parts of the country two-year colleges are indistinguishable on the level of instruction from secondary schools. The student continues to take elective courses he did not have a chance to take when he was in secondary school. The value to any student of that kind of experience is slight. Yet in many parts of the country students are forced into these two-year institutions and have no other options open to them. The egalitarian nature of the Zacharias program would enable students who do not presently have other choices to have them. It would force many of the two-year colleges in the country, which are administered by the secondary schools and run like secondary schools, to change their character vastly. Such a change would be all to the good.

In the case of the Negro colleges—and here I would add the church schools, too, since many people go to these schools because they wish certain associations, certain identifications, and certain kinds of moral and other experiences that they would not have elsewhere—I would not in any way suggest that those factors would become less important. A study was made of where the G.I. Bill of Rights students went to school, and we learned that a somewhat higher proportion went to the Catholic and the Negro schools. I am not at all certain that it would mean the demise of these schools if we had a considerable upgrading of all institutions.

The other main point is that of foregone earnings. I am currently running a program for 125 black students who in virtually all cases have to have stipends provided to their families—their own primary family or their parental family. It would be impossible for those families to function without this supplementary help. I have managed to scrounge enough money to finance this program for this year, but I do not know how we can continue it for very long. These problems reflect the whole character of our social structure; they cannot be dealt with through the educational mechanism alone. If we had some kind of compensatory redistribution of income to low-income families, the problem would, at least in part, solve itself. Certainly on the short run it is almost inconceivable that resources would become available for dealing with the foregone earnings problem. We do deal with this in the case of graduate students, but that is the only place in higher education where we do so.

PAYNE

It seems to me that student choice in this kind of program makes a good deal more sense than parental choice, which is what has been going on in most places. The problems of precocity and dependence are likely to be better met under a system where there is a certain amount of freedom from the financial dependence on the home and the scholarship department of the institution. You have a possibility for a more self-confident student body in that way and that is a great advantage. I am worried, on the other hand, about an additional problem of freedom. The mere fact of having to start paying off loans immediately after college is one more way of closing in a student's options. It might be feasible to talk about outright grants plus loans. This would also make it possible for an economic calculation to be made that would lead to some students staying in the community colleges because they would in fact be more economical in the long run.

REVELLE

If we follow through on Mr. Meyerson's idea at least as far as the professional schools, we have to add another element to the entities that are involved in the governance of the university, and that is the professional associations. At the present time the professional associations largely determine the requirements for entrance and practice in a profession. On the whole, their influence is, I think, pernicious in professional education. Unless we can find a mechanism whereby the professional school rather than the professional society has a major voice in determining the requirements of the profession, we are likely to freeze into the Zacharias proposal not the free choice of the students at all, but the peculiar educational notions of the professional associations.

We might also look at where this kind of allocation of resources has been tried, though in a somewhat different way. In the Philippines, certain universities exist as private profit-making corporations. These institutions obviously depend on the free choice of the students, since they can somehow provide what the students want and make money at it. On the whole, they give a poor education from every point of view except the short-run interest of the students. The students receive their union card, a piece of paper that gives them status in the society. The program Mr. Meyerson is advocating should, I think, be highly experimental; it should not be considered *a priori* as the way to proceed. I was glad to see that Mr. Meyerson did comment that we probably need a wide spectrum of kinds of support. Our experience in the relations between the federal government and the universities has been disappointing. The project system for support has come about as close to ruining our universities as any single device could because it has led to a loyalty, particularly on the part of scientists, not to their institution, but to their so-called peer groups in Washington. A man in any of the scientific fields, at least until recently, could move whenever he wanted to. He could take his grant, his graduate students, and his whole apparatus with him. He was, in fact, not a member of an institution at all; he was a member of a kind of national club that cut across institutional lines. If we reason by analogy, it seems to me that any single way of supporting higher education on the part of the federal government is liable to bring unforeseen disadvantages that may turn out to be much greater than the advantages.

SPROULL

There has been a great deal of talk about Gresham's Law here today. I just want to point out that one of the problems that we all face now is that the Washington corruption of Gresham's Law—that the urgent drives out the important—is now applied to universities. Universities are the last institution in society that ought to accept or apply that law.

I do not agree with Mr. Revelle that the Philippine experience is relevant to the proposal Mr. Meyerson has made. Surely that situation reflects the free choice of parents rather than the free choice of students. If it is a profit-making institution, it is surely a place where the parents are paying for the education.

My real point has to do with incentives. We all feel that there is an institutional insensitivity and lack of responsiveness in major American educational institutions. Here I am talking about the six-million-student problem and not about the Harvard or Cal Tech problem. But how can one achieve institutional responsiveness or institutional sensitivity? Mr. Meyerson has, I think, leapfrogged his way over a vast amount of territory in saying: "Let's put incentives into the institutional support structure in such a way that the institution has incentives to be responsive and sensitive." I should like to ask what other things are happening in institutions represented around this table to increase responsiveness and sensitivity in the shorter run.

GRAUBARD:

Perhaps Mr. Metzger might comment now on his experience at Columbia.

METZGER

I am not clear on what level—descriptive or analytic—I should proceed. I assume that you do not want a blow-by-blow account of what happened at Columbia last spring. And I doubt that I can improvise a summary of all the large meanings of those events. Perhaps I would do best to seek a compromise—to tell only so much of the story as will illuminate one of its main motifs.

Let me address myself to the problem of authority—a theme which any storyteller from Columbia is likely to think of first. Last spring, a large number of Columbia students not only violated the rules of the institution, but challenged the legitimacy of the rule-makers. A self-constituted body of the faculty interposed itself between the students and the administration and attempted to mediate their differences. This *ad hoc* intervention failed, for reasons that shed a certain light on why *ad hoc* interventions of this sort often fail. The administration called in the police (not once but twice within a fortnight and each time with bloody results). Failing to anticipate, constrain, or condemn police misconduct, the "authorities" of the institution lost most of the moral credit they had left. For a time, there was no authority at Columbia, but two competing and incompetent seats of power—an officialdom that could summon force, but could not gain the consent of the governed; a student strike committee that could shut things down, but could not gain and keep allegiances, even within its ranks. Gradually, a committee of the faculty, set up by professors assembled in full strength, acquired sufficient moral standing to become, if not a new authority, then at least the instrument through which authority might be restored. It prevailed upon the trustees of the university not to press charges of criminal trespass against students accused of one offense; it supported the efforts of another body to judicialize the discipline of the university; it appointed a commission of outsiders to investigate the causes of student anger; it began the framing of a constitution that would give students and professors a more important role in the running of the institution. Whether these techniques will work—whether a calculated policy of forgiveness, a more thorough commitment to due process, a willingness to submit to outside judgment, and a more democratic form of governance will reknit our shattered community—it is still too soon to tell. The way the spring term ended admonishes against facile optimism: The official graduation ceremony had to retreat to a nearby church in order to protect itself against disruption; a radical student counter-ceremony took over the embattled campus grounds.

I think it can be said that at no other university up to that moment was the attack on authority so jugular, the crisis of legitimacy so complete. Yet, when one looks back, one finds little evidence that this attack and this crisis were anticipated. Those in charge of the university knew that students were restive, but they felt that student restiveness was a chronic illness, not one that reached climactic peaks. A minority of radical students was attacking the alleged seduction of the academy by the social institutions of war and profit, but it was believed that numbers were decisive, and that those who were complaining about the CIA, ROTC, and grades for selective service could command the soap boxes, but not win the troops. I would attribute this false sense of security in part to conceptual failings. What produces and sustains authority? President Kirk seemed to employ a "rational-legal" model: Authority, he appeared to believe, is the gift of the charter and the statutes conferred on the holder of a specific office. Vice-President Truman seemed to use a pluralistic-pragmatic model: Authority, he appeared to believe, is the product of the capacity of a system to recognize and satisfy divergent interests. The senior professors seemed to favor yet another concept: Authority, many of them seemed to believe, is an attribute of personal competence, as attested by institutional credentials and by disciplinary repute. A sanguine corollary could be drawn from each of these conceptual models. President Kirk made the Weberian assumption that as long as he stayed within his sphere of competence and obeyed the general rules, his orders would be obeyed. Vice-President Truman seemed to infer from his political science that as long as students had access to the administration and could negotiate with it for concrete rewards, they would be socialized into the going order, even as the Populists and the CIO had been in another day. The senior professors seemed to think that of all authorities, their own, a product of mandarinism and charisma, was the most natural, the most winning, and the most secure.

What these models failed to take into account was the thrust of black student militancy and the animus of white student revolutionism—two very different forces which joined at Columbia for one frightful week. To the black students on campus, who had gathered in numbers large enough to make the assertion of race consciousness a collective rather than a lonely task, academic authority was white authority and thus congenitally suspect. They did not test the moral quality of an official action by asking whether it was authorized or *ultra vires:* In their eyes, the rules, though general, were not neutral with respect to race. Nor would they automatically accord to a white professor the respect due knowledge and renown, for knowledge could be tainted by prejudice and fame could be accorded evil men. This did not mean that they would never treat with white officials. To the extent that they regarded the university as a dispenser of occupational advantages and the arbiter of racial rewards, they did conform to the Truman doctrine and bargain for specific gains. But black confrontation with white authority was no longer just an ask-and-get affair. It served an expressive function: It was a way of acting out resentments, a way of exorcising inner doubts; it involved a purging of the servile images incorporated into the black man's psyche through centuries of social subordination. To use a convenient shorthand, the black students were concerned not only with de-exploitation, but also with de-victimization. The goal of de-exploitation is a fairer allocation of resources, a more even division of the pie. In the context of the campus, it took the form of demands for greater black enrollments and for larger scholarship funds for the poor. The goal of de-victimization is to repair the psychic consequences of prolonged subjection. Whatever forms it takes, it cannot have so finite an agenda. Historically, the prime vehicle of de-victimization has been de-colonization—the replacement of the foreign superordinate by the indigenous subordinate in every position of power and prestige. The demography of this country may not permit so drastic a solution. Still there is room for colonial analogies: Population movements have concentrated blacks in ghetto pockets; administrators, social workers, and policemen, entering the "native quarters" by day and leaving them by night, do bear a certain resemblance to foreign officers, religious missionaries, and expeditionary armies. The fight for community control of schools is somewhat akin to a bid for sovereignty, although it is more partial and oblique. When Columbia decided to build a gymnasium in the park that separated Harlem from the Heights, it failed to consider these analogic possibilities. On its face, the move was not exploitative. The facility would be used by both the community and the college; located in a city park, it would not force any tenants to be relocated and reduce the limited housing stock. Ten years ago, these considerations had weighed heavily with Harlem's leaders, who had helped pass the enabling laws. But now a new set of leaders, reflecting a new black power mood, was inclined to see things very differently. To them, Columbia was a white settler's city on the hill—a Salisbury, a Johannesburg, a Nairobi—rising high and mighty over the native flats. Like them, it had seized the land around it through a policy of purchase and chicane and had expelled the native population so as to protect its safety and hygiene. Now, its appetite unappeased, it was about to appropriate more tribal territory that had struck it as desirable and green. No matter that it was willing to share the building's floor-space, the control of the building would not be shared; moreover, the very plan for sharing betrayed an *apartheid* prejudice—one entrance on the high ground for students, another for the lesser breeds below. I am not certain that every student at Columbia who was black saw the gym as a colonial intrusion. But almost every student who was black took sides with the black community, rather than with the white-led institution, once these Mau Mau symbols had been raised. To put race above status was to prove that one had not been suborned by white preferment; this was essential to self-esteem, and self-esteem was now of the very essence. (I recognize, as I say this, that Columbia had been harsh toward its neighbors, and that this imagery, though exaggerated, had a germ of truth.)

At the start of the week that shook the ivy, Hamilton Hall was seized and occupied by black militants and white revolutionaries joined together. Soon, however, this alliance fell apart. After a night of squabbling, the whites were sent out into the early morning cold to colonize another building, and the blacks had Hamilton to themselves. Why this separation? In part, because the blacks demanded autonomy. (In a crude way, the building was for them a kind of country; the negotiations for its release, a kind of foreign policy; the removal of the white contingent, an assertion of their own self-determination.) In part, because the blacks did not trust their allies. (At first, the whites opposed the barricading of the building and proposed to block administrative rooms instead, seeking thereby to avoid embroilment with the student body. The blacks interpreted this to mean that these white rich men's sons in their Skid Row clothes were willing to take the risk of words, not deeds. To prove they had the courage of their convictions, the whites jettisoned selective tactics when they struck out on their own, and the idea that confrontation should be discriminating in its choice of target fell a casualty to this contest of zeal.) But as much as anything else, the blacks parted company with the whites because of differences over ideology. Where the whites spurned the materialism of society and regarded social mobility as an anaesthetic, the blacks maintained a strong commitment to the stratification system and to conventional notions of success. Where the whites saw the enemy as "capitalism," the blacks saw the enemy as "racism," and these symbols, while they touched, were not the same. Most of all, they had different attitudes toward academic authority. The black militants wanted to face the "Man," both in order to redress their grievances and to address their wrath.

They sought, therefore, a responsible and responsive adversary. (It is interesting that, of all the student groups in the buildings, only the blacks failed to call for the resignation of Mr. Kirk.) The whites would not render the administration the tribute of being needed. In the revolutionary credo, the social system was congenitally corrupt and those who served to sustain it had to be attacked and overthrown. The weakness of university authority, a sometime source of despair to the black students, was for the whites an opening to be exploited, a point in the social organism where one could inject the redeeming plague. The blacks used ingestive and obstructive images ("let more of us in," "stop the juggernaut"), but they did not use toxic or gangrenous metaphors.

At Columbia, there existed no faculty body that could debate important academic issues, generate a consensus about them, and make sure that that consensus took effect. (There was a University Council, but it was dominated by administrators and traditionally had concerned itself with bagatelles.) Consequently, the brunt of this assault upon authority was borne by the emplaced authorities, which is to say, by two individuals—the president and vice-president of the university. To say that it was not borne well is not to ignore the difficulties under which they worked. They were— to start with—only two, hardly an optimum number for gaining the sort of intelligence and instigating the sort of argument that were needed to correct mistaken views. Men younger than they would have been overtaxed; men less able than they would have been overwhelmed. Then, too, they had inherited from the last great president of the institution, Columbia's own demonic St. Nick, the worst of all possible executive worlds—too much uncommunicativeness on high policy to receive the benefits of feedback, too little control over subdivisions to implement any central plan. In a time of crisis, this combination of an overabundance of prerogative with an insufficiency of power turned out to be particularly perverse. Added to all this were the pressures that outsiders exerted on them. Alumni who had been students in a more tranquil day saw their successors as engaging in a temper tantrum that would grow if it were in any way placated; men of property saw property rights invaded and demanded instant recourse to the law's defense; other administrators begged ours to hold the levee, lest the radical torrent engulf them too (this was a liquified version of the domino theory and doubtless just as hyperbolic). For a while, these pressures were resisted. The separation of the black students from the white students had created an all-black citadel in a predominately white institution that stood cheek-by-jowl with Harlem. To allow them to stay ran one sort of danger, but to dislodge them by force ran another—the danger of

arson and riot—and the balance of risks had to be gravely weighed.
The hostaging of a dean also bought the sit-ins time and allowed
them to spread to other buildings. But procrastination was not
adopted by the administration as a policy; to the external publics
of the university, this would have been taken as a sign of weakness,
and the regard of these external publics counted much at Low.
This is not to say that a Fabian approach would have been adopted
had there not been so much prompting from outside. I do not
know exactly at what point the president and vice-president concluded that negotiations with the SDS-dominated strike committee
were useless, that the issues of the gym and of IDA (an institute
of weapons analysis with which Columbia had nominal connection) had been raised to embarrass not reform the university,
that the longer the sit-ins lasted the more they became a counter-
government competing with the legal one for mass support, that
so ultimate a challenge to authority had to be met by something
no less ultimate—the arbitrament of force. Perhaps they reached
this point when the SDS took over the president's suite and began
to affirm the revolutionary counter-ethic that establishment
property, being theft, is therefore eminently seizable and that
privacy is never a right that can be said to adhere in official persons. With the blacks, who were less wounding in words and
conduct, the administration did make an effort to come to terms;
it would not, however, pay the ransom asked for—the abandon-
ment of the gym; and so these negotiations did not prosper. On
the third day, the vice-president told the faculty that he had
reached the end of his political string. He was about to submit
to the harsh protectorship of the police.

But a group within the faculty would not accept this, and
their intervention was to produce another chapter in the crisis
of authority at Columbia. I shall not burden you with the details
of how the Ad Hoc Faculty Group took form. Let it suffice to say
that it arose spontaneously, rather than by any plotter's will. Nor
shall I try to examine all the motives of those who joined it.
Assuredly these were varied and in certain persons quite complex. It may be enough to say that, as far as its steering committee
was concerned (as a former member of it I can describe its mind
with modest confidence), there was little sympathy for the insurrection. One fear brought us into action—the fear of violence on
the campus—and one hope sustained us through four sleepless
nights—the hope that third-party intervention, free from the
intransigencies of either side, could find a placable and equitable
way out. Subsequent commentators have charged that this was a
partial fear and a naïve hope—the Ad Hoc Faculty Group has
not received what one would call a glowing press. I do not doubt

that there is some substance to these charges. We *were* more concerned about imported violence than about the violence boiling up in our midst (though we did constitute ourselves a constabulary to try to keep the left- and right-wing students from each other's throats). And we *did* misjudge the temper of the revolutionaries, which was far more Sorelian than we anticipated. Between our desire to pacify the campus and their desire to traumatize and radicalize it, between our sense of politics as accommodation and their sense of politics as war, stretched a gap that was probably unbridgeable. Yet, it seems to me, there was more wisdom in our course than has been noticed or than even we at the time realized. When the police came with their covered badges and flailing nightsticks, when they not only made arrests but inflicted punishments—and on the innocent and the lawbreaker alike—when they disobeyed the instruction of their own officials in venting their fear and spite, they did more to jeopardize authority than ever did the students at their barricades. To have tried to sustain the life of the university around the confiscated buildings would probably better have preserved the social compact than to have invoked what turned out to be an indiscriminate and ungoverned force. Moreover, it is possible that, in time, the area of disaffection might have shrunk. By dealing substantively with the issues, the Ad Hoc Faculty Group took cognizance of an important fact—that most of the students in the white communes were not revolutionary and had not written their manifestoes tongue-in-cheek. If most shared with the revolutionaries a radical critique of society, they did not draw the same nihilistic inferences; if they agreed that the university had been corrupted, they did not agree that its improvement was beyond all hope. The very innocence of our rationalism allowed us to discern complexities—to see that the buildings had not been occupied by eight hundred anarchistic Rudds, that there were many communards who were not *enragés* and who were tense under the latter's leadership, and that time and a concessionary stance might result in their defection.

And yet I now see that our intervention was doomed to fail—not because it was inept, but because it was *ad hoc*. To salvage authority, one needs authority—or at least some authorization; to exercise power without anointment, to mediate at no one's behest, is almost to guarantee defeat. We were made aware of this in many ways. In our first phase of mediation, when we simply tried to repair communications between the students and the administration, we were seen as abdicating our role as teachers and turning ourselves into colorless connecting links; in the second phase, when we tried to impose a settlement and speak with our own

authentic voice, we were seen as making promises we lacked the
mandate to put forward and the power and stature to enforce.
By going our self-made way, we became an object of suspicion to
colleagues who valued due procedures. Some seemed to think of
us as intruders, well-intentioned perhaps but too presumptuous;
while others seemed to think of us as adventurers capitalizing on
crisis to advance our own careers. Perhaps the worst of the lia-
bilities of our *ad-hoc*ism lay in the indefiniteness of its contours.
Who belonged to the Ad Hoc Faculty Group? To what extent
did the Faculty Group speak for the faculty as a whole? The debate
over the issue of amnesty made it clear that these questions were
critical and that the answers would be indistinct. "We will not
accept judgment of punishment from an illegitimate authority,"
said Mark Rudd, referring to the corporate authority that emanated
from the legal fount. The *ad hoc* steering committee, which was
largely made up of senior faculty, proposed that the disciplinary
punishment be light (for those who voluntarily left the buildings),
but that some sort of disciplinary judgment be made—in short that
the students be granted amnesty *de facto,* not *de jure.* Critical
as they were of the administration, they did not regard its authority as illegitimate; much as they sought a settlement, they would
not agree that the revolutionaries were in the right. Doubtless, for
professors who were not so critical of the administration or were
not so eager to arrange a pact (and these included some of the
most distinguished members of the faculty), even amnesty *de facto*
went too far toward immunizing lawlessness and acknowledging
its moral claims. But in the group that called itself the *ad hoc*
membership, there was a surprising amount of "faculty" sentiment
in favor of a prescriptive amnesty. A certain part of this variance
in sentiment was clearly an artifact of composition. Existing outside the rules, the Ad Hoc Faculty Group had no standard by which
it might define itself except that of an incontinent egalitarianism.
Some who came to vote and argue had fewer ligatures to the
faculty than to the students (some indeed *were* students, with relatively minor teaching responsibilities). Some were of a rank and
office that would have barred them from a seat on the established
faculties or would have admitted them without a vote. In regular
academic governance, there may be something to be said for open
doors and an elastic franchise; in irregular modes of operation,
there is not. Because we did not know what we were, we could not
maintain confidentiality; whatever happened in our sessions was
instantly reported by double agents to the SDS. As the votes on
the issue of amnesty teetered back and forth, depending on the
vagaries of attendance, the student rebels came more and more
to believe that "the faculty" might declare itself their moral ally.

359

Clear-minded observers would have known that, whatever happened in these frenzied meetings, the bulk of the tenured faculty would not dissolve the thousand ties—personal, contractual, and customary—that bound them to the given order, and the idea that they would have preferred to live in anarchic confraternity with the students rather than in orderly relations with the legal powers should have strained credulity from the start. But crisis is not a time for clear-minded observation, and the rebelling students did believe that they would get large pickings if they stood pat.

The Ad Hoc Faculty Group failed. The lessons of its failure have not always been correctly drawn. Its failure does not prove that whenever authority shows cracks it crumbles. "United we stand and divided we fall" is a precept for preserving power, not legitimacy; a flawless alliance between Columbia's professors and administration might have brought the police in sooner, but would have made for greater difficulties when they left. Nor does it prove that mediation in a polar world is fruitless. True, our evenhanded formulas were rejected—politely by the administration, contemptuously by the students; we did seem, from each perspective, to be disingenuously partial to the other side. But one rejection after five days' trying can hardly be generalized into a law of nature, and it remains to be seen what mediation can accomplish when time is less at a premium, and there is less need for a climactic "yes" or "no." For me, the primary lesson of that failure is that structures should anticipate, not trail, events. For what we were trying to do, we needed an established mechanism that could draw on the legitimacies of tradition, that could enjoy collegial proxies, that could define itself. We needed a faculty organ; all that we could manufacture, on the spur of the moment, was a crowd.

The coda to the story I am telling involved the effort to create just such an instrument in the dark period following the "bust." On the day after the police retook the buildings, all the professors from the varied divisions of the university met together in the chapel, one of the few places free of the strains and debris of war. Only once before had they met as a collectivity; this had been on the eve of battle, when the administration had convoked them for the purpose of gaining their general support. On this occasion, the members of the Ad Hoc Faculty Group had been able for the first time to address their peers on the dangers of a stiff-backed policy and the virtues of mediation; they had not, however, submitted their proposals to a vote, fearing that a negative or closely-won result would hamper their negotiations with the students. (Whether they had thus let slip an opportunity to gain majority support for their own position, it is difficult to tell. Clearly, they had made a greater impact on their audience than their pariah instincts had supposed they would. Nevertheless, the only formal outcome of that meeting was a bland vote of confidence in the administration.) Now, in its second convocation, the assembly had to face the consequences of decisive action: almost two hundred students bloodied, four or five thousand students on strike, an armed patrol at every gateway, every civility effaced. The inclination of this body was now to find some way to go back—to retrieve a community based on shared assumptions that had so suddenly developed into a regime of force. It sensed it could not do this by rallying again to the administration; it needed its own instrumentality and one that would not be factional or outcast. Out of this sense was born the Executive Committee of the Faculty, something new under the academic sun. It was given a nostalgic mandate—"to return the university to its educational tasks." But the past could not be recreated; the very existence of this body was a rebuke to the old regime; the disaffection of the mass of students had to be coped with, not wished away. In a short time, the Committee became an advocate of reform as a key to recovery, and "restructuring" became its motto and major aim.

For all its advantages of birth, the Executive Committee of the Faculty had to struggle for legitimation. At the beginning, it did not transcend the deep divisions of the faculty. Its parliamentary sponsors, hoping to have it do so, had fixed its membership in a slate composed of old *ad-hoc*ers, staunch supporters of the administration and a few members heretofore disengaged. This *politique* approach, instead of creating a committee of the whole, created a committee of warring parts, and it took time before the conciliations of an able chairman and the unifying effects of the committee process could work to solidify the group. At the beginning, it was distrusted by the students. In an effort to restore the peace, which it saw as a precondition to reform, it became deeply involved in crisis management and lost credibility as a force for change. Moreover, its notion of the changes called for—a greater voice for faculty and students in a government that would leave old forms intact—aroused a great deal of student skepticism in quarters where "co-option" was a fighting word. It was not until the summer brought composure that a *rapprochement* of sorts could take effect. A radical, but not revolutionary student group, which had broken away from the diehard leadership, turned its energies to "restructuring" and became the critic and the partner of a faculty similarly engaged. With the Kirk administration, the Executive Committee of the Faculty had very strained relations. This was a third block to legitimacy. But for the recognition accorded it by the trustees, the Committee might have found itself in the role of its *ad hoc* predecessor. As it happened, the exigencies of the moment impelled the board to turn, not to their deputies, but to an agency of the faculty for advice. It was a marriage of convenience, not without its points of discord. The board thought the way to restore authority was to invoke full disciplinary sanctions; the faculty argued—in part, successfully—that a punitive university would be a university beset by enemies, that retribution without mercy would lead to confrontation without end. The board wanted to continue to allow the president to raise intramural punishments at his own discretion; the faculty argued— more successfully—that this was as judicially untenable as it was politically unwise. Not all the arguments were won by the faculty and not all the arguments of the faculty were sound. What mattered as much as the score on issues were the utilities gained by the debate. The trustees came to know their campus; the Executive Committee of the Faculty received the accolade of their regard. I think I have located one of the latent functions of trustees—they can validate new agents of authority when the old no longer work.

The returns are not yet in. The relegitimation of authority has not yet been accomplished at Columbia. We are only at the point where we may think that we have learned something from our distress.

DIAMANT

I have a few points at issue with Mr. Metzger on the question of legitimacy. The overt issue at Columbia was the gymnasium, and the question of legitimacy was not whether or not the gymnasium was a benefit to Harlem, but whether the Harlem community was in control of that decision. It was at this juncture that the students disagreed with the university. Mr. Metzger also remarked that *ad hoc* situations are dangerous, especially continuous *ad hoc* situations, and that we must have structures ready to deal with crisis. If I heard him correctly, he said that you do not know who you are when you are *ad hoc*. The comment upset me dreadfully because I do not think that structures can define who we are. Perhaps Mr. Metzger does not think so either since everything he was saying, while overtly calling for structure, seemed to be saying implicitly that part of the problem is that under the structure that exists we do not know who we are. Though he said that his group felt they could not give *de jure* legitimacy and *de jure* amnesty because that would have recognized the illegitimacy of the structure, what he really meant was that the group knew it was an illegitimate power structure. Their real concern with structure and with avoiding *ad hoc* situations arose from a desperate fear of having to fall back on what all human beings have to fall back on—the legitimacy inside ourselves and the legitimacy of our values, our purposes, and our goals. The defense of the administration—which the faculty was being pushed toward much against their will—meant a retreat to an identity defined by structure. In other words, they were saying: "I am a professor; I fulfill my human responsibilities partly through teaching and research" and not "I am a man." There is a tremendous difference between those things. I heard implicit in Mr. Metzger's dilemma the kind of honest intuition on his part that the power structure at Columbia was illegitimate.

SILBER

The thing that I find most perplexing about the Columbia situation is that it came so many years after the trouble at California. After what happened at California in 1964 and at Wisconsin and elsewhere soon after, most faculties and administrations immediately recognized the need to revise their rules. I find incredible the revelation, made at this conference, that there was no faculty senate at Columbia. I had taken for granted that no faculty of any standing could fail to assert its voice, however ineffectually, in a faculty senate.

At the University of Texas, we called for the development of a new set of rules in the spring of 1965. On the advice of a first-rate constitutional lawyer on our faculty, we sought a system that would guarantee all aspects of due process of law and provide the basis for court review for any decision made by the dean of students. The courts could then take jurisdiction in any case in which students were clever and determined enough to insist on court review. We assumed that they would be.

A new period then began. A committee composed of faculty and four students with alternates—the students chose their own representatives, including the president of the student body—set to work. All of the students attended regularly for three weeks, but this was a laborious job. We met two afternoons every week throughout the academic year 1966-67 and through the following summer, a season when it is generally difficult to keep faculty members in town. One of the two students who remained to the end was an alternate. The president of the student body attended less than 20 per cent of the time. The original draft amounted to something like three hundred pages of material, which we thought could be reduced by half. The university administration hired a legislative bill writer to put the deliberations of the committee into the best legal form so that the intent was clear and the wording avoided, for instance, the passive construction that specifies actions without identifying agents.

The finished document was submitted first to the students for their review and their approval. It was then submitted to the Faculty Council. Then began some of the toughest debates that our faculty has ever had. We had to persuade the old guard, who balked at any rule that would give students the guarantees of due process of law and would deprive the dean of students of some of his discretionary power. After a series of test votes on the less controversial points, we decided that we finally had the support of the majority. Then we started passing the sections one after another. It took most of the fall semester to pass the entire legislative program, at the rate of a chapter or two per session. By the time the 1967-68 faculty meetings were over, our set of rules had been passed.

In addition, our president summoned a group to discuss what we would do if disruption took place on campus. We decided that it would be a great mistake to put ourselves in the position of ordering the police on campus. Instead, we incorporated in the rules a statement on disruption on university property, and agreed that if the rules were deliberately transgressed, we would seek a court order under provisions of the laws of the State of Texas. If a judge found that there was a violation of state or municipal law, he would issue a court order that would be presented to the students involved. They would be told that if they did not obey the order they would be in contempt of court. At that point it would be up to the judge to decide whether he wanted to enforce his own court order; the decision would not be left to the university. We knew perfectly well that calling in the police would be a last resort, to be used only if the disruption became so serious that the civil authorities decided that action must be taken. The only time the Supreme Court of the United Stares failed to support Martin Luther King occurred, I believe, when he defied a court order—not when he defied an ordinance or a rule established by a bus company or a city. But when he refused to obey a court order, the Supreme Court found him in contempt on the ground that there is something ultimately legitimate about the legal system itself. So we placed our ultimate confidence in the legitimacy of the legal authority. (In doing so, I do not think that we were breaking any new ground or being particularly creative.)

These procedures were well worked out, and the students were clearly informed of them so that there could not be any uncertainty about what was permitted and what was prohibited. We wanted them to understand the nature of the legitimacy that they might bring into question: First they could test the legitimacy of the court order; only later could they come to a test of the legitimacy of the university's administration and rules.

The regents have subsequently altered some of the rules passed by the students and faculty, and the faculty has not yet been fully informed of the extent of the alterations. We are trying to have the changes clarified. Since the regents do not meet with the faculty, they rarely have any idea of the extent to which such matters have been thought through. That the regents should change these rules is a source of dismay to many members of the faculty. I think that if the regents had met with us to discuss the rules they would probably have accepted them as they were written.

We took the attitude that the right of revolution is the right of all students, but that the corollary of the right of revolution is that revolutionaries had better win. If the corollary of the right of revolution were the right of amnesty, we would have an open invitation to revolutionary activity. The only thing that protects society from the casual exercise of the right of revolution is the clear recognition by revolutionaries that most revolutions can be put down.

I should like to ask Mr. Metzger how we can account for Columbia's not having responded to what happened in California and Wisconsin. Why did Columbia not have a set of rules that guaranteed students the rights of due process? How do you account for the absence of a faculty senate at Columbia? This absence seems to me to make the central issue at Columbia one not of legitimacy, but of competence. I should hate to think that the incompetence of a president could call into question the legitimacy of the government of the United States. How then did Kirk's actions call into question the legitimacy of Columbia's administration?

MEYERSON

I want to reinforce Mr. Silber's first concern and his concluding one, but also to dissociate myself from the central part of what he dealt with. On the central part, let me be somewhat facetious and refer to an aphorism of Robert E. Lee's when he was president of Washington College in Virginia. He stated to his student body that any boy is worth more than any rule.

I find myself horrified by three hundred pages being winnowed down to half that, but I should like to go back to what I take to be Mr. Silber's concern: How odd that Columbia had not learned. As he talked, I thought back to my own freshman year at Columbia when a late and distinguished professor of classics engaged me in an argument on tragedy. He took me back by saying that the astonishing thing to him was that, having been told by the seer that he was doomed to marry his mother and kill his father, Oedipus proceeded to kill the first man he met and marry the first woman he met. I think what happened at Columbia and at other institutions is close to that.

The kind of homeostatic state we have in universities today leads to a great deal of discontent on the part of students and faculty who want something more Dionysian. The same students who come to me in wrath saying I have taken away their issues are essentially saying that they want a Columbia whether there are worrisome issues or not. A sizable number of faculty, including those who demand that the "weak-kneed administration" bring the police in, essentially wants the turmoil and the aphrodisiac effect that a Berkeley or a Columbia provides. There are those who crave the drama and the histrionics of the moment of disruption.

HURST

Determining the constituents of legitimacy involves juggling a number of factors. The experience of about 175 years of imperfect, but reasonably workable legitimacy in our legal order seems to me to indicate four constituents that are involved in some of the examples we have talked about. A legitimate social order involves the successful assertion of a legitimate monopoly of violence in one place. It is a contradiction in terms to say that you can have legitimate diverse sources of violence. Second, this legitimacy embodies the notion that we call constitutionalism in our tradition. It is basically the idea that a legitimate social order is one in which there is no center of power (defining power as actual ability to control the wills of other people) where the definition of the goals and the means to the power lies solely in the hands of the immediate power-holders. This notion is somewhat paradoxical, but a society must have organized enough diversity so that there is never any single unchecked source of power. Third, and closely related to this, is the value that is challenged by your Dionysian students, faculty, administrators, and trustees. I think our experience with social and legal legitimacy includes the idea that there is a sense in which observance of procedure is in itself a matter of substance. It is naïve at best and dishonest at worst not to see that there are substantive values in procedure and in the way in which you proceed to your value allocations. We have certain notions about what legitimate procedure is. It should be based on rational search for evidence, on an effort to apply reason to the evaluation of evidence. Evaluation, however, should be conducted with a decent deference to the dignity of the individual human being. Fourth, along with the legitimate monopoly of violence which we put in the hands of the policeman, there is the power to tax and spend. This power is a symbol of the idea that one cannot maintain a legal order by repression; it is maintained by affirmative structuring of the situations to desirable ends. Legitimacy is quickly imperiled if power is held and exercised only in negative ways. The only long-run way to maintain legitimacy is by positive responses to demands of the society.

Such a dramatic example as the Columbia situation must not blind us to the necessity of looking at other situations in normal contexts, because the legitimacy of reactions against the system has to be weighed in terms of the context of the system being reacted against. At Wisconsin we have an imperfect system, but it does provide means for affirmative response to demands. The critical fighting issue at Madison in the last couple of years has been essentially the challenge of some of our students and faculty to the substantive value of procedure. I think there has been a great deal of either naïve or dishonest belief that one must seize a building to raise the question of whether the university should hold Chase Manhattan stock because there are no procedures for getting an examination of the university's investment policy. This seems both naïve and dishonest to me because when these people first made this demand, they took over the building. In this context the situation at Wisconsin has been somewhat easier to handle than the Columbia one because if the issue comes down to a refusal to abide by imperfect but workable and rational procedures for value definition and decision, you have a concealed form of totalitarianism. We do have to be prepared at some point to assert the legitimate monopoly of violence, recognizing that this calls for great sophistication and skillful tactics because of the difficulties of controlling the police.

PAYNE

The whole discussion of legitimacy and of rules loses the interest of students rather fast, particularly when what is involved is the protection of the rear flank of the administration. Surely students have an interest in the fairness of the rules. They cannot be expected to participate in the rule-making process simply to keep business going as usual. Students do take the responsibilities of citizenship too lightly. But I am not upset that students fell away from the task Mr. Silber outlined. We are not meeting either the problem of what used to be called student apathy (and is still very much with us) or the problem of the student reaction to desperate boredom—the Dionysian impulses that Mr. Meyerson mentioned. It does not make much sense to talk about due process to people who want change. We need new forms of governance because we need new kinds of things. You have to recognize that students are interested in creation or destruction—not in any kind of stasis.

Higher Education in Industrial Societies

Participants
Joseph Ben-David
François Bourricaud
Asa Briggs
Mauro Cappelletti
Michel Crozier
A. D. Dunton
Baron John Scott Fulton
Pierre Grappin
Stephen R. Graubard
Walther Killy
Yoichi Maeda
Martin Meyerson
Elting E. Morison
Victor G. Onushkin
Talcott Parsons
Alessandro Pizzorno
Marshall Robinson
Edward Shils
Sir Solly Zuckerman

Very few of those who attended the first session of the Conference on Higher Education in Industrial Societies were personally acquainted with many of those who had been invited. It seemed important, therefore, to have some agenda prepared for the group so that the discussion might proceed more easily. A very brief agenda, prepared by Professors Talcott Parsons and Stephen R. Graubard, was circulated. It read:

Might we begin by reflecting on certain of the more important differences that presently exist between systems of higher education in the major industrial societies? These differences are explicable, in part, by historical circumstances, but also, in part, by the various current situations in the respective societies. It would be a mistake to imagine that the differences will soon be rendered insignificant. Nevertheless, all these societies are today confronted by a common set of problems, and there is increasing pressure to deal with these situations with some reference to what others are doing. Universities, less isolated than they once were, participate in both a national and an international culture.

If our first purpose is to consider how they differ, our more urgent task is to think of how they are presently faced with and responding to common problems. First, how are they reacting to the pressures imposed by numbers? Higher education, until recently, was thought to exist principally for an intellectual elite that was often also a social or political elite. Does the democratization of these institutions imperil traditions and curricula that were never instituted to serve such large numbers? Can these traditions and curricula be adapted to the needs of the new student populations? Will new kinds of institutions have to be invented to accommodate many of those who seek admission? Will new kinds of elite institutions have to be founded? How should a system be differentiated by types of institutions? What is going to happen to the old "professoriat"?

Indeed, what are the variations and changes already present? What are the implications of these changes for the professions? Ought we to anticipate a substantial transformation in the way that men and women are educated for academic life? How will the effort be accomplished to perpetuate competence among those who teach in universities? Is there likely to be increased pressure for a division between teaching and research roles? What are the principal hazards as well as the advantages of such a division? How can institutions of higher learning accede to the demands of society to educate a larger proportion of the young and at the same time maintain tolerably high levels of competence in research and training fields that are not intimately related to the education of these vast numbers?

Closely related to the issue of numbers is the larger issue of social demand. In a situation where public expenditure for higher education is certain to grow rapidly, the question of how universities or research organizations organize and maintain their independence of public authority will become more complex. Increasingly, the assumption may well develop that universities ought to "serve" the community that supports them, and not only by offering a modified apprenticeship system to the young who are being prepared for professional life. The demands on these institutions will grow not only from those who study and teach, but also from those outside who may be expected to assert a more proprietary interest in the institutions they are being taxed or otherwise pressed to support. What kinds of autonomy will universities and other such institutions be able to maintain in this situation? Are we witnessing only the beginnings of vast state-financed systems of higher education? What advantages may be expected to accrue from this new large involvement of the public in the affairs of the university? What disadvantages, if any, may be anticipated? How will the climate of opinion within uni-

versities be altered by this development? Will there be a new emphasis given to the "useful" studies, whether they be in the sciences or elsewhere, and a de-emphasis of what may be regarded as luxuries —for example, the "pure" sciences, the arts, and the humanities?

Universities have long been engaged in the training of practitioners in the principal applied professions, from the clergy through law and medicine to engineering. What is the future of this function, and how does it fit with research training and the general education of the more enlightened citizenry?

The dynamism of the intellectual world to some extent casts universities and their personnel in the role of agents of change and critics of any given status quo. Can we generalize about this role with reference to change? What are its implications for the relations of universities to the rest of society, especially government? Must they face new pressures toward intellectual as well as political conformism? But, equally, must they learn to use their enhanced influence more responsibly, and how?

Finally, are new kinds of structures developing that will make the last third of the twentieth century as significant a time in the history of institutions of higher learning as the last third of the nineteenth century proved to be? What are these structures likely to be? How will they affect the more traditional kinds? What "institutional inventions" are most urgently called for now? How can we imagine seeing them accomplished?

GRAUBARD

In the fall of 1964, in what I now think of as the pastoral period of university existence, when all was calm, and if there were clouds on the horizon, they did not appear to be storm clouds, *Dædalus* published a volume called "The Contemporary University: U.S.A." Recently I had the good or bad judgment to reread that issue. The one question uppermost in my mind was who among us saw what the likely concerns of university men would be in the year 1968. Some of those who wrote for that issue were more sanguine than they would wish to be today. But in my preface to this issue, I began with the following statement:

In a time of rapid change, when almost all institutions assume new forms or show evidences of strain in seeking to accommodate themselves to unprecedented situations, there will always be a certain amount of disagreement about what in fact is taking place. The profound transformations that have occurred in American universities during the last two decades are very reasonably the subject of discussion and controversy. While certain of these changes give promise of unparalleled opportunities for research and inquiry, making possible service to society on a scale which would have been inconceivable before the Second World War, it is not always clear what "price" is being paid for these advantages, or what their ultimate institutional and personal effects will be. It is generally assumed that most of these innovations serve to improve American higher education. The evidences of curriculum reform, new sources of financial support, and the multiplication of libraries, classrooms, and laboratories are certainly impressive; the results of this vast expansion of effort must one day soon show themselves in the lives of those who gain from the new opportunities offered.

In rereading the last sentence, I wondered whether I believed that they *must* or whether I was actually saying that they ought to. All of us are aware of the vast explosion in university populations. With this vast explosion, certain university systems, the American among them, have imagined that they could prepare for the initial demands of these new persons by a proper construction of new buildings—mostly classrooms, dormitories, libraries, and the like.

In the period before Berkeley, many universities in this country felt proud precisely because they had not been caught short in providing facilities. But it is perfectly obvious today that the problems of university education are no less serious despite those facilities. In other words, in a country like Italy the facilities do not exist. One is simply taking the old vessel and throwing numbers of new people into it, making modest curricula reforms with almost no real recognition of the new kinds of people who are coming into the universities. There one feels, and quite properly, that this essential provision for the new university population was never made. In the United States and in the United Kingdom, that provision was made; there were new buildings. And yet we all sense how acute is the problem in all of these societies—both those that have provided the physical facilities and those that have not.

It might be profitable to begin our discussion by talking about whether any of our societies have been able to provide for these vast new numbers. Have we, for example, given enough attention to what is implied when you take essentially elite institutions and attempt to make them popular institutions by simply saying that they can accommodate so many more than they had accommodated before? What does it mean when instead of a few institutions that take the bulk of those who are preparing for the positions that universities prepare for, you suddenly have a vast proliferation of these institutions? What happens in the end to the profession of teaching? Alfred Knopf, the publisher, remembers that before the end of World War I, you could bring together in a single room every historian who imagined that he was doing something and therefore had some interest in what someone else might be doing. As a result of the vast influx of students and the unparalleled expansion of university faculties, anything that we may once have believed to be true in the way of colleagueship, in the way of relations between students and faculty, is clearly in question today.

Thus, I should like to see us begin by discussing this matter of numbers. How much are we all beset by the problem of numbers? How well are any of us coping with numbers? Are we simply accommodating new and larger numbers, or are we indeed establishing new kinds of institutions where these numbers can be educated and feel some security about the kind of education that they are receiving? And most importantly, how are those who provide the education and do the research responding to this vast expansion of the university world? This issue seems to us in the United States to be critical; perhaps it is not so important abroad. Thus we might perhaps start with the problem of the democratization and popularization of our universities. This change has occurred within the adult lifetimes of people in this room.

PARSONS

Not only have the numbers increased in this country, but the people coming to institutions of higher education are from very different social backgrounds than was the case only a generation or so ago. Perhaps that is less conspicuous in the United States, because we have had a system of social stratification somewhat different from that of Europe.

375

ZUCKERMAN

May I just add a rider to what Mr. Graubard said, since he singled out the United Kingdom as being the exception? The United Kingdom did in fact try "to control" up to a certain moment in time. In practice this ceased to be possible following the governmental decision to implement the Robbins Report of 1963. Up to that moment, we had tried to assess what the rate of expansion of higher education should be in relation to the potential demand for graduates. Today we are, I think, suffering from the same kinds of problems that are being experienced in other countries; and controls are mainly financial.

BRIGGS

From what looked to be simple mathematical projections of likely future demands for university graduates, we passed in Britain in 1959 to looking at the supply of people with what were thought to be the right university qualifications from school. Then from about 1964 we started more or less gearing the number of university places to the output of people from schools who had what were held to be the minimal entrance requirements to get into universities. Given this kind of background, I believe that it is important to talk about numbers before one starts talking about social composition; and I would have a lot of *caveats* to make before I assume that the most important aspect of numbers is social. While there are certainly important changes going on in the social composition of universities—changes that may affect their mood and style—I consider that many of the changes taking place in the expanding universities work irrespectively of changes in social composition. They may, in fact, be the result of changes in the attitudes of the people who come from precisely the same groups who formed the university population before. I think one must test very carefully the assumption that the new student from the working class or the lower-middle class is responsible for troubles of universities.

PARSONS

I did not mean to imply that change in social composition is the only or even the most important consequence of the vast increase in numbers; I merely wanted to point out that it is one.

BRIGGS

I entirely agree that we ought to talk about it, but at a later point. The first issue would seem to be whether in the expansion of systems of higher education you deal with the problem of numbers simply by multiplying students within roughly the same number of units, whether you introduce quite new units, or whether you develop new institutions that are not university institutions. According to the answers that you give, a different resource allocation is involved, and you will get different kinds of universities. We have had examples in every country both of an increase in size of existing units and of new university units being brought into existence, and we should start talking about numbers within the limits of these mathematical exercises. Social composition can then be considered as we get involved in the qualitative aspects of university expansion.

CROZIER

Having faced the same kind of problem, I would like to come back to the point of social composition. Some of the trouble that has developed in French universities starts in institutions where the social composition of the people is upper-middle class. We should think about the social origin of people, but we also have to think about the place people will find in life and the way universities are preparing people for a particular social class. People at Nanterre had expectations that were not at all fulfilled. The students from upper-class origins went to the university with the expectation of a kind of elite arrangement and found something that is no longer elite at all. They were terribly frustrated, and much more so than the students from lower-class backgrounds. I would agree with Professor Briggs. I suspect social origin in itself is not so important. In France, as in England, we have not called in many people of working-class origin or from the lower income levels.

MEYERSON

I should like to return to Sir Solly Zuckerman's point on a self-regulating system that presumably existed in the United Kingdom before the Robbins Report. At the risk of being brash, I should like to suggest that so many of the ills that the United Kingdom suffers from are directly due to that presumed self-regulation of educational demand and supply. The spread of education has been, in very large measure, the key element in the economic advance of the Soviet Union, Japan, and the United States. Tremendous numbers of people have had a set of experiences that have not always led to elegant intellectual results, but they have led to two terribly important things: either to the acquisition of a whole set of scientific and related knowledge that would enable major economic advance to take place or to a change in class position and class expectation.

Half a century ago, you did have an elitist situation. This did not mean that only those who came from an elite origin were in universities, but that those who went to universities could have in the future certain elite roles in society. We are now reaching a point—the United States is probably closer to that point than any other country—in which half or more of the people will expect to have some kind of higher learning. I am suggesting that this model of mass higher education is very appropriate for a country that wishes to have a sophisticated level of economic development. One of the ironies is that so many of the protesting students are saying that they do not wish to have that kind of sophisticated economic development and would as soon dispense with it. This view is, of course, their option; it may indeed even become a societal option. Until it becomes a societal option, however, I would suggest that advanced education is the major means for transformation within the economic sphere.

The United Kingdom achieved its initial industrial advances at a time when the populace generally was not particularly well educated, and the universities utterly scorned the life of trade, the life of the economy. Today, however, economic development does demand an educational level that only universities can provide.

BEN-DAVID

Everybody assumes, because there have been troubles at certain universities, that there must be something wrong with the universities. I would put forward the suggestion that perhaps there is an ecological component here. The site of the problem may be the university, but its cause may not be. For instance, if I take the situation in the United States right now, more than 40 per cent of the age group between eighteen and twenty-two are at the universities. As a matter of fact, they are conscripted into the university; if they ever want to get ahead in life, they cannot do anything else. Thus, the population that is potentially the most active politically is at the university. They have plenty of time. They live away from their parents, usually, and have the fewest obligations and personal responsibilities. So if one had to ask oneself where a social revolution would take place in such a society, one would have to answer the university. Any trouble that gives rise to social agitation will take place at universities. Places like Berkeley and Columbia in this century are the parallel of Paris in the middle of the last century, when young people from all over France who wanted to seek a new future congregated there. If they did not find society to their liking, they made trouble.

According to a survey of a representative sample of Berkeley students conducted in November, 1964, the following distribution of answers was obtained to the statement:

Although some people don't think so, the president of this university and the chancellor are really trying very hard to provide top-quality educational experience for students here.

Forty-four per cent strongly agreed, 48 per cent gave moderate agreement, and only 5 per cent disagreed. Among militants, the percentage of those who disagreed was 12. To a question on how well they were satisfied with "courses, examinations, professors, etc.," one fifth replied that they were very satisfied and another three fifths said they were satisfied. Only 17 per cent expressed any degree of dissatisfaction. Thirty-two per cent of those who were very satisfied, 29 per cent of those who were merely satisfied, 33 per cent of those dissatisfied, and 40 per cent of those two in a hundred who were very dissatisfied were militants. [Cf. Robert H. Somers, "The Mainspring of the Rebellion: A Survey of Berkeley Students in November 1964" in Lipset and Wolin (eds.), *The Berkeley Student Revolt* (Garden City, N.Y., 1965), pp. 549-50.]

To a large extent this process is being repeated in the United States. I would not generalize this to Europe. All attempts to use the student disturbances at American universities for the purpose of constituting basic reforms at the university have failed, and we now have four years of experience. As soon as the troubles started at Berkeley, a number of disaffected staff immediately adopted the F.S.M. and pointed out the ills of the university according to their own beliefs. But according to the surveys conducted during the early stages of the movement, even the activists showed great satisfaction with the administration, the quality of teaching, and their teachers. Their subsequent apathy toward the various educational experiments is further evidence that this was not an issue.

There is no concrete sign that there is something basically wrong with the present structure of the American university, except perhaps this fact of conscription. One ought to rethink the absolutely unfounded custom that every person has to receive a formal education, a diploma, and that all have to go through this experience at the same age.

The problems in the American university reside in parts of the university and not in the whole of the university. The university's function has changed for a certain proportion of the students; even ten or twenty years ago, much of college life in the United States was very different from what it is today, especially at the elite universities. Then many people went to Princeton or Yale for the same reason that they used to go to Oxford or Cambridge: to have a good time. In the course of their stay, they also received some education, but it was not terribly important what education. This was an extension of adolescence and a kind of socialization too. Now the universities and the colleges attached to universities have completely lost this concept. They are now creating kinds of professions and an underground college culture that are potentially deviant and disruptive because many young people do not find anything that they want in a university.

Other students perhaps should not have gone to the university because they are too mature for it. I think we can recognize the type of person who is now among the university activists. These are small, marginal problems if compared to the university as a whole, but they can be disrupting and we have to face them. One should not generalize and start thinking that there is something basically wrong with the universities.

I also want to point out the problem of staff. If any generalization can be made about student disturbances here, it is this: A serious outbreak occurred in cases where a considerable number of staff not only condoned but actually implemented the eruptions. These two groups are not fighting the same war; they have quite different objectives and quite different ideas and ideals.

MEYERSON

I should like to ask Professor Ben-David why Israel is almost the single exception throughout the industrial world of a nation in which the university students have not exhibited the dissidence that we know so well from Tokyo, from Warsaw, from Prague, from the London School of Economics, from Columbia.

BEN-DAVID

Unfortunately the answer to this question is very simple. We might have the same problem as the European universities have because, from the point of view of our educational policies, we are somewhere in the Channel between France and England. Universities in Israel have expanded in much the same way as the European universities, without giving much thought to the proper facilities or to the quality of the education. We have not had dissidence simply because our students have a more serious war to fight.

ZUCKERMAN

May I refer back to Mr. Meyerson's comments? I agree with him fully that advanced university education is a prerequisite for economic advance. But other conditions are just as necessary; not one of them by itself is sufficient. The question that still comes to my mind is whether or not we necessarily need the large battalions of university graduates for economic advance. Are the bigger numbers qualitatively the same as the smaller numbers of yesterday? Mr. Graubard mentioned in his opening remarks that there was a day when one could get all the meaningful historians into a room this size. Once upon a time I knew everybody in England who was doing endocrinology; indeed, I helped start the Endocrinological Society in our country and its journal, as well as the first society in England for the study of animal behavior and its journal. I am not certain that knowledge is now being advanced at an increased rate proportional to the increase in the numbers of scientists at work. Nor, indeed, do I believe that more significant questions are being raised.

I was a member of the Barlow Committee in England, set up after World War II to consider the expansion of the universities and the need for more trained manpower. We came to a very quick conclusion; the war had shown that there were not enough scientifically and technologically trained people to deal with the technical problems that had been generated by the war and the phase of postwar reconstruction. Our recommendation was that the intake of the universities should be doubled as rapidly as possible. The committee was not a committee of scientists, and we had to make certain obeisances to old tradition, and one of them was that if the universities did increase in size, they should not necessarily be distorted from the pattern that they had enjoyed up until that moment; that there should also be an intake into all other faculties equivalent to the intake into the science faculties. Needless to say, as you well know, the intake into the other faculties was greater than the increased intake into the science and engineering faculties. I recall a friend of mine in the Treasury, who had to help persuade the Chancellor of the day that the money should be forthcoming for this expansion, warning me that as the universities expanded, we were not going to increase the proportion of first classes coming out of the universities on anything like the scale that one would expect from the increase in total numbers. Nor did we.

One problem in England may not apply to other countries. An enormous number of our science and engineering graduates has been absorbed into an aerospace industry which had grown greatly as a result of the demand brought about by the war. It is still responsible for a big intake of trained people, and this has not necessarily been to the economic benefit of the country. I mention the aerospace industry; another is the nuclear industry. At the present moment, we are spending about fifty million pounds a year on nuclear R and D of one kind or another, using the best people we can in a field where there is enormous competition and so far little payoff.

Another result of the great increase in the output of university graduates is the great increase in the volume of so-called research that is pursued. I was pleased to see that a vice-chancellor in England has recently commented that far too much mediocre research is now being done in many universities.

So I return to the basic issue: Is it not possible to conceive of some better controls than those that have been discarded? I accept that the diffuse market mechanism is no way of handling the problem. Professor Ben-David has implied that some of us who were at universities in the thirties and twenties went there because we wanted to have a good time. In those days the British universities had an extremely distinguished record in scholarship and turned out many who helped advance the economy. Even so, I would reject the older market mechanism.

After the Barlow Committee reported, I became the chairman of another committee, whose work was subsequently dismissed in something like two sentences in the Robbins Report. We had tried for every bit of nine years to devise techniques to see whether or not one could get some prevision of what the rate of expansion should be in relation to the social and economic development of the country. Most were inadequate, and the last one did not have a chance to be tried. In effect, the Robbins Committee said all such attempts are hopeless. Their report went on to say let us now throw the universities open. With what results? I am not talking now about student unrest, but of a period of very cold weather for the universities due to a lack of financial resources. The United Kingdom economy cannot sustain the rate of university growth that is now demanded, any more than it was able to sustain the rate of growth of our Atomic Energy Authority, which at one moment ran at 15 per cent. Physical facilities are falling off; staff remains a difficulty.

But what about the practical effects of the vast expansion of the universities on the economic state of the country? I have looked at some new figures that show what the immediate trends are. At this moment in time, the rate at which university-trained people are heading into industry is increasing fast, and has been going up over the past four years faster than anybody could conceive. Yet the performance of the British economy still leaves much to be desired. I, therefore, should like to know whether or not it is necessary to consider just one kind of higher education when one considers economic advance.

May I end with a tangential observation? A fortnight ago I was written to by a distinguished headmaster in England, asking my advice about a sixteen-year-old boy in his school who happens to be a brilliant mathematician. He has already taken an external degree at the University of London and got a first. The following question was put to me: Should he go to a university and possibly be destroyed trying to broaden his education? I wrote back saying be careful about broadening his education. In a century there may be four mathematical minds which can penetrate new veils and transform knowledge. Don't broaden his education at the moment: wait and find out whether the environment of a university would not blunt his genius.

I therefore return the question to Mr. Meyerson: Must we really educate the whole public as a necessary condition for economic advance? Does that mean that the doors of a university must be wide open?

MEYERSON

I thought it would be unbecoming not to defend the American national honor earlier this morning; thus, I made a case for an egalitarian mass-based higher learning. If we do not use a market mechanism or a kind of surrogate of the market mechanism, what mechanism are we to use in allocating resources for universities? Certain patterns are evolving throughout the world whereby increasingly the resources for higher learning are coming through government funds in a combination of national and state or provincial sources. Those allocations are being made not by the market, but by certain presuppositions as to what a university ought properly to be doing and what its priorities ought to be. The independent latitude of the University Grants Committee in Britain is altering considerably. The counterparts of the U.G.C. in the rest of the Commonwealth are probably becoming even more rigid. The Australian grants committee has formulae as to what ought to be, and Mr. Dunton knows the provincial formulae that are used north of the United States, formulae that build in certain sets of expectations. With the exception of only a handful of institutions, American universities, whether public or private, are now dependent on public aid. With each year that goes by, there will be more dependence on public aid. This public aid will increasingly have certain expectations built in—namely, the more students, the better; the more scientific and technical work, the better; the more students from across class lines, the better.

MORISON

If you begin with Professor Ben-David's proposition that not everybody who is at a university is appropriately there at this moment, you can begin to think about ways of dealing with the numbers problem. There are probably two parts to that question. First, what is the appropriate structure of the university if it is to be a distributor of talent? It may be overloaded now in trying to obtain too many different kinds of talent and disperse them too widely into appropriate places in the society. One has to ask oneself what the shape and character and purpose of universities ought to be today, and then one has to ask if there are many students who within this definition are not appropriately there. Where ought they to go? What appropriate alternatives are there to university training? In many instances such alternatives would require the invention of new kinds of institutions. You have overloaded the universities because there is nowhere else to go.

BRIGGS

Before we ask questions about the future, we must begin with the system as it existed before new strains and pressures were put upon it. If we are talking about whether there should be other kinds of institutions to deal with certain categories of people, then we have got to take into account the position, say, of the *grandes écoles* in France. We have got experience of alternative ways of handling groups of students in the past. Before we get to the fascinating point of the social pathology of university students at the present time, we have got to clear away the resource allocation pattern in straightforward quantitative terms. We have to face the marked contrast between, for example, the British way of handling numbers and the Japanese way of handling numbers.

After all, the notion of a university *system* is a relatively recent one. Different constellations of institutions have been emerging with uncertain goals. The first bit of sorting out that is needed is more study of the components of systems, before we get to critical points about determination of future policy. We should ask questions about whether the embryonic systems that are emerging are satisfying the needs and the demands placed upon them at the present time.

PIZZORNO

We have been talking so far too much of a university system as such and not about university relations with the society. We are looking for causes within university systems and do not see that everything probably comes from outside in a way. We should try to see if the position of the university in the society has changed very much and, more specifically, if the relationship between the university system and the professional complex has changed. I think that the real causes of the strains on university systems are changes that have taken place in the professional complex. As Sir Solly pointed out, even in a period of economic stagnation, certain industries exert more and more demand on manpower. In the thirties in Europe, there was a low ratio of degree-holders to total population and, at the same time, there was unemployment among degree-holders. Now we have an increase in the economic growth rate, and yet there is almost no unemployment among degree-holders. On the contrary, we have an increasing demand for degree-holder manpower. Somehow, the whole economic system has been distorted. You can do almost anything in a modern society, but only with very great difficulty can you keep down the output of the university. This is really the only point that the whole society agrees to accept as some sort of a constant. If we look at what happens to the ratio of administrative employees in industry, in the whole society as such, we see this continuous increase as a very abnormal phenomenon. In a way there is an artificial relationship between university and society. Much of student questioning of societal goals comes from their awareness of the artificiality of the equilibrium between society and university.

DUNTON

Mr. Chairman, I think to some extent we are talking about different things. Certainly Sir Solly is looking at something else; perhaps that is partly a reflection of the different philosophy of higher education in Britain. As in many things, Canada is between the United States and Britain so far as opportunities for numbers of people are concerned. Since World War II, the primary function of universities in Britain has been to turn out highly-trained people. The typical honors graduate of an English university is presumably capable, if he has a first or second class, of going on to professional work in that field. Even if he goes into industry, he should be capable of operating as a professional. The sociologists tell us that we are now moving into a post-industrial era. I suggest that universities always should provide opportunities for people to become highly skilled as research scientists or as historians or as classical scholars. But we should also be allowing young people to leave universities not as specialists, but with a strong ability to adapt. We deliberately ought not to train for some existing piece of research. We ought to try to sharpen their minds so that they can go on learning and do many jobs that will not necessarily be in industrial production, but in all kinds of services and activities. I suggest that one of the big questions before us is what educational opportunities in the universities should be, apart from the obvious one of turning out the people who go on to Ph.D.'s.

ROBINSON

Asa Briggs clarified the problem by stressing the idea of system. We are told from time to time in this country that California is an indication of what the United States as a whole will be like in about twenty-five years. So far as I can tell the system of higher education in California has emerged to a rather high degree in response to folk values. There has been relatively little planning, until fairly recently. But there has been a conviction that education somehow was good and should be provided for virtually everyone who manages to show that he has the capacity to operate in that kind of environment. The environment is not well defined, but someone on the outside can clearly see that there is a well-established pecking order; the natives, however, seem to go on blithely innocent of the elitist elements in the system.

To a considerable extent, it seems to me that this characteristic runs through higher education in the United States. Somehow we have convinced the citizens of Mississippi or Nebraska or Utah that they should be happy with the University of Mississippi, Nebraska, or Utah, and they send their children to it, and Harvard goes on and does its distinctive work. We have allocated certain of the most important functions of the universities to a very few universities. For the most part, these few are private universities. Indeed, Berkeley, the greatest exception to the private university-excellence correlation in the United States, was almost a historical accident, which is rapidly disappearing under the tender ministrations of the processes that are making California more like Nebraska. We have in general been willing to turn over a high proportion of the quest for knowledge to a handful of institutions. A certain amount of the purposeful quest for knowledge, which is sought by governments and corporations, we allocate to another group of institutions. The rest are large multi-purpose higher education institutions, where the central function of the faculty is simply to keep up with what is going on so that they can do an adequate and responsible job of teaching.

Such a system requires an arrangement in which the academics are not very close to the social decision-making system. They cannot be in a position to determine what should happen to whom and indeed what the system itself should be like. It is my impression that what passes for educational planning in this society has for the most part been done by people who are not learned, though many of them have gone to institutions where those wares are made available. They are not manpower planners, though some working suggestion that education and economic development may be important is surely a part of what goes into the thinking on the subject. Because academics have not played an important part in educational planning, we have escaped for the most part the propensity to make each new unit a replica of that which the academic knows. Most men's educational philosophy is autobiographical.

MEYERSON

I have always regarded California as a developing country. You have in California a history of university life and of higher education more generally that reminds me of Edward Shils' monograph on the intellectual in India. The kinds of roles that historically have developed have been very different at different points in time. At the end of the nineteenth century, Henry George, the social critic, could write that the University of California was a place where the taxes of the poor went to support the education of the sons of the rich. The shift that has taken place there has been an extraordinary one. There was a rather self-conscious view on the part of the political leaders of California that education was the second great resource of the state, the first being its climate. There is a conscious sense that certain kinds of consequences will follow if education becomes a major effort in public investment. Those claims are constantly made. Even the people who oppose the University of California at Berkeley are still very much in favor of other levels of the higher learning in California. They point to the aerospace industry in California and a whole series of economic achievements that they believe would not have taken place without huge public investment in higher education.

The notion that the pecking order of the status system of California higher education is not perceived by the members of that system is, I think, inaccurate. The students as well as the staff in the universities, four-year colleges, and two-year institutions have clear understandings of their status. You enter the university if you are in the top eighth of your class; you enter the state colleges if you are in the top three eighths of your class; and you enter the two-year colleges if you are in the residual category. If you are at a university, you can have graduate students or at least doctoral students; if you are at a four-year college, you may have a few graduate students, but no doctoral students. Thus, there are status distinctions that possibly can be hurtful.

I should modify Marshall Robinson on another point as well.

There is a fair number of public universities today in the United States that are probably equal in the level of their scholarship to all but four or five of the private universities, but those public universities may suffer a decline in the period ahead. State legislatures may become less disposed to provide funds for what they regard as erring students and erring faculty.

I think we have been dealing with global phenomena in our discussions, rather than with what happens within the components of universities. I should like to use the illustration of medicine. Most American professors of medicine and physicians will look with great pride at the Flexner report of half a century ago. This report pointed out the dismal character of American medical education, the lack of facilities, the lack of a scientific base for medical instruction. The report concluded that there had to be a tremendous diminution of the number of medical schools; indeed, the author determined that all medical schools were properly to be at universities. As a result of this report, there was a reduction in the number of medical students. The Johns Hopkins University developed the first of the great American medical schools, and it became a model for all American medical schools. It is a rare university in this country that has less than about one quarter of its budget going to the medical school within the university.

The kind of planning that took place was planning by the guild of medicine, and it was a national kind of allocation essentially in the hands of the physicians. They are, of course, thoroughly delighted with the outcome, but I should like to raise in contrast engineering, which in the United States, unlike some other countries, is located far less in the technical institutes and much more within the universities. At the time of the Flexner report, one could have argued that engineering and medicine had remarkable similarities: Universities had schools of engineering and medicine in great profusion; the resources for each were modest; students could with great ease get into either kind of school; and the scientific base for each was of a most casual character. Since then, medicine has become more and more demanding of resources and seemingly the quality has gone higher and higher. I say seemingly because one of the social consequences of the planned constraints on medicine has been an extraordinary shortage of physicians in the United States. This shortage is so severe that it is a rare city in the United States in which the hospitals could function if they did not have their medical interns and residents from Europe and from Latin America and Asia as well. In all but a handful of hospitals, very many of the medical people are now from overseas. Thus we have built up an exquisite kind of selection, as a result of which the rural areas go without medical care and hospitals depend greatly on the brain drain from abroad.

In engineering there has not been this central planning by the guild. The universities that had engineering faculties half a century ago continue to have them. If a student wishes to study engineering in the United States, he is almost certain to find an institution that will accept him. What are the social consequences of the use of that market model? During the half century you have had a sharp differentiation among the schools, so that the best engineering schools have developed more and more of a scientific base for themselves. The most capable people have come typically from a handful of engineering schools, but a tremendous number of people who fill necessary roles within the social system of the United States have gone to the lesser schools. They make up the critical middle group without which American technology could not function; in medicine there is no middle group. Indeed, the general practitioner is disappearing in the United States, so that we have the anecdote about the woman who goes to the physician with a cold and he asks which nostril is disturbing her so he can decide which of his colleagues she should see.

I could have used the case of law, rather than of engineering. The law clerks or assistants to the Justices in the Supreme Court of the United States essentially come from, at most, half a dozen of the country's law schools. There are occasional exceptions, but they are rare. But you also have endless other opportunities for legal study.

I make this case for the virtues of a kind of market mechanism of allocating places and resources as against some kind of central decision-making mechanism primarily to stimulate discussion.

PARSONS

In the medical case, should one not also mention the Rockefeller Foundation?

MEYERSON

Yes, it would not have been possible to have had the Johns Hopkins Medical School without the Rockefeller Foundation.

ZUCKERMAN

The Flexner report also had an impact in the United Kingdom. But the situation that led to the Flexner report was the feeling that there were medical practitioners who were not qualified to

389

practice medicine. There were people around who were putting the public at risk and something had to be done.

MEYERSON

That was the case. Nevertheless, the consequence of the report was the creation of a domestic corps of magnificently qualified physicians who became more and more specialized and turned increasingly to research rather than to practice, with the result that we are essentially staffing our hospitals with the very kind of people that the Flexner report was so concerned that we eliminate.

ZUCKERMAN

Flexner might have added a rider to his report saying that while we want to see that all medical practitioners are properly qualified, there ought to be a second tier of *feldschers*. We have precisely the same problem in England; if it were not for the people trained in medicine from Pakistan, from India, and from other countries, we too would not be able to run our hospitals.

MEYERSON

This issue relates to the social-class problem that Michel Crozier and others have mentioned. What should one call this second tier of engineers? Engineers or draftsmen? Given the social egalitarianism in the United States, it would be most difficult to get anyone in the second tier if it did not have professional status. Many people called engineers are performing a kind of *feldscher* role and yet we give them professional status. Similarly in medicine, we would have the greatest difficulty in creating a subsidiary group of paramedical personnel of high quality in the United States if we did not give them professional status.

BRIGGS

I think we should look at the three possible ways of extension implicit in the notion of increasing systemization. The first way is increasing the size of the individual university units within the system. Here there has been a marked divergence between the European or American experience and the British experience. There have never been very large universities in Britain; there was no great pressure on the universities that were already reasonably large to become very large when the question of expansion was mooted ten years ago. They have all grown, however, and as they have grown, they have undergone organizational strains and some changes of pattern in the process of growth. But they have not been subjected to the complete strains which have so affected European universities that, as several people have claimed, they may destroy the conception of the traditional university as it has been inherited from the past. In all systems there has been much growth concentrated within some of the existing units, but there are differences within the different systems.

The second way is creating new university units. I myself would want to draw a sharp distinction, however, between the creation of totally new university units and the upgrading of institutions that have previously had some kind of subuniversity status. Here again there are differences of approach among countries and different university systems. In some cases, new universities are being brought into existence without any system of tutelage. This was true of my own. Sussex was created because it was decided that the total number of university places in England was inadequate and that new universities were needed. Once it had actually been created, however, it was free to move along the lines that it wished; in fact, its own planning was, to a large extent, autonomous planning. It was limited planning in certain respects, but the fundamental approach to the curriculum and the organization of the university were freely determined. It is important to look into this question of the upgrading of old institutions and the making of new ones with attention to the degrees of freedom that are open to new universities.

Thirdly, we cannot forget the point raised this morning by a number of people. This concerns the third way—the creation of new institutions that are not universities in the ordinary sense of of the word. In all our countries there are institutions serving specialized, limited purposes. In England there is a whole constellation of institutions—ranging from colleges of education at one end of the scale to technological institutions of various kinds with subuniversity status at the other. These institutions fall into the higher education system as it is evolving, but do not have what is called university status. Clearly there are differences in status in different countries. In some countries, the structure allows for more or less the same names being applied to the qualifications given by these different bodies; in other countries, you have quite sharp differentiations. In all countries, I should guess that the sharpness of the qualifications has been diminishing somewhat in recent years; certainly in England this is the case.

If you look at these three ways to expand a system, bear in mind that your adaptability depends on the way you start off. If you look at the expansion process in this way, then you are dealing with questions with "ought" in them, questions about the new kind of institutions you *ought* to found, about adaptability and variation within structures.

Another set of questions concerns the disposition of resources among the different units. Clearly, in certain cases the existing units have been expanded so sharply that resources were inadequate to make the expansion pattern possible without friction. If there had been no student revolt of any kind, there still would have been financial and administrative problems arising out of growth.

Yet we have to look not only at the relationship between expansion and resources, but at the relationship between these institutions and social need. Can we, in fact, produce certain kinds of new institutions that are subordinate to or different from universities, but which will meet certain categories of need more effectively and more quickly than universities might? This problem has been posed in the United States and certainly in England, where there has been talk of the development of a completely separate non-university sector of higher education, including polytechnics and other institutions. In theory such institutions would be able to react more quickly to assessments of national need than the unisities could. I have never seen any very satisfactory figures in relation to Britain about relative costs of development along those lines. Without cost figures here, it seems to me the practical policy questions are not easy to answer.

CROZIER

I should like to comment on the policy from a slightly different point of view. Asa Briggs has emphasized the tendency of all the different institutions of higher learning to become part of a system. Higher education was integrated into a system in France much earlier than it was elsewhere. I fear it may be extremely dangerous to overemphasize the necessity to integrate. If you do, you run into problems of a different kind related to the possibility of having responsive institutions. This issue raises the difficulty not of seeing the system as a whole, but of seeing each institution as one whole system which is answering particular needs. From a certain point of view one may consider wasteful certain activities that from a a longer view would not appear to be so. Mr. Meyerson's remarks on medical education and the Flexner report are relevant here. In many different countries, once you have professions, they tend to use their monopoly over a certain kind of knowledge to their own advantage. Once you have an integrated system, it is terribly difficult to prevent monopolies from developing. So I would advocate some type of sophisticated planning to develop a market mechanism to offset the guild monopoly.

BRIGGS

I was not, myself, doing anything more than describing the problem. I am a great advocate of freedom for diversity within the system, and I am in complete agreement with Professor Crozier. For example, if a new university is tied too completely to the practices of existing institutions, it will not release the creative power open at the start of a new institution. I would, therefore, want to look closely at the conditions within which a new institution is purported to exist so that I could be sure that it would have the power to innovate. It is important for a university not to have too much of a blueprint. It is also important for it to have access to more than one source of finance. The vice-chancellor of such an institution must be an entrepreneur as well as an organizer. The danger about upgrading old institutions is that they often start with an inferiority complex and, therefore, a certain lack of creative power is built into them. From the start, new institutions of a non-university kind have been thought of as being in some sense inferior institutions. The idea that we can get around all our problems by creating a completely new genus of institutions is too simple an answer. We are striving for a system that enables a community to dispose of its resources efficiently, but at the same time allows for creative initiative within the component parts of the system.

CROZIER

The efforts to rebuild the university system in France have run into terrible trouble due to established patterns of patronage. Each new institution is an offshoot of an older institution. Most of the planning has been only a discussion about who is entitled to do what. These institutions have been completely lost as active innovators.

MEYERSON

I am fascinated that we have not yet had any discussion of an international system of higher education. In the medieval world we would have assumed that the world of learning was indeed one that crossed national boundaries. Today, when the world is much closer not only in terms of time, but in other important respects as well, we have little sense of an international university community, of an international system of universities. The medieval student normally would have expected to be at more than one institution in the course of his education; that is not the expectation today. Indeed, in some of the countries represented around this table, it is most difficult for someone who is not a citizen of that country to hold a chair. France would be a good example of that.

My next point is of a very different order. We must distinguish between system as a descriptive concept and as a prescriptive one. My own field of study is that of cities, and we do deal with systems of cities. We could describe the system of cities in each of our countries, and in each case there would be a strong reflection of a series of other patterns within our countries. It is no accident that in France the system of cities has a hierarchy that is similar to the university hierarchy with a tremendous preponderance on the primate city of Paris. But that approach is different from discussing a prescriptive system of cities. I can point to a developing country in the world that concluded there had to be a rank order of cities, and because it was missing certain cities within that rank order, it had to create them. The result was a failure in resource allocation, because there is no cosmic mandate that there must be such a sequence of cities any more than there is a cosmic mandate that there must be a certain sequence of universities and other institutions of higher learning.

Nevertheless, we are moving more and more to prescriptive national systems, because the national state is increasingly becoming the key source of support for universities. It is essential that we try to consider the allocative principles that ought best to be used. The great difficulty in trying to establish such an end system is that we tend to think of most public goods as being instrumental. If we invest so much in transportation, it will have certain tangible benefits. In higher learning we have much less sense of what these benefits are. The tendency, again, is to attempt to put them in instrumental terms. Perhaps universities can contribute to economic development or to certain other purposes, but what we must achieve is a set of allocative principles based much more on the intrinsic characteristics of education, rather than on the instrumental role that a university can play.

We now recognize that the central authority will enter more and more into the resource pattern of university life. How can we make sure that that central authority operates in such a way that we avoid a rigid system and provide an opportunity for wide autonomy? How, in Michel Crozier's terms, do we stimulate a kind of market mechanism by using public aid? A number of us in this country have sharply contended that the consumer of higher education has the best sense of what is intrinsically as well as instrumentally valuable in a university. Let the student have the vote by assessing him whatever charges there may be. If he cannot pay those charges, see that he gets sufficient funds through loans or grants or a combination. There are many dangers in that kind of quasi-market mechanism, but I should like to suggest that there are far greater safeguards in that kind of policy than exist in other methods of central decision-making.

Higher Education in Industrial Societies

One can envision a Sherman Act for higher education whereby any university that had a monopoly position in the market would be broken down and share the market with another university. I believe that the Department of Justice starts to interfere when any firm has more than 20 per cent of the market in a certain product. There is no single institution of higher education in the United States that has a monopoly position in this sense. Neither Harvard nor any of the elite institutions produces 20 per cent of a given type of product, as would be true of the University of Tokyo or Oxbridge in relation to the higher civil service.

SHILS

I want to comment on the Sherman Antitrust Act and its application to universities. The Sherman Antitrust Act was intended to curb the powerful. The proposal Professor Ben-David is making would curb the inferior institutions. It is not the leading universities that have the monopoly of the output of postgraduate students. The proportion of the output of Ph.D.'s from the leading universities is shrinking relative to the total output of Ph.D.'s in the country. In quantitative terms the center of development is moving away from the major universities. The biggest departments, with the largest numbers of Ph.D.'s, are not always the most distinguished. Would one want to break up the most distinguished departments because they are producing people of better quality? And what difference would it make to break up the less distinguished departments, many of whose graduates do useful research and perform beneficial services for society?

The question of the differentiation of the higher educational system raises the question of the flow of influence among the universities, and this raises questions of autonomy. The question of the permissible and desirable degrees of autonomy of universities has come up in our discussions repeatedly. That seems to me to be one of the central questions that we face here. As long as there was a system of units that were not highly competitive with one another, many places slumbered indifferently of one another's accomplishments and were satisfied with what they were doing. There was a hierarchy of canon; but a position lower down did not injure the self-esteem of those in the lower ranks. They were therefore immune to the pressure of the model of the greatest, and in that sense they were independent. There were centers of initiative and of creation that provided the models which then diffused to other universities. Now, because of increased dependence on central sources of finance, a new kind of system has emerged in which the different units form a whole. Of course, it can never be a totally unified system. In France until recently there was more or less a single system, but even there it was not completely a unitary system. Complete self-government or autonomy of universities has not always been a wholly satisfactory thing under all conditions; on the other hand, the complete central control that existed in France was not satisfactory either, and it has finally broken down. In reaction to the French system, everyone is execrating central control. Yet the complete freedom of a university from any sort of control or pressure from the outside might also lead to a state of slumber. The freedom of Oxford and Cambridge up until the middle of the nineteenth century was complete, except for restrictions on admitting dissenters for degree programs. What kinds of autonomy ought to be safeguarded in the growth of the national system? I agree completely with what Asa Briggs said about the need for multiplicity of sources of financial support; nonetheless, the main source will, I think, increasingly be the central government, at least as far as this country is concerned. For other countries, the central government is practically the entire source.

PARSONS

We have been talking about the institutions other than the full or standard university, and I hope this theme will not be lost sight of. The British technical colleges are one type with a relatively definite vocational focus; the American junior colleges are quite a different type. Both of these stand in the academic pecking order well below the university. In France the phenomenon is reversed; the *grandes écoles* seem to have preempted prestige away from the university. Michel Crozier's article in *The Public Interest* [Fall, 1968] points out that the universities in France are below certain other institutions in the prestige order, and that this might have been one factor in the genesis of unrest at the university level.

A somewhat similar problem arises with reference to the organizational segregation of a city. Powerful forces are operating in the American scene to pull research into the university. The Rockefeller ex-Institute/now-University case is a striking example; it does not want to remain segregated. The Soviet Academy of Sciences enjoys a special position; it is not organizationally part of the university system. This pattern is repeated in a number of other countries, with modifications of course. A colleague of mine said casually not long ago at a lunch table that with all these Columbia and Berkeley situations, there is going to be a major movement in the United States to set up separate research institutes where people are not going to be bothered with unrest. This prediction raises interesting questions as to whether or not the delicate balance between being separated and privileged and yet responsive to demands and subject to certain controls is at all stable in any of our systems. If it is not a stable balance, which way are changes likely to be going?

CAPPELLETTI

Degrees of difference emerge from country to country, but it is fairly clear that there is a differentiation of superior-inferior institutions. The technical schools arise out of the need for vocational, professional, practical training. You will train people in a more practical way in such schools, but they are not universities. At the same time, these proliferating institutions tend to become universities.

PARSONS

That tendency is very strong in the United States.

CAPPELLETTI

My second point is on research. I have spoken recently with friends at N.I.H. [National Institutes of Health] in Bethesda. I asked them what are the advantages and disadvantages of being at a research institute. They said the first benefit was that they teach very little and are free for their research. They also said that government determines the direction of their research only up to a certain degree. These men had been professors in a great American university before going to N.I.H. They all felt that their freedom for research was greater at N.I.H. than it had been in the university. Thus I should like to ask whether or not we are facing a time in which high-level research has to be concentrated in some type of special non-university institute.

MORISON

To touch on another aspect of Mr. Cappelletti's remarks, the technical schools in this country were started by and large at a time when they answered a direct need—teaching people how to run machines. They have had an interesting history since. Five or six have remained at about that level, progressively becoming third-, fourth-, and fifth-rate as intellectual institutions. Two of them have become, as it became increasingly obvious that technology rested on science, more and more speculative within the fields of science and engineering. They both also have struggled hard to retain themselves as specialized institutions, I think mistakenly. Both would do far better to become general universities for two reasons: Their research would profit by the spirit of the university, and it is excellent for engineers and scientists today to be part of a general civilizing experience. If it were my decision, I would not even consider C.A.T.'s [Colleges of Applied Technology] now. Rather, I would consider altering existing engineering schools so that in time they would become universites.

In reference to another point Mr. Cappelletti made on the creation of separate research institutes, I think we could demonstrate that research does not flourish in this country as a separate enterprise; it has to be tied in some way to the functions of learning and instruction. Moreover, the dangers of a pure research institution becoming hooked to purposive research are very great. You might wind up as a government lab with diminishing returns in your intellectual life because you would increasingly be restricting your investigation to what was needed at the time.

ONUSHKIN

I should like to make some comments on the problem of utilizing market mechanisms in education. I am not against using some elements of the market mechanism (for example, economic stimulation) inside the system of planning, but I do not quite understand who, from Professor Ben-David's point of view, would be the customer—the students or the society? If it is the students, I am against such a market mechanism, because it will not create a situation of social justice. The students who are going to buy knowledge, or the services of higher education, in any case should know that they can use the knowledge that they are going to get; inevitably this means that they should have more or less clear perspectives. If they do not know whether or not they will be able to apply their knowledge, there will be a waste of scarce resources. Perhaps the optimal situation would be the combination of central planning and the initiative of different universities, but the customer should be the society as a whole—not just individuals.

BEN-DAVID

Another point on which I should like very much for you to say something is the relationship between the Academy in the socialist countries of East Europe and the university.

398

ONUSHKIN

In developed countries, there is a tendency toward universalization of higher educational institutions. These countries, and to some extent developing countries also, are getting more and more full universities. As Professor Parsons remarked, the problem of the combination of teaching and research is extremely important, and this combination of teaching and research is one of the main features of the modern university. I cannot imagine the university without research. Yet, at the same time, in some countries, like the Soviet Union or the other socialist countries, there are special organizations that are preferred in research work and are doing only research work.

Basic research and some applied research are being done in the Soviet Union at the institutes of the Academy of Sciences and at universities. The division of labor is not strict between the institutes and the universities because the people who are doing the research at the Academy of Sciences often also teach at the university. Similarly, many university professors do research at the Academy of Sciences. At the same time, there is a system of research institutions for applied research and development; these institutions are under different industrial ministries. The Academy of Sciences is responsible for the coordination of basic research; it works together with the Ministry of Higher Education.

The money for research at the universities comes from two sources: from the Ministry of Higher Education and from industrial contracts. The State Committee on Science and Technology coordinates the applied research and development for the whole country.

Until two years ago, all the universities and the institutions of higher learning were under republican Ministries of Higher Education. At the same time, however, we had the Union Ministry of Higher Education which coordinated the work and was responsible for the development of the whole system of higher and specialized secondary education, the high standards of training of specialists, methodological problems of teaching and research, publication of periodicals, textbooks, and so on. Two years ago, the Union Ministry of Higher Education decided to have its own universities and institutions of higher learning as experimental bases. The Ministry has chosen for this purpose a number of universities and other institutions of higher learning from among the best of their kind. These are Union universities, and they are the focus of experiments—curricula changes and so forth. The Ministry generalizes the experiences and invites the republican ministers to employ them. Universities under the republican ministries certainly can also go to the Union Ministry for advice.

KILLY

Medieval conditions still prevail somewhat in Germany. All our universities are financed by *Länder*. These states are coming to realize that a modern university is an expensive affair. Some are able to finance their universities; others are not. We are moving out of this situation because the legislature is trying to help the, so to say, underdeveloped *Länder* finance their universities by supplying up to 50 per cent of the financing out of federal funds. Although the university in West Germany is a state affair, there are quite a lot of other sources of income, both official and private. Among the official sources is the so-called Forschungs-gemeinschaft, a current foundation of the German university which gets its funds from the Bund and is a self-governing body. This organization tries not only to finance research, but to emphasize certain fields and to even out differences that might arise. Foundations are not so important in Germany as they are in the United States, but the Volkswagen Foundation and, to some extent, the Thiessen Foundation are doing a lot of good things. All this is, as you know, not sufficient and we are trying to blue-print the future by means of two bodies: One body is the so-called Wissenschaftsrat, consisting not only of academics, but of public figures as well. This body has an efficient staff and tries to analyze the future but with, I am afraid, not much success. One of the main problems, especially in the sciences, is that up to 70 or 80 per cent of the financing comes from private sources, very often industry. These big industries cannot be controlled by the university and might influence the liberty of research in a detri-mental way. We are trying to get this under control, but it is going to be hard.

One drawback should be mentioned. We still have an annual budgetary system, and this is absolutely nonsensical because, as you know, we need much bigger planning, much more time for planning. I think we can, however, overcome this difficulty within the very near future. I am personally involved now in an attempt to found a private university in Germany that will have a built-in buffer between its financial sources and its governing body. I am not sure yet whether we will succeed with it.

PIZZORNO

I should like to describe just one new way of allocating money to universities in Italy, for the general pattern is not far from the German one. The new way is the pattern of allocating money through the National Research Council. There are two ways, it seems to me, in which the method of funding is particularly important. First, purpose can change because of the structure that has received the money; second, the relationship between teaching and research can change.

The National Research Council is divided into seven or eight sections with a committee for each section. The allocation is decided by the general committee of the Research Council. Only full professors can apply for research grants; if you are not a full professor, you have to have the signature of a full professor to apply.

These funds are meant for research, but everyone knows a goodly part of these research funds goes to the universities. You receive the money for a research project, but a large percentage of the project's funds goes for general expenditure which is meant for the university itself.

SHILS

What is the proportion roughly?

PIZZORNO

It ranges greatly. In sociology, we are rather honest in our accounting.

Even though there is a central planning authority here, the allocation still flows through the channels of a baronial structure. Thus, money that should go to research directly is allocated by an administration that has nothing to do with the university as such. The administration that allocates funds for research is, in fact, weaker than the universities and, through the power of the baronial structure, some money which should go to research flows into the old university system. When you have such a strong local structure at the bottom, it does not help to have a central planning authority. You cannot go against this structure; after all, this local structure elects the committee and you have to keep up good relationships with them.

To speak to Mr. Shils' point about the multiplicity of sources of funds, the money comes from many sources. Although about 95 per cent comes from the state, there is always support from local authorities. I do not see that the university in Italy is much affected by the origin of the money.

SHILS

When I raised the question about the multiplicity of sources, I had two aspects in mind: on the one side, the protection of the

401

autonomy of the university from excessive pressure from one single institution that would have its way with the university and, on the other, a tendency toward disaggregation of the university, with staff members using the university as a bookkeeping convenience. Of course, where the university is already as disaggregated as the Italian universities are, there is no *esprit de corps* anyway. Yet *esprit de corps* is necessary to a university to keep it focused on its central tasks.

GRAUBARD

Perhaps M. Bourricaud might say a few words on the situation in France.

BOURRICAUD

This topic is rather complex due to the present university conditions. I should like to start with certain little disputed points of fact. First, the *grandes écoles* are the core of the system. Second, at least until 1950, about 40 per cent of the students were registered in the faculties of law and medicine. Third, law was taught at the undergraduate level. Fourth, the research organization was more of the Soviet type than of the Anglo-Saxon type; research and university activities were clearly divided.

The university itself was run and managed according to the most tightly centralized pattern of administration. It is extremely difficult to understand how innovation or change could enter into such a picture, especially because the show was run not so much by the central authority, as by the corporate body of the professors—the academic profession.

Most of the personnel was financed through the state budget. The only way to get something new was to create new positions, although even then the procedure was rather long and complex. The initiative had to be taken by the local faculty or university group asking for the opening. The request had to be brought before the central agency, which would have to make that request in line with the budget and ask the local faculty to designate such and such a person for the post. The final decision would be made by the Ministry after a special corporate committee had been asked for advice. Thus, the whole thing was in the hands of the central administration on the financial issue and in the hands of the corporate group as far as personnel problems were concerned.

As far as research is concerned, basically two distinct branches of the state were interested. The central authority in the Ministry of Education provided the university with funds for minor research. The Centre Nationale Recherches Scientifiques was operated apart, though most of the people who were the barons within the university system were also the barons in the C.N.R.S. In the Italian system, research money has to be spent within the university structure; in the French system, it has to be spent outside. In sharp contrast to the Italian situation, no funds come from regional authorities. We have some territorial political authorities, but until now they have not made appropriations to universities. And finally, foundations are, for practical purposes, ineffective in France as the money they can spend is very small.

GRAUBARD

Mr. Onushkin, would you care to give us an idea of the situation in the Soviet Union?

ONUSHKIN

The number of students in higher education in the Soviet Union is 4,311,000; this number includes full-time students, day-time students, and evening students. There are three kinds of institutions of higher education in the Soviet Union. When I speak of institutions of higher learning, I do not include the specialized secondary schools.

The institutions I will describe are university-level institutions. First of all, there are full universities; then polytechnical institutes or universities; and third, specialized institutions of higher learning. There are forty-two universities in the Soviet Union. All the republics have their own universities, and some have several. There are 433,000 students at the universities, which means that about 10 per cent of all the students are in the universities. Despite this rather modest representation, the universities play the leading role in the higher educational system because they combine teaching and intensive research.

The universities are the only educational institutions that combine natural sciences, social sciences, and the humanities, and this is a particular feature of the university. In specialized technological institutions, for example, the social sciences and humanities are taught, but the research in these fields is not at such a high level.

The universities usually have faculties in the natural sciences, the social sciences. One of the important new features of the universities in the Soviet Union is that the leading universities— such as the University of Moscow, the University of Leningrad, and the University of Kiev—now have special institutes for improving the qualifications of the young professors or teachers from the other higher educational institutions. As you know, the young professors can carry the greater part of the teaching load of the universities. That is almost the universal situation and the reason why they do not have enough time to do research work. Thus, it was decided in 1966 by the government that it would be useful for the younger professors and, as a result, for the whole system of higher education to create special institutes to improve the qualifications of the young professors. As a rule, they spend half a year in such institutes. They do not teach at this time; they participate in discussions, do research, consult leading professors, and so on.

The polytechnical universities, of course, combine different fields of the natural sciences and mathematics. There are fifty-three polytechnical institutions in the Soviet Union.

The third part of the structure of the higher educational system is comprised of specialized higher educational institutions —technological, medical, juridical, economic, and so on. As a rule, these institutions concentrate in one definite field. Of course, the development of science and technology creates new fields; and specialized institutions, such as technological or engineering institutions, become more like engineering universities. The same is true, I should say, for medical institutions, which become more and more medical universities, teaching and doing research in different fields of medicine and in some aspects of biology, physics, and mathematics. The results of all these sciences are used in medical research.

There is a Ministry of Higher and Specialized Secondary Education in the Soviet Union, and this Ministry is responsible for the planning of higher educational developments in the Soviet Union. The Ministry is also responsible for the methodological part of higher education—the preparation of textbooks and so on. This creates a general curriculum for higher education which tends to be the same in all higher educational institutions in the Soviet Union. I should like to stress "it tends to be," for the level of training is not absolutely the same because it depends mostly on the quality of teaching staff, and this is not the same in different institutions.

Some of the universities, most of the polytechnical institutions, and most of the specialized higher educational institutions are under Union Ministry of Higher Education or under the corresponding ministries in the Republics. Some establishments of higher education are under a special ministry, such as the Ministry of Health or the Ministry of Agriculture. Some industrial ministries have their own institutions. Nevertheless, the tendency is for higher education to fall under the jurisdiction of the Ministry of

Higher Education. This means that some of the specialized higher educational institutions are under two ministries.

From this description, you can see the system of finance. Almost all the higher educational institutions are state institutions, financed by the central government or the republican governments.

The general rule is that all faculty members divide their time equally between research and teaching. Certainly this distribution of time is relative. Because universities are financed from the budget of the Ministry of Higher Education, university research is financed directly by that Ministry. But the universities also have the right to have research contracts with industrial enterprises. For some fields of research, these contracts are becoming a more and more important means of financing. Certainly, from the general point of view, both sources of funds are state sources because industrial enterprises are state organizations. There is a difference, however. The universities can choose the research projects for themselves, and they can get money for this research from an industrial organization.

One area to which a great deal of attention is devoted in the Soviet system of education is that of the continual improvement of the quality of education. The rate of scientific and technological development is so high that the universities face great difficulty in training people for the future and not for yesterday. Equally to be included in this domain is the same approach to the qualifications of the teaching staff themselves. There is also the question of the contacts between the higher educational institutions, research institutions, and industrial enterprises. The exchange of ideas in this area was one of the main foci of the reform initiated several years ago and still under way.

On one of the evenings, Dr. Pierre Grappin, the former Rector of the University of Nanterre, was invited to join the group. His account has such interest that we have given it in full, as he has revised it in fall 1969.

GRAPPIN

Nanterre was created in 1963 essentially because of the great numbers of French students. There were, of course, new principles, but the essential idea was to double the existing faculty. Those who made the new university did not make it exactly on the model of the old. The new principles that we have tried to apply consisted first in the materials that are taught. This is a very important point, as it could have a great influence on our future. In the course material, we gave a much greater place to psychology and sociology than has been done in any other French university. We had incontestably the most active departments in these fields in France. This policy responded to a real need; one for which there was a great demand among the students and one which corresponded to the character of the present world. We put the accent on the "human sciences" and the "social sciences." Furthermore, we tried to have a method of teaching that was simple and direct, close to the subject, and without constraint. In the first year, we were able to do this because we had enough professors in relation to the number of students.

It must be underlined that the environmental conditions for Nanterre were very bad. The university was a wholly artificial creation in a social context that was difficult to define. It was located in a wasteland; there were railroad lines, but practically nothing else except a few colonies of squatters living in board huts. In the first year, we were able to overcome these negative factors by giving to the professors and the students the feeling that they were in the process of doing something totally new, that they were building for the future. For this reason, we were able to obtain very appreciable results and without real opposition from the students. Thus, we were able to create a university experience which was the first of its kind in France and one which was often of interest to people elsewhere. We were able to unite the learning process and daily life for the students. We were able to create a place for the students to live near the place where the teaching went on. And we did this for a very large number of students— 1,400 in 1965, half of them girls and half of them boys. In France this was a wholly new experience. The young people who were brought to live in this place had few conveniences. This was the milieu in which the new radical opposition was born. This opposition was born among the students who lived in this place because they felt themselves without guidelines; they felt themselves to be rejected by the society and that they were living in a sort of "slum" and not a normally constituted society. This represented the essential milieu from which the disorders sprung.

For me it was a tangible reality. The first violent incident that I had anything to do with took place in March, 1967, at the Cité Universitaire. On this occasion I saw for the first time someone I did not know. I did not know him, but an employee of the house next to mine knew him. He was to become famous in the years to come; it was Cohn-Bendit. He was there in order to direct the revolt against the regulations governing the Cité. They wished the abolition of all regulations, and because of the protests, the regulations have been completely abolished. At the students' residences at Nanterre, the students can do exactly what they wish. But in March, 1967, at least in my opinion, that element was completely new.

Actually, we had attempted more than one innovation at Nanterre. We tried, for example, to introduce an element that was completely new to the French university—the students living and studying in the same place. For this change, we evoked examples from the Anglo-Saxon countries, all of which you know well. We also wanted to involve student and faculty participation in this enterprise. This succeeded for two years, but was suddenly destroyed by the boys who lived at the Cité without professors. Only students live there and no professors. These students constituted a group that was no longer amenable to anything. Quite naturally they wished to make something from the situation they were in. Starting in November, 1967, a communal society was constituted there, as if on an island.

The elements of the second milieu in which the confrontation was organized, with a revolutionary affirmation, was the milieu of department of sociology and also of psychology. I saw the first signs of the revolt when torn-up lists of students were brought to my office in order to show me that from this point on it would be impossible to have any form of regulation or central authority over the teaching that would be given.

Exactly a year ago a large movement of *revendication* began among the students. It was concerned with professional questions, those issues having to do with the university. The students also complained that there were too many of them. In 1967 there were five thousand new students, and there were close to eight thousand students already enrolled. In 1964 there were only two thousand; in 1965 there were five thousand; but at the beginning of the term in 1967 there were close to twelve thousand. This is a large number of students, given the fact that many things were lacking: We did not have enough professors or assistants to teach them, and so forth. The movement, therefore, was concerned with professional questions, those having to do with the university. Its leaders arose spontaneously—at least that was my impression—and did the best they could. This movement lasted about eight days and then it dissolved; I am not quite sure why. There were very large assemblies where I spoke; there was a delegation of students to the faculty council, and we found, therefore, a way of making contact. We instituted a mixed commission, with both students and faculty, to consider the disputed questions. It was necessary to wait several months before certain other questions once more came to the fore.

When the revolt began again in March, 1968, what was most striking was that the leaders were no longer the same as those of the preceding months. Those who had led before—and whom I knew—had almost completely disappeared. A change involving the movement's very nature had taken place. In November, 1967, we

407

had a movement within the student body that centered on questions concerning the university. In March, 1968, we saw an important, politically well-organized minority movement formed for a political struggle. Thus, the leaders were no longer the same.

In January there was a terrible battle. But in January, February, and the beginning of March, the revolt consisted of a relatively small number of organized students. By the middle of March and the beginning of April, when the students held public demonstrations or made speeches in the corridors or the classrooms, they had a very large audience of comrades. Then the movement became altogether different; a great number of students listened to speeches about razing to the ground the very principles of university education. From day to day, the demonstrations became larger, to the point where I think it would be inexact to call this a minority movement. At Nanterre a large number of students supported it, although probably for many diverse reasons.

The movement had several "natures" in the stages of its evolution. What was most striking about it was the facility with which a large number of young people—of diverse origins and of diverse aspirations—were veritably led to participate in it. They were fascinated by the idea of a social revolution and threw themselves into the movement without any kind of interior resistance, without often much sincerity, but with perhaps a kind of enthusiasm. This movement incontestably was originated by a very small number of people, but it echoed the thoughts of a much greater number.

CROZIER

I should like to add some comments on the change of mood M. Grappin has described. UNEF, the national union of students, had disintegrated, and there was general apathy. But small spontaneous groups were active on an informal basis, and the first leaders of the movement came from these groups. These leaders sought reform, but this was difficult to achieve as it would have disrupted the traditional *laissez faire* which meant a certain freedom for students. These leaders were the solid citizens of that community, but their efforts could not meet with any success because they were running against all the state machinery, because the university itself had no power of decision. Thus no solution could be found for them. The faculty and administration understood the situation, but our proposals were turned down by the Ministry.

Let us take the case of Cohn-Bendit. He could act as the victim himself. According to the compromise that was made, he was supposed to come into the third year. But since he had failed an exam the year before, he was put back into the second year. He became the representative victim and that was his first starting point. He was a revolutionary; he was agitating; he found an issue and won the support of the people who had grievances. He defeated the old leaders completely to the point that they just disintegrated and they became irresponsible. We tried in the sociology department to meet with them to discuss the situation, but they would not come to the appointments or they would disappear. We tried to meet them, but we could not find them; they did not represent anything that was real; and they were under attack from the extremists all the time because they promised a lot of things and nothing happened. After about two months of hesitation, the extremists picked up, and then the movement became something else entirely.

GRAPPIN

Last November the reasons for protesting were of a "technical" nature. The application of a new system of study made difficulties during the time of transition. These difficulties touched very few people. But the grievances they really had were much more vast, much more profound, and even these first grievances revealed the deep uncertainty felt by a great number of students about the French university system. For at least ten years, this system had remained quite extravagant; an absolutely uncontrolled number of people was allowed to enter, without anyone taking the trouble to know what they wished or what could be done with them. It is, in my opinion, a university system too far from its students.

One felt, at that moment, that these young people complained less for the precise reasons they gave than for a far more general reason—an all-pervading uncertainty. These events must be viewed with this understanding. Since January, 1969, the student movement has been led with much more political aims, in a tactic of constant provocation. They attempted to force the authorities either to abdicate or to retaliate. This movement was led, in a systematic fashion, by men who certainly had political experience and who were something entirely different than the young people who followed them. It is difficult to imagine that a young Frenchman, aged eighteen and a graduate of the *lycée,* could devise a political tactic so clever and so effective.

I was put in the position of having two choices open to me and only two: I could either annul my own position, my institution, my authority, or I could use force to enforce my power of decision. I did not wish to do either of these things, but I had only these two choices. The people who thought up this tactic were very intelligent. I do not think that the ordinary eighteen-year-old

French student is capable of concocting this. I assure you that the students I have known in the last ten years could not have conceived of a tactic like this because they were not interested in destroying the universities. Their revolutionary purposes did not concern the universities; quite a new kind of revolutionary tactic appeared among French students during the first months of 1969. These leaders felt that the French university system belonged in a museum. I understand perfectly well that the authority that reposed in me, as the head of a liberal university, depended entirely upon mutual consent, but I had no recourse, except force. From the moment people who respect absolutely nothing of a system's fundamental principles install themselves in that system, they can do anything they wish. They have absolutely no obligation to it. They pay very little—eighty francs per student. The university has no recourse: It can neither in practice limit the number of students nor forbid them to enter or to present themselves for an examination. This system depends entirely on the good faith of those concerned with it. From the moment that you find yourself confronted with people who—for whatever reason—have decided to ignore these rules, authority has no grounds on which to stand.

PIZZORNO

You said that in April the character of the *revendication* was completely different than it was later when it assumed a political aspect. In what sense do you mean "political"?

GRAPPIN

The students became radical in the etymological sense of the word. It was no longer a question of university regulations. They were attacking the fundamental principles on which the university—the society itself—was founded.

PIZZORNO

How did this attack manifest itself?

GRAPPIN

I talked with the students a great deal, even during the times of the terrible battles. They said to me that the university—all society —had to be made over. They offered as proof the following argument: You, who are an esteemed authority in the university, employ the methods of repression against us. These, I told them very sincerely, were the repressive measures they had asked for.

But the result was the radicalization of the movement. University society is the most open and the freest of all the forms of society I know. It is the form in which authority is farthest away and the most liberal; but the students demonstrated to themselves that even this society was founded on repression. In this sense, one could no longer speak of a possible resolution to the problem; the fundamental principles of society were involved. On this subject there are many possible variants: The war in Vietnam plays a role, as does the imperialism in which we are engaged. The crux of the idea is that we are a society that will use force and repression for the purpose of limiting each individual's particular talents. From that point of departure, they went on, for hours and hours, about individual creativity, a new method of teaching that would reinforce this creativity and not limit it, a new society that would be a place for creative people.

You have certainly heard discussions of this kind. The political element comes in. There was a small political faction in the large assemblies of students that was not in accord—Marxists, Maoists, Trotskyites, anarchists. The political transformation of this movement came when the movement itself became a radical critique of the society. This was the dominating theme in the end and was, incontestably, anarchistic.

ZUCKERMAN

In a way, M. Grappin answered the question I was about to put as he discussed the transformation of the attitude of the students and the emergence of a radical political objective. Given the existence of student upheavals in many countries, would you say that there is some sort of diffusion of this defiant kind of unrest? The London School of Economics is not yet out of its troubles. I should be very surprised if the political motives inspiring the young people in England were the same as those disturbing the young people in France or in the United States.

GRAPPIN

The elements most active in organizing the revolt in France were the politicized elements—the students who belonged to political groups.

KILLY

May I try to explain the difficulty? I am afraid that to an Anglo-Saxon mind this revolt is not worth being called political because it is wholly unreal. It is not of this earth.

GRAPPIN

It is.

KILLY

In your country and in mine, a strange or dangerous contamination has taken place between the political and the utopian, between the ideological grievances and the real ones.

BRIGGS

I first came across the term "imperialist-capitalist complex" in February, 1968, around the same time that the university grievances began to take political form in France. In England the language of the upheaval was exactly the same, as were the forms of organization, the talk about organization, the references to committees, to general assemblies, to coordinating committees. This was so even though only a very small minority belongs to the rebel group.

ZUCKERMAN

There is no other language?

BRIGGS

They have a language quite different from that of the 1930's. I should like to know just when communication at Nanterre between the university authorities and the students began to be increasingly difficult. I take it that in November, 1967, when the issues were essentially about the structure of the university and student grievances, there was communication; but that when the political issues began to become more prominent and different factions began to develop, each with slightly different approaches, communication began to be extremely difficult.

GRAPPIN

In November, 1967, communication did exist. M. Crozier underlined this. We not only had communication, but were able to arrive at an agreement rather easily. We had such a rigid university system that, so far as our university was concerned, we were not able to take the measures that we had been forewarned that we should take, measures that the rest of the French university system did not consider necessary. Communication was cut because of two facts: On March 5, 1968, I was besieged in my office by about fifty people, who had come to bring me a paper that I was supposed to sign, a paper that provided guarantees for freedom of political expression without reprisals. Furthermore, I was to give guarantees to the effect that there would be no reprisals in the grading of examinations.

I said I would never sign anything under duress, and that they should go back where they came from. I informed them that if they sent me an elected delegation, with men who could tell me whom they represented, I would be perfectly willing to discuss the issue. One of them replied: "From now on we will use guerrilla tactics against you. We will never tell you who we are; we will never be electorally responsible; we will have only secret and anonymous counsels." From that day on, the situation was impossible to control.

ZUCKERMAN

I should like to ask where the professors were during the month of March?

GRAPPIN

I will tell you something very funny. On March 5, two professors were nearby—one a professor of geography, the other a professor of French. The professor of geography has always testified that things happened as I have told you; the professor of French has forgotten everything.

MORISON

Much of what I have to say has, I think, already been touched on. We have spoken about the impact of research and also spent a lot of time on students, debating how the variety of students might cause the universities to alter their structure. We have also discussed other pressures of equally persistent and powerful kinds that may cause universities to rethink their structure and mission.

I should, therefore, like to begin my remarks by responding to Mr. Cappelletti's question of yesterday about the wisdom of having separate research institutions. Professor Parsons knows more about this than I and has more data, which I hope he will give. I can report, however, that historically the best work in research has been done within universities; for as long as the investigation of ideas was taken to be primarily an end in itself,

413

it was very useful to have students—not only graduate students, but undergraduate students. The exercise of converting research findings into ideas that could be transmitted to undergraduates gave a kind of validity to the work. If the training of graduate students is largely intellectual, the education of undergraduates has a moral component. The university is endeavoring to educate knowledgeable and therefore more useful citizens. The existence of this moral obligation—that is, to turn out more effective citizens—and the awareness of it anchored and stabilized research. For this reason, the history of detached institutions without students has been bad, on the whole, in terms of output.

I have some reservations now that this situation need necessarily continue in certain areas. My data are drawn from a special case, the Massachusetts Institute of Technology, where I was for twenty years. Increasingly while there I wondered whether the undergraduates were getting a reasonable return for their investment; I am pretty clear that they were not. The Institute, I should say, was without any qualification the most exciting and vivid intellectual community that I have ever been in. Most of its work was done in connection with the immediate needs in the society. It is infinitely responsive to what is going on, and the validity that the older universities found in converting their information for student use, M.I.T. found in converting information and research into immediate application in "the real world." It sustained itself effectively as a general investigating institution needing graduate students, but not so clearly needing undergraduates.

All universities have increasingly been under greater pressure to develop and refine ideas of immediate use. On the basis of my experience at M.I.T., the first question I would raise is whether or not you can sustain yourself in good health over a long period of time doing what I would call *ad hoc* research. The vividness and the excitement of that life I cannot understate, but it lacks a certain philosophical dimension, which I think is not simply confined to the Massachusetts Institute of Technology. One has to think rather more than we have of the meaning of the kind of intellectual work done in the most important fields today in the classical universities. What changes may be made in the quality of their life, in the character of the men that are doing the work, and in the general conditions in which knowledge grows?

There is a second problem not immediately so pressing or so interesting philosophically, but one that must be met in time. The projected budget for the year 1976 in high-energy physics in this country is $500 million. If you take this figure and then add to it some of the current skepticism about the returns from such research, you begin to raise questions of priority. Where, for example, does biology fit in relation to high-energy physics, in relation to geophysics, in relation to psychology? These are questions we have not had to ask ourselves up to now. Who will make this determination of priorities? Where will such determinations be made and on what criteria? We have no adequate data to enable us to make good decisions about putting funds into another great accelerator or into microbiology.

Finally, as has been reiterated over and over again, the money that is spent on research comes increasingly from federal sources and to a great extent for specific areas. What distortions will be created in the nature of our general intellectual life by this focus? As a member of the humanities, I believe this question raises issues that come close, ultimately perhaps, to the survival of humanities: The significance of history and of literature is harder and harder to discern in the present situation where money is available easily for certain kinds of things and not for others. I cannot leave this topic without saying that to the extent that the humanities have borrowed the procedures of the natural sciences and research, they have done themselves a profound disservice. One reason that the humanities account for as little as they do today in the university is the character, if not the quality, of the research and the meanings of their findings. Universities must think to an extent that they have not yet about the nature of research in those subjects that supply a general or cultural context. How far can these fields appropriately borrow from the natural and physical sciences? What kind of graduate training is appropriate in the humanities? I think we are sending out poor practitioners to deal with the questions of value in an industrial society by virtue of the kinds of things we are doing in the humanities.

Particularly in America, which has always been interested in application and engineering rather than basic science, we may be using up the reservoir of fundamental ideas. If not that, we may at least be in danger of training people who are not interested in enlarging that reservoir; we may simply be producing a group of practitioners and appliers. We may run the risk of working ourselves out of any inherited cultural context.

MEYERSON

I should like to try to tie Elting Morison's points to Ed Shils' comments yesterday on the disaggregation of universities. It is constantly claimed that the kinds of research funds that go into universities remove the academic man from the student, from the classroom, and from university loyalties. It is argued that research funding creates a set of loyalties that shift the academic man's fidelity to his research guild or to the granting agency. In the United States, relatively few universities are doing the expensive research. Probably a score of universities has the bulk of the doctoral students and the bulk of the federal research funds. Thus, the disaggregation, if it is taking place, is surely not taking place because these research funds are going into the universities. We see this disaggregation in endless institutions and not just in those institutions that receive the bulk of the research funds. Why do faculty members see their primary allegiance not to the university but to their guild? If this description is an accurate one, how long has it been accurate? When did this change take place?

We need case studies in considerable detail to decide what the transformation has been. Indeed if there is evidence of such a transformation, it is probably the result of the rise of graduate education rather than of the rise of research. If each of the 500,000 college and university teachers in the United States wrote a book every fifth year, more books would be published than are published in the English tongue. Obviously this situation has not occurred, and thus it is not writing and research activities that have caused the disaggregation. Nor am I not prepared to say that the disaggregation is all bad.

Finally, to touch on the difficulty of making large-scale allocation decisions: For several years some of us have been involved in helping to get started the two-hundred-billion electron volt accelerator in the United States. This will be the world's largest accelerator and will dominate high-energy physics. But why high-energy physics? Why this huge allocation in that direction? It is essentially because of the tremendous reservoir of goodwill that the high-energy physicists have built up for themselves. With the long history of nuclear accomplishment, how can the physicists possibly be wrong? Thus, we are breaking ground on this accelerator, and no one can predict the order of new knowledge that it will provide for high-energy physical research. Some high-energy physicists themselves feel that they have probably gone about as far as they reasonably can in uncovering new knowledge. We see the problem of a marginal determination here that quickly becomes a political determination, a political determination made not by the so-called industrial-military complex, but rather largely by the guild of high-energy physicists themselves.

ZUCKERMAN

I should like to address myself to the primary question which Elting Morison raised concerning the virtue or lack of virtue in separating research from university education. In general, on the basis of British experience, I would agree absolutely with everything that he has said. At this moment in time, research in Britain is carried out in universities and also in a number of institutes, paid for by government, which are devoted to research and not at all to teaching undergraduates. Some of these institutes are also concerned with development. There is some pressure at the present moment to attach some of them to universities or to give them certain university connections.

Let me give you an idea of the scale of the problem in the United Kingdom. Our scientific civil service employs some 12,000 professionally qualified scientists and engineers. Assuming a staff-student ratio of ten to one, this is equivalent to a student population of 120,000—something like half of the university population of England at the present moment. In other words, I am talking about a body of scientists as big as the body of scientist-teachers in the universities, if not bigger. They vary greatly in their scientific quality. The institutes lack the free flow of new young people that one experiences in a university department, and therefore a major stimulus in research. A colleague of mine, long since retired as head of a major department in Cambridge, used to judge the relative merits of candidates for academic honors by asking how fast the results of their research work were becoming incorporated in the curriculum for undergraduates.

Some of our governmental research institutes are extremely good—the biological ones, in particular, are good. These are small, and they all have to maintain close links with universities. The National Institute of Medical Research, for example, has a very close link, and in terms of achievement does much more than the others. These others, however, house the bulk of the army of twelve thousand professional scientists and engineers—institutions such as our National Physics Laboratory, our aeronautical research establishment, our radar establishment, and so forth. These institutions are not just devoted to applied work. Something like 20 per cent of their budget goes to basic research of one kind or other. Yet in general the scientific achievements of these people are poor—measured in terms of recognition—compared with the corresponding achievements of people working in universities or in institutions with close university links. I think secrecy and isolation are responsible here. Harwell, for example, thrived while it was extending and developing basic propositions of nuclear physics which had been developed mainly in universities, but when it went into the business of technological development and turned from the kind of fundamental research which one associates with a university environment, its role became so blurred as to require a new definition of its mission.

417

PIZZORNO

At least two important points were made by Professor Morison. One is the relationship between research and teaching, and the other one is the problem of incentive. I should like to describe two kinds of experiences that I have had: one in an institute more or less of the kind Sir Solly mentioned and the other in a graduate school. For seven years I worked in an institute that was supposed to do only research in applied urban studies; it had about seventy or eighty degree-holders in sociology, economics, urban design, architecture, and statistics. This institute was supported by local authorities, and rarely could one see a group of intellects of this distinction working together in an institute in Milan. The experience was interesting and distressing at the same time. The main purpose of this institute was to do research on the bad situation of the Italian cities, which meant a practical, useful type of work. Most of the institute's members were university professors. We had the right to publish everything we produced. Our official public was the public authority, but we did not care at all for their judgment. We still had the university public, our guild. We were in a very uncomfortable situation, because our real prestige came from the guild, although the immediate judgment came from the political world and the bureaucratic world to which we gave our results. The difficulties might have been tempered by putting some function of teaching into the institute.

The second experience I had for just one year at the graduate school in Milan. About thirty students were collected from all over Italy; all had done some scientific work. They were so bright and so demanding that they became the public; they became an alternative to our guild public. This was the ideal situation for teaching. Some of us devoted 100 per cent of our time during that year to this new public without doing research work just for the pleasure of being recognized by this public. At least in the first half of the year, we were pleased with this alternative public, but the public itself was not so pleased. The students wanted to have some sort of outlet of their own. They became somehow more at ease when they began to see the possibility of conducting research of their own—and not just for the purposes of acquiring information.

SHILS

I agree very much with what Professor Morison and Professor Pizzorno have said, but I think one aspect has been omitted. I hope no one will misunderstand me when I speak of the erotic aspect of the teacher's relations with students. The presence of young people—full of life and intellectual vitality—is extraordinarily stimulating quite apart from the intellectual contact. When people praise some members of the academic profession for their vitality, they often do not appreciate that much of that vitality comes from living in the animated atmosphere created by lively young people.

PARSONS

There are a number of points that I should like to speak to. First, in relation to Mr. Morison's statement, I have been engaged in a study of academic professionals in this country, and I think we have some interesting attitudinal confirmation that the combination of research and teaching is highly valued. [Professor Parsons's findings have been published in Talcott Parsons and Gerald Platt, "Considerations on the American Academic Profession," *Minerva*, Vol. 6, No. 4 (Summer, 1968).] The complications of interpretation that the data pose involve the stratification of the American system. People in the less prestigious institutions, generally speaking, have little opportunity for research, and many have very heavy teaching loads. It is not at all surprising that these people want more opportunity for research than they have. As you go up the scale, however, one finds among many scholars on fully or primarily research appointments a desire for more opportunities to teach. The general trend, as Mr. Shils noted yesterday, is for the profession as a whole to want more opportunities to do research, but this is largely a function of the stratification and the historic anchorage of the system in the teaching function, rather than of the devaluation of teaching in general. This phenomenon extends not only to graduate teaching, but also to undergraduate teaching. There has been a good deal of talk among the intellectual public about the flight from undergraduate teaching, but our evidence does not bear this out. There is certainly not an exodus from graduate teaching. But across the board, the respondents wanted their administrative loads lightened. Ideally they wanted to cut in half the amount of time they devoted to administration; this was true in all categories of institutions.

There is also a strong tendency to incorporate the whole range of the intellectual disciplines in university faculties rather than to specialize in one section. M.I.T. has moved from a technological institute to a general university with a technological emphasis. It has first-rate departments in political science and other social sciences. The California Institute of Technology is now also moving into the social sciences. You do not get in the United States schools of humanities or even schools—like the original conception of the

London School of Economics—focused in the social sciences with no natural science and little in the humanities. You get a strong tendency to the total range.

You also get another tendency, which may be motivated partly by guild considerations, to pull the professional training schools closer to the universities. This phenomenon started with the classical professional schools of medicine and law, but is now increasingly true of those in business administration and education too. I remember a former dean of the Harvard Medical School telling a story about President Eliot of Harvard. Shortly after his accession to the presidency of the university, he had the temerity not only to attend a meeting of the Faculty of Medicine, but to insist on presiding at that meeting. There was utter consternation among the medical people. They used the name of Harvard University, but they considered the medical school a totally autonomous thing. The Eliot administration brought the medical school into the university, which is a common story of professional schools in this country.

It is my impression that the strongest universities have gained greatly by being able to build on strong undergraduate colleges, and they have preserved the strength of those undergraduate colleges by and large. The University of Chicago went rather far at one time in de-emphasizing its undergraduate college and then came back again.

SHILS

It was not a de-emphasis of undergraduate education so much as it was a change from general education to preparation for more specialized study.

PARSONS

We have, I think, a cluster of aggregations in the American system that is in many respects different from the continental European system and more like the British. These aggregations are very deep-rooted in the system, and perhaps counteract somewhat the disaggregation, of which research entrepreneurship is probably the most conspicuous case.

MEYERSON

I accept Talcott Parsons' research findings, but would like to suggest that he would have discovered something vastly different as little as five years ago. For example, at one university, there were ninety-some research centers and institutes with people frequently promised a professorial appointment that could lead to an attachment to a research center or institute with little responsibility to students, undergraduate or graduate.

PARSONS

In our new sample we have data on Berkeley that have not yet been pulled out.

MEYERSON

But there are other examples of similar breaks in local fidelity. The events that started with Berkeley in very large measure have caused a tremendous sense of guilt among professors in America. Thus, throughout the country we find a widespread shift toward undergraduate teaching. The pattern of avoiding undergraduate teaching is now changing at university after university.

PARSONS

It is, of course, a variegated pattern. I have one sociological colleague who has made the assertion that nobody has ever assumed the burdens of parenthood voluntarily; of course, this is fantastically untrue. But what is motivation? It has to do, on one dimension, with the internalization of the role of the other in a dyadic relationship. Every human being has been a child and the child of particular parents. He has, in turn, internalized the role of parent. When he reaches the age when it is, in fact, feasible to be a parent, there is a strong motivational base for actually assuming that role. Every university or college teacher has been a student, and although by no means all students become teachers, among those who do there is a built-in set of needs to assume the teacher role that they experienced in relation to their own teachers when they were students.

MORISON

I want to reinterpose myself to sharpen and restate a point that I hoped that I was making. I feel that pressures are being brought to bear on the university today making increasingly difficult the task the university used to do in fundamental research. I am not to be put off by Mr. Meyerson's observation that federal money goes mostly to ten or fifteen institutions. They are the ones that set the tone for the country's intellectual life as a whole. The people in those determining institutions are subjected to strains that no human being can easily withstand—particularly when they enable them to do very interesting work. But I see a real change in the character of the people who are determining our intellectual life. They are energetic, interesting; they are people concerned with problems they believe to be terribly important; they are very bright and skilled in operations. They are a new kind of man, nervous and operational and working to the moment. And they set a tone that infects not only their own areas, but the whole spirit of the university in a way that makes me nervous about the task of protecting the quality of intellectual life in areas other than the ones in which they work.

CROZIER

We do not have in continental Europe the attitudinal aggregation that Professor Parsons has described. We have separate institutions, and there is difficulty in getting any interchange. I have been in a situation where I have suffered from not having contact with students. I could have two roles, but these two roles could not overlap. At one time in the week I was a professor and during the rest of the week I was a researcher. It was absolutely impossible to mix the two roles. If people say this is possible in France, I would challenge them. Thus, not all university systems would be amenable to the mix of research and teaching that has been advocated here. The continental European universities certainly would not be conducive to it.

We should be interested in the way the system as a whole operates. There are contradictions in any kind of institution. What is important to understand is how an institution can operate in a fruitful way regardless of these contradictions. I agree with Mr. Morison on what should be the character of basic research; on the other hand, the new roles of the operational leaders are extremely important. Behind much of this applied research, which has a lot of inconveniences also, is the challenge of the environment and the challenge of young people.

One of the achievements of American universities has been to keep the general system working and cross-fertilized in such a way that new roles develop without losing the old kinds of achievement. They manage it by recognizing the contradictions in the allegiances within the various groupings. Modern life means a lot more complexity. We must have our cake and eat it too.

BRIGGS

I am doubtful myself whether the right word is *contradiction*; perhaps *tension* might be better. It seems to me that there always are tensions in the relationship between teaching and research. Sometimes those tensions can be creative; at other times they can be positively frustrating. I am relieved that Professor Parsons laid emphasis on the aggregating elements in modern universities, because the disaggregating ones do get talked about. On the whole, however, the aggregating ones have been quite obvious. For example, in Britain when the new universities were being created, people who might previously have thought of themselves as being associated primarily with the guild began to be drawn into new sets of relationships because of the special identity of the institution that they were helping to create. The particular process of bringing people together, including people from research establishments, has produced extremely constructive interchanges.

The quantitative expansion of university places in Britain has been associated with more emphasis upon the teaching role than there ever was in previous periods. This is a difficult subject to generalize about. It seems to me that the position changes almost every year. There are always tendencies and countertendencies. I have noticed one or two tendencies that may be operating in the opposite direction from those which have been brought out in Professor Parsons' research on America at the present time. There are people in British universities who are saying—and I have never heard this said quite so strongly before—that the presence of young people is not so much a stimulus as a positive disadvantage in carrying out their own lines of inquiry. This is said particularly in some of the social sciences. There is quite a strong feeling that economists previously teaching and doing research in the university would prefer to be associated with an institute created, for example, to study economic development. This tendency is also beginning to appear in the humanities. I have heard historians wish to be free of the rough and tumble of universities at the present time. I have heard comments that during the next ten years there will be new balances in Britain between research and teaching which will involve new institutional arrangements, and that these patterns will break quite sharply with the past. We have never had the disaggregation that has happened in the continental situation. The particularity of institutions has great importance in Britain. I have not seen this sense of institutional identity breaking down much.

Sir Solly talked about the sterility and the immobility of many people in the research establishments after a certain age. The important problem here is the mobility between these institutions and the universities; there must be some kind of free passage. If you have an expanding educational system, the free passage is relatively easy. If you are not expanding so fast, you begin to encounter difficulties. Many of the people who went into these institutions were probably less interesting at the point of entry than some of the people who went into the universities. It may well be that we have got to work out systems where people can be taken out of universities and put into research places for periods of time. We need places where people can recharge.

SHILS

If a mermaid were to leave the depths of the ocean and go to live in London, she would think it was extraordinarily dry. Asa Briggs lives in a university culture that is extraordinarily unique for its preoccupation with the training of undergraduates and its devotion to the training of undergraduates. Even if there appears to be a slight falling off in that, the level of concentration on teaching even among those who allege that they are not interested at all in teaching is extremely high in England.

BEN-DAVID

If one compares Professor Parsons' study with those done on the situation in England, it is clear that the university professor there considers himself to a large extent as a teacher. Quite a few professors in Britain hardly consider themselves as researchers. The whole composition and self-definition of the professorial role are different in England from what they are in the United States.

I should like now to return to a point Mr. Morison made about the superiority of the university as a place for research and add a few points to it. He spoke of the philosophical depth of the research. By having to organize a course, you have to put your own work into a much broader perspective, and you have to philosophize about it to some extent. You cannot organize a field of study for teaching at a high level without having some sort of philosophy about it. You may not be compelled to do this if you are only a researcher, even a brilliant one.

The other point I should like to make concerns the unity of the various disciplines within the university. It has often been stressed that the unity of knowledge has been falling apart for the last hundred and fifty years. It probably has; nevertheless, one of the great advantages of a university is that this unity has not entirely disappeared there. All creative people I know in any field have contacts across disciplines. It seems therefore that the combination of research and teaching as developed in the best universities has been, so far, the most fruitful way to conduct research.

There is, however, a kind of technological research which is creative and vital, but for which universities provide little incentive or opportunity. Many of the publicly financed research institutes established for the promotion of useful knowledge in fields with potential applications are not very successful in this respect either. As has been pointed out by Sir Solly, some of these institutions tend to become stale and unproductive. Perhaps they should never have been established to start with. But all this leaves open the question: What is the optimal setting for creative research in technology?

MORISON

There is a puzzling aspect here. In a sense, engineering development, which is more difficult than scientific research, combines both intellectual quality and the instincts of an artist to organize random elements into a single situation that will really work. This turns out to be almost impossible to teach except in the classic artistic apprenticeship way; it cannot be taught to large crowds of undergraduates.

KILLY

The deplorable state of the continental university has been mentioned over and over again. I would be willing to give up almost everything of Humboldt's teaching except this tension or interplay between *Forschung* and *Lehre*. The second experience Professor Pizzorno described was for him an extraordinary experience. To my mind, it should be the normal experience of high-quality university work. The malfunctioning of the continental universities can be traced to a great extent to the disruption of the very sensitive balance between teaching and research. The productive tensions such a balance might produce are destroyed from the beginning because continental universities are places of anonymity. There is no relation whatsoever between the so-called teacher and his so-called pupil, and there could not be a satisfactory relation for the obvious reason of numbers. As long as we do not succeed in getting rid of this climate of anonymity, millions of marks will be spent in vain.

I was impressed by the obvious changes in the Soviet system, which are changes to the good and intensify the tension between research and teaching. Remembering what Mr. Parsons said about the psychology of teaching, the main reason for this combination of teaching and research is for me not a psychological one, but a very material one. I cannot conceive of any productive work being done in a humanistic field without a colloquium, without the criticism of students. I could not live without my four or five assistants, and I greatly deplore that they are being alienated, not to say devoured, by their teaching loads.

The humanities simply cannot exist in an anonymous academic society. But there is another reason for the low ebb of the humanities which might be specifically modern. Only in rare instances do the humanities produce operational leaders.

PARSONS

I think that Mr. Killy has made a most interesting statement. I just wanted to say, first, that I do not think for a moment that the psychological factor I mentioned stands alone. I think Professor Ben-David made an important point in speaking of the pressure that teaching gives to deepen, broaden, and clarify thinking. I have had occasion to be concerned with sociological aspects of law, and I have been much impressed with the parallel between teaching and the procedure of adjudication. The courts must adjudicate, with very few limitations, any dispute that is brought before them; they cannot stay within a closed world of deductive propositions from a few premises, because they have to face new problems all the time. This is also one of the main functions of teaching; bright students will always ask the difficult questions, and you are not allowed to evade them. This forces the teacher to take into consideration things that he would otherwise have neglected. The motivational reasons why academic people are willing to expose themselves to the punishment of dealing with really bright students are another aspect of this whole question.

FULTON

I started as an undergraduate at sixteen in a Scottish university. People came there from very mixed backgrounds—from homes that had nothing but the Bible and from much more sophisticated families. You were suddenly confronted with the great master. He produced an astonishing proportion of scholars by bringing the light into their eyes at the right time. Then I went to Oxford at a time when the scholarship by modern standards was rather amateurish. The teaching was student-oriented, but there were still big men around. It is not so much that this teaching orientation has been lost, but that scholarship itself has become vastly more professional in approach. People began to realize that to get a chair in another university the only thing you could transfer was your writing. The systematic development of universities did, in fact, cause teaching to be regarded with a much more professional and guild attitude. People say they are interested in undergraduate teaching, but they are interested in undergraduate teaching as a reflection of postgraduate teaching.

I suspect that a great deal of the trouble in science has arisen because the people who are teaching are the people who respect the Royal Society imprimatur. That means they are addressing themselves to 10 per cent of their students; the other 90 per cent have got to undergo being taught as if they belonged to the 10 per cent and they know that they do not. These students leave the university feeling that they are failures. This situation cannot continue without creating terrible problems. I feel very much in sympathy with Mr. Killy, and the discussion about the continental universities reinforces the point that the teaching that goes on inside the university is not for the direct benefit of the students. The challenge for the university today is to pick the undergraduate course and revise it. It is terribly difficult to be a springboard for the postgraduate training of the next generation's scholars and at the same time to equip undergraduates so that they can make their contribution when they go out into the world. These two functions must be preserved; otherwise, in the so-called tension between research and teaching, the teaching is unconsciously giving way because it is becoming a reflection of postgraduate teaching. A great many university students are not going to be the scholars of the next generation. The greatest tradition of European universities has been that they have taken seriously their concern for these students.

DUNTON

As I understood Professor Morison, the pressures on the university are making it difficult for the university to do fundamental research, to speculate about big ideas. He put the blame mostly on the public demand for *ad hoc* research, as expressed largely by big federal grants for that kind of research. I suggest that a fair part of the blame may lie with the humanists and, to some extent, the social scientists themselves. They have been inclined to award their prestige for a paper published on a new bit of information about Chaucer. We certainly want to keep adding to that stock of knowledge, but surely the important thing is for humanists also to think about the big ideas, about values. There is the desire as well as the money for *ad hoc* research. But there is along with this an enormous growing demand from the public, particularly the younger generation, for the other thing—for speculation and talk and investigation of big ideas.

Enrollments in the sciences are tending to go up not nearly so fast as enrollments in the humanities and the social sciences. And I suggest that most young people studying in the social sciences may be disappointed if they only learn the methodologies of behavioral study. The humanities and the social sciences do offer an alternative to *ad hoc* research, and one that many students are looking for.

CROZIER

I agree very much with Mr. Dunton's plea that the humanities and social sciences address meaningful problems, but I fear we may have been misled in trying to reconstruct the past with the feeling that we can do so by reconstructing the parts. We should not be seduced into trying to retrieve old relationships and the old kind of content. We must reconstruct the past to innovate.

MORISON

When I went to the university, I was taught by a group of men in the humanities—literature and history primarily. They looked upon themselves, although well-trained scholars, as protectors of the old high culture. Imbedded in that high culture was a set of moral attitudes, and these professors were prepared to take positions—that Cromwell was a bad man or whatever. From this I learned a great deal about a set of values that then related to the world around me; I also learned some historical data. In recent times, this position with respect to the old high culture has been difficult for anybody in the humanities to assume for two reasons. First, the celebrated analytical method of science began to infect the humanistic fields, and humanists began to concentrate on refined analysis; they were trained this way as graduate students, which tends to kill some of the moral imperatives or the impulse toward moral imperatives. Second, the cultural arrangements that those people taught me no longer related so directly to the conditions of society. Thus, you were in danger of becoming either the purveyor of a past that did not so obviously relate, or you were being soft in not using the critical and analytical procedures that were making great headway in other fields.

MAEDA

In the system of higher education in Japan before World War II, we had relatively small classes in the humanities; now we have mass general education. There are four hundred students in philosophy classes, and you lose the intimacy that you had before. Even people outside the university have begun to realize that the student is not a real student under such conditions. He certainly has little interest in philosophy given this experience. So we are struggling to get back to the system of smaller classes.

MEYERSON

The dissident young have what they like to call the politics of rudeness, and I should like to borrow a leaf from their book for a while and be their spokesman. Since no one else obviously intends to do so, I should like to put on the table the kind of charge that they would make to us. They would say that we are asking them to do as we say rather than as we do. They would say the discussion we have had for the last couple of hours would do justice to the late Cardinal Newman or to Humboldt. They would claim this is all liberal garbage, although they would use a harsher and ruder term. They would ask where to find that blend of research and teaching we have been discussing. Who gets rewarded at the universities in all of our countries? What do we transfer to another university? Not our teaching, but our publications. Teaching is a capacity that is judged only by hearsay. Prestige rests on publication.

I have had delegations of Oxford students visit me and say how much they resent the tutorial system. Indeed, they resent the very erotic quality Professor Shils mentioned.

SHILS

They want that atmosphere regardless of what they say.

MEYERSON

Be that as it may, we will ignore this rhetoric of the angry young at our peril. The rhetoric proceeds in many fashions: Science and technological research presumably are geared to immoral ends. They claim that we engage in these immoral activities and reward only those who have publications rather than teaching skills. They go further and condemn our humanistic bias as the bias of an elitist group concerned with the past, concerned with kinds of humanism that may have been appropriate to the class structure of the Italian Renaissance, but hardly to the contemporary world. They claim it is the bias of the verbal against the sensual; a bias that ignores the visual, the auditory, the other senses. I am hardly saying that Tokyo National University is closed because of the

429

discrepancy between what we say and what we do. Nevertheless, substantial numbers of students—and not just the most politicized —have a deep concern with an educational experience that they find very wanting.

SHILS

The students may desire a set of values rather than factual knowledge, but can we give this to them? Do we have it to give to them? Are they entitled to want it from us? The students demand all these things, but is it within the possibilities of earthly existence that they be given to them? It is certainly difficult to make young people composed and restrained in their expectations of life. We live in a most ridiculous age. The utopians from the sixteenth century to the nineteenth were in a few instances thoughtful, wise, benevolent men who wrote little essays; they had a few followers, not very many. But this contemporary utopianism has taken possession of a generation and that is very difficult to satisfy. Those who are most dissatisfied are in fact dissatisfied with our "values" so that expounding "values" to them would not please them at all.

They study social sciences in increasingly large numbers. I myself think—although my friend Professor Parsons probably disagrees with me on this—that it would be much more desirable if they did not study social sciences in such large numbers. What do they get when they study the social sciences? They come for bread, and they are given gas, which sends them into convulsions. Who are their heroes—Marcuse, the late C. Wright Mills, Eldridge Cleaver. They do not want the stuff Professors Parsons, Ben-David, Crozier, Bourricaud, and I give to them. They want something more exciting, and we are not in a position to give it to them.

We have talked about the burden put on universities by the large numbers, but we have not raised the question as to whether we can supply the teaching personnel. It is not just a question of what is called high-level manpower planning. If it were, we would only have to decide that we need so and so many teachers in this category, and so forth. Even if you could provide the magnitudes desired, can you produce the quality that is desired? I am not a romantic about the marvelous relationship between Mark Hopkins and the boy on the log. I do not think that pedagogy in the pre-Civil War period in the United States was very impressive, or after the Civil War for that matter—when a professor at Yale shot an undergraduate because he misbehaved. But is it now possible with a much more open kind of selection to produce that many teachers who will possess the capacity to stimulate and excite and who can convey the values and have the breadth which the most demanding students insist on or who will have the capacity for learning, hard work, imagination, and responsibility which we desire? Does the human race have enough of those capacities at a time when there are so many other great demands for talent in so many important fields of social, economic, political, and cultural life? The United States and other countries are increasingly undertaking more than they have the brains to do, more than they have the personality qualities to perform. So we stagger on as well as we can.

We have to listen to the rhetoric of these young people, but we also have to explain to them the determinants of the human situation. There are limits, unless you can change the genetic pool.

PIZZORNO

I should like to respond to the last exchange of comments. Before Mr. Meyerson spoke, I was uneasy because there was too much consensus in our group. Everything is not so easy as we are trying to picture it here. The problems are much deeper than shifting a bit from the research side to the teaching side. Asa Briggs commented that there are not really contradictions, but tensions. Thus we moved to the middle of the road and became very happy. I thought then that we had to see if there was not something challenging us a little more deeply than we had been willing to admit.

I will just try to take two points established in our consensus, and discuss the consequences of those two points. Everybody agreed that theoretical or philosophical teaching is more agreeable to the teacher. We seem to agree that the higher the theoretical content of the teaching, the greater the incentive for the professor to teach. I tried to link this point of consensus with the other point that came up early this morning about the erotic content of the communication between a teacher and a pupil. Let us call it emotional; it is not really erotic. Earlier the professor would have been on the sadistic side of this relationship; now he has been forced over to the masochistic side. We must somehow break the pattern. On this point I am not in agreement with Mr. Killy. Given what has happened in the last few years, we cannot now have this kind of personal relationship with students. As an element in the process of socialization today, the old Socratic relationship is too emotionally loaded. The relationship must become more formal, more sober. I do not agree with Professor Shils; students do resent this enforced paternalistic intimacy.

431

SHILS

You cannot take them at their word. They say one thing and mean another; they will even say different things in the course of a conversation.

PIZZORNO

Let me say, then, that *I* do not like to have this kind of relationship with my students. It is no longer a help to have this kind of relationship. We cannot think that we are able to socialize them by means of such a situation. *In loco parentis* is a thing of the past; we are no longer a father substitute. I personally do not like this kind of relationship with my students, nor do I think it a healthy one to have.

There should be some sort of bargaining position in our position with the students. Let us bargain, and let us give what we can in our teaching or our research. But we should not try to socialize them or to give them some sort of general moral introduction to life. They do not need this.

KILLY

The few erotic experiences I know of have never been paternalistic.

ROBINSON

I feel a need to respond to Edward Shils, and in support of Martin Meyerson. As Martin spoke, the specific items he mentioned elicited a general nodding. It was the larger and fuzzier issues about values that brought the disagreement. Professor Shils' basis retort was: Can we give it to them? But when people come to the university community and say they want to crack an atom, the first response is not essentially the negative one: Are they asking too much of us? In general, we tend to grasp at these ideas; we will go back and try. Rather than the defensiveness of Professor Shils' reply, it seems to me that our first response should be to try and find out the things we can do. The students are, after all, our basic customers; they are the people who will use the knowledge that we spend all of our time trying to uncover.

SHILS

Giving them knowledge that they can use is a different thing from what they are asking for. I do not want to overgeneralize, by any means, and say that all the students are like this, but the small minority that Martin was speaking for does not want knowledge or a technique of understanding; these students simply want to discomfort and disrupt institutions, and that has to be acknowledged. This is a small minority, but it can become quite significant.

ROBINSON

Some people want space exploration simply for militaristic purposes. We do not say, therefore, that we are not going to explore space.

BRIGGS

I think Professor Pizzorno was getting into extremely difficult territory when he implied that the relationship between the tutor and student is absolutely divorced from the structural state of the university in which the tutor and student operate. You can draw sharp distinctions between the fundamental structural problems within universities and the problems of the psychological relationships between tutors and students. In certain circumstances these relationships are impossible because of the nature of the structural setups. In this sense, we have been distinguishing too much, if you like, between the two halves of Marx—between the Marx who deals with individual relations and the Marx who deals with economic patterns of growth. We had a long discussion yesterday about patterns of resource allocation that are fundamental to the university problems in all our countries. This morning we have been discussing relationships of a psychological character between individuals and the terribly difficult problems of socialization. I do not think there are any easy answers, and I should like to experiment and to innovate, as Professor Crozier suggested. But we can separate the two discussions only if we bear in mind that we live in societies where universities have got to interpret themselves to the communities that are paying the money and where they also have got their own internal relationships to settle. To keep the two halves absolutely separate skews the picture.

All societies want scientific research, whatever their political structure. When we start talking about humanities, we get into problems of a quite different order. When Professor Pizzorno was talking, as he was in such an extremely austere way, about no possibilities of socialization, no kind of contact other than the straight communication of organizational knowledge, he was describing what to me would mean the end of the university as an institution, indeed almost the end of knowledge. Knowledge is culture, and if universities abdicate from that whole area, they are going to have a tough time indeed over the next hundred years.

PIZZORNO

You can have this socialization implicitly, but you cannot aim for it explicitly.

BOURRICAUD

I should like to put in the pot not an altogether new element, but something perhaps slightly different. I should like very much to see the crisis of the academic ethos discussed with a great deal more clarity. At the time of Durkheim, for instance, some sort of balance had been achieved between teaching and research, though the research was not of the contemporary type. For a certain set of reasons that balance has been lost, and a new situation has emerged. I would like to explore the causes for the *anomie* in which the academic profession finds itself in France today. There are two or three alienating mechanisms that would be interesting to take into account. Perhaps if we did consider these mechanisms, they would explain why one has at the same time in France a breakdown of two main components of the role (these being research and teaching) as well as a loss in status, prestige, and control by the profession. There is a great disjunction between the present state of knowledge within the profession and the type of course or teaching that is administered by the professor or teaching person in the university system. This gap has alienated the academic group from the most advanced and better informed among young people and those without the proper academic credentials. In France, the separation between the teaching people and the research people resulted to some extent from the unsatisfactory formation of the teachers and of the professors themselves.

Second, I should further like to analyze the mechanism of alienation of the teacher from the student body. In that respect, we would have to devote much attention to the lecture. It is remarkable to see how much time, for instance, a man like Durkheim devoted to writing his lectures. But of course, even in that case, this formalized rite was perhaps of more significance for the teacher or the professor than for the student body. On that score, I would agree with Lord Fulton in his previous intervention.

Third, we might perhaps explore the alienation of the university from any of the leading and deciding agencies, as it becomes insulated within its own corporate and traditional problems. My analysis is taken from the French case, which is a particular type of university pathology, but to some extent it could also apply to other cases. After that deviance mechanism has been analyzed, we might ask what sort of countermechanism could be set in motion so that we could start the operation recuperating.

Notes on Essay Contributors

MORRIS B. ABRAM, born in 1918, the former president of Brandeis University, is a partner in Paul, Weiss, Goldberg, Rifkind, Wharton, and Garrison, New York. Mr. Abram has served as U. S. representative to the United Nations Commission on Human Rights and as a member of the National Advisory Council on Economic Opportunity. He is the author of "The Eleven Days at Brandeis: As Seen from the President's Chair" (*New York Times Magazine,* February 16, 1969) and "Is Liberalism Dead: A Response to the Campus" (*Southwestern Law Journal,* October 1969).

GENO A. BALLOTTI, born in 1930, is managing editor of *Dædalus,* associate executive officer of the American Academy of Arts and Sciences, and secretary of the Assembly on University Goals and Governance.

DANIEL BELL, born in 1919, is professor of sociology at Harvard University and co-editor of *The Public Interest.* Mr. Bell is the author of *The End of Ideology* (Glencoe, 1960) and *The Reforming of General Education* (New York, 1966), and editor of *Toward the Year 2000: Work in Progress* (Boston, 1968).

PETER J. CAWS, born in 1931, is professor of philosophy at Hunter College of the City University of New York. Mr. Caws is the author of *The Philosophy of Science, A Systematic Account* (Van Nostrand: Princeton, 1965) and *Science and the Theory of Value* (Random House: New York, 1967).

JILL CONWAY, born in 1934, is assistant professor of history at the University of Toronto. She is the author of "Jane Addams: An American Heroine" (*Dædalus,* Spring 1964) and of biographical essays on nineteenth and twentieth century American women for the forthcoming *Dictionary of Biography of Notable American Women.*

RALPH A. DUNGAN, born in 1923, is Chancellor of Higher Education for the State of New Jersey. He had formerly served as legislative assistant to Senator John F. Kennedy, special assistant to President Kennedy, and U. S. Ambassador to Chile.

ERIK H. ERIKSON, born in 1902, is professor emeritus of human development and lecturer in psychiatry at Harvard University. Mr. Erikson's publications include *Young Man Luther* (1958), *Childhood and Society* (2d ed., 1963), *Insight and Responsibility* (1964), *Identity: Youth and Crisis* (1968), and *Gandhi's Truth: On the Origins of Militant Non-violence* (1969).

EDGAR Z. FRIEDENBERG, born in 1921, is professor of education and sociology at the State University of New York at Buffalo. He is the author of *Vanishing Adolescent* (Boston, 1959), *Coming of Age in America* (New York, 1965), and *The Dignity of Youth and Other Atavisms* (Boston, 1965).

STEPHEN R. GRAUBARD, born in 1924, is professor of history at Brown University, editor of *Dædalus*, and director of studies of the Assembly on University Goals and Governance. His publications include *Burke, Disraeli, and Churchill: The Politics of Perseverance* (Cambridge, Mass., 1961) and *British Labour and the Russian Revolution* (Cambridge, Mass., 1956). He edited *A New Europe?* (Boston, 1964), and, with Gerald Holton, *Excellence and Leadership in a Democracy* (New York, 1962).

STANLEY HOFFMANN, born in 1928, is professor of government at Harvard University. Mr. Hoffmann is co-author of *In Search of France* (1963) and author of *The State of War* (1965) and *Gulliver's Troubles, or the Setting of American Foreign Policy* (1968).

CLARK KERR, born in 1911, is Chairman and Executive Director of the Carnegie Commission on Higher Education. He is professor of industrial relations in the School of Business Administration and professor of economics in the College of Letters and Science at the University of California, Berkeley. Mr. Kerr was President of the University of California at Berkeley from 1958 to 1967. He is the author of *The Uses of the University* (Cambridge, 1964) and *Labor and Management in Industrial Society* (New York, 1964).

SALVADOR EDWARD LURIA, born in 1912, is Sedgwick Professor of Biology at the Massachusetts Institute of Technology. He is the author of *General Virology* (1st ed., 1953; 2d ed., 1967 with James E. Darnell, Jr.) as well as numerous articles for scholarly journals. Professor Luria shared the 1969 Nobel Prize for Physiology or Medicine.

ZELLA LURIA, born in 1924, is associate professor of psychology at Tufts University. She is the author of seventeen articles and book chapters in the fields of psychology, moral development, and child psychology.

MARTIN TROW, born in 1926, is professor of sociology at the University of California, Berkeley. Mr. Trow is currently Director of the National Survey of Higher Education for the Carnegie Commission on Higher Education and was formerly editor of *Sociology of Education*. He is co-author of *Union Democracy* (Glencoe, 1956) and *The British Academics* (forthcoming).

List of "Dialogue" Contributors

Daniel Bell
Professor of Sociology
Harvard University

Joseph Ben-David
Professor of Sociology
Hebrew University of Jerusalem

Landrum R. Bolling
President
Earlham College

François Bourricaud
Professor of Sociology
The Sorbonne
University of Paris

John Brademas
United States House
    of Representatives

Asa Briggs
Vice Chancellor and
    Professor of History
Sussex University

Mauro Cappelletti
Professor of Law and
    Director, Institute of
    Comparative Law
University of Florence

Peter J. Caws
Professor of Philosophy
Hunter College

Jill Conway
Assistant Professor of History
University of Toronto

Michel Crozier
Maître de Recherche au Centre
    National de la Recherche
    Scientifique
Director, Centre de Sociologie des
    Organisations
Paris, France

Sarah E. Diamant
Doctoral Candidate in American
    History
Cornell University

C. M. Dick, Jr.
President
Business Equipment Manufacturers
    Association

Martin Duberman
Professor of History
Princeton University

A. D. Dunton
President
Carleton University
Ottawa, Canada

Seymour Eskow
President
Rockland Community College

Edgar Z. Friedenberg
Professor of Education and
    Sociology
State University of New York
    at Buffalo

438

Baron John Scott Fulton
Chairman
The British Council

Robert J. Glaser
Dean and Professor of Medicine
Medical School
Stanford University

Pierre Grappin
Professor of German Literature
and History
University of Paris (Nanterre)

Stephen R. Graubard
Professor of History
Brown University

Hanna H. Gray
Associate Professor of History
University of Chicago

Andrew M. Greeley
Program Director
National Opinion Research Center

Jeff Greenfield
Assistant to the Mayor
New York City

Eugene E. Grollmes
Administrative Intern
St. Louis University

Gerald Holton
Professor of Physics
Harvard University

Willard Hurst
Villas Professor of Law
University of Wisconsin

Carl Kaysen
Director
Institute for Advanced Study

Dexter M. Keezer
Economic Adviser
McGraw-Hill, Incorporated

Clark Kerr
Chairman and Executive Director
Carnegie Commission on Higher
Education

Walther Killy
Professor of Literature
University of Göttingen

Edward H. Levi
President
University of Chicago

S. E. Luria
Sedgwick Professor of Biology
The Massachusetts Institute of
Technology

Yoichi Maeda
Professor of French Language
and Culture
University of Tokyo

Jean Mayer
Professor of Nutrition
Harvard University

Walter P. Metzger
Professor of History
Columbia University

Martin Meyerson
President
State University of New York at
Buffalo

Elting E. Morison
Master, Timothy Dwight College
and Professor of History
Yale University

Robert S. Morison
Director
Division of Biological Sciences
Cornell University

Henry Norr
Graduate Student
School of Education
Harvard University

439

Victor G. Onushkin
Senior Staff Member
International Institute for
 'Educational Planning
UNESCO (Paris)

Talcott Parsons
Professor of Social Relations
Harvard University

Bruce L. Payne
Instructor of Government
Kirkland College

Alessandro Pizzorno
Professor of Sociology
University of Urbino

Roger Revelle
Director
Center for Population Studies
Harvard University

David Riesman
Henry Ford II Professor of Social
 Sciences
Harvard University

Philip C. Ritterbush
Director
Office of Academic Programs
Smithsonian Institution

Marshall Robinson
Program Officer in Charge
Division of Education and
 Research
The Ford Foundation

Neil R. Rudenstine
Associate Professor of English and
 Dean of Students
Princeton University

Edward Shils
Committee on Social Thought
University of Chicago

Edward Joseph Shoben, Jr.
Chairman, Council on Higher
 Education Studies, and Director,
 Center for Higher Education
State University of New York at
 Buffalo

John R. Silber
Professor of Philosophy and
 Dean of the College of Arts and
 Sciences
University of Texas at Austin

Charles E. Silberman
Director
The Carnegie Study of the
 Education of Educators

R. L. Sproull
Vice President and Provost
The University of Rochester

Preble Stolz
Professor of Law
University of California at Berkeley

Kenneth S. Tollett
Dean
School of Law
Texas Southern University

George R. Waggoner
Dean, College of Liberal Arts and
 Sciences, and Professor of
 English
University of Kansas

David M. Wax
Assistant to the Administrator
Housing and Development
 Administration
New York City

Sir Solly Zuckerman
Chief Scientific Advisor
Cabinet Officer
London, England

440

INDEX

INDEX